Communication and Society
Series Editor: Jeremy Tunstall

The political impact
of mass media

In the same series

Journalists at work
Jeremy Tunstall

The making of a television series
Philip Elliott
(available in United States from Hastings House)

The manufacture of news
Edited by Stanley Cohen and Jock Young

Also by Colin Seymour-Ure
The press, politics and the public (1968)

---

*This book is the fourth volume in a series
edited by Jeremy Tunstall and devoted to
explorations of the interrelationships between
society and all forms of communication media.*

COLIN SEYMOUR-URE

The political impact
of mass media

CONSTABLE
London

SAGE Publications
Beverly Hills, California

Published in Great Britain 1974
by Constable & Co Ltd
10 Orange Street London WC2H 7EG
Hardback ISBN 0 09 457760 9
Paperback ISBN 0 09 459660 3

Published in the United States of America 1974
by Sage Publications Inc.
275 South Beverly Drive
Beverly Hills, California 90212
Hardback ISBN 0-8039-0347-2
Library of Congress Catalog Card No. 73-87747

Printed in Great Britain

For Judy

Contents

Foreword   page 9

Introductory note   11

PART ONE:
POLITICAL COMMUNICATION AND THE EFFECTS OF MASS MEDIA

1. The nature and production of mass media effects   15
    I. Mass media and the communication process   15
    II. The nature of mass media effects   21
    III. The production of mass media effects   23

2. The political context of mass media effects   41
    I. The study of mass media effects   41
    II. Levels of political relationships   44
    III. Summary of chapters 1 and 2   62

PART TWO:
VARIETIES OF MASS MEDIA EFFECTS: CASE STUDIES

3. *The Times* and the appeasement of Hitler   67

4. Enoch Powell's 'earthquake'   99

5. Parliament and television   137

6. Newspapers and party systems: connections   156

7. Newspapers and party systems: contexts   177

8. Mass media and British general elections, 1945–70   202

9. *Private Eye:* the politics of the Fool   240

References   265

Bibliography   284

Index   291

Foreword

Most of the studies in this book developed from an undergraduate course on politics and mass media at the University of Kent. At various stages I have also had the benefit of discussion in seminars at the universities of Cambridge, Keele and Leicester, the Central London Polytechnic and a Round Table of the International Political Science Association.

My colleague Graham Thomas generously discussed the book with me on many occasions; and I have benefited enormously from the professionalism and advice of Jay Blumler, who read almost all the manuscript, and Jeremy Tunstall, who has been involved at every stage.

Others to whom I am grateful for information, facilities or comments on particular chapters include: the BBC, Brian Bond, Christopher Booker, David Butler, Ronald Butt, the University of Birmingham Centre for Contemporary Cultural Studies, Sir Colin Coote, B. P. Emmett, Harold Evans, Peter Fiddick, Martin Harrison, Paul Hartmann, Charles Husband, Richard Ingrams, the librarians of the Institute of Race Relations, Anthony King, Iverach McDonald, National Opinion Polls Ltd., Michael Pinto-Duschinsky, Rt. Hon. Enoch Powell, MP, Richard Rose, the late A. P. Ryan, Social Surveys (Gallup Poll) Ltd., my father Philip Ure, John Whale, Hugo Young. I am grateful also to Mrs Rita Gledhill, Mrs Gill Insley and Mrs Muriel Waring for their help with typing.

Finally I should make clear that responsibility for the opinions expressed and for any errors and omissions is my own.

C.S-U.
April 1973

Introductory note

This book seeks to analyse and illustrate varieties of political effects caused by mass media. Its theme is that 'effects' has commonly been defined with undue narrowness. The questions typically posed have been about changes caused by media in the political attitudes of individuals – for example their voting intentions. Other kinds of effect caused by the same media activities – for example in the election campaign strategies of rival parties – have been over-shadowed or ignored.

Part One is an analysis of what media effects comprise, the different ways in which they are produced and the kinds of political relationship that may be affected. At each stage illustrations are offered, mainly drawn from Britain and the USA. Some of them refer to the case studies in Part Two.

The studies in Part Two explore in some depth specific examples of various media effects. They complement the analysis in Part One, each illustrating a number of its elements. The cases are not constructed, however, so that they make sense only in the light of Part One. They can be read on their own, in any order and before reading Part One – or without reading it at all.

Political communication and the effects of mass media

1

The nature and production
of mass media effects

I. MASS MEDIA AND THE COMMUNICATION PROCESS

The purpose of the first section of this chapter is to place mass media in the context of social communication processes and to consider some of the political implications of their distinctive features.

Communication is a necessary social activity. Without communication there can be no society – only a collection of individuals. In a social situation, indeed, it is impossible *not* to communicate: one cannot avoid reacting to the presence of another person, even if one is not intended to and does not wish it. In situations where people are unwillingly forced to communicate, such as long railway journeys or flights, they try to protect themselves by 'disqualifying communication'.[1]* They talk aimlessly about the weather or incoherently exchange sniffs and grunts; or they communicate non-verbally, by shifting significantly in their seats, folding newspapers and opening windows. A favourite disqualifying communication of the politician is the ritual phrase 'no comment'. It illustrates the practice well. The politican wishes to avoid communicating with the media about, say, his government's attitude to the latest airline hijacking. If he ignores the newsmen at his door they will attach a meaning to his silence. If he talks to them he defeats his object. If he says 'no comment' he tells them nothing yet hopes to avoid some of the inferences that would be drawn from silence. But whatever he does or does not do, the newsmen, by the very fact of putting themselves in a social relationship with him, make communication unavoidable. Max Gluckman has illustrated the point by reference to a different kind of ritual – Barotse marriage ceremonies. To symbolise the changed social relationships following marriage, parents stay away from these ceremonies: 'Prescribed absence from a ritual is thus a form of participation in it: though it is not a protest, it states that there is a conflict present in the social process.'[2]

If communication is inevitable in a social situation it follows that all kinds of human action may constitute 'communicatory acts' –

* References begin on p. 265

including such negative actions as silence, stillness and absence. It follows too that the definition of a 'medium' of communication is so broad as to include almost anything. All that is necessary for something to be a medium is that it link the two parties essential to communication – a sender and a receiver – and 'carry' a message. It needs no other qualities. What serves as a medium between some parties may carry no message for others; and what serves as a medium at one time may not do so at another. Many media, on the other hand, are general and continuous in their use. These obviously include the mass media as conventionally defined, including television, radio, newspapers and film.

Since communication is so pervasive we should expect communications media to be a major determinant of the nature of the social system; and since politics is a form of social activity we can expect the same to be true for the political system. What the political scientist will want to ask is, 'How far and in what ways are the political relationships of groups and individuals affected by the communication between them?'. Since communication pervades politics and anything may at one time or another serve as a medium, the question is daunting. One method of answering it, indeed, is to describe a model of the political system entirely using communication concepts. This has been done by Karl Deutsch in *The nerves of government*, but it is doubtful whether his model could be applied to an actual system. When the question is limited, as it is here, to the political effects of mass media, it is more manageable.

The distinctive features of mass media can be shown by taking each stage of the communication process in turn.

(a) Sender

We deal here with media organisations. The distinctive feature of these as social institutions is that they exist specifically in order to facilitate communication: they have no other relationship with their audiences. In practice this distinction is considerably blurred. On the one hand other social institutions, for reasons discussed in the previous paragraphs, also act as significant media of communication. On the face of it, for example, the British Parliament exists to represent the people, make laws and supervise the Executive (among other things), and the United States Supreme Court exists to interpret the constitution and judge the law. Yet we could analyse both those institutions as channels of communication between various political actors: Parliament's choice of debates helps to define the agenda of politics outside Westminster, and the Court's decisions indicate to congressmen the current limits of constitutional legislative action. On the other hand, too, media organisations do sometimes establish relationships with their audiences that go beyond the simple transmission of information. Party newspapers, for instance, have been a widespread historical phenomenon (see Chapter 6). Reading the party paper may have been part of a complex of partisan activities aimed at getting political power. Newspapers and TV shows have frequently offered advice and services, including sympathy for the lovelorn, life insurance (an idea borrowed by Northcliffe from the United States and a favourite circulation-builder in the British press of the 1930s), tests of consumer products and practical assistance against bureaucracy. Media organisations, in other words, like legislatures, may represent the people, supervise the Executive and so on. In fact they have often seen this as an important role: the *Daily Mirror* established a kind of empathy with its working-class readers in the Second World War, for instance, maintaining the interests both of men at the front and women at home. Arguably the paper played a big part in channelling the attitudes behind the landslide Labour victory in 1945.[3]

Despite the blurs it remains true that the primary characteristic of media organisations is transmitting information, while the primary characteristics of the British Parliament and United States Supreme Court are respectively to represent the people and judge the law. But this amounts simply to saying that in the dominant values of the British and American political cultures these institutions are given those roles. There is in principle nothing in its control of a medium (printing press, transmitter) to prevent an organisation having goals that go beyond 'communication'; nor in the absence of direct control of a medium to prevent an organisation like a legislature seeking goals *of* communication. Indeed the British Parliament's goal of communication with the electorate has implications for its relationship with broadcast media and for its own eventual identity that are the subject of study in Chapter 5.

In a political context this potential flexibility in the role of media organisations has important consequences. Firstly we may find that certain kinds of mass media effects may follow only indirectly from the fact that an organisation controls a mass medium. In these cases media organisations fit comfortably into models of the political system that include categories for interest groups or 'interest aggregation'. Chapter 3 contains an analysis of the part played by *The Times* under its editor Geoffrey Dawson in the appeasement of Hitler Germany in the 1930s. Dawson's influence was precisely analogous to that of, say, a trade union leader over economic policy. His sanction against the government lay not in non-cooperation and industrial action but in the need felt by the government to calculate the electoral and other consequences (including reaction abroad) of losing his support. From the government's point of view he was one more influential man with a constituency to be heeded.

The second consequence of the possible ambiguity in the political roles of media organisations is that people with different kinds of relationship to the media may perceive those roles differently and therefore be affected differently by them. In practice three broad groups can be distinguished. The views of *politicians* vary widely: Chapter 7 gives an idea of the range in different types of party system. In Britain politicians typically ascribe to the mass media an important role in political communication. A proprietor like Lord Thomson was from the start regarded with disapproval in Britain because he stressed his organisation's efficiency not at communication but at achieving a different goal – profits. Proprietors who do stress communication may still suffer criticism by politicians because their political content is low, unsophisticated or biased towards particular goals.[4] In many political systems (one-party systems, for instance) media organisations are prevented from having independent political goals at all and are incorporated in government or party machinery; or an attempt may be made to neutralise them in an institution like the BBC.

The second group are *media organisations* themselves. It is easy but obviously absurd to see these as monoliths. Even among journalists orientations vary widely. For the British national press Tunstall has distinguished three main types of goal: an audience revenue goal, an advertising revenue goal, and several non-revenue goals. Between journalists in different organisations there is an ambivalent competitor-colleague relationship.[5] These orientations are reflected in a set of news values which do not place a high stress on explicitly political subjects and which – perhaps more importantly – lead to a construction of political reality that interprets events in short-run terms and emphasises personalities, élites and the unexpected or accidental.[6] To members of the organisation other than journalists, of course, like advertising executives or production workers, the organisation's specific goal of communication may be even weaker.

Audiences, thirdly, may have an attitude towards media which varies from the other groups'. Chapter 7 refers to data which suggests that audiences (at least in industrial societies) define their use of media in terms which put little value on a political role, in sharp contrast to the politicians' view. Similarly, some of the values that are important to journalists as measures of professional competence (e.g. 'exclusives') have trivial significance for audiences. It may be, naturally, that audiences could be socialised into valuing different kinds of content so that the role they ascribed to the media coincided more closely with politicians'. But it is noteworthy that the interests of readers of *Izvestia* in the Soviet Union closely follow those of western European and north American readers. (See Chapter 7.)

(b) Message

The second element in the communication process, the 'message', is open to none of the conceptual ambiguities that blur the distinctive features of the 'senders' – and specially their political features. The most distinctive point about the message or content of mass media, as opposed to other media, is perhaps their reliance on the sense of hearing and, above all, sight. They are predominantly verbal media and are therefore well suited to politics, which is a verbal activity.

(c) Medium

The third element in the process, the medium itself, needs little attention too. The distinctive features of the mass media are obvious: their implications for the conduct of politics have received attention in the literature.[7] Between the printed word and the broadcast media there are differences in the rate at which information can be transmitted and absorbed and the receiver's control over what he uses, when he uses it and whether he uses it again. Television and cinema approximate most nearly to the illusion of transporting the audience to the 'information', rather than the other way round: television in particular, since it can be beamed straight into the living-room from the scene of action. Their speed and immediacy give the broadcast media and, in an earlier age, the press a natural lead as purveyors of news. The growth of television which, though it depends heavily on words, derives most of its appeal from pictures, represents a significant shift away from the supremacy of verbal forms of communication in politics. News priorities may be affected by the availability of suitable film or of light strong enough for filming in. Demonstrations, sit-ins and riots allegedly thrive on the attention of TV cameras; while established occasions like the American presidential nominating conventions and British annual party conferences have been substantially changed by them.[8]

(d) Receivers

Other media (for example telex) have similar qualities of speed and immediacy to those of TV and radio. What distinguishes the mass media most decisively is this fourth element in the communication process. The mass media are better than other media at reaching large audiences, more or less simultaneously. Telex is not a mass medium – though it could be – because few people have telex receivers. Books are often excluded from the definition of mass media because relatively few people read books, and still fewer read the same book at the same time.* In principle, though, books are mass media because they meet the condition that the resources required to reach a large audience are not so much greater than for reaching a small one. When an audience becomes 'mass' is obviously an arbitrary matter: a mass audience of a newspaper in societies with established TV networks is generally small compared with a peak-hour TV audience. But two other points, both of which could have political implications, should be noted. The first is that for the time being TV audiences have the unique quality of being largely undifferentiated socially, when compared with many newspapers – and specially with magazines. As electronic developments increase the range of TV channels or cassette programmes audiences may become broken down. Secondly, the mass media are mass in one direction (notwithstanding the feedback from opinion surveys). They are ideal media for demagogues and populists. The typical relation is between a small number of senders and a large number of receivers. How small a number depends partly on definition. Does one regard the Palestinians who focused the TV cameras of the world upon their killing of Israelis at the 1972 Olympic Games as a handful of people or as the representatives of thousands of Palestinians in whose names they acted? The same can be asked of any TV film of a demonstration or march. Even broadly defined, however, the audience still enormously outnumber the senders – and specially those senders who actually control what is shown on the screen.

In studying the political effects of mass media, then, we study the behaviour of certain social institutions – the media organisations. The product of their behaviour is the transmission of information, possibly as an end in itself or possibly as a means to some other end defined within the organisation. The media used for transmission are those which are most efficient at sending messages; and their characteristics include the capacity to reach large audiences fast, simultaneously, frequently, cheaply and conveniently.

---

* There is, of course, a small number of mass media books, consisting mainly in formula-written novels with vast print orders, marketed aggressively in a wide range of countries and languages and linked increasingly with serialisation, film or TV versions and promotional programmes. These occasionally include books by or about politicians – e.g. President John F. Kennedy's *Profiles in courage* and William Manchester's *Death of a president*.

II. THE NATURE OF MASS MEDIA EFFECTS

'Effect' is used in this book in a broad sense. Media have an effect in the strongest sense when their behaviour is a necessary and sufficient cause of something: that is to say, nothing else could cause it and the media need no assistance. On many more occasions, no doubt, media have an effect in a weaker sense: they are the catalyst or occasion of an event which might have happened anyway but not otherwise at that time or in that form. In this case the media are neither a necessary nor sufficient cause. An intriguing example is possibly the outbreak of the First World War. If a hotline between the European capitals had existed like the one between Washington and Moscow now, the sequence of events leading up to the declaration of war might not have taken place: it was a product of the communications system of the age. In a weak sense we could therefore claim that the communications system 'caused' the outbreak of war: yet we should certainly not want to argue that it was a sufficient cause, nor that the war would not have broken out sooner or later anyway. At most the communication system provided the occasion for the war starting in August 1914.[9]

In between the strong and weak sense of effect are two others. Media may be a necessary but not a sufficient cause. For example Enoch Powell acquired the status of a major independent political figure in Britain in 1968 as the result of intense, sustained publicity for his views on immigration: yet that status depended also on the distinctive character of his views and the existence of a political crisis that gave them point. (See Chapter 4.) Alternatively media may be a sufficient but not a necessary cause. William Howard Russell's dispatches from the Crimea shocked public opinion into demanding better nursing conditions for the British army; yet the same result could in theory have been achieved by different forms of pressure.

All those senses of 'effect' are included in this study. At its broadest 'effect' is defined here as any change within the political system induced directly or indirectly by the mass media.

In what, next, do effects consist? In the first place, any effect must be an effect upon an individual. Three different degrees of intensity can be distinguished: *increments of information*, which confirm or modify *attitudes*, which may or may not modify *behaviour*. All those changes consist in a change in the relationship between the individual and some other individual or individuals: the affected person knows more about the others and perhaps feels differently about them and may even behave differently towards them, as a result of the communication process. Even when we talk about the effect of mass media on institutions we are still really talking of their effects on individuals: 'the effect of mass media on Parliament' means some kind of change caused by media in the political relationship of Members of Parliament to each other or to non-members.

It is worth distinguishing, secondly, between *primary* and *secondary* effects. A primary effect takes place when the person affected has himself been involved directly in the communication process. A secondary effect takes place when individuals or groups not involved in the communication process are affected by changes in individuals who are. Such an effect might involve a changed relationship either with the person primarily affected or with some third party or parties. This distinction can be made clearer by an example. It was often claimed that the ability of the Johnson administration in the United States to sustain the war in South Vietnam was hampered by television coverage which 'brought the war into your sitting-room' and mobilised public opposition. If the claim was correct the effect of television was this: the news coverage had the primary effect on individual viewers of creating or confirming anti-war attitudes and (for some people) behaviour. The secondary effect was on the Johnson administration's relationship to the U.S. forces and the Vietnamese: it lost the capacity or conviction necessary to fight the war on the maximum scale. There may also, no doubt, have been a secondary effect in the form of a changed attitude on the part of the administration to those individual viewers who were the subjects of the primary effect.

These distinctions are worth making because they help to show that the notion of effects can quickly and without undue stretching become quite complex; whereas it will be argued below that the bias of media research has conventionally limited itself to a rather narrow definition.[10]

Finally, only certain kinds of changed relationship are at issue because we are concerned simply with the *political* effects of mass media. We should note that the parties to a relationship may not agree whether it is political. The primary effect of a particular communication may thus be political and the secondary effect not, or *vice versa*. For example reading about a certain parliamentary candidate might make a constituent decide to campaign actively on his behalf, with the secondary consequence of a temporary reduction in the social activities enjoyed with his family. Or news items about, say, environmental pollution might increase public knowledge of its dangers, which politicians would then articulate as a policy issue.

III. THE PRODUCTION OF MASS MEDIA EFFECTS

What is it in the communication process that produces these changed relationships which constitute media effects? The answer depends partly on the elements of each particular communication and partly on its 'communication context' – its relationship to other communications.

(a) The particular communication

The essential point here is that an effect may be caused by all or any of the elements of a communication process – sender, message, medium and receiver. In primary effects the effect may be on the receiver or on the sender (or both); in which case the effect is likely to stem only from three elements at most – i.e. excluding whichever is the affected element. Nonetheless it is possible to find situations where a receiver may be affected not only by a sender, message and/or medium but also by his own awareness of being a receiver. Jay Blumler's study of producers' attitudes to TV coverage of the 1966 British general election provides an example. Producers' resistance to adverse comment from the parties about programmes was stiffer than it might have been: 'Since no member of the *24 Hours* staff had an office to himself, the reactions of a receiving producer to telephoned party comments were immediately visible to many of his colleagues. Those responses, then, were inevitably conditioned by the reference group norms of a circle of dedicated television journalists.'[11] In secondary effects, of course, this consideration does not apply, since the individual or group affected is not a direct element in the communication process.

It is impossible to generalise about which elements most commonly produce effects: in many cases it would not be possible to separate them anyway. The relationship of political parties and newspapers provides an example. The analysis in Chapters 6 and 7 raises the question, 'What was the effect of the development of the mass press in the nineteenth century upon the growth of modern parties?' Whatever the answer, it is unlikely we could satisfactorily separate effects caused by the control of party papers (sender, medium) from those of their contents (message) and the existence of mass readerships (receivers). The example illustrates another point: the effective elements may vary greatly with the kind of changed relationships one is interested in. If one is interested in broad effects on political culture (i.e. aggregate effects on individuals, and with the stress on the individual's relationship to the total political system) one may be conscious of changes induced by the use of a particular medium which, to someone interested in a short-run change in a certain individual, seem less significant than the effects of a particular message. The classification of relationships is discussed in Chapter 2 (section II): the selection of illustrations here is arbitrary.

(*i*) *Sender*. Who says something may be much more effective than what he says. Harold Wilson forbade any discussion of devaluation of sterling as a policy option after the Labour Government took office in 1964: newspaper stories saying even that the word had been uttered in cabinet could have started a run on the pound making the policy difficult to avoid.* When devaluation did take place three years later the preliminary discussions were limited to a handful of civil servants and ministers. The cabinet itself was excluded until the decision had been taken: by Wilson's own account it was asked only to *confirm* the decision.[12] Because devaluation, at least in a system of fixed exchange rates, is such a classic case of a self-fulfilling policy option, those with authority to implement it simply cannot afford to have people know they contemplate it. Discussion by people remote from that authority, in contrast, might be harmless. A speculative story in an uninformed newspaper might rouse no interest in financial circles, while the same story by an authoritative journalist, well known to have sources in the Treasury or the Government, might create consternation.

Another example, analysed in detail in Chapter 3, is provided by reaction to the support of *The Times* for the appeasement policy in the late 1930s. The editor was known to be a good friend of the Prime Minister and Foreign Secretary. His views on how to deal with Hitler coincided exactly with theirs. The result was that abroad *The Times* was seen, not least in Germany itself, as the Government's mouthpiece – a guide to present and future British intentions. Occasionally this led to dramatic results; the most sensational being the consequences of a leading article in September 1938, published at the height of the Czechoslovak crisis. The article was interpreted throughout the chanceries of Europe as signalling the British Government's preparedness to see Czechoslovakia dismembered rather than risk a European war. Other papers supported appeasement as strongly as *The Times*; and the *New Statesman* had in fact

* Cf. George Brown, *In my way* (1971), p. 105: '(Devaluation) was a very difficult subject to discuss because it was absolutely essential that nobody should know that it was being discussed . . . The Prime Minister and the Chancellor were not unnaturally always terrified lest talking, or even thinking, about devaluation should alert the world to what was going on and give our friends the "Gnomes" the opportunity which would force that result'.

made the same suggestion about Czechoslovakia at an earlier date. But the historical prominence of *The Times* and its editor's privileged position in the political élite compelled attention to its views. On a more modest scale *The Times* has persistently been assumed abroad to stand in a privileged relation to the government. Twenty years after the Czech crisis an article speculating that Harold Macmillan was about to replace Selwyn Lloyd as Foreign Secretary led to exactly the same reaction at a European security conference Lloyd was attending in Geneva. Whether or not Macmillan had been intending to dismiss Lloyd, it was certainly impossible for him to do so for the time being after that! Indeed he went out of his way to declare publicly in the Commons next day that he looked forward to working with Lloyd for a long time to come.[13]

The history of *Private Eye* illustrates the importance of a sender in rather a different way. Chapter 9 suggests that this magazine, the leading product in the print medium of the 1960s 'satire boom', played the role of Fool at a feudal court. Because it made no pretence at distinguishing truth and falsehood, fantasy and reality, it could occasionally state truths about people which would have led to massive libel damages if published in any magazine that expected to be taken seriously. To sue *Private Eye* in the early 1960s, unless one wished to play the Fool oneself – or to risk looking one – was out of the question. The Fool was beyond the reach of normal social rules. Because of the role they defined for themselves, in other words, information published by the editors of *Private Eye* had to be treated differently by readers, and specially by the people *about* whom it was written, than information in ordinary journals.

(*ii*) *Message*. The obvious fact that mass media messages have effects does not need illustration, particularly as so much empirical work has concentrated on measuring precisely this kind of effect (see Chapter 2, section I). What needs stressing, as research has again and again shown, is that the screens of selective exposure, perception and retention, through which a message has to pass in order to affect someone, are substantial; so that the meaning of the message transmitted by the sender may bear little relation to its meaning for the receiver.

(*iii*) *Medium*. The characteristics of the medium by which a message is transmitted can have considerable effects. A few examples were touched on in section I. They need little elaboration here beyond reference to some of the studies later in the book. The medium is critical because it so easily affects the behaviour both of sender and receiver, as well as giving distinctive shape to the message.

Chapter 5 considers some of the reactions of M.P.s to the prospect of televising House of Commons proceedings. Instead of being interpreted to the public by the craftsmanlike hand of the parliamentary reporter, debates would now appear raw on the screen, albeit in the form of minced extracts. Would M.P.s be obliged to modify their well-tried procedures and habits because these were incomprehensible if not absurd to the viewer, even though for the most part they were functional (even the schoolboy boos)? Would everyone rush to speak, eager to show their constituents they were busy and thereby giving the whips a new tool of pressure? Would the remaining spontaneity of debate evaporate because M.P.s talked over the heads of their colleagues to the constituencies beyond? Would Ministers hog the floor, to the disadvantage of the Opposition front bench, let alone the backbenchers? Or would the aggressor in debate – the destructive critic – have all the advantages, so that governments appeared for ever on the defensive? Would Prime Ministers tend to appoint the telegenic to ministerial office? Would Parliament, in short, become more of a theatre and less of a workshop (whatever the present balance) – and all because television poked its cameras out of the panelling? One might think the changes good or bad. The fact remains, they would be the product simply of a new medium.

Television has had effects on election campaigns too (Chapter 8). One small illustration in Britain is the institution of daily press conferences, normally at the party headquarters in London. These qualify aptly for Daniel Boorstin's definition of 'pseudo-events'. They tend to be a roundabout of ritual trivia as journalists and cameramen traipse from one conference to another, bouncing the comments of the rival spokesmen off each other, looking for the indiscretion or the original quote. They flourished partly because of the needs of television. In the U.S.A. television time, there for the buying, has made an enormous difference to electioneering for both state and national office. It has helped to shrink the sprawl of geography and encourage image-building and packaged candidates (including the alteration of physical features – tooth-capping, hair-dyeing, etc.). If assassination of presidential candidates increased much more it is probable that campaigning would be carried on almost entirely on television. Nixon's 1972 campaign went quite far in that direction anyway. Outside elections television has tipped the balance of power between Congress and the President in the President's favour.

The effect of particular media is manifest at the broadest and the narrowest levels of analysis. Is it possible in the television age for a democratic society to sustain an aggressive overseas war? Would television coverage have changed the length or outcome of the Korean war? What if the cameras had been in strength at Hiroshima and Nagasaki? At completely the opposite end of the scale one may consider a modest effect of the difference, as media, between the small circulation, broadsheet 'quality' papers in Britain and the mass circulation tabloids. Their various specialist correspondents regularly have encounters with ministers. At some, at least, of these the difference in the type of paper is reflected in the different concern and behaviour of the ministers. The tabloids want a good quote, and the minister wants a good image in return. The 'quality' papers want a dialogue, and the minister shares their concern for analysis and issues.

(iv) *Receivers*. The most important effects of the receivers in a communication process are secondary effects: they stem from the calculation of some third party or group about the importance to attach to a sender or message by virtue of the audience concerned. One reason foreigners paid attention to *The Times* in the 1930s was that its readers included many of those exercising political and economic power in Britain. The controllers of other papers often received political rewards, if they sought them, because their readers were strong in number if not individually. Even in the 1960s, long after the heyday of the press barons like Northcliffe, Rothermere and Beaverbrook, who were politically ambitious yet independent of party, Cecil King, controller of the *Daily Mirror* and *Daily Herald*, was offered a junior post in Harold Wilson's Labour administration. He had no parliamentary or political experience whatsoever: his weight rested roundly on his direction of the entire Labour mass circulation national daily and Sunday press.

The weight to attach to particular contents of mass media depends also on the type of audience. If circulation is limited, items may be ignored to which persons concerned would otherwise have to respond. Enoch Powell's speeches on coloured immigration into Britain are an outstanding example (examined in detail in Chapter 4). One speech in particular attracted such massive coverage that within a few days ninety-six per cent of the respondents in an opinion poll claimed to have heard of it. Moreover the coverage interpreted the speech as a threat to Edward Heath's position as leader of the Conservative Party. Although Powell had often deviated before from party orthodoxy the public attention to this one occasion forced Heath to reply with a decisive act asserting his authority. He sacked Powell from the Conservative shadow cabinet within thirty-six hours of the speech.

The same principle lies behind the traditional practice of exposure journalism: because information is published to a certain kind or size of audience from whom someone would have preferred it concealed, that person is obliged to behave differently. Where the exposure does not carry moral overtones it is better described as *disclosure*. Often this consists simply in publishing information sooner than its 'owners' would have liked, as in the case of Harold Macmillan's cabinet reshuffle in 1962, which is described in the next section.

Where someone wishes to prevent information being distributed he may have to make nice calculations about the costs incurred. The experiences of *Private Eye* (Chapter 9) again illustrate the point well. Its significant readership and reputation in 1962 enabled it to publish libels without serious risk of retribution. Exactly the same was true of the virtually private newsletter *Westminster Confidential* (circulation about two hundred) which was the first medium to publish rumours about possible incompatibilities in the private friendships and public office of Macmillan's War Minister John Profumo. Government leaders took a calculated decision not to squash the rumours at that source, since legal action would probably have been counter-productive and led to more publicity.[14]

(b) The communication context

Acts of communication do not take place in a vacuum. The effects of a particular communication – whichever elements of the process produce them – are also determined by its relationship to other acts of communication. This relationship has three aspects: *timing*, *frequency* and *intensity*. One or all of these may be very important.

(*i*) *Timing*. The time at which a piece of information is transmitted may make all the difference to its significance. The timing of communication processes is probably one of the most important determinants of mass media effects. Yet it is largely neglected in research. Where timing is important the most trivial increment of information may change the course of events, without any need for those changes in attitude which so many researchers look for. On the other hand the effects of timing are not easy to pin down. At the microscopic level of day-to-day changes in the political relationships of individuals the effect may perhaps be almost continuous, if rather weak. But the clearest examples to quote are at the other end of the scale – once-for-all effects, often of a crude or general nature. In theory one could distinguish, too, between the consequences of timing and of sequence; the former relating a single communication process to the concerns and activities of those involved, while the latter measured the significance of the *order* in which a set of communications took place. In practice, however, both are referred to as the effects of timing in the illustrations that now follow.

The Zinoviev Letter (*1924*). This episode is worth tracing in some detail, for it is a classic case of effectiveness caused by timing. The authors of the most exhaustive inquiry into it conclude: 'publication of the Zinoviev letter constituted the biggest election campaign "windfall" for the Conservative Party in this or any other century'.[15] If the letter had remained secret for another five days its impact would have been completely different, if not insignificant. Whether it actually lost Labour the 1924 general election seems extremely doubtful. But in the Labour movement particularly it was for years believed to have done so. The letter dominated the 1924 campaign from its publication on Saturday 25 October until Polling Day on the 29th.

In its short life the first Labour Government, existing on the sufferance of the other two parties, trod extremely delicately. Russian affairs were a subject of some of its bolder initiatives. Besides the important symbolic gesture of giving the Soviet régime diplomatic recognition, Ramsay MacDonald negotiated commercial treaties settling Tsarist debts in return for a £50 million loan. Relations with Russia were thus bound to be an election issue. From the beginning of the campaign the overwhelmingly Conservative national press, led by the *Daily Mail* (with, at 1·8 million, twice the circulation of its nearest rival) attacked Labour persistently for these policies and tarred the party with the communist brush. The publication of the Zinoviev letter was thus the climax of a Red Scare not the beginning of one.

The 1,200-word letter, marked Very Secret, bore the address of the Third Communist International, the organisation in Moscow responsible for international communist tactics. Signed by the president, Grigory Zinoviev, it was directed to the Central Committee of the British Communist Party. Its theme was the necessity of stirring the British proletariat out of its habits of compromise and into revolutionary action. The party was to 'strain every nerve' in favour of the Anglo-Soviet treaties; encourage exchanges of British and Russian workers with a view to spreading Leninism; and concentrate on forming cells in the armed forces – 'the future directors of the British Red Army'.[16] It now seems clear the document was a forgery, as many people in the Labour movement claimed at the time. It was probably drafted by Russian émigrés in Berlin and planted in the European intelligence network. It reached the Foreign Office on 10 October. MacDonald, who doubled as Foreign Secretary and Prime Minister, received it with routine papers on 16 October while campaigning furiously in Scotland. He minuted that its authenticity must be established with great care and a draft note of protest drawn up meanwhile to send to Rakovsky, the Soviet chargé d'affaires in London. On 23 October MacDonald, by now in Wales, saw the draft and sent it back with alterations. On 24 October the *Daily Mail* procured a copy of the letter for itself. The paper had known about it previously and had already published hints which made clear to the Foreign Office that Conservative Central Office also had a copy (or at least knew of its existence). Probably because they feared the Labour Government would be badly embarrassed if the *Mail* published the letter before it was officially released – the Conservatives could claim Labour had intended to hush it up till after Polling Day – the Foreign Office released it on the afternoon of the 24th. This was done without MacDonald's knowledge: the Permanent Under-Secretary was completely satisfied about the letter's authenticity. The text of the note to Rakovsky was also released.

The next day, Saturday, saw a deluge of publicity. The *Mail* had seven decks of headlines:

CIVIL WAR PLOT BY SOCIALISTS' MASTERS
Moscow Orders To Our Reds
Great Plot Disclosed Yesterday
Paralyse the Army and Navy
And Mr MacDonald Would Lend Russia Our Money
Document Issued by Foreign Office
After 'Daily Mail' Had Spread the News

The *Mail*'s treatment was the most strident, but the entire press gave it blanket coverage. With the exception of Labour's *Daily Herald* (which had one-sixth of the *Mail*'s circulation) the letter's reception was uncritical. The *Herald* alone declared outright that it was a forgery; but thereafter the paper was inevitably thrown on the defensive. The ramifications of the affair filled the remaining days of the campaign. MacDonald's reaction was slow and clumsy. He made no comment at all until the Monday night, leaving Conservative campaigners like Birkenhead and Churchill to ram home their advantage while Labour waited bewildered the entire weekend for a lead. Papers stepped up their news from Russia. *The Times* discovered ANOTHER RED PLOT IN GERMANY. The *Express* carried a banner across every page on Polling Day, saying in red ink: DO NOT VOTE RED TODAY.

If the Zinoviev letter had been published *after* the election or not at all, what would have been the difference? Baldwin allegedly thought the letter 'materially assisted' but did not 'vitally affect' the Conservative victory.[17] Labour lost 50 seats but gained more than a million votes. The Conservatives gained 155 seats and 2½ million votes. The Liberals lost over 100 seats and were reduced to a rump of 42. It may be that the ability of the Conservatives to form a majority government was decided by the letter. In the longer run it is also arguable that the episode reversed the trend towards acceptance of the Soviet régime: Russian isolation was perpetuated, and that proved a bad handicap when Europe had to handle Nazi Germany.[18] It may be, too, that Labour's feeling of having been tricked out of office blinded the party to the need for reconstruction internally and prevented the leadership from realising its own loss of contact with the rank and file.[19] Finally the episode spawned in party activists a suspicion that the Conservatives would always look for a stunt to frighten voters with the spectre of a revolutionary Labour government. The possibility was taken very seriously in 1945, and even in 1950 platform speeches were fraught with warnings.[20]

Other examples of the importance of timing can be quoted more briefly.

The Times' leading article on the Sudetenland (*7 September 1938*). This incident is analysed at some length in Chapter 3. In September 1938 Hitler was in the process of bullying the British and French into accepting the dismemberment of Czecho-Slovakia, on the grounds that the German-speaking people in the Sudetenland wished incorporation into the Reich. The crisis lasted some six months, from April 1938 onwards. Hitler achieved his goal in the Munich agreement within the time limit he had set himself – 1 October. At first Britain and France had stood firm in support of the Czechs. The importance of *The Times'* leader of 7 September was that, in the words of Anthony Eden, it was 'a loosening of the stone that sets off the avalanche'. The article raised the possibility that the secession of the Sudetenland Germans might not be a bad idea. The prestige of *The Times* meant that the suggestion was immediately taken by the French, Germans and Czechs themselves to emanate from Downing Street. It did not, in fact: but it did prove to be the 'solution' that was eventually imposed. The paper had made exactly the same suggestion at an earlier stage, on 3 June. Then the reaction had been of little consequence. Now, at a stage when the German determination was harder, Czech resistance beginning to crumble and the crisis that much deeper, the implications of the article were enormously greater. A significant detail confirming the importance of the timing was that Geoffrey Dawson, *The Times'* editor, was much taken aback by the general uproar: for he judged the article by its substance and not by its context.

The Bay of Pigs invasion (1961). In April 1961 anti-Castro forces, organised with the help of American Central Intelligence Agency funds, launched an unsuccessful invasion of Cuba, landing in the Bay of Pigs. The affair humiliated the recently elected President John F. Kennedy: it was completely inconsistent with the foreign policy image he had sought to project, specially towards developing countries. The *New York Times* had received prior information of the invasion. But after a good deal of internal argument they decided at the last minute *not* to publish it. Ironically, of course, Kennedy wished heartily after the event that they had done so: he admitted that publication would probably have stopped the invasion and saved his administration from a disastrous mistake.*[21] The example is thus an unusual one, since it shows the dramatic consequences of withholding publication; examples more commonly illustrate the effects of *premature* publication.

Harold Macmillan's cabinet changes (13 July 1962). By July 1962 Harold Macmillan had been Prime Minister for five-and-a-half years. He had borne up the Conservative party after the traumatic Suez crisis and the resignation of Anthony Eden and brought it triumphant through the 'You've never had it so good' election of 1959. The party increased its majority then for the third election running. After that the glitter began to tarnish. Four grotesque by-election results in November 1961 reduced the Conservative vote by an average of nearly 20 per cent. Equally bad results followed in the spring, including the Liberal apotheosis at Orpington, where a Conservative stronghold was shattered by a 27 per cent Liberal swing. Local government elections were also disastrous. Pressure naturally grew in the party for changes – fresh policies and new younger faces. A cabinet reshuffle was expected anyway in the autumn; the by-elections were probably an important factor in the decision to bring them forward.

On Thursday 12 July the *Daily Mail* carried an inspired story, with the headline MAC'S MASTER PLAN, forecasting a major cabinet reshuffle by the autumn and mentioning specific changes, some of which turned out to be right. The story caused a hum of speculation at Westminster. In yet another by-election the same day the Conservative came a bad third. Friday's press excitedly expected cabinet changes by the end of the month. In fact they came that very day. Under the eagle eye of the press parliamentarians went to and fro to the Prime Minister in an embarrassing stream. An official announcement came at 7.00 p.m. Mr Macmillan had sacked

* James Reston has pointed out that other papers knew as well and did publish. *The artillery of the press* (1966), pp. 30–1. They did not carry the weight of the *New York Times*, however.

no less than 7 out of 21 cabinet ministers, including the Foreign Secretary (Selwyn Lloyd) and Lord Chancellor (Lord Kilmuir). Junior changes brought the total appointments affected to 36.

Shedding a third of the cabinet would always require a delicate touch; and even more so now, when the aim was, in the *Mail*'s words, 'to give the Government a new look and infuse it with fresh energy'. Many of the ministers were 'senior', in that special sense implying long service and loyalty, and five had offered to retire whenever the Prime Minister found it convenient. But the haste of the exercise spoilt both the impression of freshness and the dignity of the farewell to old colleagues. Instead of a reshuffle the press dubbed it a purge – 'the night of the long knives' – and conjured the images of butchery. 'The trouble from Mr Macmillan's point of view', wrote the *Sunday Times*' Political Correspondent, 'is that hostile reactions to what has been termed the "shabby and disreputable treatment" of senior colleagues have blurred the excellent effect of 90 per cent of the vast reconstruction'.[22] This was true in a variety of ways, ranging from short-term resentments inside the party to the long-term loss of confidence in Mr Macmillan's leadership. For the haste and resulting shabbiness the press, started off by the *Mail*'s speculation, took clear responsibility. The timing was critical, and Mr Macmillan acknowledged it openly. His farewell letter to Lord Kilmuir began: 'The widespread speculation in the Press and the undesirability of a period of uncertainty made it necessary to complete the reconstruction of the Government as rapidly as possible'. Of course he may have been glad to blame the press; even so, to have delayed once the speculation started would almost certainly not have made matters any better.[23]

The BBC and the devaluation of sterling (1967). Harold Wilson was woken up on the morning of 16 November 1967 by an excited phone call from Richard Crossman, Leader of the House of Commons, asking what was going on. 'I then opened my morning papers and realised why he was so upset. They carried splash stories, clearly put out from Paris, about a massive international loan.'[24] Page one of *The Times*, for instance, said: 'An officially unconfirmed report from Paris relayed by the BBC that Britain is negotiating a $1,000 million (£357 million) international loan threw politicians on both sides at Westminster into a flurry of mixed disquiet and speculation last night.' The effective decision to devalue the pound had already been taken on 13 November: it was confirmed by the cabinet on the morning Mr Crossman woke the Prime Minister up. The devaluation was not announced, however, until the 18th. The period from the BBC's report up until then was free for speculation – both intellectual and financial. The BBC's rumour implied that unusual manœuvres were being undertaken to defend the currently hard pressed pound. It led directly to urgent questions in the Commons on the following day. The answers given by the Chancellor of the Exchequer, James Callaghan, unfortunately added fuel to the fire. He was in precisely one of those situations where it was impossible not to communicate. If he had admitted negotiations were taking place, opinion might have been reassured. If none was taking place, would it have done harm to say so? In fact he said 'no comment', and that simply encouraged people to infer negotiations were taking place but had run into difficulties. That was the view of *The Times*. Harold Wilson thought Callaghan had no choice. But there was no doubt about the outcome. 'Within minutes of that answer, the world's foreign exchange markets went mad', Wilson's memoirs recall. 'But what else could the Chancellor have done? The run on sterling which then developed after a reasonably quiet day, and which intensified to record proportions on the following day, cost us hundreds of millions.'[25] The timing of the BBC's story was primarily to blame.

The occupation of Czechoslovakia by Warsaw Pact forces (1968).[26] In the early hours of 21 August 1968 the reform movement inside the Czechoslovak Communist Party, nurtured under the leadership of Alexander Dubcek since the 'Prague Spring' of that year, was brought to a halt. Russian and Polish troops landed at Prague Airport. Soon tanks from three other Warsaw Pact countries crossed the border. The pretext was that Czech leaders had asked for assistance from their allies to put down a minority of 'counter-revolutionary elements' in the party and government. 'Normalisation' was restored, but not until the Czech and Slovak peoples had made plain to themselves and to the outside world that the intervention was aggressive in intent and overwhelmingly resented. As a military operation it was a success; as a political one, a failure. The Czech mass media played an important part in relaying these feelings and countering the Warsaw Pact propaganda. At crucial moments – when the occupying forces came on the streets, when the Czech leaders issued a declaration condemning the invasion and when they were detained – radio and television managed to continue broadcasting uncensored information and pictures and to warn their audiences against the propaganda stations being set up. Furthermore their persistence meant that 'normalisation' took longer to impose. A puppet government did not quickly arise and silence the media, as the occupying powers hoped. Formal censorship, officially reintroduced on 1 September, did not at once become effective. The media continued stressing over and over again 'that Czechoslovakia had not been threatened by a "counter-revolution", that the leading politicians and statesmen had been firmly in control of the situation and that even without a military intervention they could have handled it'.

Radio and television were able to broadcast effectively for so many days because of the sympathy and assistance they received from the public (including the police), and because the technical means for clandestine broadcasting had long ago been prepared – against the possibility, ironically, of a NATO invasion. After their studios were occupied broadcasters showed great ingenuity in improvising and concealing studios in uncompleted buildings, private homes and factories. 'They not only transmitted information on internal and external affairs (which alone was a difficult task considering the lack of communication and a disrupted information system) but they did not shrink from issuing political comment, and discussed such themes as the illegality of the invasion by foreign troops, the loyalty of the majority of the people to the political leadership (of the Dubcek régime) and the adherence to ideals of a humanistic and democratic socialism.' One television journalist has described how he and a few colleagues worked. On the 21st they managed to film the advancing tanks, though an East German soldier spotted them and confiscated most of their equipment at gunpoint. Then they established themselves in a clandestine studio. 'Wearing dark glasses, carrying our equipment in shopping bags, we roamed through the streets. We were handed various resolutions in the factories and plants we visited and these formed the raw material for our reports. At 10 p.m. there was a curfew. It was during this time that we worked hardest. Our studios were visited by prominent guests, who had to stay with us in our improvised offices . . .' On the 28th they reluctantly obeyed a Central Committee order – given under the terms required by Moscow – to stop.

In this example too, then, it was the timing of media activity that was critical: media continued to reach audiences successfully – including abroad – far beyond the point at which they became embarrassing to the aims of the occupying powers.

(*ii*) *Frequency.* By frequency of communication is meant its repetition in more or less the same form over a period of time. The effects of this are rather general: for one cannot regard messages as being repeated, even if they are routine matters like the weather forecast or *Yesterday in Parliament* on the BBC, unless one defines them in general terms (i.e. no two editions of the weather forecast are identical). The effects of frequency thus feature often in fairly broad discussions about the effects of mass media on social or political systems as a whole. (See Chapter 2, section I below.)

Without being quite as broad as that one may suggest the following illustrations.

The climate of politics. This is something wider than specific issues; a matter, rather, of the whole agenda of politics at a particular time. It is difficult to believe that this is not affected by the regular drip of mass media contents. Euthanasia in the 1960s was a taboo political issue in Britain: would it be twenty years later? Much social legislation in 1964–70 concerned subjects like homosexuality and abortion for which there would not have been a climate in the 1950s. Over a slightly longer term, the acceptance of, say, Keynesian economics, comprehensive education and motorists' breathalyser tests surely all owed something to the sustained attention given to them in the mass media. Shifts in the climate can sometimes be marked by institutional changes: for instance the relative status and space in their media given to different specialist correspondents is one barometer. In the 1960s Education and Economics correspondents flourished: Commonwealth correspondents slipped back. Politicians notice the climate too. In an unusually explicit acknowledgement of this kind of media effect Lord Boyle, when asked about the determinants of cabinet business, replied (on the strength of his experience in the Macmillan and Home governments): 'The Cabinet increasingly, as the years go on, tends to be most concerned with the agenda that the press and media are setting out as the crucial issues before the nation at any one time.'[27]

A 'Westminster view' of British politics. The construction regularly put up on the nature of British politics by the mass media stresses heavily the 'Westminster' as opposed to the 'Whitehall' elements. The power of Parliament, and the extent to which it figures in political processes at all, are arguably emphasised more than they should be if an accurate impression of events is to be given. If that is so, the frequency of media coverage has much to do with it. Parliamentary debates often provide the lead story in British newspapers, and the 'quality' papers publish a full-page précis daily.

Various explanations of this situation can be offered. The status of the Lobby correspondents, focusing on Westminster, remains high in the journalistic profession. Journalism and parliamentary politics overlap often as careers. Parliament is highly accessible as a news source, specially compared with Whitehall and the unpredictable if not necessarily sinister activity of interest groups. Parliament, in return, is most anxious to communicate with the public: as elected representatives its members must communicate if they are to attract any attention. Their appeal to the people and to 'public opinion' is one of their few effective sanctions. For the M.P. knowledge is power; if he sees his job as representing constituency interests and supervising the several types of executive power, he must have information. Exactly the same is true for the media organisations. The argument can be taken a step further, for the frequency of communications about parliament has a secondary effect on parliament itself. Since parliament depends on contact with the electorate it is probable that all this media attention does in fact increase parliament's effective power: the media's view of politics is thus to some extent self-fulfilling.

'*Negative frequency.*' The above examples suggest that the primary effects of the frequency of communications about a subject are to define the matters that audiences think *about*, even if they do not determine audience attitudes towards them, let alone their behaviour. It is important to note that frequency has an effect in inverse ratio on subjects that are *not* communicated. For every Ibo baby fed out of funds collected after media coverage of the Nigerian civil war, some other child in a part of the world untouched by the zoom-lens of TV war reportage starved. In the 1950s and 1960s mass media audiences cared nothing about the problems of Northern Ireland because they were told nothing about them. Overseas subjects provide the best examples because there is so much to leave out and relatively little regular space for overseas news in the media. But the principle obviously holds for domestic subjects too. For example the British government had an easy time implementing its policy of entry to the EEC in 1971–2 (once the parliamentary arithmetic was assured) because with a single exception – the *Daily Express* – the entire national press supported the idea. The government did not need to sell it at all, still less out-argue an opposition and counter the unfavourable interpretations and information that might have been adduced. The press sold the policy for them. Similarly the United States media seem in retrospect to have been unduly slow to criticise the Administration's policy in Vietnam in the early 1960s (with a few minor exceptions).

(*iii*) *Intensity*. Much of what has been said about the effects of frequency applies also to the intensity of communication processes. Intensity refers to the relationship between a communication and other communications going on at the same time. For example if one story completely dominated the press we should say it was communicated more intensely than when attention was shared between several stories. In practice the connection with frequency is close, for if one is interested in a wide time-span – a general election, for instance – communications may derive part of their intensity from what are, strictly speaking, sequential and not simultaneous communications.

General elections in fact provide various illustrations of the effects of intensity. On a broad scale, the mass media are extremely important in focusing public attention on an election: they help to make it a genuine process of popular political control (or to foster a myth, if one prefers to look at it that way) and to confirm the legitimacy of the political institutions. A crude indicator of intensity in the 1970 British election, for instance, is the simple statistic that 82 out of 135 lead stories (61 per cent) in the nine major national dailies in the three weeks before Polling Day were about the election. (Many of the exceptions were about the football World Cup.) The contrast with the lack of attention given to local government elections is extreme. So is the contrast between the voting turnouts – about three times as high at general elections. There is a chicken-and-egg problem about the role of the media in contributing to this discrepancy. But it seems plausible to suggest that the intensity of media coverage does make a difference to the size of the poll; and marginal differences can decisively affect the results.

On a more detailed scale the nature of media coverage can make an important difference to the course of the campaign. Indeed it is no exaggeration to claim that 'the campaign' exists only as a construct of the media: they give to the disconnected though more or less coordinated activities of the participants a kind of scrap-book tidiness, laying out the pieces in patterns, with prominence to some while others are tucked away at the back. The central question about this kind of effect is thus: 'How far does the media coverage coincide with the party leaders' own strategies for the campaign?' Is the same balance struck between issues and personalities and between particular issues and particular personalities? Brief illustrations can be drawn from press coverage of the 1970 election. Labour's strategy was for a 'quiet' campaign: they wanted to fight on their record and cash in on recent improvements in the British economy. Conservatives wanted to stress the economy as a major issue on several grounds – inflation, strikes and what they saw as Wilson's complacency about the balance of payments. How did newspaper performance fit those aims? Generally the press was against a 'quiet' election and in favour of debating issues – a pro-Conservative factor. Without exception they agreed that the economy was the issue to put first – another pro-Conservative factor covered with great intensity during election week. During the campaign there was a four-day strike of national newspapers – a pro-Labour factor inasmuch as it contributed to 'quietness'. The mass circulation press tended to presidentialise the campaign by projecting the issues in personal terms, particularly emphasising the party leaders. Since opinion polls showed Wilson rated much higher than Heath as a personality and leader, this factor was pro-Labour. Substantial attention was paid to the maverick campaign of Enoch Powell – up to twice as much in some papers as to the entire Liberal party – and on radio and television the Powell issue took up about one-fifth of all election coverage. Although cool in tone this attention threatened to distract from the Conservative onslaught on the economy issue. Major attention was also given to the opinion poll forecasts: 30 per cent of all lead stories on the election in the major dailies and Sundays in the three weeks before polling day were about them. These indicated a clear Labour victory – a pro-Labour factor, since they led to speculation about Heath's future as Conservative leader. Finally more papers were rooting for the Conservatives in the leader columns, and with more vigour, than for Labour. Overall one was left with the impression that the performance of the press – and the relative intensity of different subjects – coincided more closely with Conservative strategy than with Labour. That is not to say, of course, that it changed large numbers of votes or won the election for the Conservatives in some simple sense. But it affected the course of the campaign, the subjects the election was perceived to be 'about' and the relationships of the participants. After all that coverage, for instance, might Enoch Powell have been strong enough, if the party had lost, to force his way back into the Conservative leadership – if not to become leader himself?[28]

Enoch Powell in 1968. Powell's attraction for the media in 1970 stemmed from his activity in 1968. This has served as an illustration of earlier points. It is worth mentioning again because it was the intensity and the timing of media coverage of his outspoken views about immigration that created a crisis of party unity for Mr Heath and obliged him to sack Powell from the Shadow Cabinet. Moreover Heath's position was weakened however he reacted. Inside the Shadow Cabinet Powell would have remained a personal threat and a drag on party policy: outside, he would have less authority but be less subject also to control. Powell ensured maximum coverage by distributing copies of his speech direct to Sunday newspaper editors in good time for publication, and by timing it to fit in with recent concern about Kenyan Asian immigration and with the forthcoming parliamentary debate on Labour's Race Relations Bill.

Crisis definition. The claim that Powell's media coverage created a crisis for Heath can be generalised. When is something a political crisis? One answer is: when the media say it is.[29] Lord Boyle has been quoted as saying the cabinet uses as one guideline for the priorities of its business (apart, obviously, from routine and administrative matters) the agenda set out by the media. Crisis definition is simply an extension of this idea; and since 'crisis' denotes something unexpected and urgent the intensity of media coverage particularly contributes to it. The effects are heightened, furthermore, because crises demand immediate response – and normally action not words. Obviously the situations themselves that become crises are not necessarily created by the media: but the fact that they *become* crises, involving the investment of time and resources in their solution (at the expense, by corollary, of other activities) normally has a great deal to do with the media. Several of the case studies in this book illustrate the point: the famous *Times* leader on the Sudetenland (Chapter 3); the Profumo affair in Macmillan's government (Chapter 9); and Powell's case above all (both his own behaviour and the Kenyan Asians' plight which preceded it; Chapter 4). A checklist of the crises facing the government at any time would show that most of them involve intense media coverage. Differences in the checklists of ministers and the public would probably refer mainly to foreign affairs and security matters. It is worth noting, too, that crises often spill over into the media and become crises *for* them. Their role becomes a subject of attack, like the *New York Times* after the publication of official documents about Vietnam in 1971. In Britain in 1962 a tribunal of inquiry set up by the government to inquire into allegations arising from the detection of a spy in the Admiralty (the Vassall Tribunal) took on the colour of a witch hunt against the press and led to the imprisonment of two journalists for refusal to disclose to it their sources of information.

2

The political context
of mass media effects

The previous chapter sought to explain what mass media effects consist in and how they are produced. This chapter considers the question: 'what kinds of political relationship may be affected and with what results?' As the foreword to Chapter 1 stated, the essential argument of this book, which the case studies are intended to illustrate and support, is that mass media research could approach that question on a very much broader front than has been customary. The bulk of this chapter puts forward a simple set of categories within which a wider range of studies could be classified: it is illustrated again partly from the later chapters and partly from separate examples.

I. THE STUDY OF MASS MEDIA EFFECTS

Several surveys are available of the main traditions in mass media research, and a summary here would be redundant and inadequate.* The argument that research has been unduly narrow rests on two assertions. Firstly, studies have concentrated upon *primary effects*: that is, upon changes induced in individuals directly exposed to the media. The secondary effects – their consequences for other individuals or groups associated with the affected persons – have been emphasised less. Secondly, research has stressed effects upon one particular kind of political actor – those who comprise the *mass audience* ('the voter', 'the electorate', 'the manual worker', etc.).

Nothing illustrates these assertions better than Lasswell's well

* A thorough, concise and accessible introduction is Denis McQuail, *Towards a sociology of mass communications* (1969) which itself contains a full annotated bibliography. Other useful summaries and surveys are in J. D. Halloran, *The effects of mass communication; with special reference to television* (1965); J. D. Halloran, *The effects of television* (1970); J. T. Klapper, *The effects of mass communication* (1960); M. L. DeFleur, *Theories of mass communication* (1966); J. Tunstall (ed.) *Media sociology* (1970); D. Chaney, *Processes of mass communication* (1972); Walter Weiss, 'The effects of the mass media of communication', in G. Lindzey and E. Aronson, *Handbook of social psychology*, Vol. V (1969, 5 vols.).

known paradigm of the communication process, first published in 1948:

Who
Says what
In which channel
To whom
With what effect?[1]

Corresponding to each question is a field of analysis: control, content, media, audience and effect.

The construction of this formula, which became the model for much research, was narrow and static; and it focused inquiry predominantly upon audiences. The first four questions each describe an essential stage in a communication process, corresponding to the equally simple formulation 'sender, message, medium, receiver'. The question 'With what effect?' corresponds to no such essential stage: it is a different type of question, tacked on the end, hanging in space. Lasswell could as well have asked instead or in addition questions like 'How often?' or 'With what intention?' By picking out one question for special emphasis he narrowed the area of inquiry down. To answer the four questions about the elements of a communication process one has to concentrate solely on the process itself: to find out about content, one examines content; about senders, one examines senders. But to find out about effects, what does one examine? There is no group or object integral to the communication process corresponding to the 'effect' question. The answer depends entirely upon the prior questions 'Effect of what kind upon whom or what?' Yet these questions were not asked by Lasswell. In their absence the obvious approach is to refer his 'effect' question to the receiver of a communication – that is, to analyse the effect on audiences, the last stage in the process and the one immediately preceding the 'effect' question. This approach in turn contributes to a static view of communication processes, often referred to as the 'hypodermic' view. Someone 'jabs' a message into an audience: the audience is immediately affected by it.

Research projects in this tradition typically studied short-run, clearcut, relatively simple acts of individual behaviour. Several factors contributed to the tradition. They included the development of reliable sampling techniques (i.e. a more rigorous methodology than was available to answer wider questions); the influence of 'stimulus-response' theories of psychology; and both commercial and political interest in the potentialities and dangers of mass persuasion. In the study of politics an obvious illustration of the tradition and its limitations is the subject of elections. How do mass media affect elections? The natural interpretation of that question for Lasswell would be 'Do mass media change votes?'. Many studies have sought to answer that question: indeed it must be the most studied question of all about the political role of media. But, as Chapter 1 and Chapter 8 suggest, such an interpretation is not just unnecessarily narrow but even dangerous. For it invites the easy and superficial conclusion that if media exposure by the electorate, studied over a few weeks or months, has changed few votes, 'the effect of media on the election' is insignificant. An alternative interpretation of the question might be this: 'What is the function of media in the electoral process?' Lasswell's question sees media as communication channels, carrying messages which may or may not 'affect' the audience. The alternative makes no assumption that the effect of the media is limited to the potency of their messages (and of the media themselves). It leaves open the questions 'Effect of what kind upon whom or what?' When these are answered the function of mass media may be seen as far wider and more significant in the electoral process.

Those limitations of the research tradition in 'audience effects' are well known; and obviously they should not obscure the fact that within their limits such studies have built up – sometimes very skilfully – a considerable bank of data about the ways in which people accumulate information and the circumstances in which mass media may successfully change people's attitudes. The general drift of findings has confirmed that producing changes of opinion, particularly in an intended direction, is difficult and changes of behaviour even more so.[2] The early 'hypodermic' studies have given way, too, to different types of inquiry such as the 'uses and gratifications' approach, which puts less emphasis on 'what the media do to people than on what people do *with* the media'; the outstanding example in British political science being the work of Blumler and McQuail (1968).[3] There has also been a growth in studies of those parts of the communication process taken implicitly for granted by Lasswell's paradigm. Media organisations, in particular, are no longer treated as monoliths; and studies like Halloran, Elliott and Murdock's *Demonstrations and communication* (1970) have attempted to look at whole communication processes rather than particular elements. The general direction in which mass media research is moving is towards a greater awareness of the social context in which communication takes place. The 'effects' of mass media should no longer denote the limited meaning implicit in the older tradition. The result of that tradition has been to leave us with a thoroughly incomplete and misleading picture of how media effects operate and how politics works.

II. LEVELS OF POLITICAL RELATIONSHIPS

How, then, are we to answer the question posed at the start of the chapter – 'What kinds of political relationship are affected by mass media and with what results?' It has been postulated that every effect acts initially upon an individual and consists in a modification of his relationship with at least one other individual. The most limited political relationship that mass media may affect, therefore, is a bilateral relationship between two particular individuals. At the other end of the scale lies the political system considered as a whole – the totality of members of society in their interacting political roles.* The most extensive effect of mass media is thus upon the political system. Between those extremes lies a large number of groups or institutions. We can therefore classify mass media effects according to three levels: individual, intermediary group or institution, total system. Effects consist in changed relationships within one level or between one level and another, with the following combinations of pairs:

> System/Individual
> System/Institution
> Institution/Institution
> Institution/Individual
> Individual/Individual

(Since there is only one 'total system' there cannot, of course, be changes within that level. 'Effects on the system' turn out to be effects upon the relationship of individuals or institutions to the system – i.e. to changes *between* levels.) In practice, obviously, communications may affect more than one of those pairs at the same time: the detailed case study on Enoch Powell shows this very clearly (Chapter 4). For purposes of illustration, however, the examples below are limited just to pairs.

Levels of relationship are easy to distinguish. But what about the *terms* of relationship? Mass media effects comprise changes in knowledge, attitude or behaviour. Where they have a political

* Definitions of the concept 'political system' vary more in the meaning attached to 'system' than to 'political'. For present purposes the usage of Gabriel Almond and G. B. Powell is suitable though its looseness may offend sociologists: 'The political system includes not only governmental institutions such as legislatures, courts and administrative agencies, but *all structures in their political aspects.* Among these are traditional structures such as kinship ties and caste groupings; and anomic phenomena such as assassinations, riots and demonstrations; as well as formal organisations like parties, interest groups, and media of communications'. *Comparative Politics* (1966), p. 18.

quality those changes alter the relative 'weight' of the respective parties to the relationship in the balance of forces that govern the course of political events. For example, changes in viewers' attitudes as a result of the famous Kennedy–Nixon television debates in the election campaign of 1960 changed the relative weight of the two candidates.[4] In this specific sense of changing political 'weight', media can be said to have *objective* effects. But those are not the only effects people are interested in. The question 'Effects of what kind upon whom or what?' tends to expect a secondary and subjective answer. That is to say, people attach to the 'weights' affected by mass media varying weights (or significance) of their own. The full significance of media effects depends ultimately on the kind of political questions one is interested in. Do mass media encourage violence? Different research projects are equivocal about this; but some suggest no more than that latent violence may be made manifest by media among a small minority of audiences.[5] Are the political effects then negligible? If we are concerned with the political system as a whole, or with some of its institutions, or with the electorate, we may say yes. But suppose a Lee Harvey Oswald is one of that small minority: and suppose the object of his hate is not some insignificant voter but the President of the United States? Surely we do not then give the same answer, for the political role of the victim attaches priority in our minds to a completely different set of concerns.

Once we go beyond calculation simply of changes in the relative political 'weight' of parties affected by mass media, then the question 'What kind of political relationship do media affect?' becomes a question not about mass media at all but about the study of politics and the varieties of political theory. What constitutes a significant effect to one person may seem trivial to another. What were the effects of media coverage of Enoch Powell's immigration speeches? The answer depends on whether we are interested in Powell, Heath, the Conservative Party's electoral prospects in 1970, the party system at large, the Home Office, British political culture, race relations in Wolverhampton, the growth of revolutionary consciousness in the working class, the presentation of politics in terms of personalities or of issues, or something else. It would be absurd to try and reduce the preoccupations of students of politics to a few generalisations that would fit in with the categorisation above of levels of mass media effects. The examples below refer more or less explicitly to a variety of common themes, like the responsiveness of leaders to led, political stability and change, élites and social class, and functionalism. Given the bias of research towards studying primary effects upon individuals, the bias here is towards intermediary groups and institutions: the influence of mass media upon such topics as the role of parties, interest groups and the institutions of government is the great neglected area. For the same reason, individuals discussed below are mostly members of a political élite not anonymous units in a random sample. The examples are tabulated in a matrix in Figure 2.1 and elaborated under their separate headings. The detailed case studies in later chapters can be fitted into this scheme but have not been written exclusively to do so.

(a) *Political system and individual*

The most general form in which an individual's relationship to the political system may be affected by mass media is his perception of politics. Who are political actors? Do they control events or are they controlled by them? Is politics an estimable activity? What is a political issue? Awareness of and answers to such questions will partly be conditioned by qualities of the media themselves, such as their tendency to define events in short-run terms and their need to reduce subjects to convenient symbols for easy assimilation by audiences. Journalistic news values tend to stress élite individuals, negative events, human interest and topics that are culturally proximate. The significance of all these qualities becomes more explicit when a controversial subject arises. *Media coverage of Northern Ireland* (from 1969) provides an example. The media faced a difficult task. Their audiences were largely ignorant – Ireland had not been on the 'agenda' for nearly 50 years. There were few immediately recognisable symbols and stereotypes. The media themselves were largely ignorant too.* Widely divergent constructions were put upon events by various of the participants and by observers in Britain and the Irish Republic. A bomb is a bomb. But when newspapers juggled with less solid facts they found them no less explosive. Were those who made the bombs terrorists or freedom-fighters? Even the use of names – Derry versus Londonderry being the classic case – implied a value judgement (cf. west Germany and West Germany in the 1950s). The difficulties of the media in knowing whom and what to believe and what sort of context to place their reporting in were reflected in the cross-pressures that squeezed them on the spot, where the army might fling charges of 'treason' at them while the provisional IRA alleged Protestant bias. All the time, moreover, daily deadlines hampered attempts to put the contemporary issues in a historical setting and clear the smoke of the latest bomb from readers' eyes.

* The *Sunday Times* blamed itself for this fact in an editorial on the occasion of its 150th anniversary (15 October 1972).

FIGURE 2.1

EXAMPLES OF MASS MEDIA EFFECTS: CLASSIFIED BY LEVELS OF POLITICAL RELATIONSHIP

	Institution/Group	Individual
Political system	Entrenchment of the British monarchy Acceptance of the British judicial system and forces of law and order Role of parties in political systems TV's effect on the British Parliament Acceptance of the importance of general elections in Britain	Media coverage of Northern Ireland (1969–) Northcliffe's impact on the political system (from c. 1896); his own political career Enoch Powell in British politics (1968–)
Institution/Group	Relative strengths of political parties Effect of televising parliamentary debates upon Government and Opposition Effect of *Times* Sudetenland article (1938) on relations of European governments Institutional consequences of media's power to define political crises Effect of *Sunday Telegraph* disclosure of secret document on Nigerian/British govts Balance of power between President and Congress in the USA	Media role in protecting citizens against bureaucracy; consequences for relations of individual bureaucrats and the bureaucracy Resignation of Hugh Dalton from Attlee govt (1947) Resignation of J. Profumo from Macmillan govt (1963) Enoch Powell in the Conservative party (1968) Downfall of Senator Joe McCarthy (1954) Richard Nixon's candidacy as Vice-President (1952) Decline of Sen. Muskie's presidential aspirations (1972) Macmillan's cabinet purge (1962) Resignation of George Brown from Wilson govt (1968)
Individual		(Nixon/Eisenhower relations (1952)) (Brown/Wilson relations (1968)) (Powell/Heath relations (1968)) Kennedy/Nixon tv debates (1960)

One step beyond an individual's perception of politics is his acceptance or rejection of the legitimacy of the political system he perceives. The most plausible hypothesis *a priori* is that in advanced industrial societies mass media tend to reinforce the legitimacy of the system, or at most to be reformist. If they were extremist they might either lose their audiences or, if they kept them, drag the established political institutions in their wake, so that the thread of legitimacy was not broken. A broad example that supports that hypothesis is *Lord Northcliffe's effect on the political system* (from *c.* 1896). Northcliffe's name is associated with the transformation of the British press into a shape which it still retains. The narrow, small circulation journalism of the Victorian daily press was changed in a matter of years into mass circulation popular journalism. (Sunday journalism became 'popular' much earlier. It thrived on a diet of sport, sex, and crime. Many people in the nineteenth century who could buy a paper one day a week could not afford or did not want a daily. *Lloyds Weekly News* was already selling 100,000 copies in 1854, at a time when most dailies sold between 3,000 and 8,000, and in 1896 it became the first paper to sell a million.) Few of the innovations originated with Northcliffe himself. Most came from the United States; many of his most important associates were Americans or had American experience. So did the technical developments which made large print runs (i.e. large circulations) possible. The changes were only successful at all because the growth of the economy had provided a potential market for cheap daily papers and an advertising industry to feed it. Northcliffe's significance lay in being the first person to exploit the situation effectively with a daily paper and in building an organisation that towered over his competitors'.

At the heart of that organisation was the *Daily Mail*. Hence the growth of the popular press is often dated from its first appearance on 4 May 1896. The first number sold 397,215 copies. Within four years it was printing in Manchester as well as London and had a circulation of nearly one million. Compared with the heavily political Victorian papers it was lively, entertaining, full of snippets of inconsequential news, with particular appeal to women and those in the lower middle classes beginning to acquire purchasing power and leisure time. 'You could search the Victorian newspapers in vain', Northcliffe reminisced years later, 'for any reference to changing fashions, for instance. You could not find in them anything that would help you to understand the personalities of public men. We cannot get from them a clear and complete picture of the times in which they were published, as one could from the *Daily Mail*. Before that was published, journalism dealt only with a few aspects of life. What we did was extend its purview to life as a whole.'[6]

The rise of the popular press was certainly of revolutionary importance in a media context: as well as the changes of style and content it introduced a low-price, large-sale strategy; a new stress on profit; growing dependence on advertising; greater difficulty of entering the market; a different type of journalist; and two widening gaps between 'serious' and 'popular' papers and between national and provincial ones.* But the political consequences were overwhelmingly conservative. Although the new press was independent of party control and not entirely Conservative with a capital 'C', the values it represented were firmly in support of the existing social and political system; and of course its dependence on the existing economic system was complete. The *Mail* aped its betters. Its masthead said it was 'a penny newspaper for one halfpenny'. Northcliffe aimed it at the £1,000 a year man ('. . . well . . . they like to imagine themselves £1,000-a-year people').[7] It was the paper for those with aspirations – people who accepted society by and large as they found it, who enjoyed identifying with the personalities they read about in the gossip column, and who wanted to get on. When the Lib.–Lab. members were elected to Westminster in 1906 the *Mail* had a momentary fit; the class it represented was a cut above organised Labour. Not until the strained growth of the *Daily Herald* in the 1930s and the *Mirror*'s massive success in the 1940s was the working class wealthy and educated enough to sustain a popular paper. The *Mail* appealed to a class with conservative instincts. Northcliffe steered and interpreted them in a manner which must surely have sustained the legitimacy of the political system.

Northcliffe's control of an enormous newspaper empire – in the days before the electronic media, moreover – obviously affected his own relationship with the political system too. Whether papers could influence attitudes in a more 'hypodermic' manner in those days cannot be known. But politicians certainly thought it wiser to assume they might. The possession of papers therefore brought political power. First it brought membership of the House of Lords. Then came political office; never the really high office Northcliffe coveted – a seat in Lloyd George's war cabinet or membership of the British delegation to the Paris Peace Conference in 1919. But as Director of the British War Mission to the United States in 1917 he had considerable status and a real job (though it was also convenient to Lloyd George to have him out of the way); and in 1918 he was director of propaganda in enemy countries.

The distinctive quality of Northcliffe's political power, however,

---

* Hitherto the latter distinction had lain between *London* and provincial dailies; the point being that henceforth the London papers increasingly swamped the provincials on their own ground.

and the fact which makes it appropriate to look at his role in the political system as a whole, is his relative independence from any of the system's constituent institutions other than the press itself. Northcliffe depended on no intermediaries – in particular on no party. His links joined him, or so he might fancy, direct to the people. For their instincts, as his soaring career confirmed, he had a remarkable feel. Like party politicians he could claim responsibility to a constituency – the vast numbers of readers who voted with their pence. The party politicians, of course, did not see it that way: they resented his detachment from intermediary institutions, with their trammels of organisation, compromise and discipline. He played the kingmaker in the First World War, contributing to the triumph of Lloyd George as Prime Minister over Asquith. After the war he forsook Lloyd George and pursued a relentless vendetta against him. ('I would as soon trust a grasshopper', said Lloyd George.) But at the level of political infighting and jockeying for jobs his power was insubstantial; and at any level it was only as great as politicians believed it to be. They never feared him enough to grant him executive authority. In the last resort a media tycoon's bluff could always be called.

Enoch Powell's relationship to the political system (from 1968) shared a few of the same important features (see Chapter 4). Like Northcliffe he developed a 'constituency', consisting in the support of a large but indeterminate number of people who felt their views on certain issues – notably immigration – to be unrepresented. These people came from both parties: the opinion polls showed it, and in the 1970 election both sets of party managers wavered in their opinion whether his unorthodox campaign would gain them votes or lose them. Unlike Northcliffe, of course, Powell had to win his media coverage. This made him relatively weaker, though his skill in securing it was remarkable – especially when the external conditions were right, as they were for the Birmingham speech in 1968. On the other hand he had the strength, unlike Northcliffe, of having worked his passage inside the party system and, for a time, into the cabinet. His populist constituency was a supplement to his parliamentary one. Together they enabled him to stand in the historically not uncommon pose of a prophet armed; a public figure distant from party yet not over the hill, and waiting for the call that might one day draw him to power. Such a position is exceedingly difficult to achieve, let alone maintain. Access to the media may be an essential instrument: it certainly was for Powell.*

* Churchill, in the wilderness in the 1930s, never lost access to the press both through the reporting of Parliament and his own journalism. But he never had access at that time to the radio.

(b) Political system and institution

The entrenchment of the British monarchy. Not only is the monarchy the institution least subject to criticism and unfavourable publicity in the mass media: it attracts, on the contrary, a regular flow of approving publicity that becomes a flood on occasions like the investiture of the Prince of Wales in 1969. The investiture was preceded by two showings of a long television documentary, *Royal Family*, and three of a half-hour interview with Prince Charles. On the day itself there were live TV transmissions on two channels for over six hours, with 90-minute edited highlights presented at staggered times in the evening on all three channels. Radio also presented live coverage followed by recorded highlights. Coverage in the press was correspondingly intense (e.g. $12\frac{1}{2}$ pages in the *Daily Mirror* the following day).[8] The effect of this characteristic media attitude, it may be suggested, is to confirm the entrenchment of the monarchy as a social institution with quasi-political functions. The legitimacy of the political system, broadly defined, is embodied by the monarchy – and probably reinforced by it. Blumler and his colleagues found that the percentage of a sample who thought the British political system generally worked 'very well' or 'fairly well' rose from 60·4 per cent before the investiture to 68·6 per cent afterwards. Popular attitudes to the monarchy exhibit relatively little disapproval, and that which exists does not coincide sharply with normal political divisions. Conservatives and Liberals in Blumler's sample were more Royalist than Labour supporters but the difference was one of degree. More marked were variations in the approval of different age groups: 59 per cent of the 18 to 24-year-olds agreed that the Queen was 'a symbol of Britain at its best' – a figure which progressed to 86 per cent of the over-65s. Out of 26 opinions about the Queen, some of them critical, the suggestion that she 'prefers one political party to another' received least endorsement of all (18·0 per cent). Blumler interprets his evidence to support a religious analogy of the role of the monarchy. 'It is as if the Investiture brought to the fore a profound emotional commitment to the Monarchy, to the representatives of which the vast majority of people were prepared to extend an exceptional degree of respect'. Many other communication channels contribute to this attitude. It is likely that at the very least the media confirm it.

The same argument can be advanced in a rather weaker form about the effect of the mass media on *the judicial system and the forces of law and order*. Journalists' fear of the severity of the law of contempt (exaggerated, in the view of some jurists)[9] has led to serious criticism of the courts being extremely rare in the mass media, except in generalities. One of the distinctive features of the underground press in the later 1960s was their criticism in this area. (*Private Eye* adopted the habit too, in a fairly mild form.) Unlike the monarchy the courts need respect in order to function properly: they depend heavily on symbols like the wig and gown and various ritual procedures that stress the impersonality and indifference of justice. Lack of media criticism may therefore be correspondingly more important to them. The police have some of the same characteristics. Public goodwill is important to them and may be harmed by criticism, though criticism may of course be justified. In the 1960s the volume of criticism grew very substantially.[10]

◊ *The role of parties in political systems.* The range of relationships between individual newspapers and parties and between press systems and party systems is very wide. (See Chapters 6 and 7.) There is a chicken-and-egg problem about how far the importance of a particular party has been caused by its relationship with the press. But there are certain recurring patterns of association that justify advancing at least the following hypothesis: control of a newspaper tends to promote a party at the point of development and to confirm its position when established. Even if in fact there is no causal connection the behaviour of politicians wherever newspapers exist has unquestionably been affected strongly by the belief that there is: they have poured money and energy into the press.

The reasons for supposing that newspapers can promote party aims are rooted in the similarity of the institutions: the functions of parties are highly compatible with the capabilities of newspapers. The cooperative needs of a party are helped by the newspaper's obvious advantages as a highly flexible, cheap and penetrating medium of communication. Papers are verbal, and politics is a verbal activity. Parties and papers alike seek common ground among people in order to maximise their appeal: the same social forces therefore tend to find expression in parties as in papers. As Chapter 7 shows, movements of all political colours have founded papers at the start of their existence. Indeed production of a newspaper has often been the basis if not the sole form of party activity. 'The formation of a party – if this party is not properly represented by a well known newspaper', wrote Lenin before the Russian revolution, '– remains to a significant degree just words.' Hitler – and Mussolini even more so – used papers to help build up their parties; and papers formed the basis of independence movements in many colonial territories, and of the Black Panthers in the USA. Well established parties, it is clear from the evidence of many political systems, do not positively need to control papers. Nonetheless papers are frequently used, especially in one-party systems, as an instrument for transmitting the directions of the leadership and as a forum for discussion. So far as can be judged, parties without papers would invariably prefer to have one if they could.

The effect of television on Parliament. The British Parliament has been much more suspicious than most other European and north American legislatures about the consequences of allowing its proceedings to be televised. (See Chapter 5.) The arguments about it in the 1960s and early 1970s mainly turned on the question how these might affect its role in the political system. The aims of everyone were the same – to maintain Parliament's position as a sovereign representative assembly, exercising control over legislation and the different arms of the Executive. Some people argued television was therefore essential, even if nuggets of tradition were cast out and parliamentary procedure changed. They saw the alternative as decay: other institutions open to television would usurp Parliament. Indeed television itself would do so, with its widening range of political programmes. Others argued, in contrast, that televised proceedings would be altogether harmful: they would turn Parliament into a theatre not a workshop, and the advantages of closer contact with the people would be insignificant if not a sham.

The argument is inconclusive. But whether it let the cameras in or not, Parliament was likely to change as a result of the growth of television. In the early 1970s, moreover, there was a little evidence to support the 'decay' theory. Several TV programmes about critical issues like the EEC and Northern Ireland were broadcast, with politicians taking part, in 'grand inquest' form and amid much previous and subsequent press discussion; all of which seemed more appropriate to a parliamentary occasion.

General elections are another obvious example, already quoted, where the popular importance attached to a political process is heavily reinforced by the mass media.

(c) Institution and institution

Several examples previously mentioned find a natural place under this heading too. *The relative strength of political parties* is one; though it must be stressed that media do not appear to change parties' electoral support much in a direct and short-run way. If media win elections it is more likely to be the result of, say, changing differential rates of turnout between the parties on Polling Day. *Televising parliamentary debates* is another example: it might well be that the balance of advantage in debate between Government and Opposition would shift – though in which direction is a matter of dispute. Again, *The Times, leading article on the Sudetenland* shifted

the relationship between the British Government and other governments concerned in the Czecho-Slovak crisis in 1938: their expect-
tations about British intentions changed.

The media's power to define crises also affects the relations between
the government and institutions involved in a crisis, or between
different branches of government. The institutions concerned may
find themselves the focus of intense, often hostile publicity and
pressure: for instance, if British power workers take industrial
action in winter, a stream of media stories is apt to follow about
old people dying of hypothermia caused by power cuts.[11]

The Sunday Telegraph and the Nigerian civil war (1970). On 11
January 1970 the *Sunday Telegraph* published a confidential British
government document called 'An appreciation of the Nigerian
conflict', written by the Defence adviser to the British High Commission in Lagos. The war happened to end in a Federal victory next
day, but the incident took on lasting significance when some of
those responsible were prosecuted under the Official Secrets Act.
The Labour Government was still in power and the *Sunday Telegraph*,
whose editor was one of the defendants, was a strongly Conservative
paper. Another defendant, Jonathan Aitken, who actually passed
the document to the newspaper (having been shown it by a colleague
of the author) was a prospective Conservative parliamentary
candidate.* Some commentators (including Aitken) suggested the
prosecution was brought basically on political grounds because the
Government had been embarrassed by the publication. In the event
the prosecution failed. The judge passed strong remarks about the
need for revising the Official Secrets Act, and a committee under
Lord Franks was shortly set up to make recommendations.

It never became entirely clear how and why the prosecution was
brought. Michael Stewart, Foreign Secretary at the time, denied
later (when out of office) that publication had embarrassed the
Government. But there is no doubt that it did change the relations
between the Government and the Federal Nigerian Government,
however briefly. For their part, the Nigerians reacted quickly and
angrily. The British Government had taken the Federal side in the
war, yet the report was critical of their management of it (e.g.
wastage of ammunition). The Defence adviser who wrote it was
expelled from the country within 24 hours. Michael Stewart conceded
that the *Sunday Telegraph*'s action 'could have endangered goodwill
between Britain and Nigeria'. But 'Fortunately it didn't do any
harm, because the end of the war came at the same time'.[12] The

* The third defendant was Colonel Cairns, Britain's senior member with the
neutral international observer team in the civil war, who originally set the train
of disclosure in motion.

effect of disclosure was thus softened by the coincidence of timing: had the war continued the effect might have been more serious. Even so, the relations of the two institutions suffered momentarily.

Relations between the American President and Congress. Television, both by its nature as a medium and because of the way it is organised in the United States, has shifted the balance of power towards the President.[13] The President has a direct link with the people: he needs no sympathetic journalists or party organisations as intermediaries. Kennedy exploited the televised press conference technique skilfully – so much so that Johnson did not give a single televised conference for 17 months after he took office. Straight face-to-the-camera talks have been commonly used in crisis situations (and are a simple extension of F. D. Roosevelt's radio 'fireside chats'). In 1970 Nixon even invited the cameras to witness his formal veto of a particular congressional Act, in a pointed demonstration of constitutional powers. Then the President, obviously, is 'news' on any number of occasions which he can turn more or less to political advantage. He can also, through his aides, manipulate news by techniques of leaking, kite-flying, denials and so on. Moreover he can use all of these methods to distract attention from Congress's attempts to focus the cameras on itself. For example during the televised Senate hearings on Vietnam in 1966 Johnson, embarrassed by criticisms of the war, chose to attend a conference in Honolulu in the alleged hope of upstaging them.[14] Similarly he generated a variety of news stories in Washington one day in 1967, merely in order to draw publicity away from Senator Robert Kennedy, who for the past two weeks had been preparing the media for a major anti-Johnson speech that day.[15]

By contrast the opportunities for Congress to exploit television are limited. Coverage of regular proceedings is open to the same problems as in Britain. Individual Congressmen, unless they are presidential aspirants or in the very limited group of elder statesmen, cannot easily get national coverage. The most satisfactory weapon against the President is simply the televised Senate committee hearing. (The House of Representatives does not allow its committees to be televised.) Very occasionally these attract extensive live coverage – for instance the Vietnam hearings in 1966 and 1968 and, classically, the 1973 Watergate hearings. But, effective as these may be, they are a blunt instrument. Congress speaks with a variety of voices, the President with one. The President sticks to high ideals, while Congress squabbles over details.[16] Of course the President's advantages, one should add, are no guarantee that his policies will prevail. Indeed exposure might be counter-productive if it unrealistically increased popular expectations of his power to get things done.

Nonetheless the growth of television can be said in general to have strengthened the Presidency vis-à-vis Congress.

(d) Institution and individual

Because of their focus on the individual many traditional 'effects' studies could provide examples under this heading. Changes in voting behaviour, for instance, involve changed relationships between the individual voter and the institution of party.

Studies of the watchdog role of mass media could provide other examples. This role often consists in exposing unfairness in the bureaucracy, with consequential redress for aggrieved citizens. The impact of exposure does not depend on the appeal solely to 'public opinion' but also to political élites, including particularly MPs and perhaps other civil servants as well. In 1967 the establishment of a Parliamentary Commissioner for Administration in Britain (modelled on the Scandinavian Ombudsman) institutionalised the watchdog idea. The press obviously continued to exercise their own watchdog function but they also made a contribution to the effectiveness of the new institution. The Parliamentary Commissioner was given no statutory powers of redress and depended entirely on the sanction of publicity: any publicity beyond Parliament, where he reported to a Commons committee and in certain cases to individual MPs, was in the gift of the media.* In the nature of this process the focus is on the individual citizen. But the product of redress may be a changed relationship between the bureaucracy and the offending bureaucrat as well. Careers can be blighted by the public exposure of error, even if they are almost never brought to a premature end. The private exposure of error is bad enough, given that civil servants value highly the opinions of their colleagues and of institutions with which they deal.†

The main illustrations under this heading are drawn not from

* Frank Stacey (1971), pp. 247, 318. Stacey thinks the Commissioner should publicise his reports on cases more effectively. At present it is up to the MP responsible for initiating a case to decide whether to release the Commissioner's report to the press.

† Cf. Anthony Crosland, interviewed about his experiences as Minister of Education: '. . . a really bad mistake is known all round Whitehall – the gossip that goes on is something absolutely out of this world. I once had some totally wrong advice on a highly technical subject, and as a result looked an absolute fool in Cabinet . . . There was a quite formal inquiry in the Department on what had gone wrong, and the official responsible didn't recover for six months – he came near to a nervous breakdown, simply from the humiliation within the circuit. So although there's no press publicity, there's a great deal of informal publicity within the official's own group. And people of course mind desperately about that.' Boyle & Crosland (1971), pp. 180–1.

these categories but from political élites. MPs in general, for example, derive a good deal of information about the activity of their party leaders from the press. Barker and Rush have shown also that the biggest single source of M.P.s' information about their constituencies comes from the local press.[17] The particular examples that follow, however, are drawn from more specific situations than those. Some of the most abrupt are the result, as in the watchdog category, of mass media exposure (though the media were rarely more than a contributory cause). *The resignation of Hugh Dalton as Chancellor of the Exchequer* (13 November 1947) is a simple example. The opportunities for individuals to profit by advance notice of budgetary measures have led to an extremely high value being placed upon budgetary secrecy. In 1947 Hugh Dalton was actually on his way to the Commons chamber, only a few minutes before his budget speech was due, when he encountered the correspondent of a London evening paper. In the course of a brief conversation, which Dalton wrongly thought was covered by the Lobby correspondents' convention of secrecy, he disclosed a few important details. These duly appeared in the Stop Press of a limited number of copies of the paper that went on sale before Dalton reached that part of his speech. Even so slight an indiscretion – the result simply of a misunderstanding – seemed to Dalton to require resignation: his immediate reaction to the publication – which he did not hear about till next day – was to say to his colleagues, 'This means that I must resign my office'.* Some people have argued that he was not reluctant to go.[18] Either way, this incident precipitated his departure.

The resignation of John Profumo as War Minister (1963) was less abrupt but no less closely linked to mass media exposure.[19] Rumours that Mr Profumo's friendship with a girl might involve a security risk, since she was also associated with a naval attaché at the Russian embassy, were published in the press in an oblique form but very intensively for a week. Fear of the libel laws prevented explicit allegations. The rumours were then scotched by Mr Profumo publicly in Parliament. Some two months later, however, he admitted having partly misled the House in his explanation and resigned. But for the initial publicity the affair might never have come to light and his political career would not have been ruined.

Sometimes the intensity and timing of media coverage provide equally clearcut examples. The coverage of *Enoch Powell's speeches on immigration* (1968) changed his relationship with the Conservative party significantly and gave him a populist base. One of the doubts

---

* Hugh Dalton, *High tide and after* (1962), p. 276. Dalton returned to the cabinet in the unimportant office of Chancellor of the Duchy of Lancaster on 1 June 1948, staying until the 1950 general election.

about *the proposal to televise Parliament* was that it might provide opportunities for M.P.s with appropriate skills to seek the same result from Westminster; the doubt being whether Parliament was the right forum for such an attempt, rather than a belief that populism was necessarily evil.

The downfall of Senator Joe McCarthy (1954), another politician with a populist streak in his career, also owed something to mass media coverage of critical intensity and timing. McCarthy's ruthless search for communist skeletons in the bureaucratic cupboard culminated in a series of televised confrontations between a special Senate investigating committee and members of the Defence services. His reckless charges and smears in the eye of the camera marked the start of his decline – not so much because the public turned against him (the polls did not show an immediate drop in popularity), but because his technique alienated congressional colleagues. They used it as part of the case against him that was organised after the hearings and resulted in a Senate resolution of censure.[20] McCarthy died a few years afterwards.

The Army–McCarthy hearings spread over several weeks. Two years earlier *Richard Nixon's 'Checkers' speech* (1952) had shown how one brief television performance could make or break a career.[21] Nixon had been chosen as Eisenhower's running mate on the Republican presidential ticket. One of the main themes of their campaign was 'corruption' in the Democratic administration. Yet in mid-campaign the *New York Post* discovered that 76 Californians had put together a private expense fund for Nixon. Pressure mounted for his withdrawal. At Eisenhower's suggestion he gave a half-hour television broadcast, six days after the affair broke. 'Maybe after the programme we could tell what ought to be done', Eisenhower said.[22] Advance publicity and the importance the question had assumed ensured Nixon a larger television audience than a campaign speech had ever before commanded – perhaps as many as 25 million people. The broadcast was a triumph for Nixon and the Republican party. He told of his humble beginnings and hardships, his war record and his devoted wife, his modest lifestyle, his integrity and his acceptance for his children of the gift of a cocker spaniel puppy, Checkers – which he did not intend to return. The talk, plainly, was an advertising agency's combination of 'market-tested symbols to convey his personal honour and love for his country' and a routine speech attacking the Democrats and praising Eisenhower.[23] He finished with an appeal to the audience to send their views about whether he should withdraw to the Republican National Committee. The result was a deluge of support. Nixon flew to meet Eisenhower, who publicly embraced him with the words 'You're my boy!' From then on, Nixon's position on the ticket was secure and he became a positive asset, a public figure in his own right.

Few examples can match that one for directness on a grand scale. But *the decline of Senator Edmund Muskie* (1972) as a Democratic presidential aspirant may serve as a matching example of the power of television cruelly to break a career. Muskie had run as vice-presidential candidate with Hubert Humphrey in 1968. In 1972 he started as front-runner for the presidential nomination. Then came a fatal incident. An extreme Republican newspaper, the *Manchester Union Leader* of New Hampshire, launched an unpleasant attack on his wife during the Primary election there. The publisher, William Loeb, had a reputation for invective: Eisenhower, for instance, he called a 'stinking hypocrite'. On 26 February Muskie tramped through the snow to the *Union Leader* building, followed by some 60 slightly startled newsmen and supporters, and delivered an emotional rebuttal. Loeb had abridged as a 'guest editorial' a *Newsweek* article about Mrs Jane Muskie, itself condensed from another magazine, in which she was reported to have shouted 'Let's tell dirty jokes' to reporters on her campaign bus, and to have admitted a preference for two drinks before dinner and a crème de menthe after. Loeb also alleged Muskie had insulted Maine's 17 per cent of French Canadians, who comprised 40–50 per cent of the Democratic vote, by calling them the pejorative name 'Canucks'. (Maine was Muskie's home State.) Standing outside the building in a near-blizzard Muskie launched into Loeb: he was 'a liar' (four times), a 'gutless coward', a 'person who doesn't walk, he crawls'; his paper was 'garbage'. Muskie denied the charge about French Canadians. Then, as he read out the title of the 'guest editorial', his voice broke. Three times in as many minutes he broke down. After one embarrassing gap a supporter shouted 'Who's with Muskie?' and the crowd cheered until he composed himself. Such an outburst of course played into Republican hands. Charges of weakness, emotionalism and unsuitability to have his finger on the nuclear button naturally followed. The incident was recorded on TV and repeatedly broadcast. From that moment the Muskie campaign rolled rapidly downhill.*

Harold Macmillan's cabinet changes (1962) could be quoted again under this heading. The manner in which the changes were conducted (for which the press shared responsibility) weakened Macmillan's position in his party. Another example can be taken from the Wilson administration: *the resignation of George Brown as Foreign Secretary*

---

* Sources: *Christian Science Monitor, Guardian*, 27 February–1 March 1972. Accusations later followed that the incident was set up by Republicans aiming to discredit Muskie. *Sunday Times*, 5 November 1972.

(1968). By his own account the mass media appeared to play some part in this.[24] His general reason for leaving was the belief that decisions were being taken without the knowledge or approval of appropriate ministers and in an increasingly 'presidential' style by Mr Wilson. Among the more serious incidents that gave him this impression was the cabinet decision at the end of 1967 to stop arms sales to South Africa. In Brown's view a decision had implicitly been reached to continue sales and the issue was a dead one. Then while he was at a NATO meeting in Brussels the subject blew up in the parliamentary Labour Party and pressure mounted to force a decision against sales. Brown felt that advantage was taken of his absence to pre-empt the decision, even though the formal cabinet meeting was delayed for his return. Soon after reaching Dover he saw the newspapers, which suggested he was being isolated by the Prime Minister. By the time he reached London he was therefore 'already feeling pretty sore'. The subsequent cabinet meeting was 'pretty tense' and the decision was postponed until Monday. 'During the weekend, however, the press publicity, the leaking and the briefing continued and by Monday morning it was pretty evident that it was no longer possible for a balanced argument to take place, or for there being any chance of a decision on merit being taken.' Brown and his supporters were reduced to 'a pretty small minority, and we were no longer able to carry our colleagues with us'.[25]

Brown clearly believed opinion was mobilised against his position in this sequence of events. While he does not ascribe a motive to the press, it is plain that his version sees the press as oiling the wheels – helping to define a crisis situation and working to the advantage of those who wished to reverse a decision that had seemed to be settled. Both in the broader sense of contributing to his growing mood of resignation, therefore, and in the narrower sense of defeating him on a policy issue, the mass media affected Brown's relationship to the cabinet.*

(e) Individual and individual

Many of the examples quoted under the last heading could find a place here, since institutions are composed of individuals. Richard Nixon's 1952 television triumph affected his relationship with Dwight Eisenhower in a literal way, as well as raising his stature in the party. George Brown saw his defeat on the South African arms

* For a very different account of this episode, see Harold Wilson (1971), pp. 470–6, Wilson ascribes a similar role to the press – but working to precisely the opposite effect to that perceived by Brown.

issue as to some extent a personal matter between him and the Prime Minister.[26] There is no need, then, to quote examples under this heading at length.

A final reference in this chapter to the case study of Enoch Powell may be forgiven, for the immediate reaction of the mass media to the timing and substance of his Birmingham speech on immigration in 1968 was to interpret it as a threat to Edward Heath personally. The *Sunday Express* headline, for example, was: POWELL RACE BLOCKBUSTER: A CRISIS FOR HEATH. The lead story began: 'Mr Edward Heath has been catapulted into the most testing crisis of his career as Tory leader by the stark warning which Mr Enoch Powell yesterday gave Britain on the race issue.' Heath had to take correspondingly strong action and sacked Powell from the Shadow Cabinet. This in itself weakened his position. Opinion polls showed that it was an unpopular move with three out of five Conservatives; and a poll six months after the event found that the proportion of people who thought Heath would make the better Prime Minister was only slightly greater (41 per cent) than the proportion preferring Powell (37 per cent).

The other example that can appropriately be quoted here is the *Kennedy/Nixon television debates* (1960). Despite the great volume of research these generated in the American social sciences industry no firm conclusions can be drawn about their impact on voting intentions.[27] The four hour-long 'debates' (they were in fact more like question and answer sessions) attracted huge audiences: somewhere between 85 and 120 million viewers saw at least one of them.[28] The election was so close that any of a large number of factors might have been critical in determining the result. But there is no doubt that voters, commentators and the candidates alike *believed* the debates were crucial. Kennedy told his press assistant Pierre Salinger, 'We wouldn't have had a prayer without that gadget [television].'[29] Robert Kennedy, his campaign manager, said: 'It wouldn't even have been close without the debates. Jack's appearance on TV and the way he handled himself was the big factor in our victory.'[30] Nixon too thought Kennedy got a big advantage from the debates.[31] Surveys showed that voters in both parties thought Kennedy benefited from them most and that voters said the debates had helped them make up their minds.[32] Whether that was true or not was much less clear. Katz and Feldman, in a 'survey of the surveys', felt confident only in the conclusion that the debates accelerated the rate of consolidation of Democratic support behind Kennedy. On the other hand the subjective estimates at the time gave an undoubted fillip to Kennedy's campaign – by stimulating volunteer workers, for example.[33] His mere appearance – a relatively inexperienced Senator alongside Nixon the Vice-President – had the halo effect of increasing his stature. In this sense Nixon's worst mistake was to have agreed to the debates at all. Because of what people believed (rightly or wrongly) about voters' reactions, the debates thus shifted the balance between the candidates. Before the debates, Theodore H. White wrote, 'Nixon was generally viewed as being the probable winner of the election contest and Kennedy as fighting an uphill battle; when they were over, the positions of the two contestants were reversed.'[34]

III. Summary of chapters 1 and 2

The argument of these first two chapters may now be summarised briefly.

Communication is essential in society: man cannot exist as a social entity without it. Communication processes can therefore be expected to have a great effect upon the nature of a society, including its political system. Even when inquiry is limited to the effects of mass media, those effects may be very wide. Media are so deeply embedded in the system that without them political activity in its contemporary forms could scarcely carry on at all. In practice researchers have defined 'political effects' in rather narrow terms, referring typically to media-induced changes in the political attitudes of individuals considered in isolation. A wider conception of the effects of mass media might take account of the following aspects of political communication processes.

(a) The nature of media effects

(i) Media may be a necessary and sufficient cause of a political effect; a necessary but not a sufficient cause; a sufficient but not a necessary cause; and the catalyst or occasion of a political effect.

(ii) All political effects are initially upon individuals. They consist in increments of information, which may or may not modify attitudes which may or may not modify behaviour.

(iii) Political effects may be primary (i.e. on an individual directly concerned in a communication process) or secondary (i.e. upon individuals not directly concerned in that process).

(b) The production of effects

Media effects so defined may be produced by:

(i) One or more elements of a particular communication process: i.e. sender, message, medium, receiver;

(ii) the communication context: i.e. the timing (and sequence) of that communication; its frequency (strictly, its similarity to previous communications); its intensity (in relation to other, possibly competing, communications).

(c) *The political context of effects*

(i) Effects of a communication process may vary according to the level of political relationships considered. These relationships may be between individuals, institutions (or groups) and the political system, in a variety of possible combinations.

(ii) The significance of media-induced effects on those relationships will depend upon the virtually endless range of political questions in which an inquirer may be interested.

PART TWO

Varieties of mass media effects: case studies

3

The Times and the appeasement of Hitler

Few words can suffer so fast and full a change of common usage as 'appeasement'. When Hitler came to power in 1933, Britain aimed to appease Germany – and with it the whole of Europe. To appease meant literally 'to bring about a peaceful settlement', and who would not aspire to that? Yet by the outbreak of war, appeasement was generally reviled. 'Appeasement from weakness and fear is alike futile and fatal', Winston Churchill reflected in 1950. 'Appeasement from strength is magnanimous and noble . . .'[1] By 1939 the word symbolised the first of those attitudes. Appeasement had come to mean peace at any price: the sacrifice of morality to myopic expediency, 'a nervous, jerky, guilt-encumbered affair; not a confident philosophy but a painful surrender to threats'.[2] At each new initiative by Hitler, specially after Neville Chamberlain succeeded Stanley Baldwin as Prime Minister in 1937, the British Government yielded ground, rationalising its attitude by reference to a faint hope that Hitler now was satisfied. Hitler flouted the Versailles Peace Treaty of 1919 by building up an army and air force; marched into the Rhineland in 1936 without a finger lifted against him; annexed Austria in the Anschluss of 1938; secured the position of Czecho-Slovakia by the Munich agreement of September 1938 (the apotheosis or nadir of appeasement); and invaded that country in March 1939. Only then did Chamberlain make his stand. He offered to Poland, Roumania and Greece a firm guarantee of help against German aggression: and this, of course, led Britain into war.

The purpose of this essay is not to trace the course of appeasement[3] but to analyse the role played in it by *The Times*. That role has been credited with enormous importance. Anthony Eden's memoirs describe as 'a national misfortune', no less, the lack of a post of Foreign Editor on the paper in the Munich period.[4] Lord Vansittart, Permanent Head of the Foreign Office in the 1930s, believed that the ignorance of *The Times* 'told against us throughout the vital decade'.[5] In his popular history of British journalism Francis Williams attributed to the editor, Geoffrey Dawson, 'an influence on great events . . . certainly far larger than that of any other newspaper editor, or proprietor of modern times.'[6] The first part of this study examines the grounds for such judgements and seeks to interpret the paper's role. The second part considers the criticisms that have been made of it and their underlying assumptions about what ought to be the role of a paper like *The Times* in relation to government policy.

I. THE INFLUENCE OF 'THE TIMES'

Certainly there was no more plausible, articulate, staunch, convinced supporter of appeasement than *The Times*. 'I shall always be an impenitent supporter of what is called the "Munich policy"', wrote Geoffrey Dawson in his last letter to Chamberlain before the latter died.[7] Remarks like 'Personally I am, and always have been, most anxious that we should "explore every avenue" in the search for a reasonable understanding with Germany' litter the pages of Dawson's diary and correspondence,[8] while this extract from a leading article at the time of Munich by Barrington-Ward, Dawson's like-minded Assistant Editor (and successor), has the serenity of a man at peace with his undoubting conscience as the savage drags him to the pot:

> The Prime Minister has set himself to get the work of a peace conference done before the next war, and not after it. He cannot dictate the outcome of his exertions. But one thing can be said now, even if he should fail. He has striven to the last by all that one man's energy, resource, and indifference to calumny could do, to hold up and reverse that same fatalistic slither into the abyss . . . which carried agonised Europe helplessly away in late July and early August 1914. To have moved with, and not against, the tide of events, would have brought this country by now into the worst of all perils, the peril of war upon a confused issue fastened upon an unconvinced and disunited people.[9]

When appeasement died with Chamberlain's guarantee to Poland *The Times* changed its attitude too. The paper 'could not write of the pledge enthusiastically', its official history comments, 'though it stood behind its purpose'.[10] The belief that Hitler would keep promises and had peaceful intentions was finally abandoned.

That appeasement was overwhelmingly popular with the electorate and its political leaders – at least until after Munich – is not in dispute. Great significance was attached to the famous East Fulham by-election in 1933, when a pro-rearmament Conservative candidate was trounced in a safe Conservative seat by a pacifist Labour candidate. The activities of the Peace Pledge Union in 1935, collecting 11·5 million 'votes' for its 'Peace Ballot', also symbolised, in those days before opinion polls, the strength of public feeling.[11] *The Times* had the same reasons as everyone else for supporting the policy. Natural hatred of war was reinforced by memories of the First World War: Barrington-Ward himself had done the improbable thing of surviving as a junior infantry officer throughout it.* Development of aircraft had added an unknown quantity to war: the devastation of Guernica in the Spanish Civil War had shown the numbing potentiality of aerial bombardment. The pace of her rearmament rapidly took Germany past Britain and France; and this very weakness itself became a reason for appeasement, to 'gain time' for catching up.

Those who wished to rationalise appeasement more completely found further arguments. What were the alternatives, for instance? By 1937 collective security through the League of Nations could no longer be taken seriously, while alliances with other powers meant penetrating the isolationism of the USA or linking up with Russia or making a firm commitment to France. The first seemed improbable; about Russia there was still a sniff of the Red Peril to British Conservative leaders;† and France seemed militarily and politically unreliable.

One crucial factor making appeasement the most attractive of these alternatives was the feeling that Germany in fact deserved the generosity of appeasement: the harsh dictated terms of Versailles – disarmament, large reparations, loss of territory and colonies – seemed unreasonable. As Gilbert and Gott point out, the appeasers could argue that 'where the Nazi programme was violent, Germany was not alone to blame. It was England who had helped to drive Germany into confusion and anarchy, by agreeing with France to the severe terms of Versailles. By a policy of understanding and conciliation England could remedy her fault. A sense of guilt drove the appeasers into a one-sided relationship with Germany, in

---

* He earned the M.C., D.S.O. and three mentions in despatches. See Donald McLachlan's biography of him, *In the chair* (1971). This book provides far the best understanding of the *Times*' appeasement policy. F. R. Gannon's survey of *The British press and Germany 1936–1939* (1971) also dispels a number of myths about the press in those years.

† See, e.g. the diary of Thomas Jones, 25 May 1936: 'Dined at the Astors. Bullitt, the U.S.A. Ambassador at Moscow there, and made our flesh creep with his Bolshevik stories'. Thomas Jones, *A Diary with letters* (1954), p. 210. After an academic career Jones became deputy secretary of the Cabinet, 1916–30, and thereafter the close friend and confidant of Baldwin, as well as continuing to move widely in political and government circles.

which it was always to be given the benefit of the doubt. Hitler's outbursts were not treated as the ravings of a wicked man: they were the understandable complaints of a man who had been wronged.'[12] Dawson and Barrington-Ward were ever ready to make allowances on these grounds.

With strict adherence to Versailles breached, the logical distinction between appeasement and non-appeasement in fact vanished. It was a matter simply of how far one would go. Apart from the wide range of minor arguments – the policy could quite easily be justified consistently at the time – the other factor weighing heavily was the attitude of the Dominions: until the unprincipled aggression of the Nazi régime was beyond every doubt, their willing support in another European war could not be certain.

In retrospect the factual bases of some of the appeasers' arguments are questionable. From some moral standpoints they were always objectionable. But at the time they could be held without the least cynicism to coincide with popular feeling and the best interests of Britain, Europe and the Empire.

The attitude of *The Times* was decided very largely by Dawson and Barrington-Ward.* The *History of The Times* acknowledges, without going into detail, that there were 'resignations from junior members of the staff' over the Munich agreement, and that 'some of the seniors were unhappy'.[13] One 'unhappy senior' was Colin Coote, leader writer and former Liberal M.P., and a convinced opponent of appeasement. He thought the atmosphere in the office in the late thirties was 'quite horrible'. He decided not to resign after consulting Churchill, who said he would prefer to keep 'a friend in the enemy's camp'. Coote recalls that several others in the office were also 'deeply distressed'.† Such concern seems to have caused Dawson no prick of discomfort. The paper had always had a strong corporatist tradition, typified by the anonymity of its writing and the donnish quality of its procedures.‡

Dawson's position as editor was exceptionally strong. He had first

---

* Just how far Barrington-Ward was responsible did not become clear until the publication of *In the chair*, Donald McLachlan's biography of him. See e.g. pp. 99ff.

† C. Coote, *Editorial* (1965), pp. 170–1. Coote also credits the historian E. H. Carr, brought in as a consultant on foreign affairs, with influence in the paper's appeasement policy. His chapter on 'The Nightmare Thirties' contains other useful comments on the press. Coote later became editor of the *Daily Telegraph* from 1950 to 1964.

‡ An honorary degree from Oxford, the ex-editor Buckle wrote when Dawson was awarded one, was about the highest recognition to which an editor of *The Times* could aspire. Wrench (1955), p. 316. The paper had strong links with All Souls too.

been appointed to the post in 1912 by Northcliffe, with whom he eventually fell out over policy, resigning in 1919. After Northcliffe's death in 1922 the paper was bought by Colonel J. J. Astor and Mr John Walter IV (a descendant of the founder). Since they planned to restore it to its 'steadier' traditions of pre-Northcliffe days, an obvious step was to invite Dawson back. Determined not to run into difficulties again, Dawson drew up strong and explicit conditions of appointment. Astor and Walter agreed to them and Dawson became in the phrase of *The Times History* 'an autocrat over the whole of the editorial content of the paper . . .' He had 'a free hand', to quote the euphemism employed in the negotiations,[14] and he used it to imprint his policy on the paper regardless of disagreement. Coote describes leader-writing under him thus: 'You wrote your leader, left it for typing with the editor's secretary, and had no right to resent anything subsequently done to it.' Since Coote felt so strongly about appeasement, the Editor agreed that he should only be asked to do leaders on British rearmament – which was 'Dawson's insurance against disaster arising from his pro-German policy'.[15] In the same vein Liddell Hart, the paper's Military Correspondent, has recalled a revealing discussion with several senior staff during the Czecho-Slovak crisis in 1938: 'I expressed strong criticism of *The Times* leader that morning, and was rather surprised to find that the others agreed with my criticism. So I said "If you all share my view, who does hold the view taken in today's leader?" At that one of them replied: "Only one man for certain – B. W. Geoffrey Dawson perhaps!". It was a very significant comment.'[16] Liddell Hart too found that on occasion his leaders were doctored, and several times he considered resigning (Munich 'nauseated' him).

Dawson seems a predictable supporter of appeasement. He had a comparatively superficial understanding of European politics (and he knew no foreign languages). He seems to have been more interested in whether the right person was doing a job than in the job itself. He had all those qualities – judgement, balance, clarity of thought, articulateness – which in principle seem so desirable in public men but in practice may be so negative. His first-class mind enabled him nimbly to conduct the semantics of argument about the justification of Germany's foreign policy. The one visionary idea which captured him in his youth and held him ever after was the Empire. This, intellectually, was the key to his commitment to appeasement.

Dawson as a young man was good proconsular material: clever but not odd; gregarious but not insensitive; sound, conscientious, responsible; good to work over or under. A scholar of Eton and Magdalen, Oxford, he got Firsts in Classical Mods and Greats and joined the small élite of prize Fellows of All Souls. Though he thought at one time of the Indian Civil Service, in the end he took the Home Civil Service exam, always a very tough competition. He won the last place in 1898, at the age of twenty-two, and was appointed to the General Post Office; which, one may hazard, disappointed him no end.

The turning-point in his career was the South African War. At its outbreak in 1899, Dawson was working in the Colonial Office. This, under Joseph Chamberlain, was an exciting place to be: it is not surprising that Dawson, with his Oxford record and connections and with friends elsewhere in Whitehall, succeeded in getting transferred there.* Towards the end of the war he was made one of Chamberlain's Private Secretaries, and from there he was recruited, in 1901, to the staff of Lord Milner, Britain's High Commissioner in South Africa. Milner's 'Kindergarten' is one of the most fascinating élites of young Englishmen this century. All were fired with the imperial enthusiasm of their formidable master. Most went on to win great distinction in a variety of conventional fields: Dawson at *The Times*, Sir Herbert Baker as (literally) an architect of Empire (and of the Bank of England), L. S. Amery as politician, Lionel Curtis (known among them as 'The Prophet') as Scholar, R. H. Brand as banker, Lord Lothian as politician and Ambassador to the USA. Their experience shaping the future Dominion of South Africa linked them with a life-long Arthurian bond, institutionalised in the influential quarterly *Round Table* and the regular associated 'Moots'. (A Camelot analogy is scarcely too far-fetched.) When Milner went back to England in 1905, many of the kindergarten stayed behind in seats of influence. Dawson became editor of the *Johannesburg Star*, thus setting foot on the path to *The Times*. That path was quite short, and within a few years he was the regular *Times* South African correspondent. On leave in 1908 he met and impressed Northcliffe.† Two years later he left South Africa for good. He spent 1911 and 1912 'attached' to the Imperial and Foreign Department at *The Times*, effectively being groomed to succeed G. E. Buckle as editor. This he did, aged 38, in 1912.

Nine years steeped in practical problems of Empire, at a formative stage of his life, were bound to colour Dawson's vision of the world. Obviously the commitment to imperialism mellowed: the earnestness could not survive with which he wrote to Amery in 1910, 'Remember

* The transfer on the evidence of Wrench (1955), p. 31, was very far from the the 'accidental circumstance' suggested in *The dictionary of national biography*. It seems a pure example of string-pulling.

† L. S. Amery claims to have suggested Dawson to Northcliffe as a possible *Times* editor, after turning down a hint to that effect himself. Amery, *My political life*, Vol. I (1953), p. 324.

that, one way or another, I propose to devote my life to our common cause – in journalism, politics, or any way that offers.'[17] But the commitment is clearly discernible in another passage from that final letter to Chamberlain thirty years later: 'No one who sat in this place [*The Times*] as I did during the autumn of '38, with almost daily visitations from eminent Canadians and Australians, could fail to recognise that war with Germany at that time would have been misunderstood and resented from end to end of the Empire . . .'*
Perhaps the most striking illustration of the perspective of the kindergarten is this brief comment by a member of it: 'We are not a part of Europe, even if the most important unit of the British community lies off the European coast.'[18] History went the wrong way for Dawson: he was educated to Empire in the dying days of imperialism. His energy and interest in it found outlets, as editor of *The Times* in the 1930s, in the problems of India and of Commonwealth economic cooperation. He could not bring the same skills to European problems; and it is small wonder that the imperial factor loomed large in his approach to appeasement. The other factor said to have influenced him heavily was dislike of Bolshevism and acceptance of Germany as a bulwark against Russia.†

So Dawson used his 'free hand' (brushing off some feeble tugs by Walter at his sleeve) to commit *The Times* with unshakeable confidence to the appeasement of Hitler. The shifting, expediential quality of that policy means that the paper's influence cannot be seen in simple, clearcut terms. Least of all can one say the paper persuaded the Government into adopting the policy. Baldwin, Chamberlain, Halifax, Hoare, Simon and the others needed no persuading. This is not a case of the power of the press to force a policy upon ministers through its columns. The role of *The Times* was more subtle than that.

* Wrench (1955), p. 433. The Canadian Prime Minister Mackenzie King told Churchill in the War 'that he doubted very much whether his country would have rallied to us at once' in 1938. See Lord Ismay, *Memoirs* (1960), p. 92. Cf. J. W. Pickersgill, *The Mackenzie King Record* (1960), pp. 12–13. Iain Macleod quotes Australian and South African leaders in the same vein in his biography *Neville Chamberlain* (1961), pp. 269–70. It should be added, however, that *The Times* did its bit to *produce* this situation. For example Dawson and the Canadian High Commissioner Vincent Massey tried successfully to 'mobilise' the other High Commissioners against the prospect of war over the terms brought back by Chamberlain from Hitler at Godesberg at the height of the Czecho-Slovak crisis in September 1938. See Keith Robbins, *Munich 1938* (1968), p. 291.

† Wrench (1955), p. 376. Dawson's pro-German inclinations could have been picked up in his South African days.

Negative influence

The paper's role, first of all, had a significant negative side. The absence of criticism by *The Times* against appeasement was very important. 'All the Cliveden set and *The Times* people prevented us from taking a strong line while it could have made for peace . . .', wrote the anti-appeaser Harold Nicolson bitterly in the Munich days.[19]

Neville Thompson's study of opposition to the Government's policy inside the Conservative Party confirms that the anti-appeasers never consolidated into a bloc (in sharp contrast to the opposition over the 1935 India Bill). As late as Eden's resignation in February 1938 the anti-appeasement group never numbered more than thirty.[20] In the 1930s *The Times* still enjoyed the highest status of all British daily newspapers: the proprietors' description of it as 'a national institution conducted solely in the best interests of the nation and the Empire'[21] was widely acknowledged (though anti-appeasers would question the 'best interests' bit). To have been faced by cogent, persistent criticism instead of comfortable support would have complicated the Government's conduct of policy. Instead Geoffrey Dawson was a kind of priest: public guardian of the appeasers' conscience and theologian of their policy. 'I am having a stiff fight in the Cabinet', a Chancellor of the Exchequer once wrote to Wickham Steed, editor from 1919–22; 'and your articles are the very thing I want'.* No one in the Cabinet contemplating a stiff fight against an appeasement measure could write thus to Dawson.†
On the contrary, Dawson's biographer can say that 'A study of the available material certainly gives the impression that Chamberlain (as P.M.) valued the Editor's opinion and was strengthened in his own views by the knowledge that Geoffrey agreed with his policy and would support it in *The Times*.'[22]

The significance of this 'negative' factor can be further appreciated by considering the function of a leading article. Chapter 2 pointed out that research on the impact of mass media on their audience has shown consistently over the last thirty years that mass media are more likely to reinforce opinions than convert them. Thus *Times*

---

* The Chancellor was Sir Robert Horne and the articles were about war debts. *History of The Times* (1952), p. 724.

† Liddell Hart, as Military Correspondent, did have a somewhat similar experience – but with a significantly different ending. Early in 1938 he turned two memoranda about strategic questions into articles for *The Times* with the agreement of Hore-Belisha, Secretary of State for War, who 'felt that this course would aid his arguments in the Cabinet'. The articles got as far as being printed in galley-proof, but neither was published. *The Liddell Hart Memoirs*, Vol. II (1965), p. 144.

leaders on appeasement probably did not convert its readers: these came from the professional and political upper middle classes who were largely predisposed towards appeasement already.* The leaders must certainly have confirmed that inclination by articulating the policy, reasoning it out and giving it a halo of authority. Appeasement was precisely such a 'nervous, jerky' affair as needed no straightforward conversions: rather, *The Times*, oiling the machinery of approval by the slow drip of argument, reinforced what a later age would call 'the consensus' about appeasement.

But the leading article has another function: to clear the mind of journalists themselves. It is a touchstone by which they can continually adjust both their view of events and their criteria of what matters (and should be reported) and what does not. Journalists probably value leading articles more than their readers. They are particularly valued in 'quality' newspapers, a *genre* existing in some form in many countries. These impute qualities of rationality and judgement to their readers that are equally stressed in their own approach to journalism.[23] The corollary of ex-diplomatist Nicolson's despair of *The Times* was a gratitude among the practitioners of appeasement that they could drink deeply in the paper and assure themselves of the good taste of the wine.

One phrase that has settled into the commentaries well illustrates the disquietening effect which the government might have felt if *The Times* had been opposed to it: 'The Corridor for Camels'. In 1935 the enforcement of peace by collective measures under the terms of the League of Nations still seemed a practical possibility. When Mussolini threatened to invade Abyssinia Sir Samuel Hoare, the Foreign Secretary, made a stirring speech to the League Assembly in support of collective security against aggression and pledging Britain to play her part. On 3 October Italy attacked Abyssinia. Within months the League had organised partial sanctions against her. But the British Government was not committed to the necessity of backing them with force (specially if crucial oil sanctions were to be imposed). In December the French press published proposals agreed between Hoare and the French Prime Minister Laval, who leaked them in the hope of ensuring their acceptance by the British cabinet. The Hoare-Laval pact amounted to the acceptance of an Italian victory on generous terms, including the cession of much Abyssinian territory. In return, Abyssinia was to receive a narrow

* Survey figures quoted by Political and Economic Planning in its *Report on the British Press* (1938) showed that more than half the families in the top 10 per cent. of the population (classed by income) read *The Times*. (In London the figure was 70 per cent.) Almost the whole *Times* readership was in the top 20 per cent. 70 per cent of the readers were men.

strip of land giving an outlet on the Red Sea at Assab. It was not even certain whether she would be permitted to build a railway along it – hence 'the Corridor for Camels'. *The Times* invoked this phrase in a damning leading article. Some of the press, notably the high-circulation *Daily Express* and *Daily Mail*, accepted the deal. Most, like *The Times*, condemned it. M.P.s were inundated with hostile letters; Baldwin's support drained away. At the last minute he repudiated Hoare: Laval's tactic had backfired, for the cabinet had not, of course, endorsed the proposals before they became public. Hoare resigned and Anthony Eden became Foreign Secretary.

The Times obviously could not claim to have shifted the government singlehanded. Given the paper's status, its biting criticism was undoubtedly a significant factor. Thomas Jones noted at the height of the crisis that 'public opposition has been mounting throughout the Press of the country led by *The Times*'.*[24] Harold Macmillan describes *The Times* as the government's fiercest critic, 'and for Dawson to attack Baldwin was indeed like Brutus turning upon Caesar'. Some of the younger cabinet ministers (Walter Elliott, Oliver Stanley, Ormsby-Gore) exerted pressure through *The Times* against Hoare, Macmillan suggests; and had the storm been only among left-wing critics or fanatical League of Nations supporters 'the Government could no doubt have ridden it out'.[25]

If *The Times* had fought appeasement it might have been a catalyst for opposition. From the depths of their gloom† the anti-appeasers may have tended to overestimate the direct influence of *The Times* for evil and therefore its unused potential for good. Whatever the outcome might have been, the fact remains that in supporting appeasement *The Times* effectively smoothed the path of the government.

Influence on 'opinion abroad'

There was one area, however, in which *The Times* was more directly influential and made the government jittery. This was the effect of another facet of its 'national institution' status: 'opinion abroad'

---

* Jones also notes that Dawson sought an interview with Baldwin and failed to get it.

† During the appeasement of Hitler over Czechoslovakia Harold Nicolson noted in his Diary for 20 September 1938: 'The morning begins by Baffy Dugdale (a niece of A. J. Balfour) ringing me up. She said she had been sick twice in the night over England's shame, and that at breakfast she read *The Times* leader. She came upon the words "The general character of the terms submitted to the Czechoslovak Government could not, in the nature of things, be expected to make a strong *prima facie* appeal to them". Having read these words she dashed to the lavatory and was sick for a third time ...' Nicolson (1966), p. 355.

always assumed that *The Times* spoke with special knowledge of government intentions, if not with government approval. The American journalist William Shirer noted in Berlin that the paper had 'an immense circulation' there in 1936.[26] What *The Times* said, therefore, mattered to the Government: it could provoke shifts in foreign attitudes. 'Always on any international issue', wrote Lord Halifax from experience, 'the Foreign Secretary knew that, whatever might be the disclaimers, much foreign opinion would go on believing that the voice of *The Times* was the voice of the British government.'*

The situation was exaggerated by Hitler's sensitiveness to foreign press criticism.† A favourite theme in his speeches was 'the international press campaign against peace'. In the Reichstag on 20 February 1938, he saw no reason for Anglo-German conflict: 'But what does poison friendly relations between the two countries, and consequently causes trouble, is an absolutely intolerable Press campaign which is being conducted in France and England under the slogan of "liberty for expression of personal opinions"'.[27] As late as 23 August 1939, Hitler blamed on the British press the imminence of war, insisting to the Ambassador, Henderson,[28] that the press had fabricated the German threat to Poland and had thus needlessly provoked the British Government's guarantee against aggression.[29] Some of the anger was no doubt simulated (specially in public), but not all. In his despatches to the Foreign Office Henderson constantly preached the desirability of not inflaming Hitler. In the middle of the Czech crisis, for example, he wrote: 'I do wish it might be possible to get at any rate *The Times*, Camrose, Beaverbrook Press, etc. to write up Hitler as the apostle of Peace. It will be terribly shortsighted if this is not done.'[30] There was little the Foreign Secretary could do; though in response to one such plea at an earlier stage in the crisis, he did gather editors together and urge that 'it was essential that the efforts of all well-disposed persons' should be concentrated on smoothing the path to negotiations.[31] Reflecting later on his experiences, Henderson concluded that the press 'handicapped my attempts in 1937 and 1938 to contribute to the improvement of Anglo-German relations, and thereby to the preservation of peace'.[32] He had even tried, without much success, to

---

* Wrench (1955), p. 12. For the same reason the Foreign Office News Department took special pains after 1937 to see that the official point of view was correctly conveyed to the paper's diplomatic correspondent. McLachlan (1971), pp. 128–9.

† Mussolini was also sensitive. See e.g. *Ciano's Diary* (1947), p. 11, 14 January 1939: 'I accompanied the Duce to the station on Chamberlain's departure. He is furious about the British Press in general . . .'

persuade those responsible for submitting British press cuttings to Hitler 'to put some of them in the waste paper basket before they ever reached him'.[33]

Foreign Office documents of the time provide many examples of this German sensitiveness: for instance the Paris embassy reports Ribbentrop (by now Hitler's Foreign Minister; but earlier ambassador to Britain) complaining to the French Foreign Minister in 1938 about British press attacks on Hitler; and in March the same year there were official German protests at British press comment on the Austrian Anschluss.[34] The documents also illustrate in various ways the special position of *The Times*. British missions abroad often seek confirmation from the Foreign Office of items in the paper. Then in June 1938 we find Halifax writing to Prague and Berlin to deny that a *Times* leader on Czecho-Slovakia 'in any way represents the views of His Majesty's Government' (President Beneš 'had already realised', Prague replies);[35] while after the British guarantee to Poland, Roumania and Greece in 1939, the Roumanian Foreign Minister tells the British Ambassador he is 'unpleasantly impressed' by a *Times* leader that was uncomfortably reminiscent of the one (discussed below) that foreshadowed Czecho-Slovakia's doom the previous year.[36]

The amount of *Times* influence abroad is inevitably imprecise. One politician who evidently believed in it strongly was Anthony Eden. A letter from him as Foreign Secretary to Chamberlain in 1937 is a good example: 'Unhappily this *Times* correspondence on the colonial question has without doubt encouraged the Germans to think that we are in a condition to be bullied on that issue. This is the worst possible frame of mind to allow the Germans to be in. I asked Dawson some time ago to stop this correspondence, without success . . .'[37] When Eden had been a junior minister in 1935 the belief was just as strong. He toured European capitals in the spring, whipping up support for the League of Nations in the face of Hitler's recent proclamation of conscription and rearmament. On 4 April a *Times* leader described the German rearmament proposals as constructive and welcomed the end of what it called 'the Versailles habit of mind'. Eden described this leader to the cabinet as a calamity. In every capital he had been claiming the demands were unacceptable, 'But *The Times* regards these as "constructive proposals", and Europe regards *The Times* as the organ of His Majesty's Government.' The Ambassador's telegrams had shown how much harm the leader had done in Berlin:

I can undertake that it will have done as much, or more harm in Moscow, Warsaw and Prague, to say nothing of Paris and Rome.

It is little use for members of the Government to make long journeys if a part of the confidence they have striven to create is thus
to be destroyed. If we are to pursue an effective policy in Europe,
it is essential that it should be made clear that *The Times*, with its
defeatist leaders, does not represent His Majesty's Government. If
this is not done, all our efforts will be in vain . . .[38]

The greatest example during the appeasement years of this foreign
view of *The Times* was the notorious leading article about the
Sudetenland in 1938. 'No single factor contributed so much to the
disasters of last September', reflected the *Spectator*, 'as *The Times*
leader on the 7th of that month, suggesting that Czecho-Slovakia
might be wise in her own interests to let the Sudeten-German areas
go'.[39] Wheeler-Bennett concluded in his study of the Czech crisis
that the encouragement which the article (and a similar French one)
gave to Hitler and the Sudeten Germans was beyond doubt.[40] The
dismemberment of Czecho-Slovakia was the last, most desperate
stroke of appeasement, settled in the tension of Munich after war
had seemed inevitable. The crisis spread over some six months,
intensifying from April onwards. The issue on which it turned was
the right of the $3\frac{1}{4}$ million German minority in the Sudetenland area
of Czecho-Slovakia to have self-determination, and therefore possibly to demand secession and join the German Reich. Czecho-
Slovakia had been created after the First World War out of part of
the old Austro-Hungarian Empire (under which the Sudeten Germans
had lived for centuries). It had a strong army, a strategic position in
Central Europe and mutual assistance treaties with France (1925)
and Soviet Russia (1935). For Hitler the Sudeten question was
simply a pretext to crush it. He achieved his goal by 1 October 1938
– the date he set himself – without a shot fired. The general influence
of *The Times* was towards 'a peaceful outcome' throughout the
crisis: the leading article of 7 September was just a very glaring
example of it.

In April the Sudeten German leader Henlein, prompted by
Hitler, demanded automony for the Sudeten areas and the revision
of Czech foreign policy. The French Prime Minister and Foreign
Secretary, Daladier and Bonnet, assured Chamberlain in London
that they were ready to fight if Czechoslovakia was attacked.
Chamberlain, however, would not do more than undertake that
Britain 'could not guarantee to remain aloof' in that situation.
In May a border incident in which two Sudeten Germans were shot
led to fears of a putsch in Prague. The firmness of the British and
French in warning Hitler of the consequence if he should intervene
held the situation steady for the moment. On 4 August a British

mission under Lord Runciman arrived in Prague to provide advice and assistance in negotiations between the Czech Government and the Sudeten leaders. On 24 August Chamberlain told Henderson in Berlin to prepare the ground for a possible meeting between him and Hitler.

The Czechs made a substantial concession on 4 September. Beneš, the President, refused any foreign policy change but conceded the Sudeten demand for autonomy, From this point onwards events gathered momentum. The importance of *The Times* leading article of 7 September lay in the widespread assumption that it foreshadowed the British view. It created in observers at home and abroad both a belief that the Government would not stand up to Hitler and, in consequence, a resigned expectation of that result. That it was actually a self-fulfilling prophecy is unlikely. The Government needed no hand on the tiller but its own.

The story of the leader can be traced fully in *The Times History* and Dawson's biography.[41] The last paragraph began by accepting as natural the Czech desire to retain its foreign policy. What caused such a sensation was the next passage: if the Sudetens asked for more than the autonomy Beneš conceded, did they want to stay in Czechoslovakia at all? In that case, the critical sentence ran, 'it might be worth while for the Czecho-Slovak Government to consider whether they should exclude altogether the prospect, which has found favour in some quarters, of making Czecho-Slovakia a more homogeneous State by the secession of that fringe of alien populations who are contiguous to the nation with which they are united by race.'[42] Shorn of verbosity, this meant 'Perhaps the Sudetens should be allowed to secede'. Indeed, the leader ended, the advantages to Czecho-Slovakia of becoming a homogeneous state might 'conceivably' (a last minute addition by the editor) outweigh the disadvantages of reduced size. By 1 October this policy had been forced by her supposed allies, France and Britain, on the helpless Czech leaders, after the 'personal diplomacy' of Chamberlain. It was the fruit of his comings and goings to Hitler at Berchtesgaden (15 September) Godesberg (22 September, where Hitler demanded immediate German occupation of the Sudeten areas) and Munich (29 September, when that demand was effectively granted after nearly a week in which British and French refusal to do so looked like precipitating war).

The immediate consternation caused by *The Times* leader can be illustrated from many sources. 'There was a hubbub, as I fully expected', Dawson noted in his diary: '. . . reactions in Prague and Berlin, and the Foreign Office went up through the roof.'[43] Jan Masaryk, the Czech Minister in London, hastened to Whitehall, and in the afternoon the Foreign Office issued a statement that *The Times* leader 'in no way represents the view of His Majesty's Government'.[44] Lord Runciman, whose mission had barely started work, telegraphed from Prague that the article 'has added to our difficulties. We are dealing with the matter here, but it would be useful to caution them (*The Times*) against adventurous speculations at a time when we are hoping to make some progress.'[45] Maisky, the Russian Ambassador, told Halifax that in his view the article had had the worst possible effect. The attitude of Halifax was the same: 'I told him [Maisky] that I did not in any way disagree with his judgement in this matter.'[46] (Dawson himself, however, was left with a different impression after lunching with Halifax, who 'did not seem at all to dissent from my views . . .'*) Other Cabinet ministers were equally upset. Duff Cooper thought the leader 'very mischievous'.[47] Inskip told Tom Jones he regretted it 'like everyone else'.[48] Walter Elliott called Dawson 'one of the biggest fools in Christendom' for writing it at that time.[49] Eden, who had resigned as Foreign Secretary in the spring, noted that '*The Times* bloomer may be a loosening of the stone that sets off the avalanche'.[50] From abroad the Paris Embassy reported inquiries from the French Foreign Office about whether the leader expressed the Government's view.[51] The delegation to the 19th Assembly of the League of Nations reported that, in the French Minister Bonnet's view, 'an already extremely serious situation had been aggravated'.[52]

A note in Harold Nicolson's diary can be taken to illustrate the reaction of many other politicians: Colin Coote, the *Times* leader writer, was, he told Nicolson, 'appalled by the lack of responsible guidance in Printing House Square. Nobody semed to realise the amount of damage which such an article would cause.'[53]

The BBC reported the appearance of the leading article, and the rest of the press pounced on it as a misrepresentation of the British point of view and a damaging indiscretion. Obviously there was much discussion of whether it was 'inspired'. Many people believed it was.[54] *The Week*, a magazine widely read by 'informed' people, attributed the suggestion to the German Embassy. The Embassy itself, however, reported to Berlin that it had possibly originated from 'the Prime Minister's entourage' but was not inspired by the Foreign Office.[55] Maisky refused to believe Halifax's denial to him that it was inspired.[56] That it was not inspired by anyone makes no

---

* *History of The Times* (1952), p. 935. Liddell Hart says Dawson felt sure that Halifax was 'privately in agreement, even though [he] was expressing the opposite view to the representatives of the other countries concerned'. Liddell Hart (1965), Vol. II, p. 160. Harold Macmillan, on the other hand, says the leader 'struck a cruel blow, which Halifax had deeply resented'. Macmillan (1966), p. 572.

difference.* The situation was one where people's reactions are governed by what they believe, not by what is proven true; and *The Times* had no reason at all to be surprised if people thought the article inspired. It was the price of being an 'Establishment' paper, both in the broad sense of representing the interests of a governing class and in the narrow sense implied by the Editor's range of contacts. Others on the staff had good contacts too. With Dawson's knowledge and approval Liddell Hart, at the same time as being Military Correspondent, was, for nine months from June 1937, 'Private Adviser' to Hore-Belisha, the War Minister, whose views on strategy he did much to shape.[57] With that sort of arrangement possible, naturally observers would read special meanings into the paper.

It is not hard to feel some sympathy with *The Times* in this incident. Though unfortunately phrased, as Dawson admitted, the article did not positively *recommend* secession – only that it should not be excluded as a solution if all others failed.† Precisely the same suggestion had been made in a leader by Barrington-Ward on 3 June. This too had been repudiated by the Foreign Office privately through diplomatic channels. A final irony was that *The Times*' suggestion turned out within weeks to be the policy approved overwhelmingly in the press and by the public. To *The Times* the Sudeten problem was one more result of the deficiencies of Versailles. Though that treaty had made much of the principle of self-determination, 'the wishes of the Germans in Bohemia, as of their fellows in Austria, were never consulted'.[58] It was perfectly reasonable that the omission should be rectified. The reaction to the leader of 7 September owed more to timing – its appearance at a crucial stage of the crisis – than to substance. It remains a classic illustration of the way in which those involved in the formation and execution of policy – in Britain and overseas – had constantly to count into their calculations the columns of *The Times*.

Influence through 'access'

The most penetrating kind of influence of *The Times* in the appeasement years is the most difficult to convey, for it consisted in the close, continuous movement of Dawson and Barrington-Ward

* R. A. Butler, a junior minister at the Foreign Office at the time, remains convinced that Halifax at least knew the article was to be written, and that he saw Dawson leaving the Office on the 6th after a long interview with Halifax. Lord Butler (1971), pp. 68–9.

† 'It was not worded *quite* as I should have done if I had had rather more time to revise it', he wrote to his Proprietor, Astor. *History of The Times* (1952), p. 935.

among the appeasers. Dawson had, more than any other journalist
and most politicians of the day, the power of *access* to the policy
makers (not forgetting those in the Dominions). For example
Churchill, the arch anti-appeaser, former holder of high office and
Prime-Minister-to-be, had worse sources and less direct access.
Where Churchill kept abreast of foreign policy through Vansittart,
the permanent official at the top of the Foreign Office, Dawson had
the ear of the Foreign Secretary himself.

Such access had been traditional in *Times* editors (if they wished
it) and is one of the reasons for the paper's historical pre-eminence.
Something of its flavour can perhaps be gauged by this extract from
a generous letter to Dawson, as incoming editor, by his predecessor
G. E. Buckle (written – a pleasing touch – from the Athenaeum):
'. . . You will find a favourable reception from Balfour, Lansdowne,
Bonar Law, Austen Chamberlain – and of course Curzon, Milner
and Selborne, whom you know well, on the one side; and from
Morley, Grey, Asquith and Haldane on the other. The Archbishop
of Canterbury, whom I know well, will be very ready to help you.
I have also bespoken the friendly interest of Stamfordham, the
King's Private Secretary.'[59] Dawson himself could have drawn up
an equivalent list of leading politicians for his successor. In the
appeasement years he was 'specially intimate with Stanley Baldwin
and more intimate than most with Neville Chamberlain'.[*][60] Wrench
describes him as remaining in close contact with the latter during
his three years as Prime Minister;[†] while Vansittart claims that
Baldwin relied heavily on Dawson and once said to him, 'It is easier
for me to talk these matters over with you than with any of my
political colleagues.'[61] While Eden was Foreign Secretary, Dawson
had 'many talks' with him.[‡] Halifax, Eden's successor in February
1938, had long been one of Dawson's closest friends: it was only
natural that when Chamberlain decided to go to Berchtesgaden in
September 1938, 'Edward [Halifax] imparted this momentous news
to me at the Foreign Office in the afternoon under seal of secrecy
till released.'[62]

On 24 September when Chamberlain was due back from his

* Chamberlain was intimate with very few people. Dawson probably saw
more of Baldwin in retirement than of Chamberlain.

† See, e.g. Diary, 22 September 1938: '*The Prime Minister's second meeting
with Hitler* . . . drove down to Heston to see Neville Chamberlain off to Germany. There was no great crowd there . . . but I think he was glad to see me, and
was very appreciative of the support of *The Times*.' Quoted, Wrench (1955),
p. 377.

‡ Wrench (1955), p. 364. e.g. Diary, 21 April 1937: '. . . To the Carlton Annexe
to lunch with Anthony Eden and discuss the state of Europe . . . He himself was
in very good form and thoroughly sensible.'

second flight to Germany (Godesberg) we even find Lady Halifax twice ringing Dawson up for 'news' – 'Edward having left the house at 9 and not been heard of since'.[63]

Such associations were naturally repeated many times over with a wide range of public men of varying importance – though including few Labour and industrial leaders. Lord Boothby dubbed Dawson 'Secretary-General of the twentieth-century establishment', and the phrase fits well.[64] Dawson's diary lists endless clubland lunches (often *tête-à-tête*), visits to hear the Prime Minister in the Commons, assignations in Downing Street* or Foreign embassies ('Looked in on Joe Kennedy, U.S. Ambassador, on my way to the office . . .').[65]

This kind of merry-go-round of activity is symbolised by the idea of 'The Cliveden Set'. Complex political ideas or institutions quickly become reduced to symbolic phrases if they do not already have a convenient name. In this way, they easily can be used, albeit crudely, in the currency of day-to-day discussion. 'The Cliveden Set' was a phrase penned by Claud Cockburn, editor of *The Week* and formerly a *Times* Foreign Correspondent, to head 'a longish think piece' in his broadsheet 'about the nature and aims of those in high places who were working, sincerely perhaps, but as it seemed to me disastrously for the "appeasement" of Adolf Hitler'.[66] Cockburn has described how he published basically the same article three times inside a few weeks. Not until the third time, when 'The Cliveden Set' was given it as a heading, did it command attention: and then 'The thing went off like a rocket'.[67] The phrase, narrowly speaking, took its name from the Thames-side mansion of Lord Astor (brother of *The Times* Astor, who seldom went there).[68] Those entertained by the Astors, there or at their London house, included Chamberlain, Dawson, Barrington-Ward, J. L. Garvin (editor of Lord Astor's paper *The Observer*), Hoare, Lord Lothian, Lord Halifax and many others – not all of whom shared the Government's attitude to Germany.†

* Cf. Thomas Jones (1954), p. 202 (20 May 1936). 'I fixed a talk tomorrow with G.D. on the state of the world'.

† Thomas Jones, who seems to have combed the Visitors' Book, says Chamberlain spent five weekends at Cliveden in the decade 1930–9. Dawson, however, was 'a regular visitor'. Baldwin spent the weekend before he became Prime Minister (on 7 June 1935) at Cliveden, constructing his Cabinet. Thomas Jones (1954), pp. xxxv, xxxviii. Jones gives a colourful account of the weekends at the house and stresses the wide range of political views represented among guests: 'The so-called "Group" has as much unity as passengers in a railway train. Several of them never mention politics at all and confine their observations to golf, others to books, some to gardening. Those who are active politicians are engaged in criticising one another for the most part.' p. 403. Christopher Sykes' biography of Nancy Astor takes an equally sceptical view of the 'Cliveden Set'. *Nancy: the life of Lady Astor* (1972).

The phrase quickly took on a broader connotation and, as Cockburn points out, ceased to represent a particular group of individuals but became 'the symbol of a tendency, of a set of ideas'.[69] To the extent that there was a 'Cliveden Set', however, Dawson was clearly a member of it. Gilbert and Gott suggest that Lothian's house Blickling was as much a centre of appeasement, and that Cliveden 'prompted' the policy only in the sense that a prompter does not write a play 'though he can often speed it on its way'.[70] The fact that Cockburn and others sedulously ascribed more influence to the set than it really had contributed to popular belief in Dawson's power.* 'This "Cliveden gang" business is becoming tiresome,' he confided in his Diary.[71] He also featured in an *Evening Standard* Low cartoon (Shiver Sisters Ballet, 1938) showing members of the set dancing to Dr Goebbels' tune.

Influence as a pressure group

Dawson's connections – and by 1938 he had had 26 years in the editorial chair (excepting the brief post-war interregnum) to develop them – were so interwoven with the politics of the day (specially Conservative politics) that it would be impossible to estimate 'Who influenced Whom' in any simple sense. Rather, one must say simply that as events took their course throughout the appeasement years, Dawson was never far away, listening, noting, arguing.†

These connections meant that Dawson's role (and that of *The Times* as an institution) should in this form be seen as precisely similar to that of any pressure group in the political process. Dawson had no party, Trade Union, parliamentary or business 'constituency'. His constituency was the readership of his paper; and Prime Ministers needed to bear that in mind when dealing with him, just as Baldwin, say, had to calculate feeling in his party in the Hoare–Laval affair. From time to time, therefore, one can find specific examples of Dawson being treated not as a journalist in the sense of a reporter or commentator, but as a pressure group leader. An excellent example is the reconstruction of the government by Baldwin on the retirement of Ramsay MacDonald in June 1935. Dawson had a long talk with Baldwin in May: 'Tom Jones, whom I'd just met in the Athenaeum, suggested that I should have a talk with him and I called, without warning, on the chance.'[72] They discussed whether Churchill should be given office (Baldwin thought he

---

* Dawson's role in the Abdication Crisis in 1936 had brought him publicity in the United States. For some American comments, see Wrench (1955), p. 366.

† His connections were just as important, of course, during the First World War. See Wrench (1955), e.g. p. 132.

would be a 'disruptive force': Dawson agreed); whether Lloyd George or other Liberals should be included; and whether there was 'anything to be done with reasonable Labour' (Dawson thought it 'hopeless': Baldwin was less sure). When Baldwin got down to filling posts early next month he made Hoare Foreign Secretary. According to Hoare, Baldwin at first said he did not know whether to offer him India or the Foreign Office. Hoare said he would prefer India. Baldwin's response was 'a knock on the table with his pipe' and a promise to think it over. Next day, 'his mind had definitely moved towards the alternative of the Foreign Office. I gathered he had consulted several friends, including Lothian and Geoffrey Dawson and that they had pressed it. They had found him more than half-converted to their view, and it needed little further persuasion to convince him. He accordingly offered it to me . . .' It was not in the least unnatural, in the view both of Prime Minister and Foreign Secretary to-be, that the Editor of *The Times* should be consulted before the appointment. Dawson's standing is described here by Hoare just as if he were one more interested politician with an axe to grind.* Examples can be found in Wrench's book of Chamberlain and Halifax behaving in the same way. Halifax discusses with Dawson the problem of finding the right man from the Labour Party to take over the embassy in Moscow; while Chamberlain, in the early days of the war, calls Dawson to Downing Street to explain why he had formed a larger war cabinet than the paper had advocated that day and 'to give me his general ideas' about Hitler's most recent speech.[73]

Dawson's connections imply one other conclusion. That is: for purposes of defining 'influence' over a government the boundary between what is published and what is left out is more or less arbitrary.

Permeating the political atmosphere as he did, Dawson gathered and 'published' news by letter, telephone and word of mouth as much as in his columns. His leaders no doubt were read with the kinds of effect described above. But, even had he wished, Dawson could not have published more than a fraction of the news and letters about Germany and foreign policy from sources and correspondents at home and abroad. Certainly the type of publication associated with ideas of exposure may influence governments. But influence through the power of access does not depend on the sanction of mass publication, though of course it may do. The

* Vt Templewood (1954), p. 109. Compare Michael Astor's comment on the standing of Lothian: 'the danger of Philip Lothian's position was that although he had no actual responsibility for government he had the ear of men who wielded power.' Michael Astor (1963), p. 145.

influence is akin rather to that of a man who, by the contribution of his wits or knowledge, helps another to complete the clues of a crossword puzzle. Dawson's critics, as will be argued below, claim that such influence is not journalistic. It was influence by a journalist, nevertheless.

The role of *The Times* in the appeasement years can be summarised thus. Its total commitment to the policy smoothed the Government's way in implementing it; added to its authority in the community; hampered and disheartened its opponents. The authority with which *The Times* was held to speak abroad obliged the British Government to be continually alert to its opinions. The longstanding position of Dawson in the governing élite gave him the power of access to the members at its centre and caused him to be granted the same influence as a party politician or pressure group leader. He must bear a corresponding responsibility for the events of the appeasement years.

II. JUDGEMENTS ON 'THE TIMES'

Naturally, in view of its role, *The Times* has been included in the blanket criticism of appeasement. But criticism has gone further than blaming it for backing the wrong horse. A. J. P. Taylor, in his *English History 1914–45*, damns Dawson curtly out of hand: 'He turned *The Times* into a propaganda sheet and did not hesitate to suppress, or to pervert, the reports of his own correspondents.'[74] Francis Williams has objected that Dawson was 'a committed man': 'It was an honourable commitment, but it was not a journalistic one and in the end it led Dawson into courses contrary to the principles that should sustain journalism at its highest levels . . .'[75] Similarly Liddell Hart felt Dawson tried to make the paper into 'the cabinet behind the Cabinet', instead of giving priority to its function as a newspaper.[76] *The History of The Times*, published only a few years after Dawson's death, also criticises the paper's support for appeasement, but in terms of changes of structure and journalistic practice. Not until the publication of Donald McLachlan's biography of Barrington-Ward (1971) and F. R. Gannon's study of *The British press and Germany 1936–1939* (1971) was a more considered view taken and the paper's conduct defended (specially by McLachlan).

The criticism of backing the wrong policy does not need discussing here: the reasons why people supported appeasement were indicated earlier on. The criticism that the paper's influence was somehow improper or 'not journalistic' deserves examination. It implies that the role described in the previous section could and should have been different.

The criticism can be divided into two parts: firstly that Dawson used improper *means* to achieve influence; secondly that he sought influence towards improper *ends*. Taylor is implicitly concerned with the first (though too precise a set of unstated assumptions should not be hung on his one brief comment). He does not suggest that it was improper of Dawson to promote appeasement, but just that he went improperly about it ('suppression' and 'perversion' of news). Williams, *The Times History* and Liddell Hart are more concerned with the second criticism; though in arguing his case Williams relies also on the first.

Williams' argument does not refer only to Dawson's behaviour over appeasement, but that aspect is certainly crucial. The nub is that Dawson became personally much too close to the government. Partly this was because he was committed 'socially', in the sense of being deeply involved in the activities and values of one rather narrow though admittedly very influential social class; and partly because he was utterly convinced of the rightness of appeasement.*

He became devoted more to the success of that policy than to the maintenance of journalistic values: he lacked the element of detachment. He was faced with the classic dilemma between the national interest and a sectional interest (though there is no way of knowing if he ever posed it to himself in these terms). He believed that the wellbeing of Britain, Europe and the Empire depended upon the success of appeasement, and that *The Times* could be effective in its achievement. How then was he to behave? Was he perhaps to sacrifice the success of the policy by offending Hitler with the bare truth about Germany? Or to outrage journalistic norms by judicious choice and presentation of news? Williams has no doubt that he chose the latter and was wrong to do so. He accepted the limitations, duties and liabilities that governments accept and that his great predecessor Delane had said *The Times* must never accept.† The duty of the journalist, Delane had written,

---

* Lord Brand, Dawson's friend since Kindergarten days, wrote an illuminating comment to Halifax's biographer: 'Baldwin, Dawson and Halifax all had this in common. They were all English country gentlemen, all good public school men, and all good churchmen. They seldom visited Europe, or knew what Europeans were like. None of them could have the slightest conception of the enormity of Hitler. Their whole upbringing conspired against understanding that such people could exist, and that the Nazi State was a lunatic State.' The Earl of Birkenhead *Halifax* (1965), p. 422.

† Both Delane and Dawson were offered Civil Service jobs by the government of the day. Both declined them.

was 'to seek out the truth above all things and to present to his readers not such things as statecraft would wish them to know but the truth as near as he can attain it'.[77] In Williams' view, 'Dawson was too much committed to statecraft for that journalistic compulsion to hold his fidelity'.[78] In addition to this Williams believes that: 'The influence that a great editor exercises should be in the open. Much of Dawson's lay behind the scenes.' He behaved as though he were a 'superior civil servant'.[79]

The conception of the role of *The Times* upon which those criticisms rest derives straight from the middle of the nineteenth century, when the pre-eminence of *The Times* was indicated by the fact that its circulation was three times bigger than all other London morning papers put together. It amounts to a belief in the paper as, in political terms, an 'opposition' (though not, of course, an 'alternative government'). The author of *The Times History* measures Dawson's performance critically against it too. He should not have committed the paper totally to appeasement, the *History* argues: the paper should never commit itself totally to any government policy and ignore the bad sides. But the commitment is explained by the *History* in structural more than sociological terms. Great stress is laid, for instance, on Dawson's failure to appoint a Foreign Editor after the expert Harold Williams died in 1928. Instead Dawson combined the job with his own, which might conceivably have worked if Empire problems had predominated but meant that the paper was ill-equipped to cope with European ones.* The *History* complains that Dawson failed to perpetuate a machine with which *The Times* could have forged a policy that was independent of the government sources used by Dawson, that was therefore truly its own, and that it could have pressed on the public.† Not just any old independence though: the nineteenth-century concept of the role of *The Times* protrudes sharply in this casual comment – breathtaking by any less exalted standard – in the *History*'s discussion of the Sudetenland leading article: 'That there was in Printing House Square *no specialist with a completer understanding of European and World politics than a Prime Minister or a Foreign Secretary* was the result of a defect in

---

* Vansittart's view on this – the view of a professional diplomatist – runs: 'Dawson kept the whole field under the survey of his impressive sketchiness, and relied on Barrington-Ward who was wrong-headed on the highest and therefore most hopeless grounds. Neither Dawson nor Ward . . . had a tithe of Wickham Steed's experience.' Vansittart (1958), p. 364. Steed was Editor from 1919–22.

† The *History* sees 'no sign', for instance, that Dawson consulted Tory or other statesmen who were known to oppose appeasement. *History of The Times* (1952), p. 1008.

the organisation of Printing House Square that originated with Dawson's recall in 1922.'*

The *History* condemns Dawson further, like Williams, for trying to do the Government's job: 'to assist a government of whatever complexion to find a national policy had become one of the important functions of *The Times*'.[80] 'Unenlightened public opinion was sovereign master of both the Government and the paper.' The Government had some excuse: it had to take account of the ballot box. *The Times* need not, but it had nonetheless 'capitulated' to the mood of an uninformed ostrichlike electorate swollen by recent franchise extensions. The paper's true usefulness, in contrast, would have been in standing aloof from contemporary politics and politicians and defining clearly the direction in which the world was moving, the decisions to be taken and the worse as well as the better implications of government policies.[81] The *History* concedes implicitly, however, that the nineteenth-century standard could no longer be met in full anyway. In Barnes' and Delane's day, 'the public' was a small informed body capable (in theory) of sophisticated judgement. It made sense then to believe that 'by making all he knows the property of the nation' a journalist could instruct and appeal to 'the enlightened reader' who could then form a clear and accurate idea of his duty and his interest, which in turn the paper would reflect. The size of Northcliffe's empire meant that he was able still in the First World War to preserve that sort of stance. In the thirties, however, no paper or group of papers had anyway the strength to succeed in *organising* popular support for a strong, independent foreign policy. Instead papers took over policies formulated by the parties and were content to win support for them in the country.

The *History* thus partly blames Dawson directly for *The Times* failure to take an independent line, and partly it sees him as the victim of changes in the political system which inevitably modified the paper's role. The main difference of view from Francis Williams' is that the *History* makes no attempt to distinguish 'open' influence from that 'behind the scenes'.

Dawson's behaviour was thus improper or 'not journalistic' in relation to a very ambitious, partly outmoded standard. Its ambition can be seen in a further remark from the *History*: '. . . Even had the Editor differed from Baldwin and Chamberlain (about Germany)

---

* Ibid. p. 931. Author's italics. The kind of thing which might have been done differently, perhaps, was the appointment of a permanent Military Correspondent. Not until 1934 was Liddell Hart appointed to the post, at the behest of Barrington-Ward. Until then Dawson left the post vacant because he thought it unlikely there would ever be another war. Liddell Hart (1965), Vol. I., p. 73.

he would have argued that it is no use telling politicians to do what politicians had decided is utterly impossible. There is force in the argument, except to an Editor who has made his newspaper an instrument that creates conditions in which a statesman might decide otherwise.'[82] It was the paper's own traditional standard, however, and its own *History* not surprisingly applied it. But it is a highly exceptional standard, if wholeheartedly applied. Even other 'quality' papers did not necessarily aspire to it, particularly those with any tradition of partisanship. If wholehearted commitment to a policy, and hence on occasion to a government, were always to be 'non-journalistic', there would remain little journalism in the history of British newspapers. *The Times* standard is the basis of its self-professed claim to be a national institution; of Eden's cry that its lack of a Foreign Editor was a national misfortune; and of Coote's being appalled at the lack of 'responsible guidance' in the Czecho-Slovak crisis. It was this standard which enabled Northcliffe to talk – quite seriously – of bequeathing *The Times* to the British Museum: not because he wished it to go into the refrigerator of British Culture, but because he liked the system of trustees that administered the museum. Astor and Walter indeed implemented something like that scheme: shares in the paper could not be sold without the approval of a committee consisting in the Lord Chief Justice, the Warden of All Souls, the President of the Royal Society, the President of the Institute of Chartered Accountants and the Governor of the Bank of England. Lord Thomson carried on the same idea – though the Monopolies Commission thought it was mere window-dressing[83] – by nominating four 'national figures' to the eleven-man Board of Directors.

The other part of the criticisms of *The Times* alleges the use of improper means. Taylor's tart accusation raises three questions: Was *The Times* in the appeasement years a 'propaganda sheet'? Did Dawson, as Taylor claims, *turn it* into whatever it was? Did he really 'not hesitate' to suppress and pervert reports? Whether it was a propaganda sheet depends of course on the meaning of propaganda. In the literal sense it was manifestly 'propagating' the Government's policy; though it was certainly not a *tool* of the Government, and Dawson and Barrington-Ward reached their positions on appease-ment by their own routes, as we have seen. In the context it is propagandist *means* that are at issue and on which the answer depends. In the modern sense of the word, propaganda denotes a particular kind of persuasion: not the attempt to persuade by reasoned argument after a full statement of facts, but by the use of non-rational appeals to the emotions. If the result is achieved more efficiently (and in propaganda the end justifies the means) it may be that the appearance of rationality should be given to the process by the selective use of fact and argument.

What evidence is there that Dawson edited *The Times* like that? One commonly quoted piece is a damning passage in a letter from Dawson, in May 1937, to his Geneva Correspondent, G. E. Daniels, temporarily in Berlin: 'But it would really interest me to know precisely what it is in *The Times* that has produced this antagonism in Germany. I did my utmost, night after night, to keep out of the paper anything that might hurt their susceptibilities. I can really think of nothing that has been printed now for many months past which they could possibly take exception to as unfair comment.'[84] The *History*'s comment on this is: 'The Times Correspondents in Europe felt bothered by the practice of excluding anything that the Germans might choose to regard as "unfair" from both the leader and the news-columns of the paper. It looked to them as though correspondents' messages were being "trimmed" to fit a policy. In fact, messages were cut or omitted from time to time in accordance with what was accepted by the Editor as the requirements of diplomacy.'[85] Not only did Dawson leave things out: he put things in. 'I spend my nights taking out anything which I think will hurt their susceptibilities', he wrote to Lord Lothian about this time, 'and in dropping in little things which are intended to soothe them'.[86] Despite this policy, within three months of that letter to Daniels, the Berlin Correspondent, Norman Ebbutt, had been expelled by the German government because of the unfavourable nature of his reporting. A first attempt at pressure was met with resolve in Printing House Square. During the three following days there was a sudden and violent German press campaign against Ebbutt and other foreign correspondents, and an article on Goering's organisation of the German steel industry on 13 August provided the pretext for his expulsion. Despite a Nazi tip that it would be considered an unfriendly act towards Germany, 50 foreign correspondents went to see him off at the station. That was a measure of Ebbutt's prestige. The young American journalist William Shirer, whose *Berlin Diary* is a classic of those years, had noted soon after his arrival in 1935 that 'Ebbutt is by far the best-informed foreign correspondent here';[87] and when Ebbutt left Shirer reflected that the Nazis had 'hated and feared him for years because of his exhaustive knowledge of this country and of what was going on behind the scenes'.[88] Ebbutt himself confided to Shirer in 1935 that *The Times* did not print all he sent and did not want to hear 'too much on the bad side of Nazi Germany', and that he was talking of quitting.* By 1937

* Ibid. p. 42. Cf. the comment by Alexander Werth, the *Guardian*'s man in Berlin in February 1933, to his editor: '. . . Ebbutt . . . showed me the article

he was telling the United States Ambassador Dodd that the paper refused to print more than half his stories;[89] and he often complained to Vansittart about the same sort of thing,[90] and to colleagues when on leave.

The Times was certainly not toadying: even the 'toned down' reports were still resented as 'aggressive'. It was a question at worst of the paper telling the truth but not the whole truth. As Martin Gilbert concedes, 'Even *The Times* gave prominence to stories of religious persecution inside Germany';[91] and William Sharf's exhaustive study of *The British press and Jews under Nazi rule*[92] compliments the paper on its courage. McLachlan claims, in addition, that the real cause of Ebbutt's expulsion was less his own writing than the paper's strong and persistent exposure of German bombing in Spain, which provoked a furious attack on the paper by the official German News Service. Moreover it is certainly not true that the reports of foreign correspondents were never before sub-edited to take account of repercussions. During the editorship of Buckle there were some 'rare precedents' of this kind.[93] There were others during the brief editorship of Steed. For example, at the time of the Washington Naval Treaty in 1921, which agreed ratios for the size of the United States, British and Japanese navies, the Anglo–Japanese Alliance of 1911 came up for renewal as well. 'The Washington Correspondent was unequivocal about the unpopularity of the Alliance in America: his messages were published, *though the trenchancy of his phrasing was editorially minimised.*'[94]

Taylor is thus wrong in suggesting Dawson *turned* the paper into a propaganda sheet; and the evidence is very slight – though admitted even by McLachlan to have 'some substance' – that news presentation was sometimes angled slightly in this period to fit policy goals.[95] Ebbutt, according to the recollection of colleagues, 'wrote too much anyway and so was always being cut down';[96] but cutting for reasons of space was quite a different matter from intentional bias. Liddell Hart suffered the frustrations of similar treatment, which he has documented fully in his memoirs. His own writing (even when it was not a leader article) was less to do with 'facts' in the sense of events or things and more a process of analysing implications and consequences. This, indeed, was what caused his difficulties. 'For a long time past', he wrote to Barrington-Ward in November 1938, 'I have felt that the foundations of our national security were slipping, and that there was an increasing risk of the structure itself

---

he wrote on Monday, and it was pretty violent; yet, at the London end, they cut out everything that was in the least likely to offend Hitler.' Quoted in David Ayerst (1971), p. 508.

crumbling. The chance of averting the danger must depend on prompt and adequate recognition of the cracks. This in turn depends on those who have studied the subject being allowed to point out the flaws before they are beyond repair.'[97] But he was not able to point out the flaws: he was 'repeatedly gagged' when trying to say anything that ran counter to the editorial line.[98] In March that year, for example, he expressed his concern to Barrington-Ward 'that the great central body of thoughtful opinion represented in the readers of *The Times* has never had the Imperial Defence issues clearly set out for their consideration. And that I have not been allowed the opportunity of doing this.'[99] His articles were increasingly cut or discarded.* His expertise was ignored: the notorious Sudetenland leader, for example, was written without reference to him about the strategic implications. Looking at it from Dawson's position, however, the trouble was that Hart was 'viewy'; and the Editor could not abide correspondents who 'spatchcocked' (as he called it) comments into the paper or tried to write like columnists.

Dawson and Barrington-Ward agreed to the exceptional arrangement of letting Hart write up to a dozen pieces a year for papers not in competition with *The Times*. Earlier he had suggested in vain that controversial articles could perhaps be published under his own name.† The new arrangement worked satisfactorily for some months, but the continued incompatibility of the paper's views and his own led to a mutually agreeable separation at the end of 1939.

Another incident often quoted to suggest Dawson's propagandist bias stemmed from the resignation of Duff Cooper, First Lord of the Admiralty, after the Munich agreement. The Lobby correspondent Winn reported the speech enthusiastically. 'I never saw what he wrote,' Duff Cooper recorded in his Memoirs, 'but it did not accord with the policy of the paper. Not only did the editor suppress it but he inserted a concoction of his own in which the speech was described as "a damp squib" and headed it "from our lobby correspondent".'‡ Winn felt so strongly about this that he

* A leader-page article about the Air Defence implications of the Munich agreement was published on 23 October, 'but, to my dismay, with cuts and alterations that were bound to diminish its effect'. Eight critical articles were not published at all in 1938 (up to the beginning of November). Ibid., pp. 178–9.

† Ibid. p. 179. McLachlan, arguing that what Hart wanted of *The Times* was never quite the job the paper wanted of him, suggests that 'thirty years later the office would have used Liddell Hart as a columnist, giving him regular space to air his own views over his own signature, while maintaining in the leader columns an editorial view which might or might not be different'. McLachlan (1971), p. 156.

‡ Cooper (1953), p. 250. Gannon points out that in fact the phrase 'damp squib' appears nowhere in *The Times* account, and Cooper's speech was reported in two columns of the parliamentary pages. Gannon (1971), p. 66.

resigned (having first secured a job on the *Daily Telegraph*), telling Dawson that he could not continue to serve a paper 'which was the first responsible advocate of secession [of the Sudetenland] and still has hopes of a genuine friendship with the Nazi régime'.[100] This was the occasion more than the cause of his resignation (contrary to the impression left by Francis Williams' account);[101] and the episode appears in a completely different light in Dawson's diary. Like him, Dawson heard Duff Cooper's speech: but he found it 'not very impressive'. 'I had a bad time with tendentious Political Notes and Sketch', he noted, 'and at midnight received a long and pompous letter of resignation from Anthony Winn.'[102] Whether it was Dawson or Winn whose account was 'tendentious' could never be anything but a matter of opinion. What is quite clear, however, is that Dawson was perfectly within his rights in sub-editing the piece. It was an example of ordinary journalistic practice, done in good faith.

One more incident commonly quoted against Dawson involved the paper's correspondence columns. In July 1939, when war seemed close, *The Times* printed a letter from the veteran Liberal journalist, J. A. Spender, deploring an attack on the Prime Minister's foreign policy by the Liberal leader, Sir Archibald Sinclair: at this time national unity should be the aim. Nine prominent Liberals, led by Asquith's daughter Lady Violet Bonham Carter, sent a dissenting reply which stated that if the Prime Minister wanted to show national unity he should include the anti-appeasers Churchill and Eden in his cabinet. Dawson replied privately, explaining that he had already decided not to have a correspondence on the subject of Churchill and therefore would not print their letter – at least not in full. The authors then sent their letter, with a statement that *The Times* had refused to publish it, to the news agencies and a number of papers. It featured widely in the national and provincial press, and was then published in *The Times* without the Churchill paragraphs, as a news item. *The Times* explained its attitude in a leading article. A newspaper agitation for Churchill would, because of his controversiality, be both mischievous and futile: 'To those of us who feel intensely that Mr Churchill may well be needed in a Government again, and that his recent services as a detached critic of the present Government have not been negligible, such a public controversy over his personal merits is altogether deplorable. His friends have already done him infinite harm.'[103]

For this exercise of editorial discretion *The Times* was roundly attacked by its contemporaries, generally on the grounds of having abandoned the duty to give space to letters which did not coincide with editorial opinion.[104] In fact the paper was fully alive to the potential value of Churchill (though Dawson, according to Coote, 'disliked and despised him');[105] if 'bias' can be detected, it was if anything in the other direction. Questions of 'balance' in letter columns are inevitably subjective. Less than a year earlier we find one of the staunchest anti-appeasers, Duff Cooper, prompting Halifax (already Foreign Secretary) to use his influence over Dawson and stop a correspondence in the paper at a point when the Czechoslovak crisis was mounting to a climax, about the desirability of the Sudetenland seceding. Halifax spoke to him 'very strongly'. 'It was too late to stop the edition, but Dawson had promised to do his best to "bottle up" the correspondence . . .'[106] Dawson might well feel anti-appeasers judged his use of the letter columns in terms of the optimum promotion of their own policies.* At the very least, it is difficult to assert that Dawson used the columns as an instrument of propaganda.

There is a more general difficulty about any allegations of the subordination of journalistic values to a policy goal, such as Williams and Taylor make. This is the fact that 'journalistic values' themselves depend upon some ultimate goal. To print news of any kind about Germany in the appeasement years involved a prior decision that Germany was important and the 'suppression' (through lack of space) of news about somewhere else. Why was Germany important? Because its actions could affect Britain's security. Why did Britain's security matter? Because it just did. Here was the ultimate value – and one from which, no doubt, a number of British inhabitants dissented. In a simple and strict sense, then, every journalist subordinates means to ends and lacks a 'journalistic commitment'. Francis Williams' distinction is not one of kind, but of degree. Even so, there is a substantial degree of difference between printing news about Germany because it is *relevant* to the goal of appeasement and printing it (or omitting it) because you believe it promotes that goal. (Whether it does or not is immaterial: here it is the intention that matters.) The case against Dawson on this ground probably stands.

There is a similar difficulty about Williams' complaint that Dawson's influence was not 'open'. *The Times History* quite rightly does not recognise any such distinction. To think that a journalist can become disembodied and exist only in the page of print is, as a critic once wrote of the Lobby correspondents, to expect him to be

* Not only the letter columns. The allegation of *The Times*' 'irresponsibility' in the Czech crisis by Eden, Walter Elliott, Coote, etc., all assume precisely that function they are otherwise so quick to condemn – namely that *The Times* *ought* to have had regard to the consequence of its actions for government policy: in other words, that 'closeness' to the Government entailed nothing improper.

'the original invisible man'. Contact of a journalist (however 'disinterested') with a source is inevitably a two-way process. The source will react to *his own* communication of fact or opinion to the journalist, even if the journalist has given no fact or opinion to him. As the last section argued, the dividing line between matter published and withheld is arbitrary and often unimportant in point of influence. The leading article may be merely the extension to a wider audience of the dinner-table conversation with a group of influential public men. To quote a real example, Dawson on 26 September 1918 put down on paper the case for an early general election. He did not have it set up in print: he sent it privately as a memorandum to the Prime Minister.* Is that to be held improper? Again, when the leadership of the Conservative party was under discussion in 1921 Wickham Steed (then Editor) recorded that 'Austen [Chamberlain] sent a man to me to say that Austen hoped to be elected leader of the party, and to ask whether *The Times* would support him. I said *The Times* never supported any persons on personal grounds, but that there seemed to me to be no one else in the running, and that Austen was obviously entitled to the job, if he wanted it.'[107] Was Steed to reply that Chamberlain must wait till his opinion was expressed in a leading article?

Steed in fact seems to have been a master at the use of nicely timed publication and non-publication as a means of pressure (particularly in the Irish problems that were so prominent in his years as editor).[108] Steed was particularly close to Bonar Law during the momentous days in 1922 culminating in the decision by the Conservative party to reject their leaders, break up Lloyd George's wartime coalition and fight the forthcoming general election in their own colours. Steed's intervention was one of several that were critical in coaxing Law to attend the meeting and oppose the Government.† Steed believed the night before that he had persuaded Law to go. He printed an item to that effect. Law rang up just after the edition went to press. Steed told him of the item. 'But I have not yet decided to go', answered Law. Steed again pressed him to attend, in the interest of 'healthy party government', and promised the backing of *The Times*. 'He thought from the tone of Bonar Law's final remarks that he was likely to attend,' and left the news item in.[109] Law went to the meeting and his opposition to the Government was probably decisive.

* Wrench (1955), p. 167. Wrench also says that throughout the First World War Dawson periodically circulated to a small group of friends a survey 'explaining what was happening behind the scenes', p. 398.

† The result of the meeting was that Law became Prime Minister. He resigned with ill health in May 1923. According to A. J. P. Taylor, Beaverbrook gave 'the final push' that took Law to the meeting. A. J. P. Taylor (1972), p. 198.

The allegation that Dawson used improper means to advance his appeasement policy is valid only in an extremely narrow way. He himself did not turn the paper into what it was. To say that 'he did not hesitate to suppress, or to pervert' the reports of his correspondents is highly misleading, as is the phrase 'a propaganda sheet'. If *The Times* did not claim such high standards, and if the appeasement policy had turned out successful, it is probable that Dawson's limited news bias and lack of 'journalistic commitment' would have called down on him only a tiny fraction of the criticism he has in fact received. Even this criticism, however, is an acknowledgement of the important role of the paper in the appeasement years.

4
Enoch Powell's 'earthquake'

Enoch Powell made a speech on immigration to a small audience of Birmingham Conservatives on 20 April 1968. The result, to quote the word Powell himself used later, was an 'earthquake'.[1] The Conservative party's tender unity on the issue was badly bruised. Powell was sacked immediately from the shadow cabinet. A great surge of popular support swept over him. Dockers and meat porters marched to Westminster; many token strikes took place. Powell received 110,000 letters in the next few weeks. His popularity leapt in the opinion polls. He acquired a populist base that established him as a major political figure independent of his party.

All this was occasioned by the mass media. Intense coverage meant that the speech before an audience of 85 reached 96 per cent of the adult population (according to a Gallup poll) within a few days. The coverage was not entirely accidental: Powell's skills as a communicator enabled him to exploit the media at the same time as the media 'exploited' him.

Several aspects of the interaction of mass media and politics are illustrated by a study of the speech and its aftermath. Why did Powell win such publicity? What were the effects on immigration and race as an issue, on Powell and the Conservative party, and on Powell's role in the 1970 general election?

I. POWELL'S BIRMINGHAM SPEECH: MEDIA COVERAGE

(a) The immigration and race relations background

The disturbances in Notting Dale in September 1958, after which nine youths were convicted of assault on coloured immigrants, symbolise a turning-point in British race relations. Previously Commonwealth immigration was a peripheral issue: government policy was decided by extraneous factors. In the next ten years it moved to the centre. 'Since 1964', the Institute of Race Relations' survey commented in 1969, '. . . immigration and race relations have been accepted as one of the range of policy issues occupying a permanent place in political debate'.[2] After Notting Dale the first landmark was the Commonwealth Immigrants Act 1962. This introduced a voucher system to regulate the flow of immigrants, many of whom were coming from the West Indies and, latterly, India and Pakistan. In 1956, the peak year, nearly 40,000 had arrived. The figure dropped but then soared to new peaks in 1960 and 1961. By 1961 the total coloured population of England Wales born overseas, according to the Census, was 336,000, compared with 74,500 ten years earlier.* The Act replaced an informal system of 'voluntary controls' by the Commonwealth governments and was introduced (against bitter Labour opposition) after mounting Conservative pressure. Once in office the Labour party back-pedalled but tried to take a more positive view by passing a Race Relations Act (1965), designed to reduce discrimination in public places through the principle of conciliation and the machinery of a Race Relations Board. At the same time, however, the government tightened immigration controls, reducing the vouchers for people with jobs assured and special skills and completely discontinuing vouchers for the unskilled. This led to a very rapid drop in voucher-holders – a little over 6,000 in 1967, compared with 30,000 in 1963. But the regulations permitting dependants to join immigrants at a later date meant that the figure for dependants continued to rise until 1967. *Colour and citizenship* estimated that the total coloured population in England and Wales by 1966 – for various reasons a difficult calculation – was 924,000.[3] In the two years following the Race Relations Act negotiations were carried on with industry and appropriate interest groups by the government prior to further constructive legislation. This was to cover employment, housing and all commercial and public services and to extend enforcement procedures. It duly emerged as the Race Relations Act (1968). But its thunder was largely stolen by the 'Kenya Asians problem'.

At the time of independence late in 1963 large numbers of Asians living in Kenya opted to keep 'U.K. and Colonies' citizenship. They were given (with other aliens) two years in which to apply for Kenyan citizenship. In 1967 new legislation provided that those who had not taken up this option could work in Kenya only on a temporary basis, while Kenyanisation of jobs proceeded. In 1965 and again in 1966 more than 6,000 Asians had used the opportunity to settle in the United Kingdom. After the new legislation 1,500 arrived in the month of August alone, 2,661 in September, 1,334 in November and 2,294 in January 1968.

The position of these Asians was the subject of a sustained and urgent campaign in the autumn and winter of 1967 led by Duncan

* E. J. B. Rose et al. (1969), p. 72. 171,800 came from the West Indies, of whom only 15,300 had arrived by 1951. 81,400 came from India (30,800 in 1951) and 24,900 from Pakistan (5,000).

Sandys, Sir Cyril Osborne (an anti-immigration campaigner of long standing) and Enoch Powell. The subject received extensive coverage in the press; and some papers – notably the *Daily Telegraph* and *Daily Express* – used the imagery of floods, tides and stampedes.[4] Failing to persuade the Kenyan government to moderate its policy, the cabinet capitulated on 20 and 22 February and legislated to prevent the Asians coming in such numbers.[5] Strong opposition was immediately roused in many different quarters, and the temperature about immigration rose. In the view of *Colour and citizenship*, the Act gravely compromised the credibility of the government's whole integration programme.[6] It was in this context of intense activity and feeling – a period when, to quote Paul Foot, 'the press crawled with stories of racial conflict'[7] – that Mr Powell made his speech.

(b) Mr Powell's position

By the time of his Birmingham speech Enoch Powell already had a growing reputation for unorthodox opinions that distinguished him in some fields from his colleagues in the shadow cabinet. Ten years earlier he had resigned on a point of policy from a junior post at the Treasury in Mr Macmillan's government, along with the Chancellor, Peter Thorneycroft, and his colleague Nigel Birch. He returned to the Government as Minister of Health in 1960 but showed his independence again by declining, like Iain Macleod, to serve under Sir Alec Douglas-Home in 1963–4. When Sir Alec stepped down shortly after the election defeat, Mr Powell stood as a candidate for the leadership. He received 15 votes, against Mr Maudling's 133 and Mr Heath's 150.* From then on he pursued an increasingly idiosyncratic line – but on economic policy and defence, not on immigration. In the 1966 election campaign, for instance, he made only one speech on immigration. It caused no noticeable embarrassment, in sharp contrast to his anti-American remarks about the Vietnam war, which Mr Heath had publicly to disown.[8]

In 1968 Mr Powell had certainly not been associated in the minds of the public or the press predominantly with strong, let alone eccentric, views on immigration. At constituency level Paul Foot found no evidence that he had made any complaint when, for example, the number of immigrant children in Wolverhampton schools doubled from 1,000 to 2,000 between 1962 and 1964. 'Certainly before 1959', Foot claims, 'and most probably after it, Powell took

---

* One commentator wrote later that he knew at least one M.P. who voted for Powell 'not out of conviction but for fear that he might suffer the humiliation of a single figure return'. Ian Trethowan, *The Times*, 26 April 1968.

not the slightest interest in immigration into his constituency and the multiple problems arising out of it.'[9] At the national level Mr Powell made no public statements about the dangers of immigration in the years of maximum inflow between 1954 and 1964; and his support in 1964 for immigration control was mildly worded – 'an expression of mainstream opinion in his party'.[10]

The fact that he did not broadcast them does not apparently mean that Mr Powell had no views on immigration. For tactical reasons he preferred to advance them privately so long as the Conservatives were in office: 'I thought that such a fundamental change in the law as [immigration control] was a monkey which was easier caught softly.'[11] If the Conservatives were re-elected in 1959, they would be obliged to introduce legislation, and he saw no value in making a 'harouche' about it (like Sir Cyril Osborne) in advance. After the election Mr Powell rejoined the government himself and, according to Foot, became a firm advocate of control on such bodies as cabinet committees.

Out of office after 1964 it was a different matter. Even so, in the broad sweep of his speeches and journalism immigration did not stand out. After the crushing Conservative defeat of 1966 the speeches became more radical, but none of them dealt with immigration in the entire fifteen months after the election.* All that Paul Foot could find in this period was a long leader-page review by Mr Powell in the *Daily Telegraph* of Rex and Moore's book about Sparkbrook, Birmingham.[12]

In the latter half of 1967 Powell did begin to speak and write about immigration. On 9 July he wrote an article in the *Sunday Express* headed CAN WE AFFORD TO LET OUR RACE PROBLEM EXPLODE? (Riots in Detroit gave the subject topicality.) On 7 October he discussed repatriation in questions after a speech at Gloucester (the local paper highlighted this more than the speech). On 18 October he made the first major speech calling for controls over the entry of Kenyan Asians. He made it during – but not at – the Conservative party conference, which it completely upstaged. Duncan Sandys and Sir Cyril Osborne were associated as much, if not more, with the Kenyan Asians campaign, but Mr Powell was clearly beginning to be linked with it too. He achieved further attention by a speech at Walsall on 9 February 1968 that foreshadowed in style and content the Birmingham speech. It received splash treatment on page 1 from the *Daily Express*; the *Mirror* gave it two inches on the back page, and the *Mail* and *Sun* gave it a full column on an inside page.

* An indication of the scale of his activity at this time is that in the first seven weeks of 1967 Mr Powell made 26 speeches, 15 of them in public, 10 of them in private, and all carefully prepared. Foot, p. 100.

By 20 April, therefore, Mr Powell had a public reputation for general independence and outspokenness, but one that was only now being acquired in the field of immigration and race relations.

(c) *The Birmingham speech, 20 April 1968*

The speech[13] contained some three thousand words. It was three times as long as the published extract of the Walsall speech, made available by Conservative Central Office, but its contents covered very similar ground.

Mr Powell began with the reflection that 'the supreme function of statesmanship is to provide against preventable evils . . .' The discussion of future grave but, with effort now, avoidable evils 'is the most unpopular and at the same time the most necessary occupation for the politician'. He then told how one of his constituents, 'a middle-aged, quite ordinary working man', had said to him that he would not be satisfied till his three grown-up children had settled overseas, since 'in this country in fifteen or twenty years' time the black man will have the whip-hand over the white man'.

'I can already hear the chorus of execration', Mr Powell went on. 'How dare I say such a horrible thing? How dare I stir up trouble and inflame feelings by repeating such a conversation? The answer is that I do not have the right not to do so . . . I simply do not have the right to shrug my shoulders and think about something else.' In some parts of Britain 'thousands and hundreds of thousands' were saying and thinking the same thing as his constituent. There would be $3\frac{1}{2}$ million Commonwealth immigrants and their descendants in Britain in fifteen or twenty years' time, occupying 'whole areas, towns and parts of towns across England'.* How could the prospect be reduced? 'By stopping, or virtually stopping, further inflow, and by promoting the maximum outflow. Both answers are part of the official policy of the Conservative Party.'†

'It almost passes belief', Mr Powell remarked, 'that at this moment twenty or thirty additional immigrant children are arriving from overseas in Wolverhampton alone every week – and that means fifteen or twenty additional families of a decade or two hence. Those whom the gods wish to destroy, they first make mad. We must be mad, literally mad, as a nation to be permitting the annual inflow of some 50,000 dependants, who are for the most part the material

* The reliability of Mr Powell's estimates was often challenged. See Smithies and Fiddick (1969), pp. 46–7, 141–52.

† Smithies and Fiddick suggest that 'the adjective "voluntary" instead of "maximum" would have helped Mr Powell to express more closely the policy of his party'. Ibid., p. 48.

of the future growth of the immigrant-descended population. It is like watching a nation busily engaged in heaping up its own funeral pyre.' The 'total inflow for settlement' should be reduced at once to 'negligible proportions', and a policy of encouraging re-emigration, with generous grants and assistance, should be pursued with urgency and determination. '. . . Suspension of immigration and encouragement of re-emigration hang together, logically and humanly, as two aspects of the same approach.'

Mr Powell next turned to the pending Race Relations Bill. 'There could be no grosser misconception of the realities than is entertained by those who vociferously demand legislation as they call it "against discrimination" . . . They have got it exactly and diametrically wrong. The discrimination and the deprivation, the sense of alarm and of resentment, lies not with the immigrant population but with those among whom they have come and are still coming. That is why to enact legislation of the kind before Parliament at this moment is to risk throwing a match on to gunpowder. The kindest thing that can be said about those who propose and support it is that they know not what they do.' The existing population 'found themselves strangers in their own country. They found their wives unable to obtain hospital beds in childbirth, their children unable to obtain school places, their homes and neighbourhoods changed beyond all recognition, their plans and prospects for the future defeated . . .' And now an Act of Parliament was to be passed to give 'the stranger, the disgruntled and the *agent provocateur* the power to pillory them for their private actions'.

To illustrate the sense of being 'a persecuted minority' that was growing among 'ordinary English people' in the immigrant areas, Mr Powell quoted at length a letter from a correspondent in Northumberland about an old-age pensioner in Wolverhampton (Mr Powell's constituency). She had lost her husband and both sons in the 1939–45 war. She turned her home into a boarding-house, worked hard, paid off her mortgage and began to put something by for her old age. ' "Then the immigrants moved in. With growing fear, she saw one house after another taken over. The quiet street became a place of noise and confusion. Regretfully, her white tenants moved out." ' Immigrant families tried to rent rooms, but she always refused. ' "Her little store of money went, and after paying her rates, she has less than £2 per week . . . The telephone is her lifeline. Her family pay the bill, and help her out as best they can . . . She is becoming afraid to go out. Windows are broken. She finds excreta pushed through her letter-box. When she goes to the shops, she is followed by children, charming, wide-grinning piccaninnies. They cannot speak English, but one word they know. 'Racialist', they chant. When the new Race Relations Bill is passed, this woman is convinced she will go to prison. And is she so wrong? I begin to wonder" '.

Finally Mr Powell raised the question of integration, fearing the growth of 'vested interests in the preservation and sharpening of racial and religious differences, with a view to the exercise of actual domination, first over fellow-immigrants, and then over the rest of the population'. 'The cloud no bigger than a man's hand' had recently appeared in Wolverhampton. For such elements the Race Relations Bill was 'the very pabulum they need to flourish'.

'As I look ahead', Mr Powell concluded, 'I am filled with foreboding. Like the Roman, I seem to see "the River Tiber foaming with much blood". That tragic and intractable phenomenon which we watch with horror on the other side of the Atlantic but which there is interwoven with the history and existence of the States itself, is coming upon us here by our own volition and our own neglect. Indeed it has all but come. In numerical terms, it will be of American proportions long before the end of the century. Only resolute and urgent action will arrest it even now. Whether there will be the public will to demand and obtain that action, I do not know. All I know is that to see, and not to speak, would be the great betrayal.'

(d) Media coverage of the Birmingham speech

Despite the similarity of its themes to the Walsall speech, the Birmingham speech received much more attention immediately and in its repercussions. The most dramatic measure of it was a Gallup poll taken a few days later. In answer to the question: 'Have you heard or read about Mr Enoch Powell's speech on coloured immigrants?' 96 per cent of the sample replied Yes and 4 per cent No.[14] In the following weeks Mr Powell received about 110,000 letters of which barely 2,000 expressed disapproval of the speech. Many of the letters had more than one signature, and it seems likely that the number of correspondents was nearer 180,000.[15]

The speech, delivered on a Saturday, received saturation coverage in the Sunday press. As Table 4.1 shows, three papers published virtually the full handout – a rare event even for the weekend speech of a Prime Minister or Opposition leader, let alone a middle-ranking politician like Mr Powell. Other papers gave it exceptionally full treatment according to their resources. Only in the *Sunday Mirror* was the proportion of the speech reported in direct quotation or *oratio obliqua* less than three-quarters.

As the headlines imply, the reports uniformly construed the speech as a shock for the Conservative party and for Mr Heath personally;

TABLE 4.1

SUNDAY PAPER COVERAGE OF ENOCH POWELL'S BIRMINGHAM SPEECH, 20 APRIL 1968, AND AFTERMATH

Paper's circulation (in thousands)	Paper's political tendency	April 21					April 28		
		Page one headline (unless otherwise stated)	Leading article	Total words in report of speech*	Total words in direct or indirect quotation (% in brackets)	Feature linked to Race Bill	Page one headline (unless otherwise stated)	Features	Leading article
News of the World 6,191	Con.	'Race Speech Uproar'	Against Powell's language	1,320	1,150 (87)	Yes	'Cast Your Vote On Immigration', 'Colin Jordan Thrown Out' (2nd story)	Pro-Powell article by Nabarro Letters	Criticizes Powell sacking
The People 5,533	Lab.	'Race: Powell's Speech is A Shocker'	Against Powell	540	400 (74)	No	'Fascist Boss Thrown Out'	Political column Letters	Pro-immigration control and moderation
Sunday Mirror 5,138	Lab.	'Enoch: River of Blood Race Speech – for full report see Page Two' (Box on P. 1)	Against Powell	800	440 (55)	No	'Enoch's Ally Is Thrown Out'	Political column Letters	None

Sunday Express 4,238	Con.	'Powell Race Blockbuster: A Crisis for Heath' (2nd story)	None on Powell	1,080	1,080 (100)	Yes	'Sir Alec Steps In To Defend Enoch Powell'	Political gossip	Pro-Powell
Sunday Times 1,461	Con.	'Explosive Race Speech by Powell' (2nd story)	Against Powell	1,840	1,737 (94)	Yes	'Heath Calls For Calm and Wins Over Hecklers'	2 political columns Powell profile Immigration	'Voices of Reason'
Observer 903	Lab.	Powell Stokes Up New Tory Storm on Immigration' (2nd story)	None on Powell	1,950	1,865 (96)	Yes	'Fears Behind White Backlash'	Powell profile	Survey of race relations problem
Sunday Telegraph 713	Con.	'Mr Powell Forces the Race issue: Emotive Speech'	None on Powell	1,840	1,816 (99)	Yes	None on Powell	Political columns Immigration	Pro- moderation Immigration

* The actual number of words in Mr Powell's speech was 3,184.
SOURCE of readership figures: JICNARS, April–June 1968.

TABLE 4.2

DAILY PAPER COVERAGE OF ENOCH POWELL'S BIRMINGHAM SPEECH AND AFTERMATH

(Page 1 headline except where indicated)

	Daily Mirror (Lab.)	Daily Express (Con.)	Daily Mail (Con.)	Sun (Lab.)
Mon. 22nd	'Sack for Powell In Tory Race Row' (Hostile leader)	'Heath Sacks Powell Over Race Speech' (Pro-Powell leader)	'Powell Sacked For Race Speech' (Hostile leader)	'Heath Sacks Powell' (Hostile leader)
Tues. 23rd	'Heath Slaps Down Powell Innuendo'	'Tory "Cabinet" Backs Heath'	'Powell Swipe – Then Heath Wins Vote'	'Powell Accuses Heath of Cowardice'
Wed. 24th	'Thousands Back Powell With Strikes' (Hostile leader)	'Race Bill Stirs Up Tory Storm' (Pro-Powell leader)	'Hogg Takes It Off The Boil' (Leader on Race Bill)	'24 Tory MPs In Vote Revolt' (Hostile leader)
Thurs. 25th	'"Back Enoch" Immigration Man is Suspended' (Pro-Powell leader)	'Airport "Back Powell" Man Suspended' (Pro-Powell leader)	'Callaghan Orders Airport Race Inquiry'	'Callaghan Acts In Airport Race Row' (Hostile 2nd leader)
Fri. 26th		'Back-Enoch March May Shut The Docks'		'Powell Pulls Out of Varsity Speech'
Sat. 27th	'Racial Agitators Lead "Back Enoch" Strikes, Says Heath (page 2)			
Mon. 29th				'Arrest Powell, Say 1500 Quiet Marchers' (Hostile leader, page 5)
Tues. 30th	'We'll Pay Immigrants Fares Home – Callaghan'	'Immigration: New Storm' (Callaghan)		'Callaghan Offers Fare Home to Immigrants'

Mon. 22nd	'Why I Spoke Out – Enoch Powell' (Leader hostile to language)	'Mr Heath Dismisses Mr Powell For "Racialist" Speech' (Hostile leader)	'Heath Sacks Powell For Race Speech' (Pro-Powell leader)	'Powell Out of Shadow Cabinet. Heath Attacks "Racialist" Speech' (Leader: 'An Evil Speech')
Tues. 23rd	'Powell Accuses "Too Cool" Heath' (Leader on Race Bill)	'Mr Powell Accuses Mr Heath of Bowing to "Clamour": Tory Leaders Still Torn Over Policy on Race Bill' (Leader on Race Relations)	'Powell Rebukes Heath On Race' (Leader hostile to language)	'Mr Heath Gets Full Backing From His Shadow Cabinet'
Wed. 24th	'Hogg Lashes Out At "Disloyal" Powell' (Leader on race)	'22 Tory M.P.s Abstain In Race Bill Vote' (Leader on Race Bill)	'24 Tories Abstain on Race Bill: 3-fold Demand for Effective Policy: Powell Votes With Party Line' (Leader on Race Bill)	'24 Tories Abstain Over Race Bill: A Majority of 104 for the Government' (Leader on Race Bill)
Thurs. 25th	'Immigrants: The Voice of Britain' (Poll) (Leader on immigration)	'Mr Callaghan Suspends Immigration Officer'	'Airport "Revolt" on Immigrants: 39 Officers Write to Powell: Discipline Inquiry by Callaghan' (Leader: 'Race and Conscience')	'Widespread Split Over Powell's Race Speech' (Leader on Race Bill Vote)
Fri. 26th			'Brown Accuses Powell: "Opting In" to Race for Leadership: Commons Storm on Airport Inquiry'	'Midland Tories Cheer Heath Over Powell Dismissal'
Sat. 27th	'Now Ennals Stirs It Up – "Dockers Are Like Nazis"'	'Mr Heath Lays Blame On Racialist Agitators'	'Powell Dockers Jeer Mikardo: Heath Attacks "Nasty Vicious Reaction"'	
Mon. 29th	'Anti-Powell Protest Is a Wash-Out' (page 2)			'Ministers Act to Cool Race Feeling' (Leader: 'Appeal for Tolerance')
Tues. 30th			'Fare Home Aid for Immigrants'	

several stressed that he had known nothing of it in advance. It was set in the context of the forthcoming Second Reading debate on the Government's Race Relations Bill, in anticipation of which most papers carried feature articles. Some of these showed signs of last-minute rewriting. Powell's language and tone were picked up both in the reports and in the leading articles that four of the papers carried. Only one of these (*News of the World*) gave him much support. At lunchtime on Sunday Powell went on the BBC radio current affairs programme, *The World This Weekend*, to defend himself. Later he gave a Midlands ATV interview.

Sunday's papers were only the beginning of Powell's coverage. The repercussions of his speech bumped along throughout the following week and over the next weekend. (See Table 4.2.) On Monday every newspaper headlined his dismissal from the shadow cabinet and carried a matching editorial. On Tuesday they all led with his confident, almost patronising letter to Heath in reply. On Wednesday the lead in all except the *Guardian* was the Race Relations Bill debate, which the weekend's events completely dominated. The action was shifting beyond Westminster too. Token strikes and protests, mainly in sympathy with Powell, were reported all over the place. Wednesday's *Sketch* captured the tone: 'Dockers, engineers, tanker drivers, gas plant staff, brewery men, factory workers. They all stopped work yesterday to stage some of the strangest strikes ever seen in Britain. The "We Back Powell" strikes.' On Thursday every paper (except the *Sketch*, which had a poll about immigration) led with the story of 39 immigration officers at London Airport who had sent a letter of support to Powell: now their organiser had been suspended pending a Home Office inquiry. Only on Friday did Powell leave the headlines in most papers, though even then he remained on page one. On Saturday a speech by Heath condemning 'racial agitators' behind the strikes made the headlines quite widely. Dockers had been on the march again too. The Sunday papers, naturally, were full of analysis. Their news pages mostly led with another speech on immigration by Heath, at a meeting from which the National Front leader Colin Jordan (described tendentiously in the *Mirror* as 'Enoch's Ally') was ejected. The leader columns were full of appeals for moderation and calm. The features profiled Powell (and Mrs Powell), considered his future and that of the Conservative party, and analysed various background aspects of immigration and race relations. After the weekend a few stories about anti-Powell protest marches appeared; and a remark on BBC-TV's *Panorama* by the Home Secretary, Mr Callaghan, in which he appeared to extend the government's plans for financing voluntary repatriation, brought the story briefly back into the headlines on Tuesday. Radio and TV had of course been equally busy throughout. Powell was interviewed on *Panorama* on the Monday after his speech, for example; and the current affairs programe *Twenty-Four Hours* chased round unsuccessfully looking for the original harassed 'little old lady'.

The balance of this massive coverage is not easy to judge in pro- and anti-Powell terms. The subject had altogether too many strands for unqualified approval or disapproval. Besides, the really striking aspect, from which the important political consequences flowed, was not the quality but the sheer intensity of reportage. As a commentator in *The Times* remarked, 'Over the past six days Mr Powell has stirred the national emotions more than any other single politician since the war. Not even Aneurin Bevan at his most acerbic so inflamed opinion – and so cut across traditional political loyalties. The dockers have backed Mr Powell. The bankers never marched for Mr Bevan.'[16]

For the moment Mr Powell had attracted to himself almost as much attention from the mass media as would be possible to grant.

II. Explanations for the coverage

Why the earthquake? Enoch Powell himself was surprised at his publicity: 'I was not aware that this speech, in which I said very much what I had been saying in many previous speeches, would have the far greater impact . . .'[17] The only theme at Walsall missing at Birmingham was the Kenya Asians; and the only new matter at Birmingham was the Race Relations Bill. Why, then, comparing the reaction simply to those two speeches and leaving aside the many earlier speeches on defence or economics, did the Birmingham speech win so much attention?

The answer may be sought in three directions. None by itself provides a sufficient explanation: taken together they probably provide as precise an explanation as can be found. The speech seems to have been made at exactly 'the right moment': it was the result of a collision between public attitudes to the state of immigration, the aims and technique of Mr Powell and the news values of the mass media.

This argument can best be developed by separating each factor into underlying and immediate causes.

(a) Underlying causes

Attitudes to immigration and race relations. The attitude survey conducted for the Institute of Race Relations inquiry, *Colour and citizenship*, showed 'a widespread tendency to hold stereotyped views about minority group members'. The great majority of the public, 'poised somewhere between the extremes of tolerance and irrational hostility . . . can be moved in either direction by argument or by appeals to their emotions or to their fears'.[18] The *New Statesman*'s commentator, Alan Watkins, seemed confident that this kind of explanation accounted for Mr Powell's publicity: Mr Powell had 'quite deliberately, decided to exploit the one issue on which many people are scarcely rational'.[19]

Hugo Young, a *Sunday Times* journalist, also picked on the strength of people's opinions as a factor giving race a special significance for the press. People do not perceive the subject as too remote or complex; and government policy has frequently changed. These two factors, Young argued, make the subject volatile and put it in a different category from most others. That effect is reinforced by the lack of any standard criteria for reporting race: there is no 'agreed definition of the basic nature of the information' – in contrast, say, to the monthly trade figures.[20] Following this argument, one would expect to find wide variations in media treatment of race: sometimes scant attention and sometimes, as in Powell's Birmingham speech, saturation.

If people have strong opinions on race it can be argued – albeit impressionistically – that some of the strongest were not expressed in the early 1960s. Smithies and Fiddick make the point succinctly. Why did the speech excite Fleet Street? 'The fact that it was on the dynamite issue, the one everybody traditionally "keeps out of politics", was a sure start'.[21] Students of race relations talk of the 'liberal hour' of general agreement about the direction of policy in the two years up to 1968.[22] Anti-immigrant views in the mass media were associated with extremist figures like Colin Jordan or Sir Oswald Mosley, sounding echoes of discredited political movements of the 1930s. With hindsight one can argue that, even making allowance for Mr Powell having created some of the very opinions he claimed to reflect, there was no 'dialogue' about immigration in the 1960s in the institutions of organised political opinion – whether newspapers or political parties – and that one stream of opinion went undiscussed. A symbol of this is the attitude of the BBC. In the mid-1960s there appeared in the *BBC handbook*'s official statement about political neutrality the reservation that the Corporation felt no obligation to give space to racialist views. Liberal-minded producers felt that to focus on racial problems in a current affairs programme like, say, *Panorama*, might simply stir the problems up. The issue was thus neglected, or disreputable opinions about it were ignored. One of the criticisms of Mr Powell was that he lent respectability to such opinions. Yet for that to be so, the opinions must have existed. They can only have been 'dynamite' in 1968 if they had not been defused by the therapy of open discussion. For this reason some of the broadcasting executives felt their earlier attitude was a mistake. If the issue had been 'kept out of politics' and Powell was challenging that fact, the mass media were bound to take notice.

As well as being strong and on some sides suppressed or inarticulate, an important characteristic of attitudes on race was that coloured minorities were perceived by many people in hostile terms. One line of argument attributes this to historical factors: 'Our whole way of thinking about coloured people, influenced by the colonial past, constitutes a built-in predisposition to accept unfavourable beliefs about them.'[23] But explanations for prejudice are obviously advanced on many bases in addition to that,[24] and the mass media themselves can plausibly be claimed to share responsibility.

The substance of hostile attitudes can be studied in detail in *Colour and citizenship*. The survey found from its sample in five 'immigrant boroughs' (with a national control sample) 'a great deal of widely diffused confusion, anxiety and misunderstanding about the migration, its composition, and the background of the migrants, making up a predisposition towards rejection. In such circumstances, it is hardly surprising that hostile stereotypes, which seem to justify rejection in more specific terms, are common.'[25] By their tests the general incidence of prejudice was as follows: Prejudiced – 10 per cent; Prejudiced-inclined – 17 per cent; Tolerant – 35 per cent; Tolerant-inclined – 38 per cent.[26] Examples of specific attitudes were that 53 per cent of respondents regarded coloured immigrants as their inferiors and 36 per cent as their equals, and at least 60 per cent thought that each of three coloured groups (West Indians, Indians and Pakistanis) took 'more out of the country than they put into it'.[27]

In 1968 the cultural image of coloured immigrants, to put it shortly, was that of a 'threat'. This was a fear that Mr Powell's speech did nothing to dispel.

Mr Powell's aims and techniques. 'I didn't make the same speech over and over again, but I made the speech on the same point and calculated to bring out the sense of oppression, the sense of being victimised which is felt in these areas.'[28] Enoch Powell's remark to David Frost, made in the context of a comparison of the Birmingham and Walsall speeches, does not explain why the Birmingham speech was an earthquake and the others not, but it shows plainly how his aims coincided with the image of coloured immigrants as a threat. In the 1950s he had not wanted to make a 'harouche' about immigration, but now he did. He was actively seeking publicity.

Powell's gifts as a publicist undoubtedly contributed much. His feel for language was important and struck a chord with journalists. Alan Watkins wrote in the *New Statesman* that Mr Powell's speeches in the previous four or five years 'are among the few contemporary political speeches that bear re-reading'.[29] Smithies and Fiddick, both journalists, comment: 'It has long been known that Enoch Powell is one of Parliament's "speech-makers", a man who, when he wishes, can produce an oratorical technique in the classic tradition'; and that 'beneath the classical exterior lies a feeling for the guts of the English language that Aneurin Bevan himself would recognise'.[30] Butler and Pinto-Duschinsky, in their study of the 1970 general election, attribute to 'the power of his tongue and the richness of his pen' Mr Powell's acquisition of 'a new status' after 1963–4 and of his consequent ambitions for his party leadership.

Powell's feeling for language extends to a well developed awareness of its potentialities. 'A politician's business is with words', Terry Coleman reported him saying in an interview in 1970 for *The Guardian*; 'With words as opposed to action'. The title of the 1966 Conservative election manifesto, 'Action not words', was about the silliest title a manifesto can ever have had.[31] Politicians, he wrote at the time of his Birmingham speech, try 'to provide people with words and ideas which will fit their predicament better than the words and ideas which they are using at the moment'.[32] The politician's role, therefore, was in his view not so much to change opinions as to crystallise them.[33] Similarly politicians were concerned with prophetic utterances, in the strict sense of 'a speaking forth, not a telling in advance. Not a telling of the future, but putting into words a sense of what is striving to become'.[34] Again, when pressed by Coleman about his extended use of hearsay evidence in the Birmingham speech – the letter from Northumberland about the little old lady in his constituency – Mr Powell argued that he was not quoting it to justify his claims but to illustrate them: whether or not it was checkable could make no difference to its usefulness. Coleman asked: 'Had he no objection, then, to the tone of the words of the letter, which was written as if by a pop-paper columnist?' 'No. I was much struck by their truthfulness as a description of what I knew to be happening.' Again, if he knew himself, why not use the best evidence? 'Because I was using the best words.'[35] It is in keeping with those views that when Mr Powell began to tread his independent path after Mr Macmillan's resignation in 1963, he should describe the process as 'talking politics': 'There comes a time in the life of a party when it needs to talk politics again; when it once again needs to tell itself and others, loud and clear, what it stands for; when it needs to say plainly what it wants and aims at and what kind of future it wishes for the nation . . .'[36] 'Talking politics', to Powell, meant going back to first principles and challenging the conventional wisdom of his party, regardless of the practical effects. This was an activity to which he was well suited. By temperament he was more interested in national than local issues. (Even at election times, Paul Foot has pointed out, his speeches hardly ever referred to local issues.[37]) Secondly, his sense of history enabled him to escape the narrow perspectives of the present. Asked by David Frost in 1969 what were his greatest achievements so far, he ended his reply: 'On the political side, I think I have severely damaged the prices and incomes policy, and I think I have given a good shake to the complacency with which people were assuming that a planned economy and a largely and increasingly nationalised structure of industry had come to stay and were inevitable. Let me put it this way: I think I've shaken some inevitabilities. I hate inevitabilities.'[38]

The procedure for 'shaking inevitabilities' was that Powell used his gifts of expression to the full in speech after speech that challenged official Conservative policy.[39] According to one commentator, the reason why he stood for the leadership against Heath and Maudling was to maintain the consistency of his idiosyncratic line.[40] He developed at this time the distinctive style of his speeches – the massive presentation of an argument, combining the tension of a platform speech and the content of a treatise. Without opposing Heath after 1965, 'he constantly prodded, pressured and thwarted him', to quote Butler and Pinto-Duschinsky, 'while carefully promoting his own personality among party activists and expressing his distinctive philosophy of government non-interference with market forces'.[41]

Mr Powell's political technique and purposes were always likely to appeal to mass media. The *Sunday Express* described him in 1968 as 'controversial, brilliant, stimulating, devastatingly original'; an article they were publishing by him was 'fresh, penetrating and provocative'.[42] Stale adjectives those might be: but they applied to Powell's technique as to few other British politicians in 1968; and they were characteristics journalists prize.

The implications of Powell's technique – particularly the implications of his view of language – are complex. At one level they lead into questions about his philosophy of politics: his view of the influence of ideas, of causation, of historical inevitability, of dialectic in politics, of illusion and reality.[43] At the level of everyday activity they led to allegations of boatrocking, propaganda and demagogy. Strictly speaking a predicament exists, no doubt, even when people have inadequate words and ideas to analyse and express it. But when a politician gives them words, as Powell said politicians do, he may look, through the spectacles of practical politics, as though he is *creating* a problem rather than just defining or highlighting one. Similarly when Powell 'prophesied' he put into words 'a sense of what is striving to become'. But would this thing strive successfully without his help? Does not this look, also through the spectacles of practical politics, like self-fulfilling prophecy? Powell was often accused of precipitating the Kenya Asian crisis, in part, by predicting that it would happen. Again, the distinction between quotation in evidence and in illustration, drawn in Powell's discussion with Terry Coleman, is clear enough in close argument. But will the distinction always be clear in the platform speech? May not the confusion of fact and fiction follow; or at least the destruction of a true sense of proportion? These dangers arguably were not always avoided in Mr Powell's speeches. They were part of the price of his publicity.

Mass media news values. There is no need to discuss here the general criteria of news value in British mass media. The stress on conflict, deviancy, cultural proximity, unpredictability, human interest, simple themes, the involvement of élite individuals, are all clear enough. We need look only at their application to race relations.

'In the last five years immigration and race relations have rivalled almost any other subject except natural disasters for prominence in newspapers and on television', commented the authors of *Colour and citizenship*.[44] There seems no dispute, among journalists and students of race relations alike, that the subject was highlighted because of its supposed inherent conflict. 'Because much of what we call news arises from conflict', Harold Evans, editor of the *Sunday Times*, wrote, 'stories with an ethnic tag look more like news because they are thought to imply some conflict of interests.'[45] 'Many events are felt to be newsworthy which, if they did not ostensibly have a racial dimension, would simply not be news', said Hugo Young in his essay about the Kenya Asians; '. . . everything to do with coloured people takes place against an underlying premise that they are the symbols or the embodiments of a *problem*. Whether we like it or not, that is the state of public opinion as perceived by news editors; and that is what tends inevitably to influence professional news judgement.'[46] *Colour and citizenship* noted 'a tendency to sensationalise, to pick out the most prejudiced elements in a story, and to print scare headlines'.[47] Hartmann and Husband argue that 'the way race-related material is handled by the mass media serves both to perpetuate negative assumptions of blacks and to define the situation as one of inter-group conflict'.[48] They quote examples of the use of such headlines as 40 INDIANS 'INVADE'.[49] 'The word "invade" manages to imply that society is somehow threatened by them.'[50] Their survey of secondary school children showed that media-supplied information about race-related matters carried the inference of conflict more often than that from other sources.[51] Harold Evans quotes examples to illustrate also two other criticisms: irrelevant ethnic identification (e.g. in court and crime stories) and 'the way racial stories tend to be reported against only the flimsiest background of verifiable fact'.[52]*

When the journalistic appeal of Powell's technique and his 'boatrocking' party position are added to this conception of race as a subject that fits traditional media values of 'good news', one can expect the newsworthiness of his speeches to be greatly increased. When they are put in the context of prevailing public attitudes on the subject, as described in the first section, it becomes difficult to imagine anything that would better fit the definition reached in Jeremy Tunstall's study of political newsgathering: 'the type of domestic political event most likely to become news is conflict between leading personalities over issues which can be easily dramatised as relevant to large numbers of audience members'.[53]

(b) Immediate causes

The arguments in section (a) seek to explain why Powell's speeches in general got so much attention. But why was the Birmingham speech in particular an 'earthquake', when the Walsall speech was not? The arguments in this section try to answer that question.

Attitudes to immigration and race relations. Powell himself ascribed the impact of his speech to the climate of April 1968. '. . . That impact . . . very largely arose out of the political conflict at the time between a government which was introducing the Race Relations Bill, and an opposition which was opposing it.'[54]

Two circumstances made the climate of April particularly sensitive for race relations. The first, as the quotation indicates, was the Government's introduction of its long awaited Race Relations Bill, the 'constructive' counter to its tougher immigration measures. The Second Reading was due on the Tuesday after Mr Powell's weekend Birmingham speech. The speech would inevitably be interpreted in the context of the Bill; and in the context also of a somewhat embarrassed Conservative shadow cabinet (of which

---

* The views in the above paragraph are highly consistent with the findings of the Kerner commission set up by President Johnson to inquire into the 1967 riots in American cities, *Report of the National Advisory Commission on Civil Disorders*, Washington, D.C., 1968. The Commission found, for example, that the disorders were less destructive, less widespread and less of a black–white confrontation than most people believed; that some papers printed scare headlines unsupported by the mild stories that followed, and that despite the general good intentions and efforts of the media the overall effect of their coverage was 'an exaggeration of both mood and event'. pp. 201–3.

Mr Powell was of course a member – for a few days yet). The campaign against the entry of the Kenya Asians had built up pressures on the right wing to oppose the Bill outright.[55]* On the other wing was a smaller group of 'progressive' Conservatives arguing for conditional acceptance. (They included most of the fifteen who had voted against the Second Reading of the Kenya Asians Bill). Both views were represented in the shadow cabinet. Mr Heath achieved a fragile unity by tabling a reasoned amendment, drafted in a shadow cabinet sub-committee of which Mr Powell was a member, that accepted the principle of legislation but not the methods of his specific Bill. The 'progressives' were to be allowed to vote with the Labour party if they insisted. In a situation of such delicacy Mr Powell's speech might be regarded as an open challenge; certainly as having implications for the Conservative leadership and policy going far beyond its actual substance.

The second factor affecting the climate was simply the Kenya Asians upheaval. This raised in an intense form the popular image of a coloured immigrant 'threat', all the worse for having been unexpected.† A good impression of the near-hysterical, alarmist quality of the press coverage, especially in the *Daily Express* and *Daily Telegraph*, and of the preoccupation of all papers with the issue, is gained from Hugo Young's analysis. In terms of media news values the issue was unquestionably a winner. It was all over by the time of Powell's Birmingham speech but it had, so to speak, prepared the ground for him.

Mr Powell's aim and technique. Powell's critics accused him of demagogy, inflammatory propaganda and McCarthyite tactics.‡ In a speech countering his Birmingham points in detail, Roy Jenkins described what he saw as the dangers of Powell's technique. About the 'little old lady' he said: '. . . The story could not be checked, although most strenuous efforts were made to do so. The woman was never found, although, possibly, without ever existing, she has achieved a national fame and impact. This is the dreadful danger of

---

* In the end 45 Conservative backbenchers opposed the Bill on Third Reading, against the Leadership.

† The *Daily Express*, searching the basement in case anybody else was lurking there, emerged on 1 March with a headline: A MILLION CHINESE CAN ARRIVE HERE NEXT WEEK IF THEY WANT TO.

‡ See, e.g., Alan Watkins, *New Statesman*, 26 April 1968: 'He is now, in fact, the most dangerous type of demagogue'; Ian Trethowan, *The Times*, 26 April 1968: 'To some of his critics he is at best a fanatic, at most a demagogue . . . Four years ago I heard Mr Goldwater's speech accepting the Republican presidential nomination, and the similarities are inescapable'; Peter Jenkins, *The Guardian*, 13 June 1969: 'The McCarthy in our Midst'; Paul Foot (1969), p. 138.

this kind of propaganda. You need nothing to begin with except a suspicious atmosphere and a readiness to believe rumours. Then you give widespread publicity to an unsubstantiated story. Then a lot of people write in and tell you some more stories. Then, without check- ing, you use these. Then you are well on the way to creating a climate in which all sorts of rumours are passed round as absolute truth and a minority group is built up as the scapegoat for most of the troubles of the country. It was a technique which was used with deadly effect and devastating consequences against the Jews in Germany 35 years ago. It must never be allowed to gain a foothold here.'[56] Similarly Quintin Hogg remarked: 'If one is going to say, and goodness knows many of us have thought, that the streets of our country might one day run with blood . . . then surely one ought to consider whether in the more immediate future, one's words were more likely to make that happen, or less likely to make that happen.'[57]

Powell may have been surprised by the enormous scale of his publicity, but there is much evidence to suppose he courted it. In the Race Relations debate the following Tuesday, Mr Hogg, speaking as Opposition spokesman on home affairs, complained (in the speech just quoted): 'It was not as if my right hon. Friend did not know what the effects of his remarks would be. He did, because he said in terms that he could imagine the outcry he would cause. He did not come to me. He did not give me a sight of what he was going to say. He did not ask my advice, though, goodness knows, that advice is fallible enough . . . He sent a hand-out to the Press, by-passing the Conservative Office. He said what he did without a word to any of his colleagues that he was going to say it.'*[58] Powell thus went over the heads of the established national institutions of party and Parliament and sought to appeal to the people through the mass media direct. He neither informed nor consulted his leader and the official party spokesman, despite the sensitiveness of the subject (though he was strictly within his rights not to do so, since he intended the speech to be in support of party policy). He did not wait to argue his case in Parliament, despite the imminence of a debate. He did not inform Conservative Central Office: its officials learnt of the speech only by accident, when the head of the information department, Gerald O'Brien, telephoned the editor of the *News of the World* on the day the speech was to be delivered, about an article on the same subject by Edward Heath which the paper was publishing next day.[59]† The Walsall speech had been given to Central Office in advance as

* Hogg also mistakenly suggested that Powell was responsible for summoning two television networks to cover the speech.

† Heath's article began, with – in the circumstances – shattering irony, 'Nothing is more explosive than race'.

well as to the party's area organisation, and it had been distributed
to the press in the usual way with extracts of other weekend speeches.
The Birmingham speech was distributed through the Press Association
by the area organisation alone. The full text, not an extract, reached
the press in time for the midday editorial conference of the Sunday
papers. Smithies and Fiddick write: 'There was no question of the
significance of what he was to say slipping past a reporter, or the
full power of his words being lost in compression on the way to the
newspaper offices. By the morning of 20 April, Enoch Powell had
the editors of Britain's Sunday newspapers over a barrel. They knew
every word that was to be uttered, knew it was controversial, knew
that every other editor knew.'[60] If that procedure had not been
followed, how much less coverage would there have been? The
speech would have been left to such reporters as went to Birmingham
for that purpose; mainly local men of varying quality, who would
have had to wait until the afternoon to telephone their copy and who
would probably have felt ridiculous anyway if they had given more
than a concise report. The speech would have landed on the news
editor's desk late and looking distinctly scrappy.

The content of the Birmingham speech also appears well calculated
to attract sensational coverage. In dismissing Powell from the
shadow cabinet, Heath described it as racialist *in tone*. It was less
any significant deviation from the letter of party policy (not itself
very cut and dried) that was intolerable, than the language and the
approach.* The most noticeable difference from the Walsall speech
was the extended use of personal anecdote. In Walsall a brief,
passing reference to a school with 'one white child in her class' had
attracted disproportionate attention. Mr Powell, as he admitted in a
newspaper interview (*Daily Mail*, 11 July 1968), was well aware of
the publicity-winning benefits of couching an argument in intimate
human terms. At Birmingham he exploited the method more fully.
His search also for the 'best words' rather than the best evidence
led him to the long letter about the harassed old lady. That and the
anecdote about the constituent who feared the black man would
soon have the 'whiphand' took up nearly a quarter of the whole
speech.

Both these features – the skilful mechanics of publicity-seeking
and the inclusion of ripe anecdote – help to explain further why
Mr Powell attracted more attention at Birmingham than at Walsall.

Mass media news values. The extent to which the speech met the
requirements of a good news story should not need further elaboration. It contained statistics, but they were not indigestible; finely

* Mr Powell discussed this point in his own defence, in his third major speech
on immigration in 1968, at Eastbourne on 16 November.

turned phrases and images ('the Tiber foaming with much blood' was particularly memorable); and a dramatic personalisation of the themes. It was by a shadow minister. It was strong, original, controversial and appeared to challenge party policy; and it read well. Mr Powell told David Frost he would have changed only two things in the light of events. He would have made clearer than he did the fact that the story about the old lady was all in quotation and not his own words; and he would have put the quotation about the Tiber (from Virgil's *Aeneid*) in the original Latin in the hand-out, as in fact he spoke it.[61]

To drive home the speech's journalistic appeal fully, we can perhaps refer once more again to the two emotionally charged anecdotes. Table 4.3 compares the proportion of its report that each paper gave to those stories with the proportion they took up

TABLE 4.3

PROPORTION OF ANECDOTES IN REPORTS OF ENOCH POWELL'S
BIRMINGHAM SPEECH, APRIL 1968

Name of paper	Total words in report of speech	Words on 'whiphand' anecdote	Words on 'old lady' anecdote	Total words on anecdotes
		(Percent in brackets)		
News of the World	1320	211	240	451
		(16)	(18)	(34)
The People	540	234	75	309
		(43)	(14)	(57)
Sunday Mirror	800	105	23	128
		(13)	(3)	(16)
Sunday Express	1080	105	276	381
		(10)	(26)	(36)
Sunday Times	1840	236	151	387
		(12)	(8)	(20)
Observer	1950	166	357	523
		(9)	(18)	(27)
Sunday Telegraph	1840	194	410	604
		(11)	(22)	(33)
Text of speech	3184	264	461	725
		(8)	(14)	(22)

in the speech itself. With two exceptions (one of them a tabloid, the *Sunday Mirror*, which might have been expected to behave differently) the press gave the anecdotes disproportionate space. Indeed *The People* gave them getting on for three times too much. On the basis of conventional news values this is the pattern one would expect.

In summary, we may explain the coverage of Powell's speech by reference to the underlying circumstances of popular attitudes to the subject, of Powell's characteristics and of prevailing media news values; reinforced by more particular circumstances that combined to generate the 'earthquake' after Birmingham.

We can turn lastly to the effects of the speech.

III. POLITICAL EFFECTS OF THE BIRMINGHAM SPEECH

The speech provoked certain immediate reactions. These in turn were analysed and discussed in the mass media and themselves contributed to the wider and longer-term repercussions.

The effects can be examined under three headings: *Immigration and race as an issue; Mr Powell and the Conservative Party; Mr Powell and the 1970 general election.*

Immigration and race as an issue

As we have seen, immigration and race had been on the agenda of British politics for several years before 1968. In February 1966 Gallup polled the question 'Which of these things would you like to see Mr Wilson concentrate Labour policy on?'. 'Keep strict controls on immigration' (47 per cent of the sample) came third, after 'Keep full employment' (50 per cent) and 'Raise old age pensions' (49 per cent). Ten other topics trailed behind. (House building – 40 per cent – was the closest.) It would thus be wrong to see Mr Powell's speech – even his earlier Kenya Asian speeches – as introducing a new issue. But the speech did focus attention on the issue, as the previous sections tried to show, with a new intensity. It had the effect of raising the issue in the constantly shifting rank of political priorities. On three dates in 1968 Gallup asked respondents what was the 'most urgent problem' facing the government. 'Economic affairs' was easily top each time. In February 'Immigration' was named by only 6 per cent. In June, several weeks after Mr Powell's speech, it leaped to 27 per cent – the nearest rival being 'International affairs', named by only 10 per cent. By October the relative positions remained the same but the intensity of concentration on immigration had dropped. The poll reflected this: the issue was down to 20 per cent.

The second characteristic of the intensity of focus on immigration was that Mr Powell's emotionalism (critics stressed the tone more than the content of his speech, it will be recalled) appeared to provoke an emotional response. In the months after the Birmingham speech 'discussion has definitely become more frank', Dick Pixley, a Jamaican BBC producer, suggested. 'Private attitudes have been popping open like night flowers all over the place: attitudes which had never been given public face or expression before.' The coloured community, he claimed, partly welcomed this, for now 'there is something to discuss'.[62] Other commentators might have inclined less to the imagery of budding flowers than bursting boils. The *Observer*'s post-mortem began: 'Mr Powell has uncovered feelings and attitudes about coloured immigrants which have surprised and shocked many people by their volume and intensity.'[63] The *Economist* talked of 'the sheer nastiness of the creatures who have come scurrying into the daylight now that he has raised the stone'.[64]

Some of the emotion emerged in the reported behaviour of groups and individuals. Powell's enormous mailbag has been mentioned. More surprising were the strikes and demonstrations in his support. On the Monday after his speech pro-Powell petitions were organised at factories in Birmingham, Bolton and Wednesfield; and 50 steel erectors went on strike at Rugeley. On a small scale such demonstrations continued throughout the week. The real sensation, however, came when a number of dockers estimated at from 1,000 (*Daily Mail*) to 2,300 (*Daily Express*) marched in Powell's support to the House of Commons. Next day it was the turn of 400 Smithfield meat porters. On Wednesday too the letter of support from 39 Immigration officers at London Airport was sent. The *Sun* calculated that the cost of pro-Powell strikes was already £100,000 and could be trebled by the end of the week. On Thursday a 20-year-old librarian leapt to the floor of the House of Commons from the Strangers' Gallery and broke a leg. It turned out later that he did it as a 'logical extension' of the dockers' actions (the alternative he considered was a one-man sit-down in the middle of Kingston High Street). On Friday more dockers marched and 4,400 went on strike. Anti-Powell feeling took longer to emerge. Three hundred Birmingham educationists sent him a letter on Thursday deploring his speech. The same day 500 LSE students marched against him. On Sunday a protest march took place to Downing Street (attended by 'less than 1,000' – *Sketch* – or 'more than 2,000' – *Guardian*).

The emotionalism can also be inferred from the pollsters' results, which tended to show a very strong first reaction to Powell's speech, followed eventually by more moderate attitudes. Ninety-three per cent of those polled by NOP on 23–4 April 1968, only a few days after the speech, thought there should be 'a drastic reduction on further immigration'; only 5 per cent disagreed. Eighty-three per cent of Gallup's sample at about the same time thought controls on immigrants were 'not strict enough', 12 per cent 'about right' and 1 per cent 'too strict'. Over the months up to the 1970 election, however, the number of people who in general agreed with Powell's views greatly decreased, as Table 4.4 shows. Similarly NOP data on

TABLE 4.4

Q.: 'IN GENERAL, DO YOU AGREE OR DISAGREE WITH MR POWELL
ON THE QUESTION OF COLOURED IMMIGRANTS?'

Percentages	May 1968*	Nov. 1968	June 1969	Feb. 1970
Agree	74	58	64	48
Disagree	15	26	24	31
Don't know	11	16	12	22

* The question at this date was: 'In general, do you agree or disagree with what Mr Powell said in his speech?' (i.e. the Birmingham speech).
SOURCE: Gallup.

the question of repatriation showed a swing in favour after Powell's speech, but by the end of the year it had been more than counteracted.

The first effect of the Birmingham speech, then, was as a catalyst, provoking an intense, if temporary, discussion of the immigration issue in the mass media, a corresponding awareness in the public and a heightening of the emotional atmosphere. In at least one Midlands school a big increase in racial tension and a knifing incident were ascribed to the effects of the speech. In a nearby Adventure Playground 'problems were now defined in terms of colour'. A doctor in the west country reported that some of his West Indian patients were frightened to come to the surgery because of hostility from whites.

The second effect was a consequent tendency to accentuate, if not polarise, differences of attitude. Powell might presumably argue that he was simply crystallising attitudes on behalf of people who had not succeeded in voicing them before and that the differences already existed. But now they were more widely known (or believed) to exist, and the temperature was certainly raised. Indeed Powell claimed in a speech at Eastbourne on 16 November 1968 that the reaction after Birmingham 'revealed a deep and dangerous gulf in the nation . . .'* A set of semi-articulate attitudes and racial preju-

* Reprinted in Smithies and Fiddick (1969), pp. 63–77. The gulf was between 'the overwhelming majority of people throughout the country on the one side, and on the other side a tiny minority, with almost a monopoly hold upon the channels of communication, who seem determined not to know the facts and not to face the realities, and who will resort to any device or extremity to blind both themselves and others'. p. 65.

dices, hitherto associated with cranks or extremists, were now lumped together under the catchword of Powellism.* His own authority might be transferred, by a halo effect, to the 'nasty creatures' the *Economist* spotted scurrying from under the stone. Mr Powell himself felt the blast normally aimed at them. 'In the seven months which have elapsed since I spoke', he said at Eastbourne, 'I have been the target of endless abuse and vilification. No imputation or innuendo has been too vile or scurrilous for supposedly reputable journals to invent or repeat.'[65]

The tendency towards polarising attitudes was quickly seen. Within a week of the speech 50 delegates from 20 Indian, Pakistani and West Indian organisations met to set in train a Black People's Alliance against racialism. Later on Pixley detected a 'mild drawing together of the coloured communities'.[66] Gordon K. Lewis felt a 'new atmosphere of truculence' among immigrants.[67] *Colour and citizenship* referred to the 'shake given to the kaleidoscope' of race relations themes by the events of early 1968.[68] The effect of Powell cannot be separated clearly from other factors in a discussion of those themes and of the deterioration in race relations later that year.[69] But two further suggestions can be made.

It can be argued, firstly, that Powell succeeded, as an indirect result of his speech, in pushing Conservative policy towards a harder line on immigration. At speeches just before the Party Conference in 1968 and in Walsall early in 1969 Mr Heath shifted party policy by proposing that the same laws should apply to Commonwealth immigrants as to aliens (which would make their citizenship rights conditional), that work permits should be more tightly supervised, and that the right to bring relatives should not be absolute. Paul Foot puts the blame on Mr Powell;[70] and so, from a Conservative rather than a Marxist standpoint, does Maurice Cowling. Cowling's argument is that by appearing as an extremist 'Mr Powell enabled Mr Heath to present as an act of judicious moderation a policy which, if Mr Powell had not eased his way with Labour voters, would have been stigmatised more successfully than it was as vile, racialist, Tory fascism.'[71] By February 1970 Gallup found that 'Restricting immigration' was second on its list of policies that would most increase the chances of the Conservatives winning the next election.† Too literal an attribution of responsibility to

---

* See Paul Foot (1969), p. 116; E. J. B. Rose (1969), p. 106: 'It was not merely that the solutions now proposed were those that had previously been heard from street-corner orators; the style in which they were advocated was also one previously the prerogative of Sir Oswald Mosley'.

† Reducing taxation was easily top, named by 64%. Restricting immigration was named by 42%. Abolishing SET was third (40%).

Powell would be an over-simplification; but that his speech (and its repercussions) played some part seems most likely.

It is arguable, finally, that Powell's speech reinforced the 'hostile' bias of the immigration issue at a time when the Government was hoping to remove it. This was true at Westminster, in the media and probably among the public. The point here is that the debate on race relations in Britain, as one would expect from the attitudes described in previous sections, had become defined as 'hinging on immigrant numbers and the threat to existing social patterns, rather than on integration, housing or other issues'.[72] Governments could be criticised for acquiescing too long in that definition.[73] Now, at the very moment when the Labour Government was seeking to change it, the Government's measure was overwhelmed by a new surge of emotion and anxiety. Powell's speech, in the words of *Colour and citizenship*, 'illustrated in the most striking way possible the submergence of constructive initiatives by the reimposition of the immigration frame of reference'.[74] In the media, as the headlines quoted in Table 4.2 showed, the 'constructive' Race Relations Bill was swamped, at its Second Reading, in the wash of Powell's 'immigration-fixated' speech. The debate itself was dominated by Powell, even though he did not speak – and not least of the reasons was the impact of a moderate speech by Mr Hogg directed specifically at him.[75] When Roy Jenkins replied in great detail to Powell, in a speech on 4 May, the media coverage was much less than for Powell: 'It was the familiar phenomenon of the attack making news and the defence being regarded as non-news.'[76] Powell's speech, by its very attractiveness to the media in terms of their traditional news values, at least confirmed existing prejudices and possibly invigorated them by its emotive style.

Mr Powell and the Conservative Party

The effects of his speech upon Powell and his party must be seen in the context of what has been said in earlier sections about Powell's view of politics – his determination to go back to first principles after the loss of office, to 'shake inevitabilities' and to challenge conventional wisdom even to the extent of standing for the leadership of his party in a hopeless situation.

The immediate effect of the Birmingham speech was to lose Powell his seat in the shadow cabinet. Strictly, the speech should be seen as the *occasion* of his dismissal. His continual boatrocking in tricky waters, despite a warning from Mr Heath after the 1966 election that he must stop if he wanted to keep his seat, meant that his latest speech on a sensitive subject at a sensitive moment, was going too far. His failure to consult – even to inform – his colleagues (however

much that was technically within his rights) and the other circumstances surrounding the speech (such as its clash with Heath's
article in the *News of the World*) was intolerable. Had it gone largely
unnoticed by the mass media or been treated in the normal way like
his earlier speeches, even the Walsall one, Heath might have ignored
it. But Powell's unprecedented coverage, which lost none of the
emotionalism of the speech, obliged Heath to act. The mass media
clamorously defined the situation as a crisis for him: the *Sunday
Express* story was typical. Headlined POWELL RACE BLOCKBUSTER:
A CRISIS FOR HEATH, it began: 'Mr Edward Heath has been catapulted
into the most testing crisis of his career as Tory leader by the stark
warning which Mr Enoch Powell yesterday gave Britain on the
race issue.'[77] Heath therefore had to act correspondingly. Having
telephoned most of the shadow cabinet after seeing the Sunday papers
and having established that his colleagues felt things had gone far
enough, he decided to dismiss Powell. He summoned the Chief
Whip, who drove down from the north of England, and the dismissal
was announced that evening: 'I have told Mr Powell that I consider
the speech he made in Birmingham yesterday to have been racialist
in tone and liable to exacerbate racial tensions. This is unacceptable
from one of the leaders of the Conservative Party and incompatible
with the responsibility of a member of the Shadow Cabinet.' The
statement also set out the Conservative position on race and immigration.[78] It was the *tone* of the speech, one cannot stress too highly,
that was objectionable: and for the tone reaching the wider public
so distinctly the mass media were responsible.

The second effect of Powell's publicity – reinforced, of course,
by his dramatic dismissal – was to make him a political figure of
importance in his own right. The poll in Table 4.5 shows this most

TABLE 4.5

Q.: 'WHEN YOU THINK OF BRITISH POLITICIANS, WHO ARE THE FIRST
NAMES THAT COME TO MIND?'

Percent naming	
Wilson	56
Heath	31
Powell	26
Castle	9
Brown	8
Home	4
Jenkins	3
Callaghan	2
Benn	1
Macleod	1

SOURCE: Gallup, Feb. 1969.

dramatically. Powell's name became fixed in the public mind almost as clearly as Heath's and on a completely different plane from that of any minister (apart from Mr Wilson), let alone any other Conservatives. Equally, Powell rapidly became first choice to succeed as party leader, should Heath resign (Table 4.6); a choice

TABLE 4.6

Q.: 'IF MR HEATH WERE TO GIVE UP THE LEADERSHIP OF THE
CONSERVATIVE PARTY, WHO SHOULD TAKE OVER FROM HIM?'

Percent Naming	July 1966	July 1967	Feb. 1968	Mid-April 1968	May 1968	July 1968
Maudling	25	16	18	20	18	14
Macleod	9	10	10	10	7	9
Home	4	7	9	10	8	7
Powell	3	–	–	1	24	13
Hogg	4	6	4	6	5	6
Lloyd	3	5	4	5	1	2

SOURCE: Gallup.

whose massive endorsement, though it declined rapidly, surely reflects his publicity at the time. Another regular Gallup poll, which asked respondents to name the first three people they would put in a Conservative government, showed a similar rise in Powell's popularity, matched by a reduction in the number naming Heath.

Powell now had, to quote Paul Foot, what he had sought for so long: 'extensive publicity for his every speech and statement. The cuttings libraries of the national newspapers had to open new folders for Powell. The mass media from all over the world rushed to comment on this new phenomenon in British politics.'[79] In particular, his remarks on race were assured of automatic consideration in the future even when, in the view of some commentators, he had nothing new to say.[80] It would be wrong, however, to give the impression that his every comment was reported in a kind of Pavlovian reflex. The *Sunday Times*, for instance, found the decision how much to *go on* reporting him more difficult than the original decision to splash the 'earthquake'. Whenever Powell spoke on a Saturday his speech was always examined closely for accuracy and tendentiousness before the length of quotation was determined. The speeches themselves became more complicated and repetitive. After Eastbourne, therefore, his coverage in the press at large was variable and at a much lower level of intensity (except in the 1970 election).

Accepting this moderation of coverage, it remains true that Powell was made into a symbol entirely by the efforts of the mass media, acting as loudspeakers for his speeches to modest provincial audiences. In Parliament, the representative assembly for debating national issues, he was totally silent on the subject until November 1969 – eighteen months after the 'earthquake'. In 1968 he had decided not to take part in a debate precisely because it fell just before the speech which he was due to make at Eastbourne on 16 November and which he dared not 'kill' by anticipation. This was significant. Parliament depends greatly on mass media for its public impact and ranks high in media political news values. But the structure of debate, with a regular alternation of a large number of speakers on the same topic, prevents the kind of massive, concentrated coverage Powell's declamatory performances outside Westminster gained.

Powell, in effect, won himself a national constituency; a platform in the media from which to state his views on most subjects with the certainty of having an audience. Thus for the Eastbourne speech in November (the next after Birmingham), the media were fully prepared: since the press handout mentioned the name and address of the source of one of his anecdotes (about immigrant intimidation of an old lady) journalists had already interviewed him (and other people he named to them) by the time Powell spoke. Although subject no doubt to personal abuse, Powell must have felt well pleased that his campaign to stir up Conservative ideas achieved such publicity up to the next election.

Powell's prominence, we have seen, was shown clearly in the polls. They also showed its implications for party unity and Mr Heath's leadership. Heath had a chronic unpopularity problem anyway. From the time of his election right up to taking office in 1970 the NOP monthly poll hardly ever showed more than 45 per cent of its sample saying they were satisfied with him as Leader of the Opposition. Very often the figure was in the middle or low thirties (including most of 1968) – even at times when the party as a whole was well ahead of Labour. In an NOP sample taken in July 1967, as many as 32 per cent of the Conservatives thought he should not continue as leader (55 per cent thought he should).

Dismissing Powell was in itself unpopular. Sixty-two per cent of NOP's Conservative respondents (60 per cent of Labour) thought Heath wrong to do so; and 75 per cent of the Conservatives (58 per cent of both Labour and Liberal) said that on the whole they agreed with Powell's views on immigration anyway.[81] In October 1968 48 per cent of Conservative respondents thought the party had been an ineffective opposition: 29 per cent named poor leadership as the reason, and 14 per cent poor policies.[82] Periodically after the Birmingham speech NOP asked: 'Who do you think would make a better Prime Minister – Mr Heath or Mr Powell?' The answers in Table 4.7 suggest that among all voters in the aftermath of his speech

TABLE 4.7

Q.: 'WHO DO YOU THINK WOULD MAKE A BETTER PRIME MINISTER – MR HEATH OR MR POWELL?'

| | All | | | Con. | | | Lab. | | |
	Sept. 1968	Jan. 1969	Oct. 1969	Sept. 1968	Jan. 1969	Oct. 1969	Sept. 1968	Jan. 1969	Oct. 1969
Heath	41	49	50	50	60	59	36	43	44
Powell	37	34	35	34	30	32	39	37	36
Don't Know	22	17	15	16	10	9	25	20	20

SOURCE: NOP

Powell came close to 'defeating' Heath, though not among Conservative voters; but that as time passed Heath's support steadied.

Whether Powell in 1968 tapped an existing source of attitudes or created them, the fact that he, rather than someone (or no one) else, came to symbolise them was the result of his media coverage. Once this 'constituency' was won, the media felt justified in continuing to pay him attention. The effect on Heath's leadership, at the level of parliamentary politics, seems to have been embarrassing more than dangerous. Butler and Pinto-Duschinsky believe that 'at no time was Mr Heath in direct danger of losing his position. The major risk was of backbiting which would give the public a picture of a party divided and incapable of governing.'[83] They estimate his personal following at Westminster as probably less than a dozen, and once he became associated mainly with immigration the group's influence in economic affairs declined.

His expulsion from the shadow cabinet did not mean Powell was effectively drummed out of the party: Central Office continued to process his engagements in the constituencies (where he was much in demand) and to distribute most of his speeches. But the element of detachment brought by his dismissal (he was now beyond even the appeal to unity), plus the ease with which he could command public attention, enabled one to begin thinking of him as a prophet armed; waiting either to take over a Conservative party shattered by some future disaster discrediting present orthodoxy, or to lead a new coalition of political forces. The ambivalence of this position is nicely illustrated by Powell's role in the annual party conference. 'The presences and absences of Powell', wrote George Gale (a Powell supporter), 'dominated the 1968 and 1969 Conservative Party conferences at Blackpool and Brighton.'[84] In 1967 he had upstaged the Scarborough conference by stirring the Kenya Asian issue in a speech at Deal. In 1968 he made an intervention about immigration, all the more dramatic for being very brief, which brought a third of the assembly cheering to their feet and necessitated a plea from the chairman (Mr Hogg) not to overdo it.[85] Powell left his card, but he did not come to the feast.

This independence became much more marked in the role Powell played in the general election of 1970.

Mr Powell and the 1970 general election

After Wilson and Heath Enoch Powell was easily the most prominent figure in the 1970 election. Although this was obviously not a direct result of the Birmingham earthquake, that speech was one of the earliest and strongest links in a chain reaction. Without the background of 1968, Powell would not have become established enough to play a part in the election as a figure in his own right. For the media themselves the experience of 1968 conditioned them to expect Powell to behave in 1970 as a boat-rocking independent, bidding for the leadership in anticipation of a probable third consecutive Conservative defeat, and therefore demanding comprehensive coverage. (It was only natural, then, that the Press Association assigned one reporter each to Wilson and Heath for the campaign but to Powell two.)[86]

Powell not surprisingly defined his campaign strategy differently. He planned to concentrate four major speeches, presented in the style that had been so successful, into the last week of the campaign, with the aim of taking the headlines away from Mr Wilson at the critical moment. On 11 June he spoke in Wolverhampton on immigration, casting doubt on official presentation of the facts. On the 13th, in Birmingham, he attacked 'the enemy within' – the small minority whose 'organised disorder and anarchist brainwashing' were undermining the habit of law and order. On the 15th, in Tamworth, he attacked the idea of British membership of the EEC; and on the 16th (polling day was the 18th) he exhorted his constituents to 'Vote, and vote Tory'.

But there was plenty in those speeches to rationalise the view of Powell as an independent. He began the Tamworth speech by saying that on several important national issues 'the electors find themselves confronted with a virtual unanimity between the official parties and often between the respective candidates in their own constituencies. The party system seems no longer to do its work of offering a choice between policies.'[87] In the 'Vote Tory' speech he stressed the ostracism he had suffered at Westminster after his

Birmingham speech and the certainty – whatever else might be clear
– that he would not be invited to join a Conservative government
after the election. By contrast he drew strength from the tide of
encouragement and reassurance, 'which rose and fell but never
ceased . . . from strangers, from the general public, from the ordinary
people of this country'. Both the other speeches deviated from party
orthodoxy on immigration and Europe. There was the evidence of
his election address too. This outlined similar themes and, significantly, omitted the fact that he was the Conservative Party candidate. Butler and Pinto-Duschinsky were left with the impression
that he was 'the one articulate politician to attempt a breakaway
from the sane colourlessness that had characterised the consensus
politics of the sixties'.[88]

To interpret Powell's actions as stressing his detachment from
party was perfectly consistent. It did not necessarily follow that he
was making a bid for the leadership, but this was uniformly inferred
in the mass media. Their behaviour also did not match his strategy,
in that he became headline news long before he evidently hoped.
The tone of his election address, published on Saturday 30 May,
was bound to attract attention in the Sunday papers, only two
of which played it down; and the heavy papers and the Conservative
Sketch commented on it on the Monday. What really blew the
headlines up, however, was a violently worded attack of him on
3 June by the Labour minister Anthony Wedgwood Benn. 'The flag
of racialism which has been hoisted in Wolverhampton', said Benn,
'is beginning to look like the one that fluttered twenty-five years ago
over Dachau and Belsen.' This of course had a ping-pong effect,
with large coverage for reactions to the speech as well as the speech
itself.

From now on Powell was a subject of news as well as a source.
His four big speeches, coming a few days later, duly made the impact
on the media that was intended. The first one (11 June, on immigration) was made during a four-day national newspaper strike from
10 to 13 June. Despite the fact that the broadcasting organisations
must have been aware of having an effective national news monopoly,
an enormous proportion of their space that evening was devoted to
the one subject of the speech and its repercussions. It received
50 per cent of BBC 1's main 8.50 p.m. election coverage, 75 per cent
of ITV's *News at Ten* and all of BBC's *Campaign Report's*.

That evening was the extreme case of Powell's broadcast coverage.
But others of Butler and Pinto-Duschinsky's statistics also make
impressive reading. Powell was quoted more often on news bulletins
on BBC 1, ITN and radio than anyone except the three party leaders
(and in point of duration he received slightly longer attention than

Mr Thorpe). In himself and as an issue he ranked first in a list of 16 on those bulletins. His views and their reverberations took up about one-fifth of all broadcast election coverage.*

Powell's press coverage reflected the same news values. Its weight is less easy to convey in a few brief statistics, though one startling figure is that except in the *Guardian* his coverage was more than that given to the entire Liberal party – twice as much in some papers. The important difference in the press was the existence of explicit editorial comment and partisanship. No one had much to say in Powell's favour. Conservative papers handled him so as to minimise the possible danger to the party; and of Labour papers only the tabloid *Sun* resorted to sensational headlines like THIS MAN IS DANGEROUS. In the leader columns Benn's speech was condemned as warmly as Powell's, and Powell himself was treated coolly, with varying degrees of disapproval and dismissal.[89]

More significant than partisan pointers was the interpretation of Powell in press and broadcast media alike as an independent, populist politician with his eyes on the Conservative leadership. Both major parties regarded his publicity as a nuisance and potentially dangerous. Nicely symbolic is that the fact that, in contrast to the full coverage by the broadcasting organisations, none of the political broadcasts organised by any of the parties mentioned Powell once. Wilson was allegedly displeased with the 'Belsen' speech. Transport House 'let it be known that Mr Benn had spoken out of turn'.[90] For Labour the fear was that Powell appealed to some of their working-class supporters, specially in the Midlands. If the Conservatives were to be split, it should preferably be by somebody else. The Conservatives themselves were considerably more worried. Some months later William Whitelaw, Chief Whip until the election, remarked: 'The great thing you have to do with someone like Enoch in your party is to keep your nerve and keep the leadership's nerve.'[91] The leadership knew that Powell might split the party in two, not vertically but horizontally, inserting himself between the current orthodoxy of the leaders and a potentially Powellite rank and file. The more attention he won in the media, the further would the campaign be diverted from the Conservative strategy of ramming home the economy as an issue. Yet the media insisted on attending

---

* Butler and Pinto-Duschinsky note, ibid. at p. 208: 'Mr Powell himself filled only a fraction of this time; it was the comments of Messrs Benn, Callaghan, Heath and others which forced the question into pre-eminence on all channels. From the publication of his election address right through to Mr Powell's complaint about his colleagues' treatment of him, his name was rarely out of the bulletins . . . Mr Powell's appearances produced the most dramatic and compulsive viewing of an otherwise grey campaign.'

to Powell. They wanted the leadership's reactions to his election address, to Benn's outburst, to the big speech on immigration on 11 June. Heath found that at his daily press conferences on 12 and 13 June 'the journalists refused to be interested in any other subject than Enoch'.[92] On Sunday the 14th Heath issued a statement through the Press Association designed to forestall further questioning; and at the Monday press conference he used it to silence inquiry.

The first effect of Powell's coverage, then, was to include in the media map of the campaign an area which the leadership of both parties defined as a possible minefield in the path of victory. (Conservative opinion poll evidence suggested that four-fifths of a snap poll on 15 June took the same view – even though almost two-thirds thought Powell was talking sense in the particular speech in question.[93]) The second effect derived from the image of Powell sustained in the media, particularly since 1968, as a threat to Heath's leadership. The opinion polls, which received unprecedented emphasis in 1970, appeared to predict a safe Labour win and naturally tended to encourage 'Heath succession' stories. Far from being seen as stealing Wilson's thunder, Powell's big speeches at the campaign's end were construed on TV and in the press as shots across Heath's bows, a sign of the cannonade that would sink him when the election was lost. Thus *The Times* devoted almost its entire feature page to Powell early in election week, as THE SPECTRE THAT HAUNTS HEATH. The paper's lead story two days before polling day (CONSERVATIVE ANGER WITH POWELL OVER RIFT ON IMMIGRANTS) reported the 'extreme anger' of Tories over what they saw as an 'open fight' for the leadership; and next day a page-one story about Heath's press conference said: 'As speculation began about his future as party leader if the Conservatives lose heavily in Thursday's general election, Mr Heath firmly shut off all answers about Mr Enoch Powell and his opinions on immigration.' Similarly the Sunday before the election the *Sunday Times* was already looking ahead: the toughest fight in opposition would be 'Powell and the leadership'.

Those were effects on the shape of the campaign. But did Powell make a difference to the election result? Which party was right to be anxious about him? After the election National Opinion Polls asked people whether Powell had made them more likely to vote Conservative or less: 37 per cent said more, 23 per cent less.[94] How this translated into votes cannot be known. In the 30 or so constituencies with Powellite Conservative candidates the average swing to Conservative was exactly the same as elsewhere. On the other hand in nine Midlands and northern constituencies with high immigrant populations the swing against Labour was well below average and the turnout well above.[95] In other words, it may be inferred that Powell mobilised support for the Labour party among the coloured community there. None of those seats would have gone Conservative on the national swing anyway, however, so the importance of this factor is slight.

The overall effect of Powell on the election result thus remains a matter of guesswork. Whatever it may have been, it would have been impossible without his media coverage. Even supposing the effect was neutral, Powell's impact on the course of the campaign was real enough; and had the Conservatives lost, its consequences might have been very much more drastic both for himself and the party. Powell's debt to the media can be underlined by contrasting him with the independent candidature of Desmond Donnelly. Donnelly had never had a position in the Labour party like Powell's in the Macmillan government, but he was quite a well known figure and a successful journalist. Having left the Labour party in 1968 he launched a National Democratic Party, which promised 40 candidates in 1970 and in the end fielded five. Donnelly polled 20 per cent of the vote in his old seat at Pembroke, but national media coverage of his campaign was virtually non-existent. If he had fought explicitly outside the Conservative party, Powell's coverage would no doubt have been less, for the crucial 'challenge to Heath' orientation of the media would have been less easy to focus. But Donnelly had nothing like Powell's 1968 earthquake behind him: he lacked the genuine populist basis that justified media attention to Powell and rationalised those other characteristics that appealed strongly to the journalistic sense – the clash of personalities, the rhetoric, the platform drama, the identification of clearcut, gut issues. (It was the reverberations of Powell, one must remember, that attracted much of the attention.)

In 1970 Powell came nearer than anyone else, including the Liberal and Celtic nationalist parties as well as Donnelly's abortive organisation, to winning wide support for an alternative to the two big parties. The nature of his appeal fits tidily into Butler and Stokes' analysis of the circumstances in which large shifts of opinion between parties take place in Britain. Such shifts, they write, 'will happen when an issue evokes strong attitudes in much of the electorate, when the distribution of attitudes towards it is strongly skewed (as is true of all the great "valence" issues of modern politics), and when the parties are clearly differentiated in relation to it in the public's mind'.[96] If Powell is regarded as a party, the 1968 earthquake meets these conditions perfectly. Immigration – the subject to which Powell was most firmly attached in the popular mind – evoked very strong attitudes. Butler and Stokes note that it had 'explosive possibilities' even in their first survey in 1963. (It evoked overwhelming disapproval, few 'Don't Knows', much spontaneous elaboration by respondents, etc.)[97] These attitudes were indeed skewed: that is, opinion was heavily weighted on one side – in this case, against immigration. Until 1968, however, the parties were not clearly differentiated in the public mind. Powell's achievement, then, with the necessary help of the media, was in differentiating himself by the Birmingham earthquake. He attracted to himself the massive shift of support that the parties denied themselves by maintaining a bi-partisan policy on immigration.

Powell was still capitalising on this success in 1970. The parties were not differentiated widely on issues in the way that the media traditionally felt parties ought to be at elections. (See Chapter 8.) Powell was. The limitation of his position was that no other issue than immigration met the other two of Butler and Stokes' conditions as well. (The EEC, for instance, on which Powell in 1970 was a 'deviant', did not evoke particularly strong attitudes. Even the law and order issue did not really catch light.) Detached from the Conservative party altogether, Powell would in fact have had little more hope than Donnelly of launching an effective new party in these circumstances. Inside the party his challenge was blocked by lack of support at Westminster: only a major electoral defeat in 1970 might have changed that. Either way, in 1970 as in 1968 his position depended utterly on the power of publicity. No one knew this better than Powell himself. His final speech in the 1970 campaign began thus: 'For twenty years a majority of the people of this constituency have given to me the most precious privilege that a man can seek in a free country, the opportunity to be heard; to be heard in Parliament, but also, because of the unique nature and prestige of Parliament, to be heard outside. In recent years the voice which you have given me has carried further and further, until, without office or any other position or assistance except what you gave me, I have been able to be heard by my fellow countrymen from one end of the country to the other, and the response and echo has returned to me from hundreds and thousands of homes.'[98]

5

Parliament and television

Parliamentary broadcasting was quite widespread by the 1970s. In December 1968 the Inter-Parliamentary Union (IPU) gathered information about it from 50 countries. No less than 29 of them transmitted live or recorded radio broadcasts of debates, and 21 of these did the same with television. Only Denmark had full television coverage and only four countries (Australia, Denmark, New Zealand and the Philippines) had full radio coverage. Most countries simply broadcast recorded extracts, on their own or inserted into news and current affairs programmes. Committee proceedings were broadcast only in nine countries: the best known example was doubtless the United States Senate committee hearings (the only kind of broadcasting in Congress).[1]

Britain was one of the more conspicuous countries with no form of parliamentary broadcasting at all. She was therefore probably expected to heed particularly the remark of a Finnish MP at the IPU's subsequent symposium on the subject. Legislatures must keep themselves in the public eye, he explained: 'the lover who disappears from the sight of the loved one will soon lose his place in her heart'.[2] A member of the House of Lords made the same point with British phlegm a few years earlier: 'Parliament must work with the tools of the age or it will sculpt no monuments for the future.'[3]

Both those quotations show why the question of televising proceedings could rouse such passion in the British Parliament and was not treated as the trivial distraction it might seem. Discussion took place sporadically throughout the 1960s;[4] and during the 1964–70 Labour Government, when there were more parliamentary innovations than at any time since 1945, the Commons came within a single vote of agreeing to televise its proceedings privately for a trial period. A similar proposal for a public experiment was defeated in 1972 by 26 votes.[5]

The subject was controversial because it easily reduced to basic questions about the relationship of social institutions and media of communication. Put briefly, which is 'bigger' – Parliament or television? Parliament, constitutionally, is the representative body of the electorate, to which the Cabinet is responsible; a deeply entrenched institution claiming sovereignty in the law. Voting in a parliamentary election is the only political action most people ever perform.[6]* For most people too television is the main source of political information;[7] a pervasive medium, powerful in that it communicates fast, wide and directly and involves the senses both of sight and sound. Is Parliament bound to be changed by the development of television: or can it shape and limit the medium to its own ends? Some commentators argued that televised proceedings were 'inevitable'. The most plausible view is certainly that media of communication are primary and social institutions subordinate: for Parliament is an institution whose activities and democratic authority depend essentially upon communication with the electorate. In practice, however, the relationship of media and institutions is less simple. Even if media are 'bigger' in principle, there is plenty of room for institutions to modify them – particularly when a medium is developing its potential as political television was in the 1960s. The argument about broadcasting Parliament in those years makes a concise case study of the tensions involved in the relationship. In this chapter the attitude of Parliament towards broadcasting is first examined; then the effects of the medium upon Parliament itself. Finally the arguments used in the 1960s are analysed against this background.

I. EFFECTS OF PARLIAMENT ON BROADCASTING

The whole structure of British broadcasting, of course, is governed by parliamentary statute. Root principles like public ownership, non-partisanship and the ban on 'editorialising' are not at issue here so much as the control exercised by Parliament over the broadcasting authorities' behaviour towards Parliament itself.

With a few exceptions broadcasting had until the early 1960s been seen overwhelmingly as a threat to parliamentary politics, a view in which the BBC for many years acquiesced. Behaviour at general elections provides a good example. The Representation of the People Act (1949) put severe restrictions on the amount that could be spent in 'promoting or procuring the election of a candidate'. The BBC feared election programmes might tend to do this, particularly if candidates (or perhaps still worse, one but not all candidates in a constituency) appeared in them. Until the 1959 election, therefore, the BBC maintained absolute silence about the campaign in its news bulletins and discussion programmes. The parties' own political broadcasts had the air to themselves. Due to the initiative

* If discussing politics and following it in mass media is defined as political action, then that is in fact the most common kind performed.

of the independent companies this policy was abandoned in 1959 and elections since then have seen a variety of broadcasts.[8]

Parliament approached the question of broadcasting its proceedings with equal caution. As an institution it is geared to deliberate and gradual processes of change – a pattern into which radical innovations like this one do not easily fit. As early as 1925 one or two individualists broached the topic in the Commons but were stalled by the Prime Minister.[9] Similar requests, including one for cine-filming, met with blank refusal in the 'thirties and several times during the war.[10] Even a proposal by Winston Churchill to record some of his wartime speeches for broadcast was withdrawn when certain Members indicated their hesitation about a precedent with propagandist peacetime implications.[11] After the war a few further requests were rebuffed by Mr Attlee.[12] The Beveridge Committee on the future of broadcasting dismissed the idea in 1949 as having probable effects 'which most people in Britain would think harmful'.[13]

Interest in televised debates built up around 1959, partly perhaps as a result of commercial television's pioneering coverage of the Rochdale by-election in 1958; partly because the opening of Parliament was televised the same year; and possibly too because the medium now reached the majority of the population (75 per cent of households had TV in 1959 compared with 40 per cent in 1955).[14] Several Labour leaders went on record in favour, largely, in the case of men like Aneurin Bevan, because they believed it would counter the conservative bias of the press (to which, having lost three successive elections, the party was sensitive).[15] Other influential voices began to be raised. By 1963 Iain Macleod, then leader of the Commons, agreed there was much to be said for the idea. Jo Grimond, the Liberal leader, was firmly in favour. (Both of them were good parliamentary and TV performers.) By then, too, the parties had been able to taste the quite pleasing experience of their annual conferences being televised, and articles and pamphlets arguing the case had begun to appear.

When the Labour party formed a government after the general election of 1964 it was therefore not surprising that a Commons select committee investigated the question of televised proceedings. It came out against continuous live broadcasts but suggested that a closed circuit television experiment lasting several weeks should be undertaken, so that M.P.s could decide whether to make permanent arrangements to supply the BBC and ITV with recordings for use in edited form.[16] On 24 November 1966 this proposal, the product of much careful argument and research – and put to the House by its leader, Richard Crossman – was rejected, on a division that cut clean across party lines, by 131 votes to 130.[17] Some M.P.s who supported it may have stayed away in the mistaken belief that it was bound to be accepted and that their votes would not be needed.

Meanwhile the House of Lords explored the possibility of broadcasting too. Perhaps because they felt they had less to lose, the motion for an experiment was easily carried.[18] Early in 1968 four different kinds of broadcast were tried out: a continuous closed circuit performance for two days, an edited version of one day's debates reduced to 30 minutes, a 10-minute summary, and an even shorter 5-minute summary suitable for insertion into news bulletins. The peers' reactions, *The Times* reported, ranged from 'terrible' to 'excellent'. But even the most unfavourable impression could always be swept away by enthusiasts with the argument that the House of Commons would be much more successful. For example the Government leader in the Lords, Lord Shackleton, said he was 'a little bit disappointed'; but he thought 'the Commons would come over a great deal better because they move much more quickly, particularly at Question Time'.[19] *The Times* reporter felt that only the 5-minute version would really be worth having: 'Here we had a far stricter assertion of news values and audience interest, with the right pace of picture and voice.'[20]

Although the Commons had rejected television they did proceed, a few months after the Lords' experiment, with one of their own in radio.[21] For four weeks proceedings in certain committees as well as debates in the House were recorded and then edited into half-hour and 15-minute summaries. Reaction to these was not unfavourable.[22] A sub-committee of the committee responsible for the trial warmly recommended making such programmes regularly available for broadcast. The committee as a whole, however, rejected the idea on the grounds that public money should not be spent on 'a project which is known to be controversial'.[23]

One more attempt took place before the 1970 general election to get the cameras into Westminster. A Labour backbencher tried on 21 November 1969 to have the narrow 1966 decision reversed.[24] He proposed a motion in almost identical terms to the previous one. Being a Friday morning, when many M.P.s had already left London for their constituencies, the debate faded out without a quorum.

The Fourteen Day Rule. The best example of all to illustrate Parliament's negative attitude towards broadcasting is the extraordinary history of the Fourteen Day Rule. This involved a fruitless effort by the institution to remain 'bigger' than the new medium in a situation that forced it at last, Canute-like, to yield. Until its later stages the rule was never very precisely drafted, but its essence was this: the BBC was not allowed to broadcast discussions on any subject to be debated in Parliament within the next fortnight, or on any legislation currently before either House. The result was that programmes were continually being replanned or withdrawn. On the BBC's estimate, at any one time 'some hundreds' of items in various stages of preparation were potentially vulnerable. Cancelled items often had to be replaced by something 'of much less concern and value'; and programme producers developed the habit of ignoring 'risky' subjects in favour of 'safer but less significant enterprises'.[25] When the rule became formalised into a legal obligation the wastage increased (hitherto, for instance, the Budget had not been included); but much of the time, as before, the public did not know what they were missing. The external services alone of the BBC were exempt from the rule.

Incredibly the BBC Governors invented the rule themselves in 1944, in a defensive spirit typical of their pre-war attitude to powerful outside bodies. Their aim was to prevent pressure by ministers who wanted to broadcast on the eve of debates about current legislation which, as the wartime coalition began to strain, might be controversial. The Governors passed a broad resolution that included other broadcasts in addition to ministerial ones. After the war the rule was put into a general 'aide-mémoire' about political broadcasting agreed between the BBC, the Government and the Opposition. This was really the turning-point for the BBC, since the agreement introduced safeguards against controversial ministerial broadcasts and thus removed the danger that the Fourteen Day Rule was invented to combat. From now on the rule was maintained at the insistence of the party leaders. Trying to wriggle out of it, the BBC promised to stick to factual or explanatory statements about relevant subjects if the rule was abandoned: the parties were not impressed. The BBC gave earnest assurances that it had 'no intention of becoming an alternative, simultaneous debating forum to Parliament': the parties noted the fact.[26] The Beveridge Committee recommended the rule's abolition in 1951;[27] but successive governments did nothing. In 1953 the BBC said flatly that it wanted the rule dropped and asked for the parties' agreement: the period of a fortnight was arbitrary, the public thought it was absurd and wrongly blamed the BBC for its continuance, and it was difficult to administer because broadcasts were planned before the parliamentary timetable.[28] Despite the BBC's promise not to include M.P.s in discussion programmes during the appropriate periods, Government and Opposition were still immovable.

Now the BBC acted unilaterally. It announced its intention to withdraw the rule. The party leaders advised it not to. The BBC proposed a looser version, which the parties again rejected. The

BBC said that if there was to be a rule they would prefer it to be a legal directive by the Postmaster-General under the Corporation's licence. The Government accepted this suggestion and a directive was issued (covering the ITA as well) on 27 July 1955. The BBC published a statement that they accepted it unwillingly.*

The effect of the rule was to shut off the broadcast media completely from discussion of issues before Parliament precisely at the time when they were most topical – and to keep its own members away from the media too. The institution simply closed its eyes and ears and pretended the media did not exist. The party leaders' stated reason for their insistence was that the rule protected M.P.s from undue outside pressure before a parliamentary debate. It probably appealed also to party managers by removing an outlet for the views of backbench dissidents – specially as these, the BBC felt, often gave better broadcasts.[29] It was certainly not forced on the backbenchers, however. In a Commons debate in November 1955 the rule's basic principle was upheld in a free vote by 271 to 126.[30] But the motion also called for a select committee to review the method of implementing it. This recommended that any limitation should be for seven days only and not at all after a Bill's Second Reading. Then in December 1956 the Prime Minister announced the trial suspension of the rule subject to the broadcasting authorities' undertaking to continue to observe its spirit. Six months later it was suspended indefinitely.[31]

Why did the Commons change their minds? 1955 saw a new Parliament, a second, commercial, television service, an autumn Budget subject – for the first time under the formal directive – to limitations on the broadcasters' ability to cover it; and two new party leaders. All those factors may have made a difference. Sir Winston Churchill and Mr Attlee both reflected strongly the simple 'threat' view of broadcasting: either Parliament must be the grand inquest of the nation or broadcasting must. Churchill's defence of the rule has an archaic, patrician ring, asserting with purple extravagance the supremacy of Parliament: 'It would be shocking to have debates in this House forestalled time after time by expressions of opinion by persons who had not the status or responsibility of

---

* The directive prescribed: '(a) that the Corporation shall not, on any issue, arrange discussions or ex-parte statements which are to be broadcast during a period of a fortnight before the issue is debated in either House or while it is being so debated; (b) that when legislation is introduced in Parliament on any subject, the Corporation shall not, on such subject, arrange broadcasts by any Member of Parliament which are to be made during the period between the introduction of the legislation and the time when it either receives the Royal Assent or is previously withdrawn or dropped.' Select Committee on Broadcasting (1955–6), p.28.

Members of Parliament . . . I am quite sure that the bringing on of exciting debates in these vast, new robot organisations of television and BBC broadcasting, to take place before a debate in this House, might have very deleterious effects upon our general interests, and that hon. Members should be considering the interests of the House of Commons, to whom we all owe a lot.'[32] This same 'necessity of upholding the primacy of Parliament in debating the affairs of the nation', was the only justification the select committee could find for the rule.[33] Yet it was not one enforced on the press nor, obviously, on the individual.

That habit of mind had only to be changed which saw outside discussion as a challenge to Parliament, for the rule to fall away. In retrospect the episode can be seen as a natural step in the adaptation of British political institutions to the new media. The rule was a hangover from the formative period of broadcasting in the 1920s and 1930s, an age when Fascist dictators were exploiting mass media for propagandist ends and when little was known about the impact of broadcasting on individual attitudes. Its abandonment meant acceptance that the media could not easily be curbed and that Parliament must where necessary adapt without automatically fearing the consequences.

Only in one limited way did Parliament exploit broadcasting for its own positive benefit. It required the BBC to broadcast a daily impartial account, prepared by professional reporters, of the proceedings in both Houses of Parliament. As with the Fourteen Day Rule, the programme was thought up by the BBC itself. It only became a legal requirement, written into the BBC's licence, more than a year after the programme started in 1945.[34] Ever since 1929 the BBC had also broadcast a survey and discussion called *The Week In Westminster*, but this was never made obligatory.[35]

For roughly ten years after the Second World War, therefore, Parliament bent broadcasting to a rather simple and narrow conception of its needs. The Fourteen Day Rule silenced independent debate of parliamentary affairs: *Yesterday in Parliament* ensured a regular précis of Parliament's own debates. The potentialities of the media to supplement parliamentary activity and bridge the gap to the people were firmly limited. Before the war the BBC had had an equally narrow conception of its own needs. Starting with the war years, what came to be known as 'current affairs' developed and limitations like these parliamentary ones became irksome. The growth of television made them increasingly incongruous.

II. EFFECTS OF BROADCASTING ON PARLIAMENT

Is Parliament bound to be changed by television? There are strong grounds for arguing that it is. If so, the defensive reaction of the Fourteen Day Rule was vain and misconceived, but the belief behind it was correct. The argument can be developed as a powerful justification for televising debates: there may be tiresome side-effects, but the alternative is certain decay.

The argument starts by separating parliamentary functions (however and by whomever they are defined) from parliamentary structure. Historically the parliamentary idea preceded the institution.* When the institution took shape the only practical way of talking together was by meeting together. From the very start, the shape of Parliament was governed by the state of communications technology; and the nub of the present argument is the greatly reduced relevance of geography in the electronic age. At first the critical factor was the relationship of horsepower to mileage; and the parliamentary timetable was determined by the cycle of the seasons, since members could not meet at seedtime or harvest. Modern transportation has virtually eliminated such constraints, though a vestige remains in the shortness of Friday sittings, which enables M.P.s to get back to their constituencies for the weekend.

The mass media, long before the growth of television, also changed the shape of the institutution's procedures. Newspaper deadline times in the later nineteenth century meant that if speeches were to be reported they must be shorter and made much earlier in the day than before.†[36] Procedural reforms mooted in 1902 included changing Question Time, and the eventual decision to have it early in the afternoon took account of newspaper convenience.[37] 'We must arrange our proceedings, I presume,' said the Leader of the House, A. J. Balfour, 'so that they may be reported in the newspapers that have currency all over the country.' In principle the consequences of the electronic media could be more drastic. Members of Parliament need never meet together in the same building at all but could

---

* 'The parliamentary idea of consultation is older than Parliament as an institution and the seniority of the parliamentary idea is a useful reminder that institutions of government depend for their character and evolution not primarily on procedural rules and mechanisms but on the political climate in which they arise.' Ronald Butt (1969), p. 31. In this sort of argument it is worth recalling the root of the word parliament in the French word *parler*.

† Cf. J. A. Spender: 'The great moments in the [mid-19th century] House of Commons were nearly always after dinner and generally after midnight, but in these days the newspapers which impose their timetable upon Parliament are more and more aggrieved if anything important is said after the dinner-hour.' *The public life*, 2 vols. (1925), Vol. 1, p. 131.

conduct their business over closed-circuit television, just as some international companies hold 'meetings' over linked circuits. There is barely a necessary connection any longer between parliamentary activity and Parliament as a place. The connection is now one of convenience; and it is therefore more vulnerable to change. The danger for Parliament is that its functions may come increasingly to be performed through different structures. Popular expectations about what Parliament ought to be doing vary from scant awareness of its existence to the sophisticated interpretations of journalists and scholars. But in the prevailing democratic ethic almost any definition includes elements of representation and responsibility which, however crude, entail communication between Parliament and electorate. Parliament seeks to scrutinise the various branches of the executive and, by focusing the attention of more or less specialised groups of the public, to exert a measure of control. More generally, it seeks through its debates to identify and interpret 'issues of the day', placing a kind of continually revised agenda of politics before the nation. In these ways Parliament can be said to inform and educate the people. The more publicity it gets the better, for the process is circular: only if the institution is respected will popular concerns funnel up to it and take their place on the agenda. Thus if Parliament does not exploit the most vivid medium of communication available, it runs the risk of being supplanted by institutions that do: it will fail to get involved in the new sort of act that television has brought on to the political stage.

Already by the end of the 1960s such bypassing of Parliament was arguably beginning to take place. Ministers and M.P.s acquired an easy familiarity with television which was quite absent from the staged set-pieces of the 1950s. Equally, interviewers started to 'cross-examine' politicians, generally without rebuke, with a new freedom and with a concentration impossible for questioners in the House of Commons. Prime Ministers were careful to make important policy statements to Parliament first – but careful to make them on television afterwards. Even to this there were exceptions. For example Mr Wilson's Commonwealth Vietnam Peace Mission in 1965, an initiative regarded with importance by the Labour Government at the time, was announced by him on TV. The Commons, for procedural reasons, were unable to hear him until they had disposed of the comparatively minor Highlands and Islands Development Bill.[38]*

* General elections have often been announced when Parliament happened to be in recess. Already in 1951 the Prime Minister took the earliest opportunity to tell the people direct. Mr Attlee made a brief radio statement before the nine o'clock news (D. E. Butler (1952), p. 84). By 1966 and 1970 such announcements were made on television.

Lobby correspondents found that ministers made remarks off the record but then sometimes repeated them almost immediately on the air. Television programmes became a source of political news for journalists. The grand inquest of the nation more likely took place – in the eyes of the nation – on television than in Parliament. An early example from the years of the Labour Government was the way in which Michael Stewart – purposely or not – chose to make his first important speech as Foreign Secretary to a televised Oxford University teach-in on Vietnam (the first British teach-in) and not to the Commons.[39] Under the Heath Government two good examples come to mind. After negotiations to join the European Economic Community were successfully completed Parliament was to have a great debate, in October 1971. This was to be the culmination of an argument in the country. A short version of the White Paper setting out the terms was made available free in post offices throughout the land. A foreword by Heath began: 'The time has come when Britain has to make the choice whether or not to join the European Community. It will be a historic decision. And before Parliament comes to take it I am certain that there should be, throughout the nation, the widest possible discussion and understanding of what is involved.' Labour held a special party conference to decide its policy. The six-day Commons debate was not broadcast (a brief correspondence in *The Times* beforehand pleaded that it should be). But the BBC staged a debate of its own, presented in courtroom style, which attracted a peak audience of $5\frac{1}{2}$ million and lasted from 9.20 p.m. to 12.45 a.m. A thousand people in studios throughout Britain voted on the result.*

An even better example concerned the crisis in Northern Ireland. The BBC decided to mount an inquiry called *The Question of Ulster* early in January 1972. A confidential planning paper said it would be 'loosely based on the procedures of United States Senate Committee hearings'. A tribunal of eminent men, chaired by Lord Devlin, a Lord of Appeal, heard statements from eight representatives of different points of view, mainly from the Republic and Northern Ireland.[40] The tribunal questioned participants (who could not, however, question each other) and could refer to a panel of experts (constitutional lawyers, etc.). The minister responsible for Northern Ireland, Reginald Maudling, was invited to appear and summarise government policy. He refused: his Government's attitude from the moment the programme was planned was that it was highly inopportune. Pressure was put on the BBC to abandon it. The Ulster Govern-

---

* 1 October 1971. The vote came out at 34% pro entry, 52% con, 14% undecided. The main speakers were Christopher Chataway, Minister of Posts and Telecommunications, and Mrs Barbara Castle, 'shadow' minister of Employment.

ment felt the same. So when the programme took place on 5 January, lasting some three hours, the government view was represented by a filmed interview of Mr Maudling, taped not long before, and by a studio reading of one of his speeches in the Commons the previous November. The Opposition view was expressed in a film of Mr Wilson who had agreed to a special interview that morning. Both before and after the programme considerable resentment was reported among Conservatives at Westminster, not only because of predictable allegations of lack of balance (which the Stormont Government naturally felt even more strongly) but also because of the very feeling that Parliament was being usurped. Reading over the air speeches made earlier in the Commons was to blur the lines of institutional identity. So was the adoption of a parliamentary framework (specially a United States one – which might add insult to injury). Mr Maudling stated that it was no part of a minister's duty to be held responsible to television.[41] Yet notwithstanding his refusal to appear in person, which was hardly surprising, the programme may have brought home to millions of viewers the issues and emotions involved in the crisis much more effectively than would any scanning of newspaper reports of parliamentary debates.*

In other less tangible ways some of the modes of parliamentary behaviour and debate transferred themselves by the early 1970s to current affairs television. There was the balanced representation of party spokesmen (with the government having the last word); an inflexible partisanship which echoed the floor of the House more than the private attitudes of politicians; and the guiding role of programme chairmen, acting the part of Speaker and moderating the discussion. Perhaps a comment by *The Times* political correspondent David Wood caught the change. Describing the experimental 30-minute televised digest of Lords debates in 1968 he remarked: 'The contrast between most backbench speakers and the highly professional commentators who did the links was sharp, and encouraged a familiar feeling that the commentators ought to be made life peers in the next list because they are obviously much abler at the business of government than those they serve.'[42] Parliament had ceased to be the criterion of appropriate governmental qualities: the *familiar* feeling was now the one derived from observation of 'television politics'.

In the extreme case a 'bypass' situation would end in the transfer of the authority and legitimacy of the parliamentary institution to an alternative structure connected with a medium, television, that

* The BBC Audience Research Department estimated the audience to be 5,200,000.

performed parliamentary functions more efficiently.* On a minute
scale this might be said to happen every time an MP has more
opportunity to speak on television than in the House or a Committee.
Of course he might be glad to do either. But apart from being
attracted by the fees, some MPs, according to the observation of TV
journalists, feel that going on TV can help them get re-elected. On a
larger scale one may speculate how effectively Parliament would
have survived if it had succeeded in its attempts to keep out reporters
at the end of the eighteenth century. The conjecture is fanciful, but
might the arena of debate and decision have shifted elsewhere?
Once politicians recognised expediency or virtue in meeting a growing public demand for information, the institution which provided
it would have thrived. The obvious place would have been the
political clubs which flourished after the 1832 Reform Act as a focus
of party management and activity.[43] Clubs with the sort of institutionalised arrangements for debate that, say, the Carlton Club might
have developed came into existence in the Oxford and Cambridge
Unions. The requirement of election to membership even provided a
ready made framework to which the principles of representation
could in due course have been attached. Parliament no doubt
would have continued to exist to provide the *formal* process of
legislation, but it would have become, like the Privy Council vis-à-vis
the Cabinet, a residual appendage to the institutions where policies
were effectively argued out. Indeed the clubs did displace Parliament
to some extent. Political decisions were often taken in them – just
as they are taken in backbench party meetings sometimes today –
and they were then confirmed on the floor of the House.† The
Conservative backbenchers' committee, the 1922 Committee, still
bears a name derived from the famous Carlton Club meeting at
which the decision was taken to leave the Lloyd George coalition
and fight the general election of that year as a separate party. It can
be objected, of course, that the political clubs would have been no

* Much of Parliament's work, of course, does not depend directly on communication with the public at large. In the last resort, however, Parliament's
legitimacy – and hence the authority of such 'remote' things as, say, the detailed
provisions of an obscure Private Bill – does.

† Similar conjecture can be made about the monarchy. What would have
happened if the institution had failed to respond to the potential of mass media?
Would it have receded into obscurity – either in the remoteness of castled
privacy or the anonymity of reduction to the life style of 'ordinary people'?
It might have become almost as much an abstraction as the Stars and Stripes as a
symbol of national unity. Mass media have pushed the monarchy in the direction
of theatre (e.g. the Prince of Wales' investiture, and the BBC film called *The Royal
Family* which prompted facetious comments that the Corporation should make
a series); but that may be a cost of its survival, just as an increased theatrical
element might be an unavoidable by-product of a televised Parliament.

more willing to see their proceedings reported than Parliament. But the point is that the clubs can reasonably be seen as embryonic Parliaments, overlapping in their functions with Parliament just as the parties do today; so that if Parliament failed to perform a function expected of it (in this case, informing its constituents), alternative institutions already existed that could perform it instead. Television, the argument runs, is so placed today.

If one accepts the general claim that Parliament will atrophy if it does not come to terms with television, the question of televising debates is a simple matter of life and death. Any discomfort is a price of survival: the medium is indeed 'bigger' than the institution.

III. THE ARGUMENTS ABOUT TELEVISING PARLIAMENT IN THE 1960s

The controversy about televising Parliament in the 1960s was conducted, with one or two exceptions, in terms that did not make explicit the arguments of the previous section.* Proposals for broadcasting fell into three groups. Television received nearly all the attention, though most proposals could have applied equally well to radio – and some better. The commonest idea was a 'Television Hansard', an edited selection from the day's debates for broadcast in the evening.[44] As in the Lords' experiment, the programme could run half an hour or ten minutes; or there could be a five-minute summary for use in news bulletins. The most complete form of broadcast, on the other hand, would obviously be continuous live transmission on a special channel. This would be practical on radio (it is done in Australia and New Zealand, for instance); but it would be much too extravagant in television, except in the form of televising occasional unusually important debates. The third idea was for debates to be piped live on closed circuit to subscribers such as libraries, newspaper offices and universities.†

Objections to those schemes generally came under one or another of four headings. Television would change the nature of debate; it would mislead the public about the work of Parliament; it would alter the qualities required of MPs; and it would change the impor-

---

* A notable exception was Tom Iremonger. In the Commons debate on the proposal for experimental recordings he argued: 'Change was demanded in human nature and behaviour when man evolved the gift of speech. Change was demanded in human institutions when writing and printing were invented. Change will be demanded in our institutions if we let television in here . . . But I am not at all sure that we need be frightened of this change.' 24 November 1966, 736 *HC Deb.* c.1701.

† The author of this plan was William Deedes, Conservative MP and minister in the Macmillan government.

tance of Parliament in relation to other political institutions. Common to each was the argument that change would come about not as the result of a conscious decision based on relevant criteria but, on the contrary, as an undesirable by-product of the new medium. As one backbencher asked defiantly in one of the debates, 'Why should we have our changes in procedure dictated by television?'[45] Wherever television gets in, complained another, 'it wants to start moving furniture about'.[46]

'Changing the nature of debate'

Under the first heading several arguments recurred. Commenting on the Lords' experiment, for instance, *The Times* reporter remarked that any continuous broadcast of debates would surely make speakers 'change their style to address the outside audience, rather than their audience in the Chamber'.[47] This was a noticeable development when television coverage of the party annual conferences started in the early 1960s.* At its worst it could arouse fears of demagogy – the same fears which had prevented Winston Churchill recording his wartime speeches and which at least one postwar Director-General of the BBC, Sir William Haley, put on record.[48] At its least the tendency could be a distraction. In Australia an MP once interrupted his speech and said 'Milton, get my teeth ready this weekend' – a message to his dentist.[49]

If the programme was an edited version a similar possibility might be that MPs would in effect deliver two speeches in one – first a short, 'popular' summary of their argument for easy insertion into the television programme, and then a longer speech directed at the House. This might be an attractive technique for ministers, Opposition leaders, backbenchers and the editor of the programme alike. Even if that danger was exaggerated, critics feared a loss of spontaneity in the business of the Commons. Indeed Fred Peart, Leader of the House before the 1970 election, feared that even a short television experiment might reduce the informality and intimacy of proceedings, upon which members sometimes put so high a value.†

* Later on, colour television created new problems. One year the Conservatives found their conference hall carpeted in red: naturally it had to be changed to blue.

† See for example the view of Herbert Bowden when Opposition Chief Whip. The House 'has its hilarious moods, its serious moods, and very often when an important statement is imminent we are apprehensive and giggle and behave rather like schoolgirls. I think that is right. It is right that Members of Parliament should react in that way. If an important statement is expected, the apprehensions about what its effects may be on the country have their effects upon us. A great deal of that would be lost if it were felt that the television cameras were trained on us. Television would add nothing to our privileges or to our dignity.' 15 March 1963, 673 *H.C. Deb.* c.1749.

Those sharing this view found evidence in the experience of Australia, which had broadcast parliamentary debates at length since 1945. There parliamentary practice changed and spontaneity declined. The length of time MPs were expected to speak became shorter; the timetable was arranged so that important matters were considered on the days that each chamber was broadcast; party leaders invariably sought to speak at the peak listening times; backbenchers tended to be regarded as people who should speak when and for as long as was necessary to ensure that party leaders started at the best time; speeches tended to be better prepared but to constitute a set of independent statements on the subject of debate, rather than part of a genuine, continuous argument. The only real debate, it has been claimed, now takes place in debates that are *not* broadcast.[50] Some of the same effects have been noticed in New Zealand, which has broadcast debates since 1936.[51] Such objections obviously could not be transformed wholesale to the British situation – so much depends anyway on the form in which the broadcasting is done – but undoubtedly they confirmed the convictions of the objectors.

'Misleading the public'

The second type of objection claimed that broadcasting would mislead the public about Parliament. Television's compulsion to entertain would obscure the 'workshop' element.[52] At its plainest this argument suggests, for instance, that when viewing rows of empty benches in the Chamber during a debate, people would fail to realise that absent MPs were probably at that moment engaged in committee or constituency work or correspondence, and not idling away their time at the taxpayer's expense. This kind of reaction evidently followed the introduction of televised debates of the west German Bundestag in the early 1950s and contributed to their abandonment in 1958 (though the decision was again reversed in 1963).[53] Far from reflecting existing conceptions of reality, television arguably alters them. The cameras 'could make the phoney man truthful and the truthful shifty', argued one MP in the 1969 debate. They could glamorise a man or caricature him; and indeed this Member (though Labour) claimed that Sir Alec Douglas-Home had been destroyed as Conservative Prime Minister in 1963–4 by the television cameras, which in his view had totally distorted Home's personality.[54]

It is not difficult to think of ways in which the reality of debate might get distorted, even if proceedings were televised live. During a minister's speech, suppose some MPs were cheering and others booing. Which should the cameras show, without implying a judgement about the speech? Perhaps a 'balance' between cheers and boos is possible, but there would still occasionally be quite unintended, arbitrary shots which viewers, as *The Times* pointed out when discussing the Lords' experiment, would be bound to regard, wrongly, as significant.[55] If the proceedings were edited such dangers would be magnified enormously. A balance would have to be struck between liveliness and responsibility, between Government and Opposition, between party spokesmen and backbenchers, between extracts of debate and editorial commentary, between debates in the chamber and proceedings in committees.[56] All this would place a tremendous responsibility on the programme editor: many Members insisted that it would have to be exercised by someone under the control of the House.

Once again, then, the root of the objection that television would mislead the public lies in the nature of the medium as such. Parliament communicates through words: television deals most effectively in pictures. Would the cameras trivialise Parliament? Would they stress incidents of no intrinsic importance simply because they would make good viewing and alleviate viewers' boredom?

'Changing the qualities needed in MPs'

The third type of objection – that the qualities required of MPs would be changed – stems entirely from this visual characteristic of television. Was Britain to go the way of the United States, to quote Maurice Edelman again, and entrust office to people simply because they were good on television? Although few men have carved a substantial political career without some minimal competence in debate on the floor of the Commons, certainly the kind of performance that would impress on television is by no means the same thing. Some men may be good politicians *and* telegenic: but should the latter quality be decisive?

'Changing the importance of Parliament'

The objection that television might change the importance of Parliament in relation to other institutions has at its core the assumption that in recent years the seat of decision-making in British politics has moved away from the floor of the House of Commons into parliamentary committees, ministers' offices, the civil service and outside organisations. If this is true, to concentrate on televising Parliament would be to propagate a myth about Parliament's importance and to mislead the public about the institutions on which they should focus attention. People want to feel involved in Parliament and government, Fred Peart argued at the IPU mass media symposium. 'But just sitting and watching the proceedings of

Parliament is not participation. If it leads to more active participation in the democratic process, that would be good; but it must be shown – and not just assumed – that this would follow.'[57]

The arguments in favour

The arguments advanced in favour of televising Parliament reflected equally the tension between an old institution and a new medium. They fall into two categories. Some claimed the institution would not in fact respond in the undesirable ways suggested: others that it would derive real benefits.

In the first category supporters claimed that the fears of playing to the gallery, of exhibitionists dominating the cameras, of the public being misled about Parliament's work and so on were all greatly exaggerated. The select committee thought the danger would be worst under a system of continuous live transmission – probably the least likely scheme. Moreover all the party organisations felt that the annual conferences had not suffered adverse effects, and the committee's information about seven overseas Parliaments satisfied it that this kind of effect would not be significant.[58]

To the argument that spontaneity might be reduced or the qualities required of an MP subtly changed, the reply could be given that these would be a small price to pay for the advantages gained. But what were these advantages? At the most general level was the simple belief that if television could bring Parliament closer to the people it would serve the interests of democracy. Several MPs took up the point; and without developing the argument of 'inevitability' as was done in the previous section, the select committee recognised the paradox that 'the nation's most representative assembly is . . . almost the most remote from the public'.[59] On the same lines a *Times* leading article argued that politicians tended to conduct affairs at two imperfectly connected levels: at Westminster, among the professionals, and before the public, by extra-parliamentary means. From this distinction *The Times* thought Parliament tended to be the loser: 'Televising its proceedings would do something to bridge the gap and maintain its primacy in fact as well as form'.[60] This was certainly the main reason for introducing television in the view of Tom Iremonger, who initiated the debate that ultimately led to the 1966 proposals: '. . . the real discussion and decision-making must be, and must continue to be, held and done on the floor of the House' – and television was the way of securing this.[61]*

---

* Mr Grimond took the argument a step further, implying that a television Hansard might help stop the trend towards presidentialism in British government. 14 May 1963, 677 *H.C. Deb.* c.1131.

In contradiction of Beveridge's hunch in 1951 there was evidence too that televised debates would be quite agreeable to the public. In 1964 the Television Research Unit at the University of Leeds found that 33 per cent of a sample of television set owners liked the idea 'very much' and 20 per cent 'somewhat'. 42 per cent were 'indifferent'. Not surprisingly, enthusiasm was at its highest (49 per cent) among those in the sample with a high level of interest in following political argument (about one-third). Some respondents expected to enjoy the 'revelatory character' of the programmes; others hoped it would give them a clearer and more realistic impression of Parliament and politicians than the 'processed' reports presently available.[62] Experience abroad suggested these figures might well be lived up to in practice. In Sweden major debates are frequently broadcast live in full on radio and at length (though less often in full) on television. Audiences of up to 30 per cent are achieved at peak times. In west Germany, where periodic televised debates resumed in 1963, audiences of 4–14 per cent watch live afternoon and evening transmissions and up to 29 per cent watch recorded excerpts in the evenings. Both those countries and a number of others permit recorded excerpts to be used in current affairs programmes, for which the audiences may well be more.[63]

As has been pointed out, the number of countries with some form of parliamentary broadcasting was indeed remarkably high by the end of the 1960s. Supporters of the idea could thus argue that Britain had been needlessly dilatory, especially as none of the 29 countries, according to their representatives at the IPU symposium, regretted the practice at all. On the other hand the wide variations in the functions of Parliaments in different political systems (the 29 included systems as various as Albania, France, Ivory Coast and Japan) limit the usefulness of the argument from analogy.

IV. CONCLUSION

It was doubtful whether supporters of either point of view about televising Parliament in the 1960s would easily convert each other. Change of opinion was more likely to come through changes in the composition of the Commons – though the 1970 election produced an even more cautious House than its predecessor. But throughout the argument supporters and opponents of the idea alike based their claims on a desire for the survival of the parliamentary *institution* as the embodiment or instrument of the values implicit in the idea of 'representative and responsible government', and not for the survival of those values regardless of the institutional forms appropriate to the age. Even the 1966 Select Committee recommended that the House would be wise to introduce television *unless* 'the procedure, the character and the atmosphere of the House' were perceptibly changed for the worse.[64] It is the conviction of this chapter that procedure, character and atmosphere in the Commons, though they may be linked to the values of representative government, are not inseparable from them. Preserving the values need not mean preserving the institution unchanged. On the contrary, since democratic values stress communication processes, institutional forms must necessarily change in response to developments in media. If Parliaments wish to survive as democratic political institutions they must accept this situation and adapt to it. In the 1960s the British Parliament seemed to hesitate too long.

6

Newspapers and party systems: connections

I. Introduction

Why was Stanley Baldwin's complaint against Lord Rothermere and Lord Beaverbrook in 1931 – they were after 'power without responsibility, the prerogative of the harlot through the ages' – so bitter? Leaving aside the immediate reasons connected with Rothermere's attempt to influence the composition of the cabinet in advance, Baldwin was reflecting, perhaps unconsciously, a deep resentment of the fact that the press lords, by tapping rich sources of advertising revenue, had freed newspapers from their common nineteenth-century financial dependence on political parties. Among its other distinctions Northcliffe's *Daily Mail* (1896) was the first daily paper in which the public could buy shares. The new press was 'irresponsible' in the sense that it was not controlled by party politicians yet still played a political role.

Political scientists have rarely given the connection between newspapers and parties more than a nod. Ostrogorski, writing in 1902, suggested that British parties considered their papers 'their most valuable auxiliaries'; so much so that some local parties believed they need not themselves 'take any thought for political education'.[1] Despite this, he spent only two or three pages on the topic and few more about the USA. Michels at least wrote a chapter about party leaders and the press. But it lasts 5 pages out of a book of more than 400, and it is angled towards his central theme of oligarchy. The first sentence sets the tone: 'The press constitutes a potent instrument for the conquest, the preservation, and the consolidation of power on the part of the [party] leaders.'[2] The rest of the chapter compares the anonymous 'collective' party journalism of the German socialists with French individualism and discusses the implications for party organisation and discipline. None of the well known modern comparative studies of political parties, so it appears, examines the relationships between parties and newspapers any more systematically. Nor does the swelling literature of comparative politics texts.[3] Specialised country texts do a little better;

partly, no doubt, because they deal with only one party system and one press system at a time.[4] To some extent the relationship may be neglected because it is thought unimportant. V. O. Key, for example, talks of declining partisanship having turned the American press into 'a common carrier of neutral, and often meaningless, political intelligence'.[5] Almond and Coleman argue that although all the functions of a political system (recruitment, socialisation, interest articulation, etc.) involve communication, there is still a separate and distinct communication function since media have developed an ethic of 'neutrality' in purveying information. American newspapers certainly are less partisan than formerly, and this might help to account for a lack of interest by Americans. Supposing the subject was considered important, however, a very serious difficulty in studying it (which hampered the present study) is the shortage of data about newspapers. Had Banks and Textor wished to include newspaper partisanship in the *Cross-polity survey*[6] for example, they would have had to leave very many gaps.

This discussion begs the question why the relationship between newspapers and parties may be thought worth studying anyway. The reasons can be summarised as follows. First, as the incident with Baldwin indicates, there have been very obvious historical associations between press and party systems. The growth of competing political parties in nineteenth-century Europe was widely paralleled by the rise of newspapers supporting them – in Britain, France, Germany, Russia and Scandinavia, for example. The same was true in the USA and Canada. In the twentieth century newspapers have been extremely important to the development of revolutionary and nationalist movements. Lenin's influence before 1917 owed much to his control of the newspaper *Iskra*.[7] The spread of Hitler's appeal was much hastened by his connection in 1929 with the press magnate Hugenberg.[8] Mussolini's success after 1919 rested to a large extent on his pre-war reputation as editor of the Socialist party paper *Avanti* and foundation in 1914, immediately on leaving the Socialists, of the *Popolo d'Italia*. Nationalism in colonial Africa – in the Gold Coast and Nigeria for instance – owed much to the foundation of popular papers like Dr Azikiwe's *West African Pilot*.[9]

In the second place, the press in widely varying types of political system is given a role explicitly or implicitly that connects it to party. In liberal democracies the ideal was neatly defined by the British Royal Commission on the Press (1949). Political leaders should be responsible to the people; therefore 'democratic society needs a clear and truthful account of events, of their background and causes; a forum for discussion and informed criticism; and a means whereby individuals and groups can express a point of view or advocate a cause'. Efficient performance of those functions requires independence from governmental control; in which case the safeguard against irresponsibility in the press itself must be competition. 'The number and variety of papers should be such that the press as a whole gives an opportunity for all important points of view to be effectively presented in terms of the varying standards of taste, political opinion and education among the principal groups of the population.'[10] Since the bulk of political argument tends to be carried on around the poles of the political parties, any definition of 'important points of view' that is not circular will almost certainly lead one to expect the views and activities reported in the press to focus on those of the parties.

Marxism–Leninism gives an equally clear rationalisation for making the press the instrument of party, given the Communist party's central role in representing the people's interests. Before the Russian revolution, indeed, Lenin saw the newspaper as virtually a substitute for the party as an organisation. The chief means to develop a political programme and tactics, he wrote in an article in *Rabochaya Gazeta*, was 'a party organ published regularly and linked with all groups . . . without such an organ, local work will remain provincial. The formation of a party – if this party is not properly represented by a well-known newspaper – remains to a significant degree just words.'[11] In much the same way, Hitler's conviction that its own paper was essential to the progress of the National Socialist movement led him to risk overstretching the party's resources and to acquire in 1920 a controlling interest in the practically bankrupt *Völkischer Beobachter*.* He wrote in *Mein Kampf* of the duty of the state to prevent the credulous masses falling under the sway of evil leaders through the irresponsibility of newspapers. 'The state must therefore proceed with ruthless determination to take control of this instrument of popular education and put it in the service of the state and nation.'[12] The *Völkischer Beobachter* became the central organ of the party and an important property in the vast Nazi publishing organisation Eher Verlag. Nazi papers proliferated, of course, at every level and the non-Nazi press was hamstrung.

A third reason for expecting a connection between press and party systems is that the functions of parties are highly compatible with

* Oron J. Hale, *The Captive press in the Third Reich* (1964), pp. 18ff. The paper, an insignificant Munich bi-weekly, had some seven thousand subscribers. By the time of the Munich beerhall putsch attempt in 1923 circulation was 30,000; but along with the party the paper was then banned. After the ban was lifted in 1925 circulation crept back from 4,000, but the paper only started to flourish in the depression. Once in power the Nazis started a north German edition and by 1941 the combined circulations were 1,192,542. Hale (1964), p. 311.

the capabilities of newspapers. To a movement at the point of departure, as the references to Lenin and Hitler show, the usefulness of a newspaper as a focus of activity and an instrument of political education seems obvious and perhaps essential.[13] The congruence is just as great when party and press are well established. Parties exist when men cooperate to seek a common and general political goal.[14] Cooperation requires communication, whether the party is mass or cadre, open or restricted in membership and aggregating interests from the 'bottom' or imposing policies from the 'top'. Newspapers have obvious advantages as a medium of political communication, especially between large numbers of people. The reader's ability to control the time, place, rate, frequency and quantity of his exposure makes newspapers a highly flexible medium. They are cheap and penetrate communities deeply. They are verbal, and politics is essentially a verbal activity. The only social 'bias' of the newspaper, making it a less appropriate medium to some members of a society than others, is towards literacy. The less a man uses words for his symbols of expression (rather than, say, sound and tone of voice, like a demagogue) the less one may expect him to use newspapers for political communication. As to party goals, the fact that these, by customary definition, are 'concerned potentially with the whole spectrum of matters which the polity faces',[15] in contrast to the limited concerns of interest groups, coincides with the broad range of general newspaper contents. The criteria by which parties and papers judge what is important tend, by virtue of their relationship to society, to be similar. The same social forces that find expression in the party or parties of a political system tend to find expression also through the press. Where competing parties exist, one might expect to find a connection not only between individual papers and parties but also a correspondence, or parallelism, between the *range* of papers and the *range* of parties.

To explore the connection between press and party systems fully requires a much more elaborate study than can be undertaken in this book. The wide differences in the nature of both variables makes the range of relationships complex; and in particular it is impossible, by analysing just these two, to say anything confidently about the important question how far given parties or party systems are the product of newspaper activity. This chapter and the next one therefore take a fairly broad approach to the subject. In this chapter the range of possible relationships between newspapers and parties is analysed and illustrated. In the next, the discussion is broadened to examine the circumstances in which different relationships exist and by which they may well to some extent be governed. Broadcasting has been omitted. Although some of the factors that connect parties and newspapers hold for broadcasting too, it lacks the historical connection of the press and its inclusion would complicate and swell the inquiry too much.

II. RELATIONSHIPS BETWEEN SINGLE PAPERS AND PARTIES

The connection between a paper and a party can be measured by reference to three characteristics of parties: (i) *organisation*; (ii) *goals* (programmes and tactics); (iii) *members and supporters*. Here newspapers must be treated as monoliths. In fact they are complex organisations, and the connections between proprietors, news executives, journalists, circulation and advertising staff, typesetters, etc., on the one hand and parties on the other need not be uniform. The proprietor and editor of the *Daily Telegraph*, to quote an obvious British example, support the Conservative party; while its printers and production workers belong to unions affiliated to the TUC and linked to the Labour party. Sheer lack of data about the sociology of newspapers obliges one to treat them as monoliths. But in addition this treatment can be justified by the fact that papers present the reader with a single product commonly containing a single (if any) viewpoint specified as the editorial policy. It may be unclear exactly *whose* view is represented when one talks of the *Telegraph* being a Conservative newspaper; but that the *Telegraph has* Conservative views is easily established by reading the leader columns (and to some extent the news).

Judging newspapers by their public faces, then, the possible types of association with parties can be examined under each of the three headings. This is done first for Britain and then illustrated from other political systems.

(a) Britain

(i) *Party Organisation.* The closest form of connection is ownership and management of a paper by a party. In the nineteenth century this was the rule. It has become uncommon since the growth of the advertising industry to a size where papers derive anything from 40 to 80 per cent of their gross income from advertisements, and since the setting up of newspapers as public companies. At the other extreme one may find papers having no organisational connection whatever with a party. In between are many possibilities, ranging from ownership by an organisation fully under the control but technically independent of a party, through affiliation with a measure of independence, to some kind of informal, more or less close association between owners and party.

Much the best example of a 'party paper' in twentieth-century Britain was the *Daily Herald* (1912–64). For a time in the early 1930s it was the largest circulation national daily. During its first ten years it was not linked very closely to the Labour party. George Lansbury founded it in 1912 on a capital of £300 and relied much on voluntary support.[16]* The paper frequently attacked the party leadership and tried to finance its own candidates for Parliament. After the First World War, during which it was reduced to appearing weekly, Ernest Bevin became a director and brought Union financial support with him. He sought unsuccessfully to institute a consistent financial arrangement with the parliamentary committee of the TUC, but in 1922 the National Executive Committee of the Labour party and the TUC agreed to take the paper over officially.[17] Sales rose to 250,000, but continued financial problems (specially after the General Strike) led to the annual conference of the TUC voting in 1929 to enter an arrangement with the publishers Odhams. Odhams took 51 per cent of the shares, leaving the TUC with 49 per cent (and four directors against five).

Only for the brief period 1922–9, therefore, was the *Herald* fully owned and controlled by the Labour party. Thereafter it shifted along the axis towards the pole of independence, though not far. As well as retaining 49 per cent of the shares, the TUC directors were the only ones allowed to vote on political policy; and the paper's line was to be that laid down at the annual conferences of the Labour party and the TUC. (Hence in 1931 the paper stuck with the party, not with MacDonald, Thomas and Snowden.) One practical consequence of the arrangement was that until some years after the Second World War the editor attended the regular meetings of the parliamentary Labour party at Westminster. The paper thus retained a formal organisational connection with the Labour party.† But Odhams' financial control meant that when massive losses put the paper's future in question in the early 1960s the party could do virtually nothing. Odhams was taken over by the Mirror group in 1962. The possibility that the conservative Roy Thomson might buy the paper – he was known to aspire to ownership of a national daily – naturally alarmed Labour leaders considerably, and they were relieved when the *Mirror* agreed to guarantee the paper for

* G. K. Chesterton left the *Daily News* to work for the *Herald* unpaid. Hilaire Belloc contributed, and Osbert Sitwell wrote leading articles, occasionally in verse.

† The editor also had to appear every year at a private session of the party conference, to answer criticisms of the paper. Francis Williams (1946), p. 157.

at least seven years in solid support of the party.[18] Relaunched as the *Sun* in 1964, the paper continued to lose heavily. In 1969 it was sold to the Australian proprietor Rupert Murdoch, who turned it into a tabloid, and only then did it become successful.

Another paper which until its closure in 1967 was controlled by an organisation affiliated to the Labour party was *Reynold's News* (1850; latterly called *Sunday Citizen*). This belonged for some 30 years to the Co-operative Press, which was registered as a Co-operative Society and controlled by the Co-operative movement. The only daily paper surviving into the 1970s with such close organisational links to a party was the *Morning Star*. This did not belong officially to the Communist party but was fully under its control. Founded as the *Daily Worker* in 1930, it had Lenin's statement that a political movement needs a newspaper for success prominently displayed in its first number.[19] The editor at the start of the 1970s, George Matthews, was Assistant General Secretary of the British Communist party before he joined the paper.

There are many examples of British papers linked *informally* with parties through the personal support of their proprietors. Lord Beaverbrook enjoyed a political career which, while involving him frequently in intra-party struggles, committed his papers to Conservative causes. Lloyd George, after he ceased to be Prime Minister, bought the Liberal *Daily Chronicle* in 1923 and kept it till 1926. Lord Burnham, owner of the *Daily Telegraph* until 1928, was formerly a Conservative MP. So was Colonel Astor, for a time, while holding a controlling interest in *The Times*; and so too was Brendan Bracken, Minister of Information from 1941 to 1945 and controller of the *Financial Times* from 1945. The Liberal Cadbury family controlled the once powerful *Daily News*, which amalgamated with the *Chronicle* in 1930 and ceased publication in 1960. Cecil King, chairman till 1968 of the International Publishing Corporation (but only a very minor shareholder), was offered office in the 1964–70 Labour Government. IPC at that time published the *Daily Mirror, Sunday Mirror, Sun* and *People*, all of which supported the Labour party. C. P. Scott, owner of the *Manchester Guardian* from 1907 as well as editor for many years previously and up till 1929, was a Liberal MP. from 1895–1905. Ownership or control of papers by individual party leaders had ceased by the 1970s, but equally there were no known examples of papers controlled by persons supporting other parties than those supported in their papers. Links with parties appeared at most to be highly informal. Papers were no longer the instrument of their controllers' personal political advancement: while the *Daily Mail, Sketch* and *Daily Express*, for example, were all Conservative in 1970, they could not be described as linked to the

Conservative party organisationally since Lord Rothermere and Sir Max Aitken did not have or seek a party career.

Informal links with a party thus shade off into a situation where papers have no organisational links with party at all. (This need not preclude editorial support, of course.) A few papers tried to institutionalise their independence. Ownership of *The Guardian*, for example, was vested in a trust in 1936 by C. P. Scott's son John. This safeguarded the paper against unwanted takeover bids and the possibility of a forced sale to pay off death duties (a danger contemplated when Scott's elder son was drowned four months after his father's death). The power to appoint new trustees was vested in the seven trustees collectively. In 1971 these included three grandsons of C. P. Scott, three members of *The Guardian* staff and a single outsider, the Liberal politician Jo Grimond. Mr Grimond's membership could not really be said to constitute an organisational link with the Liberal party. Although formed with mainly financial considerations in mind, the trust enjoined its members to see that the paper continued to be run 'on the same lines and in the same spirit as heretofore'.[20] This meant a radical commitment, but to a set of values and not slavishly to a particular party. Indeed by the 1960s the paper's general loyalty had shifted from the Liberal party to Labour.

The Times, when bought by the Astor family after Northcliffe's death, started a scheme designed to renew confidence in it as a 'national institution' independent of personal or party gain. Colonel Astor foreswore any attempt to interfere with editorial policy, and a board of five independent figures had to give their approval before any transfer of shares could take place.* When Lord Thomson bought the paper in 1967 he perpetuated the spirit of this arrangement by making four of the eleven directors 'national directors' charged to preserve the paper's commercial and editorial freedom from outside interference. The Monopolies Commission, which investigated Thomson's plans for *The Times*' purchase, suspected this arrangement was 'window-dressing'.† Even so, it symbolised the owner's intention to keep the running of *The Times* independent of party or faction.

(*ii*) *Party goals*. Again there is a theoretical range from papers showing extreme loyalty to party goals to those with extreme

---

* These were: the Lord Chief Justice, Warden of All Souls, President of the Royal Society, President of the Institute of Chartered Accountants, and the Governor of the Bank of England.

† Report, HC 273, 1966, p. 39–40. The first four 'national' directors were Sir Donald Anderson, Lord Robens, Sir Eric Roll and Lord Shawcross.

independence. While the existence of an extremely disloyal paper
linked organisationally to a party would seem improbable, one
might on the contrary expect some papers to have great loyalty
despite complete organisational independence. Their principles
might be the same as the party's; they would simply reach the
same conclusions by their own paths. The range of goals, therefore, does not correspond exactly to the range in the previous
section.

Extreme loyalty to party is easier to prescribe than to produce,
unless party unity is very tight. The *Herald* was sometimes in trouble
with the Labour party between the wars; and during the Second World
War Bevin was annoyed by its attacks on Churchill. When the
official line is in dispute a party paper may not be able to avoid
becoming involved.

Total non-coincidence between the view of papers and parties
would be unexpected. If a paper had political views at all, they would
tend to coincide with one party more than another: as was argued
earlier, attitudes articulated through party are likely to find expression also through newspapers. There might be two exceptions to this
rule. Firstly, if British papers were the organs of narrowly based
interest groups (churches, trades unions, agriculture, etc.) they might
shift their support indifferently between the parties. But in fact,
like the parties themselves, the papers seek to transcend sectional
interests. The only exception is the *Morning Advertiser* (1794), the
daily paper of the Licensed Victuallers Society; and this is basically
a trade paper that for economic reasons happens to be published
daily, not a general interest paper happening to appeal to one trade.
Even the *Financial Times*, which in 1945, with a circulation of some
65,000, could have been classed as a sectional paper, successfully
broadened its appeal far beyond the 'City'.

The second type of total independence of a paper from party
views would exist where a paper's principles explicitly required
non-partisanship. The stance of *The Times* comes nearest to this
position: it has traditionally claimed a role above party, as the
previous section showed. The editor, William Rees-Mogg, described
this stance in 1969 as '*The Times* idea' – 'that's to say the idea of an
impartial, independent, comprehensive newspaper, which dates
back to the beginning of *The Times* and has been imitated by really
all the other great newspapers of the world'. This is 'an idea of
immense value to society. [It] gives society something against
which it can check what is going on, and rely on.'[21] Essential to this
idea is the notion of balance. Partly this implies broad, comprehensive coverage of national and international affairs. More literally
it involves an obligation that is most explicit in formal political

contests, like general elections or parliamentary debates, to give a balanced coverage of the activities and views of all sides. It even justifies also the unique *Times* letters columns that provide a regular selection of readers' views about what are (or may become) issues of the day. The notion of balance, further, attributes rationality to the reader and assumes it in the paper. Unless readers have an overall view of news and opinions they cannot judge events for themselves. If they adopt the paper's own judgements it should be through force of argument, not biased presentation: better that readers should disagree with the paper than reach agreement for the wrong reasons.* The paper's views therefore must themselves reflect a rational process of deliberation, to which considerations of party advantages are wholly inappropriate in a competing party system. *The Times* has not always lived up to this ideal (see chapter 3 for criticisms of its treatment of European politics in the 1930s, for instance); but the ideal itself supposes a detachment from party that even *The Guardian*, with its commitment to radical values, could not claim, and that newspapers in a number of other countries also share.

Apart from *The Times*, then, most British papers cluster somewhere between the extremes of total loyalty and independence. Since 1945 party loyalties have grown looser. The same liberal democratic values that ally papers to parties make them suspicious of governments; and perhaps because the functions of government proliferated after 1945, while the number of papers declined, papers came to place their major emphasis on maintaining critical attitudes to government, at the expense if necessary of loyalty to party.† The critical test of loyalty is a general election, and from 1951 onwards newspaper partisanship became less strident. Ultimate support was still predictable and consistent, as Table 6.1 shows; but in the later elections most papers made a show of balancing the issues and hearing all sides before committing themselves. They were also more concerned with telling readers to make up their own minds than bludgeoning them into following the paper's lead (see chapter 8). Between elections governments of both colours in the 1960s were

---

* Cf. William Rees-Mogg: '. . . what I think one should do is put perfectly clear, strong arguments which [readers] can agree or disagree with. I don't want to carry them along with us because we just sort of persuade them against their better judgement. The whole argument must be out in the open, they must be able to understand the argument, and they must then agree with the argument or reject it . . .'. Quoted, Seymour-Ure (1969), pp. 514–15.

† Butler and Stokes also suggest, but without giving references, that 'it is widely held that since politics began to receive extensive television coverage there has been a diminution of newspaper [partisan] bias'. Butler & Stokes (1971), p. 267.

TABLE 6.1

PARTISAN TENDENCIES AND CIRCULATIONS OF NATIONAL DAILY NEWSPAPERS IN BRITISH GENERAL ELECTIONS, 1945–70

Newspaper	Circulation in thousands; Party support							
	1945	1950	1951	1955	1959	1964	1966	1970
Daily Express	3,300 Con.	4,099 Con.	4,169 Con.	4,036 Con.	4,053 Con.	4,190 Con.	3,987 Con.	3,670 Con.
Daily Herald/Sun[1]	1,850 Lab.	2,030 Lab.	2,003 Lab.	1,759 Lab.	1,465 Lab.	1,300?* Lab.	1,274 Lab.	1,509 Lab.
Daily Mail	1,704 Con.	2,215 Con.	2,267 Con.	2,068 Con.	2,071 Con.	2,400 Con.	2,464 Con.	1,938 Con.
Daily Mirror	2,400 Lab.	4,603 Lab.	4,514 Lab.	4,725 Lab.	4,497 Lab.	5,085 Lab.	5,019 Lab.	4,850 Lab.
Daily Sketch/Daily Graphic[2]	896 Con.	777 Con.	794 Con.	950 Con.	1,156 Con.	847 Con.	844 Con.	839 Con.
Daily Telegraph	813 Con.	984 Con.	998 Con.	1,055 Con.	1,181 Con.	1,324 Con.	1,337 Con.	1,391 Con.
(Manchester) Guardian[3]	83 Lib.	141 Lib.	139 Lib./Con.	156 Lib./Con.	183 Lab./Lib.	278 Lab.	270 Lab./Lib.	297 Lab./Lib.
News Chronicle[4]	1,549 Lib.	1,525 Lib.	1,507 Lib.	1,253 Lib.	1,207 Lib.	—	—	—
Times	204 Lab.	258 Con.	232 Con.	222 Con.	254 Con.	255 Con.	254 ?/Lib.	414 Con./Lib.

Total circulation	12,799	16,632	16,623	16,224	16,067	15,679	15,449	14,908
Total Conservative circulation	6,713 (52%)	8,333 (50%)	8,599† (52%)	8,487† (52%)	8,715 (54%)	9,016 (57%)	8,632 (56%)	8,252† (55%)
Total Conservative vote	9,578 (40%)	12,503 (43%)	13,718 (48%)	13,312 (50%)	13,750 (49%)	12,001 (43%)	11,418 (42%)	13,145 (46%)
Total Labour circulation	4,454 (35%)	6,633 (40%)	6,517 (39%)	6,484 (40%)	6,145† (38%)	6,663 (42%)	6,563† (43%)	6,656† (44%)
Total Labour vote	11,633 (48%)	13,267 (46%)	13,949 (49%)	12,405 (46%)	12,216 (44%)	12,206 (44%)	13,065 (48%)	12,178 (43%)
Total Liberal circulation	1,632 (13%)	1,666 (10%)	1,646† (10%)	1,409† (9%)	1,390† (9%)	–	524† (3%)	711† (5%)
Total Liberal vote	2,197 (9%)	2,622 (9%)	731 (2%)	722 (3%)	1,639 (6%)	3,093 (11%)	2,327 (8%)	2,117 (7%)

1. Name changed to *Sun* in 1964.
2. Named *Daily Graphic*, 1946–52.
3. 'Manchester' dropped from title in 1959.
4. Ceased publication in 1960.
* Figure uncertain due to relaunching at that time.
† Includes paper(s) with divided support.

SOURCE of circulation figures: 1945, 1950: Nuffield election studies; thereafter, Audit Bureau of Circulation, excepting *Daily Telegraph* figures for 1951, 1955, 1959 (London Press Exchange).
The *Daily Worker*, the Communist daily paper, which changed its name to the *Morning Star* in 1966, is omitted: comparable circulation figures are not available. The number of Communist candidates at general elections was as often as not under fifty.

harried by papers that formerly supported them with little reservation.*

The situation in Britain at the start of the 1970s was that most papers gave general or electoral support to a party, along the lines indicated in Table 6.1, but with varying degrees of intensity. The *Daily Telegraph, Daily Mail* and *Daily Sketch* supported the Conservatives very loyally, with the *Sun* (under IPC) equally loyal to Labour. The *Daily Express* was sometimes eccentric in its conservatism (it was against British membership of the EEC, for example). The *Daily Mirror* and *The Guardian* were less close to the Labour Party than the *Sun*; and *The Times*, though conservative in tendency, kept its distance from the party.

(iii) Party supporters. For the 'parallelism' between a paper and a party to be complete, the paper's readership ought not to include supporters of any other party. Given the greater partisanship of papers themselves in the nineteenth century – especially in their contents – it may be that this situation once existed. But it cannot have survived long into the twentieth century. After 1945 only one or two papers had readers drawn mainly from one party. These were the most partisan papers – the *Herald, Sun* and *Daily Telegraph* – and their readers came from a narrow social range. Typically, the party bias of papers' readers was not weighted heavily in one direction. Table 6.2 indicates this pattern in the national daily press in 1967 and 1970. Changes for the *Sun* between the two dates probably

TABLE 6.2

PARTISAN SUPPORT OF BRITISH DAILY NEWSPAPER READERS:
PERCENTAGES IN 1970 (1967 IN BRACKETS)

	General Labour support by paper			General Conservative support by paper					
Party Support	*Daily* Sun Mirror	*The* Guardian		*Daily* Sketch	*Daily* Express	*The* Times	*Daily* Mail	*Daily* Tel.	*Fin.* Times
Cons.	22(18) 27(28)	28(30)		52(53)	54(47)	52(53)	62(56)	65(67)	72(70)
Lab.	60(69) 56(53)	52(36)		36(31)	33(33)	22(29)	28(29)	20(16)	11(11)
Lib.	7(7) 8(9)	15(19)		5(7)	5(10)	11(8)	3(8)	7(10)	11(9)

SOURCE: NOP Polling dates July 1967, October 1970.
Labour lead approx. 2 per cent on each occasion.
Figures for *The Times, The Guardian, Financial Times* may not be significant.

---

* For press attitudes in the later Macmillan years, see Butler and Stokes, *ibid.* pp. 288ff. The Wilson government – and Mr Wilson personally – were criticised much more strongly by the *Daily Mirror* than they may have expected; and the *Guardian*, which by 1960 was broadly a Labour paper, attacked it strongly too.

reflect its relaunching as a tabloid, and differences for *The Guardian* and *Times* may be a result of the small number of their readers in the samples. No paper had a majority of its readers supporting a party different from the paper's own preference. On the other hand there was only one paper (*Financial Times*) with more than two-thirds of its readers 'loyal'.

The reason for this loose connection between the party preferences of papers and of their readers – which puts a considerable gloss on Table 6.1 – appears to be that people use papers for entertainment and general information more than specific political purposes. In particular their initial choice of paper (which is important, since inertia to change papers is very high) is not made by reference to political criteria: it is a result, rather, of social class and terminal age of education. Evidence supporting these views is strong. Much of it is not widely accessible, being the product of private research by news organisations.[22] But the findings of Butler and Stokes confirm it and can serve here as illustration. Their 1963 survey, for example, showed that only a bare majority of readers, if that, named the partisanship of their paper correctly; and 'well over a third of all readers thought that their paper was neutral'. Moreover, many readers (44 per cent) were clearly aware of their paper's party bias while not themselves agreeing with it.[23]*

(b) Other political systems

Most British national newspapers, it is clear from the foregoing, are 'partisan' in only a loose sense. On the dimension of organisation they are mostly independent; on that of readers' partisanship there are broad tendencies, but they seem distinctive mainly just in comparison with one another. The strongest partisanship is on the dimension of support for party goals; and even here there are few examples of total commitment. By turning briefly to other political systems we can find examples illustrating better the full range of possible connections.

(*i*) *Party organisation.* The existence of newspapers controlled by parties is common. They can be found regardless of the nature of the party system (number of parties, ideology, structure, basis of support, etc.) and of the function of party in the political system.[24] *Pravda* is a leading example in a one-party system. *Pravda* is the

* Unpublished data from the 1963 survey showed that where one-third of respondents mentioned news coverage when referring to what they liked in their paper and one-fifth mentioned sport, only 4 per cent specifically mentioned politics.

organ of the Soviet Communist Party Central Committee. It is controlled through the Department of Propaganda, *Agitprop.*[25]* The Department had five sectors in 1966, each for different areas of media organisation. One dealt exclusively with newspapers. The Department had long been responsible for appointing *Pravda*'s editor and other senior executives. Many of these were members of the Central Committee or party office holders at one time and another. For example Leonid Ilichev, head of *Agitprop* from 1958–61 and of Krushchev's reformed Department from 1962–5, was formerly *Pravda*'s deputy editor. Apart from its power over appointments the Department exercised critical surveillance over the paper's contents. Another fact linking party and paper is that party membership among journalists is very high – 80 per cent as against 9·5 per cent in the eligible age-group of the population as a whole. The universal ramifications of the party also mean that such matters as newsprint supply and journalism training are indirectly controlled by the party. The former factor operates in *Pravda*'s favour against, say, sporting papers if there is a newsprint shortage.

Examples of party-controlled papers in more-than-one-party systems cannot be quoted here in detail. Well known names include *L'Humanité* (Communist Party, France),[26] *Arbeiter-Zeitung* (Socialist Party, Austria) and *Die Burger* (Nationalist Party, South Africa). Scandinavia has many examples.

Good examples of papers organisationally distinct from a party but in fact fully under its control can also be found in one-party systems. In Russia *Izvestia* is the government paper (officially organ of the Council of Ministers); but it is obviously controlled by the party, with the same interlocking membership of committees characteristic of *Pravda* and with the Central Committee's Department of Propaganda dominant. Indeed *Izvestia* exists as a separate paper only at the central level: in the Republics and smaller regions editions of *Pravda* and *Izvestia* appear as one paper. Apart from *Pravda, Izvestia* and perhaps *Komsomolskaya Pravda*, most important Russian papers are linked to major professional and occupational groups, themselves controlled by the party. *Krasnaya Zvezda* (Red Star), the army paper, is linked to the Ministry of Defence, *Literaturnaya Gazeta* to the Writers' Union, *Sovetskaya Kultura* to the Ministry of Culture.

Papers controlled by groups or individuals closely or loosely associated with parties are of course legion, and illustrations have to be chosen more or less at random. The commonest kind is probably the Trade Union-owned paper, which can be found in many countries

* The Department was reorganised by Krushchev, and again after his fall, and its familiar abbreviation *Agitprop* became no longer strictly correct.

with a strongly organised Union movement. A good example of a different kind of group-owned paper is *Svenska Dagbladet*, the leading Stockholm Conservative paper. This is run by a foundation set up in 1940 that gradually acquired all the shares. The self-perpetuating governing board of 10 to 15 members must be composed of 'representatives of private enterprise and cultural institutions, of public and private administration, and the Defence establishment . . .'[27] The Board appoints the editor, who decides policy within the general limits of the Foundation's Conservative founding principles.

Subsidies to papers by parties are, or have been, common in the press of Scandinavia, Latin America, Italy, Greece, Austria, South Africa, West Africa, Israel and many Arab countries. Control of papers by individuals following a political career has been equally widespread. Examples can be quoted from Nigeria before the military coups (the Lagos *Daily Telegraph*, owned by Dr Mbadiwe, 'a somewhat recalcitrant member of the cabinet'),[28] Colombia, where the two major papers, *El Tiempo* and *El Siglo*, belonged to rival party leaders and former Presidents of the Republic,[29] and Italy where one of the few Christian Democrat papers in Rome in the mid-1950s was owned by a senator of the party.[30] Papers owned by strong but 'non-activist' sympathisers, on roughly the same point of the spectrum as Britain's *Daily Mail* and *Daily Express*, are also abundant. Examples include the leading Chile conservative paper, *El Mercurio*, owned by the Edwards family; the Axel Springer papers in West Germany (notably *Die Welt* and the *Bild-Zeitung*; altogether Springer controls 40 per cent of total daily circulation); the Huitfeldt family's dominant Oslo paper, the Conservative *Aftenposten*; and the Bonnier family's Liberal *Dagens Nyheter*, the largest morning paper in Sweden.

Papers having no organisational connection with a party at all, yet taking a strong interest in politics, include many that are very important judged by the breadth and depth of their news coverage and analysis. *Le Monde* comes into this category. Sixty per cent of its shares are owned by the staff in varying proportions, and the other 40 per cent by about ten outside individuals such as university professors. Other examples are the *Neue Zürcher Zeitung, New York Times, Christian Science Monitor, Helsingin Sanomat* (easily the dominant Finnish paper: indeed the only 'national' one), *Ha'aretz* and *Ma'ariv* (the two outstanding non-party Israeli papers), the *Globe and Mail* (Toronto), the *Australian*, and the three big Japanese papers, *Asahi, Mainichi* and *Yomiuri*. All these papers see their institutional independence of party not as incidental but as an important aspect of their political standpoint.

(*ii*) *Party goals.* Papers controlled by parties are bound to support party goals. Some of the smaller Swedish provincial papers, to quote an example that symbolises the connection well, are not only owned by parties but are supplied by them centrally with leading articles.[31] *Pravda*'s policy, being governed by the Central Commitee's propaganda department, is widely taken as a lead by other papers when defining the party line. Many party announcements are published in *Pravda* verbatim. Russian papers below the national level receive directives on policy from the propaganda department. Their contents may also be investigated (a kind of policy audit) by departmental officials, and editors may themselves also have to prepare reports. In addition *Pravda* publishes its own 'review of the press'.[32] When there has been a change of leadership or direction in the Russian Government, such as followed the fall of Krushchev, the editors of *Pravda* and *Izvestia* have changed to keep them in line.[33]

At the opposite extreme, with total detachment from any party line, stand the papers quoted at the end of the previous section, sharing, largely, the rationalist ideals of *The Times*. *Le Monde* perhaps embodies them best of all. The then director, H. Beuve-Méry, described its politics opaquely to an American inquirer in 1965 as 'social liberalism or liberal socialism, as you will, to reconcile as much as possible liberty with justice'.[34] It sees its political function as a '*role de clarification*'. The Japanese papers, with the memory of pre-1945 government controls, are deeply committed to non-partisanship. In Canada the *Globe and Mail* supported the Liberal and Conservative parties twice each in the decade up to 1969. The *Neue Zürcher Zeitung* takes upon itself the role of a Swiss 'national forum' for the discussion of controversial issues. *Helsingin Sanomat*, conscious of its monopoly position as a national paper, has a daily feature printing editorials from the various party newspapers in the country.

Between the extremes of papers' total loyalty to and independence from parties is the great mass of papers more or less loyal to party (as in Britain). There is little point in arbitrarily picking out names at this stage.

(*iii*) *Party supporters.* Published data under this heading are extremely skimpy or inaccessible. Such data as exists are consistent with the view that while particular papers may have a readership that is overwhelmingly loyal to the paper's party preference, in newspaper systems as a whole there is only a tendency in that direction (e.g. France, Italy, Austria, South Africa). The British situation, in other words, may be typical of advanced industrial societies.

For the Scandinavian countries more detailed data are available.[35]

This shows, in all countries, persistent 'under-representation' in the circulation of the left-wing press measured by the ratio of circulation to votes: Many Labour or Communist voters read non-left-wing papers. (See Table 6.3.) The same is true, in party systems with more cross-cutting cleavages, in Belgium, where in the 1950s over half the Socialist voters were not buying a party paper, and in the

TABLE 6.3

LEFT-WING PARTIES
MARKET SHARE OF VOTES AND CIRCULATION:
3 SCANDINAVIAN COUNTRIES

Countries	% of press circulation I	% of votes II	% difference between I and II
Denmark (1960–6)	26·3	55·5	29·2
Norway (1965)	23·3	43·2	19·9
Sweden (1965)	22·0	52·5	30·5

SOURCES: *Scandinavian Pol. Studies*, 1968, pp. 113, 154
Anders Yngve Pers, *The Swedish Press* (1966), p. 41.
Communist parties are included in the figures.

Netherlands, where the proportion was about a third.[36] In Soviet Russia a survey in 1966 by *Izvestia*, based on 8,000 interviews and a mailed questionnaire, asked readers to rank the kinds of articles they read regularly. Editorials scored 30 per cent (i.e. 30 per cent said they read them regularly). 'Political articles' came eighteenth on the list and scored 18 per cent. Only Local Government came lower (17 per cent). 'Social Issues' (75 per cent) came top. The list shows a remarkable similarity to a non-Communist scale of news values.[37]

II. RELATIONSHIPS BETWEEN PRESS SYSTEMS AND PARTY SYSTEMS

A newspaper was defined above as 'paralleling' a party if it was closely linked to that party by organisation, loyalty to party goals and the partisanship of its readers. A press system can be defined as paralleling a party system when such links exist between each newspaper and a party. This introduction of a fourth variable – the number of papers and parties (or the ratio between them) – greatly increases the possible degrees of parallelism between press and party systems. Complete parallelism would exist if every newspaper was linked extremely closely to one or another party on the three dimensions already explored; and when, in addition, the number of papers in the system was distributed between the parties in proportion to each party's strength (measured, most conveniently, by electoral success).* Deviation from this extreme might exist on any one of the four dimensions or on some combination. This can be seen from Figure 6.1, where the possible range of parallelism is worked out. The four dimensions – organisation, goal loyalty, readers' partisanship and number of parallel papers – are lettered A, B, C, D. For purposes of simplification only two positions on each dimension are assumed possible: a 'high' and a 'low' position of parallelism. A high degree of parallelism on, for example, the dimension of loyalty to party goals would mean that such loyalty was high in most of the papers in the system. The same definition applies to the dimensions of organisation and readers' partisanship, but the definition for 'number of papers' is more complicated. In one sense parallelism on that dimension is high simply if the distribution of papers between parties is proportionate to their votes. But suppose the parallelism on the other dimensions is very much lower for one particular party than for others (even in a system where parallelism overall is high). Then it would be difficult to say that parallelism on the dimension of 'number of papers' was high, notwithstanding the fact that the proportion of papers might be 'right'. 'Number of papers', in other words, is in this sense a variable dependent on the other three. The difference can be illustrated by an example. The British press in the 1960s might be thought 'non-parallel' in both senses of the 'number of papers' dimension. In the simple sense there were 'too many' Conservative papers, given the relative sizes of the Conservative and Labour vote (and the Liberals, of course, had no paper at all). Arguably too the Conservative papers were *more* closely parallel to their party than the Labour papers.

Figure 6.1 shows that the four dimensions can be combined in 16 ways, bearing in mind that the order of combination makes no difference: i.e. ABD is no more nor less parallel than ADB. These 16 fall into five categories according to the number of dimensions

---

* Total circulation of the papers supporting any given party might be preferred to the number of papers as a measure of parallelism. But whether a party preferred the support of a large number of small circulation papers to a small number of large circulation papers would seem to depend on circumstances.

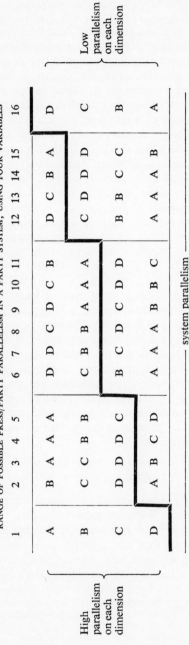

FIGURE 6.1

RANGE OF POSSIBLE PRESS/PARTY PARALLELISM IN A PARTY SYSTEM; USING FOUR VARIABLES

A: Organisational links.
B: Loyalty to party goals.
C: Party support by readers.
D: Proportionate distribution of papers between parties.

on which parallelism is high or low (0, 1, 2, 3, 4). If there were enough evidence and the 'High/Low' distinction was precisely and measurably defined, we could plot the position of different party systems in the 16 categories of the figure. In practice we can do no more than provide a few illustrations. The last category (no parallelism) can be disposed of most quickly, since few countries with properly functional parties seem to come in it. Japan is perhaps the best example. The first category (complete parallelism) can be illustrated by the plainly special case of a one-party system such as the USSR. If that category were defined strictly, as something of an ideal type, quite a lot of countries would find a place in the four compartments of the next category (high parallelism). The Scandinavian countries are good examples; also Benelux, Austria, Israel, South Africa and several Latin American countries (Chile, Colombia). The weakest links are likely to be in readers' partisanship and the proportionate distribution of papers between parties. There seems a universal tendency for left-wing parties to be 'under-represented' in their countries' presses. The 'medium' category, with parallelism high on only half the dimensions, might contain France, Canada, and West Germany as examples. In practice one would not expect some of the combinations in this category to exist: it seems improbable, for instance, that parallelism would be high in organisation but low in goal loyalty (compartments 9 and 10). The most probable combinations would seem 'high' goal loyalty and proportionality of distribution with 'low' organisation and readers' partisanship (e.g. Canada, perhaps – compartment 7); and 'high' organisation and goal loyalty with 'low' readers' partisanship and proportionality of distribution. Equally, the most likely combination in the low parallelism category would seem to be the one with high goal loyalty: the United States press, if it is regarded as 'parallel' at all, would come into this compartment.

III. CONCLUSION

This chapter needs only a brief conclusion since the next chapter takes the subject further. We need note only that the evidence (despite the abstract nature of the previous section) amply bears out the initial expectation that where parties and newspapers exist there will probably be a connection between them. Exactly what connection, however, is less easy to anticipate. The range of possibilities is clearly very broad, particularly when entire systems of newspapers and parties are considered.

7

Newspapers and party systems: contexts

In what situations are the widely varying relationships between newspapers and party systems found? The last chapter dealt only with their variety. This one considers the surrounding circumstances. Two aspects of these are analysed: (I) Characteristics of press systems; and (II) Characteristics of party systems. A connection between these and a particular press/party relationship obviously may not be causal: some other extrinsic factor could be crucial. But the analysis offers a number of generalisations, some of which might well be treated as propositions about causes. It leads to the conclusion that the interaction of parties and newspapers is a subject which ought to concern political scientists more deeply than in the past.

I. CHARACTERISTICS OF PRESS SYSTEMS

The characteristics of press systems depend on a wide range of conditions. No attempt appears to have been made yet to establish and analyse these on a global scale apart from the classification of simple aggregate data like literacy levels and number of newspapers per nation.[1] This section merely gives examples of various broad factors that may affect press associations with party systems. They can be grouped under three headings.

(a) Political culture

The important factor is the dominant conception in a society of the political role of its press. In the USSR and other Communist systems the number and organisation of newspapers are determined within a socialist framework by methods contrasting greatly with those in pluralist systems. In the Middle East and parts of South-East Asia with a wealth of newspapers, papers are widely assumed to be the personal instruments of the politically powerful. In Japan the memories of pre-1945 militarist domination, when the press had yielded to government control, led to a sharp post-war reaction of highly critical attitudes towards any government, plus a tendency for newspapers to act in concert in times of crisis.* The same attitude was reflected in the hostility of some West German papers (e.g. the Munich-based *Süddeutsche Zeitung*) to giving publicity in the late 1960s to the neo-Nazi NPD.

The variations of the perceived political role of the press in pluralist systems can be illustrated by the differing attitudes towards press subsidy schemes. In the United States the historic attachment to the constitutional principles of the separation of powers and 'checks and balances' has maintained in the public a profound conviction that the press has two important functions: one, to report and interpret the business of the Executive to the public, in a way which is more direct than in countries such as Britain, West Germany, Canada, etc., where the Executive can (indeed must) use the legislature as a major regular channel of publicity; two, to scrutinise the Executive on the people's behalf, since the President is not responsible in a day-to-day way for his actions like those other governments which depend for their tenure upon continuing support in the legislature.[2] Given also the remnants of a philosophy of free enterprise, any proposal to stem newspaper closures by public subsidy remains anathema.

In Britain the status of the press as 'fourth branch of government' can be less clearly related to constitutional principles. Acceptance of public ownership had not gone quite far enough by the early 1970s to allow a wide hearing for schemes of public subsidy, which the 1962 Royal Commission rejected as briskly as its 1949 predecessor. But they were being put forward in detail[3] and would be bound to get rather more attention as the number of papers declined.

In Scandinavia longer experience of socialist governments and a strong historical connection between a multi-paper and a multi-party system make subsidies an acceptable possibility. Sweden led the way in 1965 with a scheme (later modified) under which public subsidies were channelled through the parties according to their electoral strength.[4] In Holland, the blow struck by television against press advertising revenue was mitigated, to avoid the collapse of many newspapers, by government legislation to redistribute part of television advertising revenue to the press, with a bias towards papers that could prove they had suffered most seriously. The

* See the hostile behaviour of the press over the US Security Treaty revision in 1960; cf. the *Japan Press Yearbook 1969*, p. 25: 'It is the general custom of Japanese newspapers, with very few exceptions, to match steps and to adopt a common attitude in the face of certain social phenomena or political problems . . . As a result, the reportorial attitude and the tenor of the editorials of Japanese newspapers all tend to naturally follow the same lines.'

Italian government also sought to introduce a subsidy scheme in 1972. In all these countries, then, dominant political values stressed the need for a healthy, variegated press and (to a greater or less degree) a parallelism between it and the party system. In many other political systems, in Latin America for instance, the press has been supported (if not enriched) by overt or covert financial contributions from governments or parties.

A second aspect of political culture affecting the shape of the press and its connections with party is the acceptability of *repressive* government intervention in the press. Such intervention can be classed as political, legal or economic. Sommerlad suggests that in Latin America 'reporters or papers may seek payment from political figures or rich families not to publish a story which may be hostile or embarrassing'.[5] In a different way the British D notice system amounts also to the practice of voluntary censorship. Legal restrictions against the world's press range from simple excision of copy from newspapers (e.g. Rhodesia) to detailed restrictive press codes and harsh penalties (Argentina, Brazil, Greece). Economic control can be exercised through measures like government control of newsprint production or distribution (Mexico) and unfavourable fiscal arrangements (Greece).

(b) Geography, social structure, etc.

Several broad factors can conveniently be grouped under this heading.

Centralisation of newspapers. Not many countries have a 'national' press circulating throughout the population to the same extent as Britain's. Small geographical size, cultural homogeneity, the early development of newspaper technology, a fast communications network and the growth of a large enough advertising industry all meant that from the beginning of the twentieth century the distinction between a London and a provincial daily press became increasingly one between a national and provincial press.* Many countries have one or two 'national' papers (USSR, Egypt, Finland, France), but without the whole press *system* being 'national'. Geography is bound to be an effective barrier even where communications are very good – the obvious example being the USA. The countries with 'national' press systems most similar to the English are fairly small, like Japan and Israel.

In many countries papers from one major region – typically around the capital – have national importance. In France before the Second World War a total circulation of about 11 million was

* For evening papers the distinction remained unchanged.

divided between the Parisian and provincial dailies in a ratio of
about 7 to 4. But by the 1960s the Paris papers were selling less
than a quarter of their copies elsewhere and only a few papers –
Le Monde, Le Figaro, France-Soir – were read at all widely outside
the capital. The same pattern was broadly true of Scandinavia
(Finland's *Helsingin Sanomat* being notable as a uniquely national
paper), and of many countries in Africa and Latin America.

In the great continents or sub-continents not divided into small
nations, and in some small ones as well (West Germany, Belgium), a
more common pattern is for papers with special status to come not
from one but from several regions. In the USA the *Wall Street
Journal* is in one sense the nearest to a national paper, since it prints
in nine centres across the country, but its financial emphasis restricts
its appeal. All the other prestigious dailies remain solidly regional;
and even the *New York Times* failed in 1963 in its attempt to launch
a West Coast edition. Its history, resources and base in New York
give the *Times* great influence. But this is also enjoyed by papers in
many other regions (such as *St Louis Post-Dispatch, Milwaukee
Journal, Washington Post*). In the long string of provinces comprising
Canada the press is even more regionalised, without a paper of
similar national prestige to the *New York Times* (though perhaps the
Toronto *Globe and Mail* has approached it). The French-language
press scarcely penetrates outside Quebec: *Le Devoir*, regarded in
Ottawa as the spokesman of French-Canadian opinion, sells 5 per
cent of its copies in English-speaking provinces. In Australia none
of the long-established dailies like the *Sydney Morning Herald* and
Melbourne *Age* has ever attempted more than state-wide circulation,
though Rupert Murdoch's more recent *Australian* has succeeded
in doing so. Other good examples of regional papers with some
claim to national status can be found in India (e.g. *The Hindu*,
published in Madras and distributed by its own small fleet of
aircraft) and South Africa (*Cape Times, Rand Daily Mail*, etc.)

Decentralisation does not by itself imply any particular relationship to party: but what does seem likely is that, at least in advanced
industrial societies, a regionally based press industry cannot support
much local competition. Thus in the United States and Canada the
phenomenon of the 'single-newspaper city' is very widespread. Even
in New York the choice by the end of the 1960s was down to the
New York Times and the tabloid *Daily News* (which was so different
as not to constitute a competitor in most senses).* In the regional
press of the United Kingdom the same tendency is almost complete;
and in continental Europe it was spreading fast throughout the

* Many out-of-town papers were also available in the city centre, of course.

1960s. Local press monopoly in a competing party system, it is suggested, decreases the possibility that the paper will ally itself closely with one of the parties; 'consensus journalism' is more likely.

A final point concerns international circulations. Almost all political parties are nationally orientated: some newspapers are not. The better informed Cairo newspapers (e.g. *Al Ahram*) circulate throughout the Middle East. Singapore and Malaysian papers overlap. The *Neue Zürcher Zeitung* sells widely in south Germany. The *Christian Science Monitor* has an important European edition.

Competing media. Whether new media supplement or supplant newspapers is not always easy to tell. Where television is financed even in part by advertising revenue there is bound to be a possibility that some of the revenue will have been diverted from newspapers. At the margin this may contribute to newspapers going out of business like the Liberal *News Chronicle* in Britain, with possible implications (as in this case) for party parallelism.* It was this fear that led to the highly parallel Dutch daily press being compensated by the Government for loss of revenue after the introduction of commercial broadcasting.

Cultural differences. In many countries the organisation of the press system is deeply affected by religious, ethnic and linguistic differences. India has papers in more than a dozen of its many languages. Yugoslavia has some twenty dailies in six languages. Rangoon papers are published in Burmese, English, Indian, Chinese and Urdu. Belgium and Switzerland are two European examples of language and religion confusing party lines. In general terms, the significance of such cultural differences is that they may emerge differently in the press system from the party system. A well documented illustration is the Johannesburg *Sunday Times*. This paper was unique in the South African press of the 1960s in having a readership divided about 60:40 between English and Afrikaans speakers, rather than biased almost entirely one way or the other. Moreover 10 per cent (*c.* 200,000) of its readers were non-white. When in 1958 a section of the opposition United Party broke away to form the more radical Progressive Party the editor's decision against supporting them was based specifically on the priority of maintaining this readership pattern. Supporting the new party, even though his directors might have wished it, might damage the paper irreparably: 'It would not be possible again, no matter how many millions were spent, to create an English language newspaper in South Africa with a 40 per cent Afrikaans readership.'[6]

---

* The *News Chronicle* ceased publication in 1960.

Social class. In many countries patterns of newspaper reading are strongly correlated with social class. Sometimes this takes the form of a connection between particular papers and classes. For example in Britain – and other countries with a distinction between 'popular' and 'quality' papers – the great majority of readers of the latter come from the middle and upper middle classes. Where that distinction does not exist, different papers may still reflect the interests of different classes. In other countries, including many in the Third World, the correlation takes a different form: newspaper reading remains the preserve of the literate and well-to-do alone, and other people do not read a paper at all.

(c) Economic factors

Economic factors affect press systems at the most general and the most detailed levels. Very low gross national products make daily newspapers altogether impossible in some countries (Chad, Dahomey, Gabon); and in India, to quote a 'micro' effect, low foreign exchange reserves limit newsprint imports and hence newspaper pages. But while high newsprint consumption is positively related to gross national product (GNP), a high number of different newspapers is not. Many countries with low GNPs have a wealth of newspapers – far more than in advanced economies. Small circulations, low newsprint consumption and cheap labour enable these to survive. In industrialised societies minimum circulation needs to be very much higher, because of high printing costs, more newsprint consumption, and the high editorial costs involved in a more elaborate product; plus the historical dependence on advertising revenue which in North America and Britain, and to a less extent in continental Europe, has accustomed purchasers to regard daily newspapers as a cheap commodity. *The Times* cost the same in 1836 as it did in 1966, not least because three-quarters of the cost in 1966 was met by advertising revenue. In such a situation costs have tended to rise to meet revenue, as a result of competition and pressure on wage rates. Revenue has risen with circulation and the supply of advertising. When either or both of these become inelastic newspapers start to lose money and go out of business. In the industrialised countries circulations were elastic until about the 1950s, largely because of increased purchasing power seeping through the working classes. Advertising revenue is sensitive to short-run fluctuations in consumer demand and not subject to any particular ceiling like circulation; but the development of commercial broadcasting in the 1950s and 1960s and the slowdown in rates of economic growth at the end of the 1960s decreased relatively the advertising available for newspapers. The result was a consolidation of the number of newspapers throughout the industrialised world in the 1960s: fewer newspapers in fewer hands. Those that survived needed bigger circulations. The result of the long-run upward pressure of costs is dramatically shown by the fact that the *largest* circulation of any 'popular' daily in Britain in 1937 was lower than the *minimum* (over 2 million) regarded as necessary for breaking-even 30 years later.

The economics of newspapers thus differ drastically between industrial and non-industrial societies. In the context of parties the following implications may be noted:

Entry to the industry. To found a daily paper with any hope of success is beyond the resources of almost any individual – and, indeed, most parties – in the industrial economies. Awareness of this situation turns public attention to questions about the procedures and content of existing newspapers (e.g. opposition to Springer in West Germany; widespread discussion in Europe, beginning in the later 1960s, of co-ownership schemes and journalistic 'participation' in editorial policy making).

Monopolisation. Growth of multi-national corporations in the media industry seems also to be increasing; and a very small number of international news agencies has a virtual monopoly in the transmission and definition of significant international news. Associated with increasing cost of entry is a reduction in the number of enterprises controlling the industry. This was dramatic in West Germany, with the growth of Springer's empire. The entry of Rupert Murdoch into the British market slightly reversed the trend. In the USA it is not easy to distinguish a sense at all in which there could be said to be competition in the press. In developing countries the trend is generally far less advanced, unless there is, say, an official state monopoly.

'Personal' papers. Markets which can be freely entered – at any rate by the wealthier members of a society – still enable papers to be run, often at a loss, as the personal political instruments of their owners. This is a common pattern in the Middle East (e.g. Lebanon, Turkey), in parts of Latin America and Africa (e.g. Sierra Leone) and in Asia.

'Quality/popular' distinctions. 'Quality' papers, which tend, it has been argued, to have an ethic of non-partyism, can survive unencumbered by a popular cloak only in large markets where there are enough readers able to pay the comparatively high prices required (e.g. the 'metropolitan élite' of India); or else in smaller, wealthier markets in which the readers' purchasing power is sufficient to attract advertising that pays for anything up to 80 per cent of costs (e.g. *Neue Zürcher Zeitung, The Times*). This kind of paper is comparatively rare.

II. CHARACTERISTICS OF PARTY SYSTEMS

Party systems have been subject to much more detailed analysis than press systems and it is easier to formulate generalisations or hypotheses about party/press connections from this direction. The common categories of analysis – number of parties, ideologies, bases of support, etc. – are virtually implicit in the basic notion of party. But the author has closely followed here the terms of the comprehensive analysis in Jean Blondel's *Introduction to comparative government*.[7]* Blondel chooses as the major variable the number of parties in a system[8] and so this is now considered first.

(a) *Number and relative strength of parties*

(i) *No-party systems.* Blondel divides political systems without parties into two types: dynastic and military. About half the systems are of each type. Dynastic régimes are in a 'pre-party' situation, governed by a traditional ruler with the help, often, of a parliament chosen on a non-party basis. Military régimes are 'conservative-authoritarian' (in Blondel's terms). The dynastic ones are 'traditional-conservative'. In each case they rely on existing social structures to maintain political control: for either parties have not developed, or else they have been ousted by the intervention of the military.[9] In such a system the following generalisations are offered about the situation of the press.

In no-party systems the press typically is left in private ownership but is 'supervised' by the government. Of 19 'no-party' systems at the end of the 1960s only four had a press owned by government agencies (See Table 7.1). Iraq, for example, nationalised and reorganised its press in 1967, to produce five main dailies, all government owned. In Togo there was only one paper anyway, which was set up with government finance in a nation-building spirit after independence.[10] Four other countries had a 'mixed' press. In Jordan, the government took a three-quarters share in the ownership of all the important papers in 1967. In Qatar, on the other hand, the press was 'mixed' in the sense that one of the two dailies was government owned and the other British owned. In Nigeria and Ghana, two military régimes, some papers continued to be published privately, while others were owned by the government (and separate regional governments, in Nigeria).

In all those countries supervision was a euphemism for government

* From one viewpoint, what follows amounts to a crude attempt to incorporate into Blondel's model an institution – the press – which he omits.

TABLE 7.1

PRESS OWNERSHIP IN NO-PARTY SYSTEMS

Area	Press						Total
	Owned/Controlled by government	Mixed control	Private	No daily papers	Insufficient information		
Atlantic	–	–	1 Greece	–	–		1
Middle East & North Africa	3 Iraq (M) Libya Yemen (M)	2 Jordan Qatar	3 Iran Kuwait S. Arabia	1 Bahrein	2 Muscat Afghanistan		11
South & South East Asia	–	–	4 Indonesia (M) Burma (M) Thailand (M) S. Vietnam (M)	–	5 Bhutan Laos Maldives Nepal W. Samoa		9
Africa South of Sahara	1 Togo (M)	2 Nigeria (M) Ghana (M)	–	4 Congo C.A.R. Dahomey U. Volta	2 Ethiopia Zaïre		9
Latin America	–	–	3 Argentina (M) Brazil (M) Peru (M)	–	–		3
TOTALS	4	4	11	5	9		33

SOURCE of area categories: Blondel (1970).
NOTES: The press classification is extremely tentative. For example 'private' systems may receive indirect government subsidies or control.
'Mixed' includes *joint* government/private ownership and varied government ownership, private ownership.
(M) means a military régime.

control. In the eleven where the press remained privately controlled, supervision took various indirect but familiar forms that ensured newspapers' loyalty to the régime's goals. Outright censorship was apparently less common than self-censorship and caution induced by threats and disincentives. Thus in Greece a harsh press code, which introduced collective responsibility in press offences and even made negligent inaccuracy a crime, was not often invoked by the military government but remained a confusing uncertainty.[11] At the same time the government hit at the profitability of the strong papers by abolishing long-standing fiscal privileges. In Argentina, Brazil and Peru articles judged against the national interest might provoke the threat – or fact – of prosecution, imprisonment and closures. In Iran editions were sometimes confiscated on the streets; government advertising was essential for economic solvency.

In general, no-party régimes have left the press alone while it supported them but have jerked the reins if its hostility proved tiresome.

In the absence of party, the press reflects the interests of powerful individuals and groups. Peru's leading dailies, for example, speak respectively for landowning and export interests (mining, agriculture), importers and industrialists, and organised labour. Actual ownership (in the Peruvian example as elsewhere) is often by individuals and families, specially in countries with a large number of very small papers. Iran seems the best example of this, with some 20 dailies, all but two of which have circulations under about 10,000.

In military régimes that have supplanted party, 'submerged' parallelism may persist. Where no-party régimes have been imposed by the intervention of the military, the suppression of party names and organisation – and thus of party controlled papers – may not lead to the disappearance of ideologies and loyalties. Moreover some régimes – notably Ghana in the present context – may envisage their intervention as temporary and foresee the re-appearance of legitimate party activity sooner or later. Thus in Ghana, Greece, Indonesia, Nigeria and Peru (and possibly others) 'no-party' systems exist in which the organisation and goals of the press continue to parallel a previous party system. The parallelism probably cannot be complete, for the military régime is unlikely to countenance press support of its predecessors (e.g. Nkrumah in Ghana). Equally, goals proscribed by the ousted leader may be allowed to reappear: in Ghana the *Ashanti Pioneer*, crushed by Nkrumah as a champion of divisive regionalism, was allowed to start publishing again. In Peru the suppression of political parties did not prevent the important *Tribuna* continuing as the voice of the Labour movement and the old APRA party. In Nigeria increased governmental control after the 1966 military coup did not silence papers like the Yoruba *Daily Express*, a former Action Group organ. Before the military coup in Greece the nine Athens national dailies paralleled the party system closely. After it the four right-wing papers (with by far the lowest circulation) supported the new régime willingly; three supported it reluctantly; and the two Lambrakis papers (*Vima* and *Nea*) tried to make clear that they would attack it if they were permitted.

One-party systems. The most distinctive feature of one-party systems, according to Blondel's analysis,[12] is that they tend to be 'imposed'. That is, the régime uses a single party to secure the acceptance of its goals in the community. In radical-authoritarian régimes (Cuba, USSR) new goals are substituted for previous ones, and the party is a most important instrument in their acceptance. At the other extreme, the aim in conservative-authoritarian régimes (Spain, Portugal) is to maintain present goals, and the 'insertion' of a party is a less important instrument than existing social institutions. The difference between these latter systems and some no-party systems (e.g. Iran) is clearly very slight.

The importance of the single party to the régime is reflected in the prevalent role of the press.

In one-party systems the press typically is linked very closely to the party both in organisation and in goal loyalty. Blondel classifies 47 countries as one-party systems.[13] Five of these have no newspapers and data about the press is insufficient in nine more. Of the remaining 33, 25 (i.e. three-quarters) have a press dominated by the party and government (Table 7.2). Only Senegal (with a single daily paper, foreign owned), Rhodesia (two dailies, foreign owned) and Kenya (five dailies, variously owned) do not have at least some of their papers financially controlled by the party. In five countries the party controls only part of the press. In Spain, for instance, the Church and the influential Catholic association Opus Dei control others. In Taiwan about one-third of the 30 odd dailies are privately owned.

Communist press systems without exception are dominated by the party. In Cuba, to quote a non-European example, Castro closed many of Havana's 16 dailies and started two new ones, eventually leaving a total of five, all owned by the party or the government (the official party paper being *Hoy*).

The association between one-party systems and political values tying party very tightly to the press is further explored below under the heading of 'Ideology'.

One-party systems with newspapers not linked closely to party are normally conservative authoritarian. Here the similarity to traditional-

TABLE 7.2   PARTY-PRESS CONNECTIONS IN ONE-PARTY SYSTEMS

Area	Daily Press					
	Owned/Controlled by party/government	Mixed	No party controlled papers	No papers	Insufficient information	Total
Atlantic	1 Portugal	1 Spain	–	–	–	2
Eastern Europe & North Asia	11 Albania Bulgaria China E. Germany Czechoslovakia Hungary Mongolia Poland Romania USSR Yugoslavia	–	–	–	2 N. Korea N. Vietnam	13
Middle East & North Africa	5 Algeria S. Yemen Syria Tunisia UAR	–	–	–	1 Cyprus	6
S. & S.E. Asia	1 Pakistan	1 Teheran	–	–	1 Khmer Republic	3
Africa South of Sahara	5 Guinea Ivory Coast Mali Niger Tanzania	1 Liberia	3 Kenya Rhodesia Senegal	5 Burundi Chad Gabur Malawi Mauritania	3 Equ. Guinea Madagascar Swaziland	17
Latin America	2 Cuba Nicaragua	2 Honduras Mexico	–	–	2 Haiti Paraguay	6
TOTALS	25	5	3	5	9	47

SOURCE: For classification of countries, see Blondel (1970), Ch. 9 and Appendix, pp. 532 ff.
For data on press, sources are varied.

conservative no-party systems is most apparent. Where, in such countries as Spain, Taiwan or Mexico, the press do not attack the régime, the régime (as in Greece or Brazil) has no interest in *directly* controlling either newspaper organisation or policy. In contrast, all the radical authoritarian régimes control organisation and, through it, policy.

Whether conservative or radical, one-party régimes secure goal loyalty in the press by indirect means as well as, or instead of, by direct ownership. The limits of political expression are set in the same ways illustrated in the previous section. They include: government monopoly of newsprint distribution (Mexico); bribes and subsidies to journalists and proprietors (Liberia, Spain, Taiwan); censorship and restrictive legislation (Cuba, Nicaragua, Pakistan, Paraguay, Rhodesia, Syria, Tunisia). In Portugal (to expand the illustrations briefly) senior editorial appointments are subject to government approval. In Pakistan President Ayub suppressed the leading Bengali daily for three years for advocating Bengali nationalism. In Liberia, opposition papers were harried out of existence after 1945. Blue pencil censorship, of the kind producing blank spaces on the page, was well exemplified in the Rhodesian press after the unilateral declaration of independence in 1965.

(*ii*) *Systems of more than one party.* The analysis of these systems is naturally more complicated than of the previous ones. Blondel classifies them into Two-party, Two-and-a-half party, Multi-party with a dominant party, and Multi-party without a dominant party.[14] The distinctions are based on parties' electoral successes averaged over 20 years after 1945. In two-and-a-half-party systems the 'half' tended to obtain between 15 and 20 per cent of the votes; while in a dominant multi-party system the 'dominant' party always won about 40 per cent of the votes and was generally twice as large as the second party. Blondel also applies the concepts of *party balance* (obtaining when parties continued at almost equal strength) and *stability* (the maintenance of party strengths within the same range for the major part of the period under study). Fifty-eight countries are fitted into this classification, which is tabulated in Table 7.3.

As well as being complicated by this wide variety of party systems, the range of party relationships with the press is increased by the extra variable of party numbers: for the relationship may here include parallelism in the form of a newspaper distribution that matches proportionately the strength of the several parties. Given the number of countries involved and the difficulty of finding reliable data about the press in many of them – specially for the tricky dimension of goal-loyalty – very little can be said with any confidence.

TABLE 7.3 CLASSIFICATION OF PARTY SYSTEMS BY NUMBER OF PARTIES, 'BALANCE' AND 'STABILITY'

No. of parties per country	'Balanced' and stable	'Balanced' and unstable	'Unbalanced' and stable	'Unbalanced' and unstable	Total
Two	Australia Austria Britain Malta New Zealand USA Philippines Gambia Costa Rica Jamaica Trinidad Uruguay		Turkey S. Korea Japan S. Africa Zambia Singapore Botswana	Cameroun Mauritius Rwanda Sierra Leone Dominican Rep.	24
Two-and-a-half	Sri Lanka	Morocco Lesotho Guyana	Luxembourg Canada Eire Barbados	W. Germany Belgium Malaysia Somalia Sudan Uganda El Salvador Guatemala	16
Multi-party with dominant party			Denmark Sweden Norway Iceland Italy, Israel India, Chile Venezuela	France Colombia	11
Multi-party	Finland Switzerland	Netherlands	Panama	Lebanon Bolivia, Ecuador	7
TOTALS	15	4	21	18	58

NOTE: This table is based on the aggregate data in Blondel's appendix. This differs slightly in some cases from his text. For example, he appears to omit Malta altogether from his calculations (there is no table in his appendix), yet he refers to it in his text.

The following generalisations are grouped under number, balance and stability. They are extremely tentative; so much so that lists of countries are not given everywhere in full.

Number of parties in the system: parallelism between the range of parties in a system and the range of papers is generally high. Out of 35 countries with newspapers and available data there was noticeable parallelism in all but eight (Bolivia, Cameroun, India, Japan, New Zealand, Turkey, usa, Zambia. In Cameroun and Zambia there were fewer daily papers than parties anyway). Parallelism appeared to be relatively lowest in two-party systems: six of the eight countries were in that category (all except Bolivia and India). There was data for 15 two-party systems altogether. In multi-party systems with a dominant party (Denmark, Norway, Sweden, France, Israel, etc.) the dominance was not generally reflected closely in the distribution of press circulation between the parties. Equally the presence of a small party did not seem to imply the absence of a supportive press.

Organisational links between newspapers and parties exist slightly more often than not. Links appeared uncommon in only 16 out of 35 systems. This type of parallelism was most common in multi-party systems of both kinds (Scandinavia, Italy, Israel, Chile, Colombia, Switzerland). In two and two-and-a-half party systems it was actually untypical; being present in 10 countries and uncommon or absent from 13 (e.g. Japan, usa, Canada, Uganda).

Loyalty by papers to party goals appears strong in all systems. Any more precise statement is not justified by the data. Taking the three dimensions of range, organisation and goal loyalty and taking into account also the section on one-party systems, we can suggest that: *Parallelism with the press is stronger in multi-party systems than in two or two-and-a-half party systems; but less strong than in one-party systems.*

'*Balance' of parties in the system: parallelism between parties and newspapers is higher on every dimension in 'balanced' than 'unbalanced' systems.* Number of papers and parties: only in the usa and New Zealand, out of 12 'balanced' countries, was there little or no parallelism. Among 22 'unbalanced' countries, 5 had little or none (Bolivia, Cameroun, India, Japan, Turkey).

Organisational links were found indifferently in 'unbalanced' systems (present in 11; absent from 9). But they were found twice as often as not in 'balanced' systems (present in 9; absent from 5).

Loyalty to party goals was low only in the usa among 12 'balanced' systems; and low in 4 'unbalanced' systems (Bolivia, India, Japan, Turkey) among 21. In general then: *Parallelism of press and party systems is more often found when parties are competing at equal strength, regardless of their number, than when they are not.*

'*Stability' of party systems: parallelism between the number (i.e. range) of parties and papers appears higher in 'stable' than 'unstable' party systems.* The quantitative difference is less marked than the qualitative. That is, in 13 out of 21 'stable' systems the connection was very strong (the Scandinavian countries, Italy, Luxembourg, Israel, Chile, Ceylon, Austria, Malta, Costa Rica, Uruguay); and it was strong in 4 others. Among the 11 'unstable' systems this very strong connection existed only in 4 (Colombia, Dominican Republic, Belgium, Sierra Leone); and it was strong in 5 others.

Organisational links between parties and papers are low in 'unstable' systems and high in 'stable' systems. In 'unstable' systems the ratio of high to low was 5:6. In 'stable' systems the ratio was 15:9.

Press loyalty to party goals is high in 'stable' and in 'unstable' systems. Taking these dimensions together again we can claim that: *Parallelism with the press is stronger in 'stable' than in 'unstable' party systems.* In other words, newspapers and parties are found to have closer links in systems where the relative strength of parties changed little in the 20 years after 1945 than where changes did take place.

Analysis in terms of the number and relative strength of parties in systems with more than one party thus discloses a few general, tentative associations between parties and newspapers. These would be more striking if they were consistent; that is, if the multi-party systems were also 'balanced' and 'stable' systems. But this identity does not exist. The highly parallel Scandinavian countries, which might seem obvious candidates, were multi-party and 'stable' but not 'balanced' (except for Finland they had a dominant party). So were Italy, Israel, Chile, and Canada. Some multi-party systems that were 'balanced' were not 'stable' (Netherlands, Morocco, Guyana). Some were neither, though having some parallelism (West Germany, France, Belgium, Guatemala). A few were both but were not multi-party systems (Britain, Austria, Malta, Uruguay). It seems unlikely, even if more evidence were available, that the type and degree of party/press parallelism in a system could be explained by reference simply to the number and relative strength of the parties.

(b) Party goals and ideology

Blondel defines party goals or ideologies as concerned with policies (in the 'programme' sense), with means of implementation, and with views about political participation.[15] Description of particular cases presents familiar problems stemming from doubts and inconsistencies within parties about their ideology (and whether they even have one) and from differences between theory and practice.

Accepting these limitations, propositions can be offered under two headings. Firstly, particular ideologies might in themselves be associated with certain press/party connections. Secondly, the *range* of ideologies in different party systems might imply certain connections.

(*i*) *Association between particular party ideologies and newspapers.*
The more clearly a party is identified with an ideology, the greater is the probability of press parallelism. Newspapers can and do identify with personalities (Nkrumah, Mao, etc.). But their capabilities are biased towards the verbal activity associated with political principles and programmes. Reference to recent British general elections, for example, reveals strong editorial assumptions that there ought to be contentious 'issues' and rival 'policies' in a campaign, not simply rival candidates.[16] Apart from party leaders and senior civil servants, journalists seemed to be the main group concerned about the contents of party manifestos. The United States is another example. The main political parties are not at all clearly differentiated by ideology, and press parallelism on all three dimensions of organisation, goal loyalty and readers' support is very low.

There are no parties with an ideology that excludes press parallelism. Where 'ideological' explanations can be offered for the absence of parallelism between parties and papers the cause lies in the papers. As we have seen, some newspapers eschew party connections as compromising their independence. There appear to be no parties, however, to which the possession of newspaper support would be ideologically unacceptable.

Parties with an ideology of change tend to be linked more closely to newspapers than do others. The explanation lies again in the capabilities of the newspaper as a medium. Such parties seek to distribute new goals, intensively and extensively. Newspapers are an efficient instrument. Parties representing established goals may certainly value newspapers. But they need them less, since the interweaving strands of social communication in school, family, workplace, etc., already permeate and maintain those goals in the community.

The most obvious illustrations of this hypothesis are Communist parties. The role of the press before the revolution, Lenin argued, was 'to concentrate all elements of political dissatisfaction and protest, to fertilise the proletarian revolutionary movement'.[17] Parallelism is therefore high alike in terms of organisation, goal loyalty and – specially in the early days of a political movement – reader support. Where these parties control the régime, the connection can be established even more closely (except in reader support). Thus in Tanzania two papers were founded by TANU after independence –

one in English (*The Nationalist*) and one in Swahili (*Uhuru*) – in order to promote government policy.

It is important to note that the particular direction of change promoted by a party does not affect this hypothesis. Historically change has often been associated, since the development of modern parties, with democratic or populist movements having Socialist or Communist goals. But often change has also meant nationalism, especially in colonial countries. In India, for instance, small nationalist groups sprang up after the 1860s mainly in the urban areas; but it was not until a good enough communications network developed to support widely circulated English language newspapers that the Indian National Congress was created in 1885.[18]

In African colonies the press was often an influential catalyst for nationalism. Bourguiba's neo-Destour movement was based originally on the group who printed *L'Action tunisienne* in 1932.[19] Nkrumah's CPP was constructed round the *Accra Evening News*.[20] The NCNC in Nigeria grew from Dr Azikiwe's *West African Pilot*, the first in the Zik newspaper chain.[21] If decolonisation has been achieved, change may come to mean 'modernisation' or 'mobilisation'. David Apter writes that 'the employment of all the mass media during political campaigns, the use of journalists, cartoonists, poster-makers and pamphleteers, also helps to identify political action with modernity and to stress the instrumental role of party activity in change and modernisation'.[22]

In South Africa in an earlier generation the Afrikaaners saw the political importance of building up their own press, closely linked to their party, after the Union in 1909.

German fascism, as was shown in Chapter 6, stressed the importance of a party press from its early days. So, in the nineteenth century, did the German Social Democrats.

(*ii*) *Press/party parallelism in systems of competing party ideologies.*
The deeper the cleavages between competing party ideologies, the greater is the probability of press parallelism. This hypothesis can be illustrated by reference to South Africa. Political divisions turn on first principles dug from the very mines of society. The press lines up loyally on either side of the apartheid fence. 'Political conflicts run so deep that one is committed almost entirely to one side or the other,' the editor of the Johannesburg *Sunday Times* wrote in 1969. 'Once you are on one side, there is very little on the other that has much appeal. Since we are committed to the liberal or left side, and opposed to the Government's conservatism, the question of what principle to follow offers no problem at all. There is very seldom any scope for compromise.'[23] The Afrikaner press, we have already

seen, has always been tied extremely closely to the Nationalist Party. If anything, the *Sunday Times* is less parallel to the Opposition than are other English-language papers, because of its mixed readership. Another illustration worth mentioning is the press of West Berlin. In the cold war enclave symbolising 'western' politics to the East Berliners over the wall West Berlin newspapers speak with a stronger anti-Communist voice than the press in West Germany, which is confronted less starkly with the rival ideology.

In systems of more than one party, 'left-wing' parties tend to have the closest parallelism with newspapers. This situation is again a result of the fact that left-wing parties are normally those promoting political change, with implications already described for their connections with newspapers. (It should be stressed once more that the concern with change is the key factor: the fact that the main direction of change is 'left wing' in the 1970s is incidental.) Good illustrations of the hypothesis can be found in most of the countries of western Europe, specially those with a Communist Party (France, Italy, even Austria) and in Scandinavia.

'Left-wing' parties tend to have a smaller proportion of press circulation than of votes and parliamentary representation. This proposition certainly seems true for Europe. The explanation doubtless lies in the connection between high income and educational levels and support for non-left wing parties, and in the major indirect source of press subsidy being big business. One would expect the proposition to be accurate wherever else these conditions obtained. Epstein argues also that the non-left-wing 'western' parties commonly had no mass base; and since their members were likely to be middle class ('many chiefs but few Indians') the parties were both obliged and well equipped to exploit mass media most fully as a means of propaganda. The best European example, he suggests, is West Germany, where the low membership Christian Democrat party was quicker to exploit media campaign techniques in the 1950s than the mass-based Social Democrats: '. . . among the Social Democrats, the tradition of activist membership was less clearly compatible with broad public communication through the mass media. The old self-sufficient party of the working class provided an alternative campaign means through its internal communication network.'[24]

(c) Social bases of support for parties

The basis of support and structure of a party are so closely linked in practice that it can be difficult to maintain the analytic distinction when discussing them. 'Kinds of party membership', for example, might be thought appropriate to the category 'Bases of support': yet the topic is discussed by Blondel under 'Party structure'. Blondel's main concern with 'Bases of support' is in distinguishing 'naturally developing' from 'imposed' parties and in the process of party legitimation.[25] Parties develop naturally when they emerge from a parent group whose goals are already accepted at least by a large section of the polity. The parent groups are likely to have been originally ethnic, religious, tribal/clientèle or, in industrial societies only, class-based. Legitimation is achieved when the supporter transfers his allegiance from the parent group to the party itself; as, for instance, when immigrants transferred allegiance from their ethnic group to the Democratic Party in the United States. Parties develop by 'imposition' when a parent group already possesses the coercive power to use the party as an instrument for securing new goals not already dominant in the polity, as, for instance, in many modernising régimes of Africa or in Eastern Europe after 1945. 'Imposed' parties may gain popular legitimacy in due course.

These definitions suggest the following propositions about press/ party association.

In naturally developing party systems, politicians tend to be the clients of newspapers. The supposition is that newspapers aid the transfer of allegiance from parent group to party and reflect the broadening of group appeal implicit in the party's launching. Clearly there are many 'naturally based' parties throughout the world which are closely linked to newspapers; but the point here is that, compared with 'imposed' parties, fewer of them are able to 'command' their papers, particularly when the transfer of legitimacy is complete. In the United Kingdom the transfer was complete for the Conservative Party before 1914, and we have seen the resentment among Conservative politicians at the independence of opinion exercised by conservative proprietors like Northcliffe and Rothermere. For the Labour Party the transfer was not complete until perhaps as late as 1945; whereafter the party's command of its own newspaper, the *Daily Herald*, let alone independent radical papers, gradually lapsed. United States newspapers provide another example. The absence of nationally organised mass parties obliges American presidential candidates to campaign through mass media. But while broadcasting coverage apart from news bulletins can simply (and expensively) be bought, newspaper support is a gift held firmly in the clutch of the newspapers themselves (though presumably it may be subject to purchase of another kind).

In imposed party systems newspapers tend to be the clients of politicians. Enough has been said in previous sections to indicate the association between 'imposition', one-party systems and an ideology of change on the one hand, and close press parallelism on the other. The role of the press in the 'imposition' of the party in Soviet Russia and Nazi Germany, which has already been referred to, is a good example.

The comparison drawn by Brzezinski and Huntington in their *Political power USA/USSR*, confirms the analysis here.[26] They suggest that while mass media funnel political pressure upwards in the USA (quoting Kennedy's awareness of Negro problems as an example), the reverse process predominates in the USSR. These contrasting roles neatly fit the present distinction between naturally developing and imposed parties.

In systems of more than one party potentially 'imposed' parties sometimes exist, normally characterised as extreme right or left because of their support for different goals from those currently dominant. These parties commonly control a paper (e.g. the French and Austrian Communist parties); and it is arguable that the more they come to resemble a naturally developing party, as might be said of the French and Italian Communists, the less important is their paper as an instrument. *L'Humanité*, for instance, declined greatly in the 1960s.

Populist parties have many of the characteristics of imposed parties without always being minorities or extremist in their systems; and they too are normally paralleled by newspapers. These parties typically appeal to the urban proletariat in non-industrialised countries where a class basis for a party does not exist but the tribal or ethnic base has been eroded. They generally have radical goals (but middle-of-the-road policies if they are in government).[27] The party is often united by a charismatic leader (Nkrumah, Nasser, Kenyatta, Lee Kuan Yew) and by coercive force if the party controls the régime. The role of the press as a mouthpiece for the party could clearly be substantial (e.g. *Al Ahram* under Nasser).

Press/party parallelism on the dimensions of organisation and goals tends to be more common in imposed than in naturally developing parties. This hypothesis follows from the same circumstances as the previous one and can be illustrated by the same examples. The dimension of reader support is more conjectural. While the role of the newspaper under an imposed party seems likely to attract readers who support it, there seems no reason to suppose reader loyalty to a naturally developed party need be any less.

(d) Party structure

The three aspects of party structure on which Blondel concentrates are internal structure, external relationships and leadership patterns.[28]

To a limited extent these give rise to simple generalisations about press/party parallelism.

Blondel's discussion of internal structure is concentrated on the two spectra centralisation/decentralisation and representative/unrepresentative organs. He suggests, among other things, that authoritarian parties (excepting 'traditional conservative' ones) are more centralised than liberal democratic parties; and that the more 'programmatic' a party is, the more it tends to be centralised. On the second spectrum, he claims that internal democracy increases the articulation of supporters' opinions: it is thus avoided by 'programmatic' parties (apart from the special case of disciplined democratic centralism in radical authoritarian parties). On these suggestions we can base two generalisations.

Party/press parallelism on the dimensions of press organisation and goal loyalty will be higher in centralised than in decentralised parties. Once again the 'programmatic', authoritarian socialist or communist parties provide the obvious illustrations; though the Vatican's catholic *Osservatore Romano* is an exception to prove the rule. Once again too the potentialities of the newspaper as a focus or even substitute for party organisation can be stressed.

Internal party democracy is associated with low press parallelism on the dimension of goal loyalty. On the dimension of newspaper organisation there seems no reason to expect the same association. But where internal party debate is open and robust one may expect a parallel paper not simply to reflect it but also to take sides or dissent altogether (e.g. the Labour press in Britian in the 1960s and many European Centrist papers like, say, the *Corriere della sera* in Italy).

On the external aspects of party structure, Blondel argues that formal party membership is not a helpful measure of comparison: it is the *directness* of support that matters. Most direct support is commonly found in class-based parties, since intermediary groups are too 'abstract' to retain individual support. These tend also to be mass parties. In 'imposed' parties (as previously defined) there is an active attempt to consolidate mass support through education, propaganda, etc. In this particular analysis the usefulness of distinguishing 'social basis' from 'party structure' vanishes, and the obvious role of party in these situations has been suggested in the previous section.

Two aspects of leadership patterns may be picked out. They concern the imposed or legitimate nature of a party. Imposed parties, Blondel argues, 'need' charismatic or popular leadership more than legitimate mass parties: 'the more a party is of a legitimate mass character, the less are leaders needed to buttress it'.[29] Hence we may infer:

The more a party relies on charismatic leadership, the more likely will a newspaper parallel it. If these parties are normally imposed, the parallelism will probably exist on the dimensions both of organisation and goal-loyalty. The stress will be on transmitting goals down through the party. Thus in Nkrumah's Ghana the press was ascribed an educative role: each major area of the CPP (e.g. the Labour movement) had its own paper and editors were among the most ideologically 'advanced' party members.[30]

(e) Functions and weight of party in the political system

The word 'function' is used here in the sense common to most of the literature on parties; meaning, in effect, 'productive of consequences'.* 'Weight' is distinguished from it by reference to other structures performing the same functions. Parties might perform the *function* of recruiting political leaders but their *weight* in that function might be slight compared with, say, trade unions or the army. Blondel's section on parties concentrates mainly on 'weight' and the conditions governing it, such as a party's degree of independence from its 'parent body' (in a naturally developing system), or the extent to which it has displaced the existing social structure (in an 'imposed' system). For a catalogue of party functions appropriate to the general scale of this discussion it is convenient to turn to Anthony King's survey of the functional concepts conventionally associated with party in the academic literature.†

He lists six:

'Structuring' the vote; Integration and mobilisation of the mass public; Recruitment of political leaders; Organisation of government; Formation of public policy; Aggregation of interests.

In the previous chapter it was suggested that the performance of such functions is consistent with the capacities of newspapers; and the basic hypothesis of this section must be as follows:

The greater the 'weight' of party in the political system, the greater is the probability of press/party parallelism. If some other group than

---

* 'The word "function" is frequently employed . . . to designate a more or less inclusive set of consequences that a given thing or activity has either for "the system as a whole" to which the thing or activity supposedly belongs, or for various other things belonging to the system.' Ernest Nagel, *The structure of science* (1961), p. 525. Quoted in Anthony King, 'Political parties in western democracies', *Polity*, Vol. II, No. 2, Winter 1969, p. 119. King continues: 'Thus, the phrase "parties perform the leadership recruitment function" can be translated to read "the activities of parties have as one of their consequences (intended or unintended) the recruitment of leaders"'.

† loc. cit. King confines his discussion to 'western democracies', but it seems to the present writer that his catalogue of functions will contain parties in other systems as well. The catalogue is at p. 120.

party is performing the functions listed above, the press will tend, in consequence of its character as a medium of communication, to parallel that group.

The nature of this hypothesis effectively excludes further, more detailed hypotheses. For these would have to be about the circumstances in which parties have more or less weight and not about the press at all. We would be drawn into a much more complex and wide-ranging analysis of parties than the aims of this chapter justify. What can be said is that the 'weight' of party might be plotted along a spectrum. At one end, party would have a monopoly of the functions listed above. Closest to this situation are the 'imposed' radical authoritarian party systems, where the monopoly is held not just by party as opposed to other political groups, but by a single party. Thus we have constantly found in this analysis that the closest links between newspapers and parties (excepting the dimension of reader support that is difficult to measure) exist in such systems – in the USSR, China, Eastern Europe, Cuba and some developing countries like Tanzania. At the opposite end of the spectrum would come systems in which party is excluded altogether from the performance of the listed functions. In these 'no-party' systems, we saw earlier, the press does indeed tend to parallel the alternative groups that perform some, and perhaps all, of those functions.

It may be worth stressing that the position of party systems in between those extremes is not necessarily related to the number of parties. For example some two-party systems have great weight, as in Britain, where party has an important role in all the functions (except possibly the formation of public policy): others have little, like the parties in the USA, whose main weight is in structuring the vote and integrating/mobilising the mass public. Similarly Scandinavian parties have great weight (and parallelism) but are in multi-party systems. Finally one may also add that the performance of these six functions at all is an activity that might vary between political systems; and to the extent that they are absent the potential political role of newspapers will be changed if not reduced.

III. CONCLUSION

It was stated at the outset that this analysis would not seek to answer the question whether or how far given parties or party systems are the product of newspaper activity. Newspapers appear to be instrumental to parties in different ways in different systems and at different stages of a party's development. Even if we could be certain that answers to the question lay in the characteristics of newspapers or parties themselves, discovering them would require an elaborate research programme. Without such a programme, however, it can still be argued, on the basis of the present inquiry alone, that the failure of political scientists to take account of the press has been a major omission from the study of parties. It is all the more surprising since such studies have been one of the cores of the whole discipline. This conclusion is reinforced by the fact that the question of cause and effect by no means exhausts the subject. Another important aspect is the question what functions press/party parallelism may perform *in* the political system. Does it, for example, increase the 'weight' of party? This and other important questions have not even been touched on here but deserve further examination.

8

Mass media and British general elections, 1945-70

Studies of the part played by mass media in British general elections are mainly of two types. One, following an established tradition of north American research, concentrates on the effects of media upon individuals' political attitudes. The other, typified in the studies sponsored by Nuffield College, has provided snapshots of succeeding elections since 1945; treating the media largely as end-products and describing their pictures of the campaigns. What has been missing are studies with a broader perspective than the former and elements of comparison and historical depth naturally absent from the latter. Considering the obvious and intricate interplay at elections between the behaviour of politicians and the media, it is surprising that none has been attempted. This chapter suggests some of the lines of analysis that a deeper study might explore. The focus is upon the general question, 'What difference do mass media make to British elections?' The analysis is limited to the years 1945–70, a period throughout which electoral politics fitted the simple model of two-party competition unusually closely, yet while the balance of mass media was rudely tipped by the bulbous growth of television. The Nuffield studies, despite a number of natural shifts and developments in approach since they started, provide – as they were intended to – a valuable core of material.*

I. TYPES OF DIFFERENCE

(a) Difference in the result

The immediate (though not the only) purpose of elections is to

* The Nuffield studies, referred to in the references simply by the date of each election, are: R. B. McCallum and A. Readman, *The British General Election of 1945* (1947); H. G. Nicholas, *The British General Election of 1950* (1951); D. E. Butler, *The British General Election of 1951* (1952); D. E. Butler, *The British General Election of 1955* (1955); D. E. Butler and R. Rose, *The British General Election of 1959* (1960); D. E. Butler and Anthony King, *The British General Election of 1964* (1965); D. E. Butler and Anthony King, *The British General Election of 1966* (1966); D. E. Butler and Michael Pinto-Duschinsky, *The British General Election of 1970* (1971).

make a choice. The question whether that choice was affected by mass media is therefore of primary interest. It is natural that a research tradition grew around it. 'How and how far do mass media change votes?' is a much studied problem. The findings cannot be properly surveyed here, but their gist has consistently been that while in the long run mass media might help to shape an individual's attitudes so that he was disposed to vote a certain way, over short periods like an election campaign his opinion was more likely to be confirmed than reversed – and certainly could not be consciously manipulated. Teeming shoals of votes do not lie ready to be trawled by press magnates.

It would be a mistake, however, to jump from there to the conclusion that election results could not be altered by the behaviour of mass media during the campaign at all. Elections are won and lost by margins no bigger than a jar of minnows. To change even a few votes might be sufficient to tip the result, specially if they happened to be distributed unevenly between the parties or concentrated in marginal seats. Confirming votes, moreover, could be as important as changing them: it might make the difference between voting and abstention, and elections could be decided by margins small enough to make differential rates of turnout significant. The Labour party worries chronically that its supporters will stay at home: in two elections running the *Daily Mirror* carried a front-page polling day message – 'To Hell With the Telly Until We've All Voted' (1959) and 'Let's ALL Vote To-Day' (1964).

We must beware of generalising, then, from the relative failure of mass media at changing the opinions of individual voters to a belief that they could never change the result of an election as a whole.

(b) Difference in the salience of elections

A second way in which media could affect elections, even if they did not alter votes, is in influencing people's opinions about whether elections (in general or particular) are important and what they are for. In their surveys of the electorate in the mid-1960s Butler and Stokes found that 60 per cent of their sample had a partial or well developed understanding of popular control through a competitive party and election system and that nearly three-quarters had a substantial belief that elections make the government pay attention to what the people think.[1] A belief that the parties should alternate in office was well established – though naturally it was more strongly held by those supporting the party out of office.[2] The onset of an election made an enormous difference to people's knowledge of their M.P. In the summer of 1963 only 51 per cent of the sample could name him: even among supporters of his own party the proportion was not much higher. But when interviewed a few weeks after polling day in 1964, between 80 per cent and 95 per cent knew who their candidates had been.[3] The surveys also confirmed that voting in a general election was the only form of political activity undertaken by most people.[4]

This kind of data, plus simple facts like the contrast between the higher turnout in general than in local government elections, leaves no doubt that the electorate see general elections as important political events with far more than ritual significance. It is reasonable to suppose the mass media sustain – and help succeeding generations to create – these beliefs. For the three weeks or so of the campaign, elections displace other news, specially in the leader columns and the headlines. (Only occasionally in 1945–70 was the displacement low: in 1945 preoccupation with international relations at the end of the war overshadowed much of the campaign; and 1955 was an unexciting campaign in which papers made the election their lead story on average only four times in three weeks.)[5] Butler and Stokes comment: 'The fact that 92 per cent of our sample claimed to have followed the campaign [in 1964] is an impressive tribute to the pervasiveness of the mass media and the political socialisation of the mass British public.'[6]

To the extent that the media contributed to the sort of attitudes described above, we can summarise their functions in 1945–70 in two parts. Firstly they helped to *legitimate* both the role of elections in the political system and, by extension, the institutions of Parliament and the Executive that were linked to elections.* Secondly, they helped to *integrate* and *homogenise* the British political culture – making the election seem to about broadly the same issues and personalities at one end of the country and the other.

(c) *Differences in the course of the campaign*

A third form of possible media influence is on the election campaign itself. 'The election campaign' is an elusive concept. Butler and Stokes mention four different types. There is the 'campaign' of ordinary voters, who do nothing much at all beyond informal discussion with family and friends. There are the campaigns of the local party workers – canvassing, distributing literature – and of the individual candidates – holding public meetings, shaking hands and

* cf. A. H. Birch, Peter Campbell and P. G. Lucas (1956), p. 306: 'The particular effects that the papers may have on voting behaviour in any one election are far less important than the ways in which, through their presentation of the election, they may form their readers' attitudes to the political system.

making their presence generally felt. Then there is the national campaign of the party leaders, 'waged through election broadcasts, press conferences and platform speeches'.[7]

The mass media contribute to all those campaigns in two ways. Firstly they provide information to each type of campaigner about the progress of the other three. If 'the' campaign is considered as an amalgam of all four, then the nearest we could come to recognising it is in the artificial pattern stamped on it in the columns of the press. This information could be used, secondly, as ammunition by the different campaigners to back up their own cause and attack that of other parties.

But the value of this contribution is not the same to each level. It is useful to three but indispensable to the fourth, the national campaign. The major theme of this chapter is the contention that one cannot talk sensibly of a national campaign at all in the absence of mass media. There could still be national leaders, voicing national issues – but in local campaigns. 'It is a wry comment on electioneering and on the national press', the 1959 Nuffield study remarks of the highly publicised daily press conference at Labour's headquarters in the campaign that year, 'that parties with a membership of millions could do so much to create an appearance of nationwide activity simply by using the wits and industry of half-a-dozen people for a few hours each morning.'[8] The national campaign is formed by a continuous interaction between the behaviour of party leaders and managers and that of mass media. Three elements in it can be picked out. Firstly, some activities would not take place at all but for the existence of the media: party leaders' TV appearances and the head-quarters press conferences are the obvious examples. Secondly, other activities would take place differently in the absence of media: the style and timing of hustings speeches are an example. Thirdly, certain activities would continue much the same – leaders' electioneering in their own constituencies, perhaps – but without being reported to a national audience. In the United States the contention can be made even more strongly. Regional economic and social differences, the federal system and the local basis of much mass media all meant that a national campaign for the Presidency existed only on a very limited scale until the development of nationwide network TV and jet air travel gave it a completely new intensity. It is upon this interaction of leaders and media in the national campaign that the bulk of this chapter will concentrate.

II. Mass media and the national campaign

The approach of British media to general elections up to 1970 had several strong characteristics. There was a long tradition of partisanship in the press, somewhat modified in the 1960s; and a rule of non-partisanship in broadcasting, taken at first to Trappist lengths but complicated after 1959 by involvement in campaign reporting and analysis. The media took a predominantly national view of elections. They disliked 'quiet' campaigns. They liked clear-cut issues that plainly differentiated the parties. They were obsessed with forecasting results.

In discussing their effect on the national campaign those characteristics can be put in three groups. We can consider the effect of each in turn on such matters as the style of party leaders' electioneering, the relationship between leaders and the constituencies, the emergence and definition of issues, the balance of issues and personalities, the accuracy with which a party's intended image was projected, the coincidence between its general strategy and the picture of the election in the media, and so on. By far the most important development between 1945 and 1970 was the growth of election broadcasting, so this will be considered first.

(a) The growth of election broadcasting

This had three aspects: the rise of television and decline of radio; the break-up of the parties' monopoly; and the expansion of the broadcasting organisations' own programmes.

The rise of television and the decline of radio. Radio broadcasts by party spokesmen, talking straight to the microphone, were an important feature of the 1945 campaign. They took place nightly after the 9 o'clock news, except on Sundays and the last few evenings before polling day, and they lasted from 20 to 30 minutes.* The audience was steady, regardless of party, and averaged 44·9 per cent of the adult population. The Nuffield study considered they provided a complete answer to the question why attendance at public meetings was small and the campaign so quiet. Churchill's broadcast opening the series and Attlee's reply next evening were 'pivotal events' that set the tone of the whole election. Churchill launched his notorious 'Gestapo' charge that a socialist system could not be

* Labour's 10 broadcasts were each delivered by a separate speaker. The Conservatives gave 4 of their 10 to Churchill, Liberals had 4 and Communists and Commonwealth qualified for one each of 10 minutes by having more than 20 candidates).

established without a political police. Attlee replied 'that the voice we heard last night was that of Mr Churchill but the mind was that of Lord Beaverbrook'.[9]

These exchanges were critical, for they enabled voters from the start to dissociate Churchill as war leader, whom they could respect, from Churchill as party leader, whom they could vote against.

In 1950 television had started but none of the parties had any desire to use it. The first party television broadcasts came next year, when the audience was already three times bigger than the year before – though the broadcasts reached well under 10 per cent of the adult population. Each party had one 15-minute programme (see Table 8.1). Conservatives and Liberals used theirs for straight-to-the-camera talks by the leader. Labour, in a 'tour-de-force of television tactics'[10] put on an act by Christopher Mayhew (an experienced performer) and Hartley Shawcross, complete with cost-of-living graphs.

The growth of TV was very rapid thereafter. Audiences for programmes on the two media cannot be precisely compared between different elections since they were affected by differences in the time of broadcasting and the time of year, but Table 8.2, giving the percentage of households with TV sets, shows how rapidly the medium overhauled radio. By the 1966 campaign the Nuffield study could note that 'the "good enough for radio" spirit seemed to creep in at times' to the parties' radio broadcasts. In 1970 they reached an average audience on Radio 4 of 450,000, while the least popular TV broadcast reached 8·5 million. Butler and Stokes found that by 1964 television was well ahead of any other medium as the main source of campaign information. Sixty-five per cent of their sample named it as the most important medium: only 7 per cent named radio. The 'break-even' election seems to have been 1955. Compared with 1951 the average audience for each radio broadcast was barely a third. Television audiences, in contrast, practically doubled. The major parties had three TV broadcasts each this time and the audiences were almost the same size as for radio. The broadcasts were more imaginative in range than in 1951, using films, shopping-basket type props, discussions, interviews and question periods from journalists and 'ordinary people'. Even so, the verdict of the press was one of disappointment that they produced nothing that was 'startlingly new'.

In succeeding elections the parties chopped and changed between trying to achieve a professional effect, with the aid of advisers and elaborate preparations, and, on the other hand, resorting to extemporisation and straight talks. In retrospect both types occasion-

TABLE 8.1

PARTY ELECTION BROADCASTS, 1945–70

Election	Party	Number	Radio Total length (mins.)	Number	Television Total length (mins.)
1945	Con.	10	c.250*	—	—
	Lab.	10	c.250*	—	—
	Lib.	4	c.100*	—	—
	Comm.	1	10	—	—
	Common Wealth	1	10	—	—
1950	Con.	5	120	—	—
	Lab.	5	120	—	—
	Lib.	3	40	—	—
	Comm.	1	10	—	—
1951	Con.	5	120	1§	15
	Lab.	5	120	1§	15
	Lib.	3	40	1§	15
1955	Con.	4	80	3	60
	Lab.	4	80	3	60
	Lib.	1	20	1	15
1959	Con.	8	80	5	95
	Lab.	8	80	5	95
	Lib.	2	20	2	25
1964	Con.	7	55	5	75
	Lab.	7	55	5	75
	Lib.	4	30	3	45
1966	Con.	7	55	5	75
	Lab.	7	55	5	75
	Lib.	4	30	3	45
	Scot. Nat.†	1	5	1	5
	Welsh Nat.‡	1	5	1	5
1970	Con.	7	55	5	50
	Lab.	7	55	5	50
	Lib.	4	30	3	30
	Comm.	1	5	1	5
	Scot. Nat.†	1	5	1	5
	Welsh Nat.‡	1	5	1	5

* Described as 'ten speeches of between twenty and thirty minutes'.

† Shown in Scotland only.

‡ Shown in Wales only.

§ Sound broadcasts were repeated on the sound wavelength of the television service after the end of the day's television programmes, in addition to each party's 15-minute vision-and-sound broadcast.

SOURCE: *BBC Handbook*, Nuffield College election studies.

TABLE 8.2

PERCENTAGE OF BRITISH HOUSEHOLDS WITH TELEVISION

Year	Per cent
1950	10
1955	40
1959	75
1964	88
1966	90
1970	95

SOURCES: 1950–66, Butler and Stokes, *Political change in Britain*; 1970, derived from *Whitaker's Almanack* and *Britain 1972* (HMSO).

ally seemed ridiculous.* But they were honest attempts to come to terms with a developing medium. They mark a contrast with the generally slow, cautious reactions at earlier elections.

Break-up of the parties' monopoly. 1955 was billed in advance as 'the first TV election' but 1959 qualifies more aptly for the name. In that year the first breach was made in the parties' monopoly. Until then, elections were completely ignored in news bulletins, and programmes that might have the faintest bearing on the party balance were cancelled. The parties' own broadcasts were arranged under a system agreed in 1939 by a committee representing the three main parties and the broadcasting organisations. Other parties broadcast only on its terms. There were two main sources of inhibition on other programmes. From earliest days the BBC had a rule against expressing its own opinion on current affairs, and the same restriction for commercial television was written into the Television Act 1954. Secondly there was the Representation of the People Act 1949. Section 63 stated that only a candidate's duly authorised agent could spend money with a view to promoting his election. The press was explicitly excluded from this prohibition, but not broadcasting. There was a danger, therefore, that a candidate might be charged for the costs of a broadcast presenting him; and that a rival candidate might prosecute the BBC for contravening the Act. The Television Act 1954 placed a further restriction on ITV.

---

* In 1959 Labour beamed its programmes from the 'Labour Television and Radio Operations room', which was actually the studio set for a BBC current affairs programme and prompted a Liberal jibe at 'All those bright, young, Public School Labour boys, directing non-existent operations from a non-existent operations room'. (1959 pp. 84, 90). In 1966 the Irish Prime Minister let slip that Mr Wilson had confided in him that a political leader should try to look like a family doctor on television – 'the kind of man who inspires trust by his appearance as well as by his soothing words and whose advice is welcomed'. (Quoted 1966, p. 136).

All political broadcasts (apart from the parties') had to be properly balanced discussions or debates. This seemed to mean candidates could not be recorded at public meetings or state their views in a programme other than in debate.

As TV became widespread these restrictions began to be keenly felt, not least among politicians. In March 1958 Granada took the plunge of reporting the progress of a by-election at Rochdale. The heavens did not fall; and 'soon it became normal practice to report by-elections on the air, as well as to broadcast debates between the candidates, provided all of them agreed to appear'.[11] At a routine meeting of the Broadcasting Committee early in 1959 it was agreed that similar treatment would be given to the next general election. The principle of balance remained and party spokesmen avoided mention of their constituencies in non-constituency programmes. Within these limits the 1959 election was reported fully on BBC and ITV news and in a number of special election programmes. The parties also did their own broadcasts, as in 1955: indeed the number was nearly doubled.

Expansion of the broadcasting organisations' programmes. The elections after 1959 saw a gradual expansion in the range and discretion of the broadcasting organisations' programmes and a cutback in the parties'. In 1959 the BBC's main effort was two 40-minute 'Hustings' programmes, on TV and radio, in each of its six regions (excluding Ulster). These had neutral chairmen, and spokesmen from each of the three main parties answered questions from audiences made up mainly of party nominees. There was no attempt to take up election themes in the normal current affairs programmes like the daily *Tonight* or weekly *Panorama*. The most enterprising programme was Granada's *Election Marathon*, which aimed to give every candidate in the Granada area the chance to speak for a minute each and then have a minute's reply to the other side. Of 348 possible candidates 294 agreed to appear, but 63 of these had to stand down because their rivals had not agreed as well. Apart from this, the commercial companies' programmes were variations on the BBC *Hustings* format. In news coverage the problem of balance proved less difficult than the broadcasters expected. After the election it was found that the BBC had given 1,875 lines of bulletin space to Conservatives, 1,850 to Labour and 507 to Liberals.[12] But until late in the campaign neither organisation risked filming candidates in their constituencies with sound cameras. The ITA prohibited any presentation of voters declaring how they would vote. Shortage of equipment limited the number of politicians whose speeches could be covered each day. Those and other problems hampered the effectiveness of broadcasting coverage.

The 1964 campaign produced 'lighter, livelier and more assured' news coverage: the core on both channels was 'sound film of the morning press conferences and the travels of the party leaders, supplemented by points from other speeches, sometimes on sound film, more often read by a news reader'.[13] The two big innovations were BBC's *Election Forum* and an expansion of campaign analysis. On *Election Forum* the three party leaders answered questions sent in from the public (18,000 were received). Each had a half-hour programme to himself and got through from 21 to 28 questions. They attracted audiences from 5 to 8 million and were 'a significant political event'.[14] The campaign analyses were conducted on regular current affairs programmes which had previously dodged the election. BBC's *Gallery* interviewed party leaders, conducted regional surveys and had comments on the polls and discussions of various campaign issues. ITV's *This Week* pursued the same sort of course. Between them they brought for the first time to broadcasting the equivalent of much that had been the staple of press coverage for years. But the law retained its cramping effects on broadcasters' freedom of action, though in the face of increasing controversy. In 1966, however, the rules were significantly less restrictive. Party control over spokesmen, which in 1964 had enabled the parties to squash programmes they disliked, was now in practice 'vestigial',[15] though the parties' ban on live audiences, imposed after some rowdy heckling in 1959, was still maintained and again in 1970. 'Balance' was interpreted to cover a series of programmes not each individual programme – which released the broadcasters from problems about Liberal participation. Above all, the Representation of the People Act had been tried in the courts by the Communist opponent of Sir Alec Douglas-Home in 1964. The challenge to unseat him because of broadcast appearances failed. Broadcasters took new confidence in inviting candidates on to programmes – so long as they were recognised frontbench spokesmen – and in sound-filming candidates in the constituencies. The result was a number of mini-confrontations between party leaders, though none between the two main leaders themselves. In this election the parties again resisted pressure to cut down their own programmes, though they agreed to a reduction in the time. The pattern of news and discussion programmes began to have a familiar look. That feeling was confirmed in 1970, with *Election Forum* appearing for the third time running and the current affairs programmes like *Panorama* going through their routines of discussion and analysis. A new Representation of the People Act in 1969 had formalised the situation following the challenge to the old Act. It also included a clause enabling candidates not appearing in a programme to consent to it going on without them. The parties kept the same number of broadcasts but reduced them to 10 minutes in length. For the time being, broadcasting had evidently developed to its limit. The Nuffield study comments: 'After three elections with a steady increase in discussion between the parties, 1970 brought a clear decline.'[16]

Some of the implications of the 25 years of growth will have emerged in that summary. They can now be considered systematically.

Perhaps the most significant results followed from the development of the broadcaster's own programmes. So long as the parties had a monopoly their intentions were by definition reflected in what was broadcast (even if, as sometimes happened, the programmes were not very well coordinated with the rest of their strategy). The only distortions were those inherent in the medium itself, like the difficulty of putting across complex ideas on TV. With the broadcast media opened up (particularly television), this situation changed. The new danger was not crude partisanship. As we have seen, the organisations kept a balance wobbled by only the most microscopic inequalities. Their very success highlights the irrelevance of the activity. When it was applied to units of time, distributed like pounds of meat for the parties to cook and garnish how they liked, it made sense. Applied to programmes over which the parties had no direct control, it did not. Broadcasters might innocently serve the Conservatives grilled chops to find the party preferred them fried. In 1964 Quintin Hogg received a large share of Conservative news time. Some of his remarks embarrassed his own party more than Labour. 'Television journalists', John Whale (himself one of them) comments, 'asked one another in some perplexity: "Whose time does Hogg come out of?"'.[17] How much more might the same question be asked about the idiosyncratic electioneering of Enoch Powell in 1970 (see Chapter 4). It was this kind of problem that now worried the parties. Once the broadcasters began to exercise *their own* judgement about programme content, in other words, a purely stopwatch approach to non-partisanship was inadequate. The first important effect of broadcasters' independence, then, was that *it allowed a projection of party activities that might run entirely counter to what the parties wanted*, without any conscious bias but in a way that was impossible when party broadcasts held a monopoly. If a party's strategy did find its reflection in the news and current affairs programmes, it would be the result simply of coincidence.

It was this situation which explained the parties' concern that in the elections of the 1960s and 1970 'television's campaign was substituted for the "real" campaign'. The main argument of this chapter, as has already been stated, is that there was no such thing as the 'real' campaign. What the parties' anxiety amounted to, therefore, was that *television had come to define and shape the national campaign to a much greater extent than when it had no programmes of its own*, and in a manner formerly limited to the press.

There was an added problem, however: the broadcasters' non-partisanship was now almost a drawback. With the press, at least the parties knew that certain papers were applying criteria of campaign coverage positively sympathetic to them: what values might the broadcasters be applying? The best documented study of this question is Jay Blumler's participant-observation analysis of BBC-TV's *Campaign Report*, 13 editions of which were broadcast in the 1966 election.[18] Blumler found that producers were keen to push back the rules constricting election coverage; to promote studio confrontations between party spokesmen and, if possible, between the leaders themselves, to ensure that the Liberals did not get more time than they 'deserved'; and to prevent the parties vetoing issues they wished to cover. Two issues in particular about which the parties were lukewarm were forced to the front – Trade Unions (following sanctions against Union members for refusing to join an unofficial strike) and the Common Market. After screening a discussion on the latter, one producer explained that 'What we've achieved today is to smoke them out – to get them to participate in the programme on an issue they were unwilling to see dealt with . . .'[19] On the general approach to coverage there were two views. Some producers saw the programme as providing a service and believed the election was intrinsically important. Others argued that the election must fight its way into the programme (*Campaign Report* was contained in the general current affairs programme *24 Hours*, by ordinary news criteria, as in newspaper coverage. The latter principle had been stated officially as the BBC's approach to its first election coverage in 1959;[20] but in Blumler's view the former triumphed in *Campaign Report*. A comparison with ITV's equivalent programme showed that *Campaign Report* contained far less hard news extracts from politicians' speeches and reporters' comments – and far more magaziny items like interviews and poll analyses. There were no less than 22 'confrontations'.

In 1966 such a programme happened to coincide very little with Labour's strategy, which was for a low-key campaign based largely on the themes of 1964. The programme became a catalyst for Labour resentment with the BBC's treatment of politics. This had been working up since 1964. 'With its inferiority in solid press support Labour had come to count heavily on broadcasting to reach the voters. The trend away from straight reporting of political events towards a mixture of news, analysis and discussion stirred mounting disquiet.'[21] With some campaign strategists this evidently led to the extreme view that *any* attempt by broadcasters to go beyond the issues they themselves chose was necessarily prejudicial to them and therefore unfair.[22] These discontents were expressed in something more than symbolic form when Mr Wilson, fresh from the triumph of an increased majority, snubbed the BBC by agreeing to a victory interview only with ITV.

The experience of *Campaign Report* was the best example of the way politicians' and broadcasters' strategies could conflict without any direct party bias. But in smaller ways – or ways that might have less predictable results, like the saturation coverage of Enoch Powell in 1970 – the broadcasters' growing independence after 1959 meant a lack of identity between the strategies was virtually built into the system where previously it had been specifically excluded.

Other consequences of the growth of broadcasting perhaps had less directly partisan possibilities. There is no doubt that *the style of electioneering changed*. Already in 1945 the Nuffield study was speculating that the parties' radio broadcasts had 'revolutionised the nature of British elections'.[23] Television can hardly have done less. The changes were on every scale. Heath commented in 1966 that TV coverage made his jokes stale more quickly. Wilson discovered in 1964 that to make repartee with hecklers effective on television he had to repeat a heckler's comment himself before delivering his punchline; and several times he inserted prepared sections into a speech by arrangement with the broadcasters, in order to provide a live item for national news bulletins. Sir Alec Douglas-Home found the same year that though a speech could be made inaudible in a hall by interruptions, it could still be perfectly well picked up by the platform microphone for television.

The timing of speeches changed. When broadcast coverage started in 1959 the parties altered their schedules appropriately. Major speeches were sometimes delivered earlier than usual so that film would be ready for the late bulletins. Party headquarters adopted the technique of issuing rapid replies to their opponents' arguments (a habit that helped the broadcasters in their balancing act). By 1970 Heath's whole itinerary was planned 'with scrupulous attention to optimum conditions for filming and the timing of bulletins'.[24] Wilson often spoke too late for the BBC 8.50 p.m. news, but this simply meant that more film was used of the morning 'walkabouts' which were such a feature of his campaign.

Technical factors made a difference too. The shortage of cameras and delays in film processing that restricted coverage in 1959 gradually eased, but in 1964 it still paid a party leader to make his evening speech 'near one of the limited number of towns where film could be fed into the network for the main bulletin, provided he started promptly and included a neatly quotable passage in the first few minutes'.[25] When electronic cameras were used they tended to be left running just so that full value was obtained from the expensive relays they required.[26]*

The venue of speeches changed as well, as the above quotations show. Whistlestop tours that took the party leaders away from headquarters for a week or more vanished by 1966 (not wholly because of TV). George Brown's extended tour in 1970 seemed to be reported with the curiosity of witnesses to some dying rite. The best example, however, was the development of the parties' daily press conferences. These became firmly established, a morning sequence of three, each within easy walking distance of the others, on the initiative of Labour in 1959. They were deliberately aimed at feeding the media (the press were chiefly in mind at first) with convenient quotable and topical stories. At 10.30 a.m. the party's four-man campaign committee chose the major story for the day from items picked out of the press as suitable for enlargement. The General Secretary, Morgan Phillips, then faced the newsmen. The formula was enormously successful, simple though it was: the Nuffield study even described it as pioneering a new technique in mass communication and helping to set the tone of the election.[27] It enabled Labour to project the campaign as the party wanted it. It received more than ten times as much publicity in the first week as the Conservatives' less well planned conferences. One Conservative news editor grumbled that Morgan Phillips was so quotable that his paper was beginning to look like a 'Socialist rag'.[28] The Conservatives hurriedly vamped up their own conference (and naturally the Liberals had one too), but Labour continued to make the running. In later elections the design varied – for example in the extent to which the leaders took part (in 1970 Wilson and Heath completely dominated them). But although journalists often reported them sardonically, considering them artificial and empty, they were too convenient to ignore. They provided a unique opportunity for newsmen to question the leaders about the campaign as it developed, and for the leaders to make points to the media away from the hustings.

Some of the tendencies already described contributed to another important general consequence of election broadcasting: *it focussed the campaign increasingly on the party leaders*. This was a prospect the Nuffield study already envisaged in 1945, just as a result of the parties' radio broadcasts.[29] Technical aspects of TV were again significant. In 1966, for example, the commitment of camera teams to follow the three leaders everywhere, in case a major story broke,

* Electronics relay averaged some £1,300 against £300 for film.

still 'dug heavily into the broadcasters' resources', leaving less scope for other people.[30] Broadcasters were naturally more interested anyway in party leaders. With tiny opportunities for coverage compared with the press, they were bound to go for the big names: their near-obsession, ever since the Kennedy–Nixon debates in 1960, with engineering a TV 'confrontation' between party leaders was the logical conclusion of their situation. The party managers, knowing the vastness of TV audiences in the 1960s, were correspondingly anxious to keep a strict control over whom the broadcasters chose as spokesmen – which generally led to these being ministers or shadow ministers. The result was that an astonishingly small – and actually a *decreasing* – number of politicians were quoted in broadcast news coverage. In 1964 only 61 politicians were quoted on national radio or TV during the entire campaign: 14 of Mr Wilson's cabinet of 23 were quoted either once or not at all. In 1966 the total dropped to 56 and in 1970, incredibly, to a mere 44. Nor, of course, was this coverage equally distributed: the three leaders swamped it. Measured in length of time, Wilson and Heath took up 53 per cent of *all* the news coverage of politicians, both in 1966 and 1970.

This very sharp focus on the party leaders also encouraged a *'nationalising' tendency* that grew with election broadcasting. The 1945 Nuffield study thought the essential 'sense of constituency' in elections was threatened. The BBC *Hustings* programmes in 1959 were based on regions – but only 6, compared with over 600 constituencies. The commercial TV companies were generally unenterprising in their regional coverage, with various modest constituency surveys being the typical product. Granada's *Election Marathon*, which became a regular feature, was an exception. But the limitation of candidates to two minutes each just showed in a sense how inappropriate the medium was to a local level. ITV's news organisation had from the start been organised mainly on a national basis, and regional news bulletins, in 1964 at least, had election items only when a national leader came on tour.[31]

The tendency was shown clearly in the treatment of minor parties. The Liberals, because they managed to retain the skeleton of a national party (though the bones were bare here and there), night after night had access and coverage, being included always in the broadcasters' nice calculations of balance. Nationalist parties, on the other hand, were by definition limited to Scotland and Wales and for long were extremely poorly served. Their neglect in national news bulletins and feature programmes was understandable (in constituency items they were all right, since all contenders were on a par), but until 1966 they were not even permitted party broadcasts in their own areas (Table 8.1). In that year and in 1970 they were allotted five minutes each on regional radio and TV if they contested a fifth of their region's seats – as they did.[32] Even then they were not consulted about times, which of course could make a big difference to audience sizes. Nor were they represented on the Broadcasting Committee.

A further effect of television was that *it became itself a subject of election news.* We have seen that Churchill's 'Gestapo' broadcast set the tone for the 1945 campaign. In 1950 again the press took their cues 'to a surprising extent' from the broadcasts.[33] It was only a step from reporting these like hustings speeches to keeping abreast both of the arrangements for broadcasting them and, when the media were 'liberated', of the ins and outs of interviews and discussions. The classic illustration of this was the running battle in the 1960s and 1970 about 'confrontation'. Whether a debate between the party leaders would take place and on what terms (the Liberals' existence complicated the permutations no end) was a matter of discussion in the press in all three elections. The idea originated with the BBC in 1964, but since no party felt it had an enormous amount to gain (except the Liberals) and possibly a lot to lose, and since there was no public pressure and excuses which pinned the blame on other parties were easy to find, no confrontation ever took place.[34] In 1966 it became a major debating point early in the campaign, when ITV interviewers managed to get agreement in principle from each of the leaders. Heath issued repeated challenges, but Wilson insisted Grimond must be included. Heath naturally rejected any 'tea-party' with Grimond as an equal: Grimond refused anything less. These manœuvres were front-page news in the press. By the end of the campaign 'confrontation' and other stories about TV had taken up quite a significant proportion of their election coverage.[35*] This attention was a recognition that TV could go beyond the press as a campaign medium. The press dealt with summaries: TV with excerpts. Party leaders talked *to* the electorate on TV with a directness absent from the press (except in their comparatively rare feature articles). TV was less of an intermediary than the press.

A complaint voiced by politicians in the late 1960s was that *television trivialised politics.*[36] *The Times* repeated the charge during the 1970 election: indeed the paper had complained about it even in 1955.[37] A recurring theme of the Nuffield studies is TV's selectivity. Excerpts on TV from speeches in 1964 were mostly under 90 seconds.[38] Feature programmes could obviously come to grips better with

---

* It ranged from 3 per cent in *The Times* to 7 per cent in the *Sketch*. The figures are small; but in comparison with, say, the 8 per cent that the *Sketch* gave to constituency reports and polls and the 3 per cent which *The Times* gave to the speeches, press conferences and manifesto of the Liberal party they do not look insignificant.

subjects. Occasionally as much as 50 minutes – a whole edition of *Panorama* – was given to one subject (a decision which the Nuffield study describes, significantly, as showing courage).[39] But compared with press coverage, let alone full-length speeches, even a long programme had to be highly selective.

Nearly all the consequences of television described so far – technical developments, press conferences, the focus on party leaders – worked in one other direction too: they gave *a presidential character* to the national campaign. Parties had frequently been dominated by a single personality – most obviously, in this period, the Conservatives in 1945, who built their whole campaign around Churchill. But arguably the growth of TV meant that a party would now have less choice in the matter. Television dealt in imperatives. Leaders might dodge confrontations but not a challenge to them. If a man seemed 'good on TV', then of course the party should use him. If he was bad then a way must be found of exploiting the medium as well as possible, as the Conservatives tried with Heath in 1966.[40] The commitment of a camera team to follow each leader and the rule of balance meant that however disastrous a leader's speech might be it would still get coverage. The 1966 Nuffield study notes explicitly that TV news 'presented a strikingly "presidentialised" campaign'.[41] The fact of TV tending to be a subject of news in the press merely reinforced the development. One significant sign of its importance was the weight attached by party workers to the leaders' performances. In 1964 Home's *Election Forum* programme (answering questions from viewers and listeners) 'increased the feeling among some campaign planners and the wider public that he was a liability'.[42] In 1966 Heath's poor TV ratings compared with Wilson 'had a discernible impact on morale in the party organisation'.[43] The confrontation ritual had similar elements. Each leader had to strut and preen. He must act Goliath even if he felt like David.

(b) *Mass media values and attitudes*

Some of the points in the previous section might equally come in this one: the sections are not mutually exclusive. This one brings the press back into the analysis, and its object is to examine the implications of certain characteristics of the mass media for the national campaign.

Like broadcasting, the press in 1945–70 had a predominantly national orientation to elections. The heavy papers, reaching a minority audience, could make a fair effort at constituency reporting but the mass circulation dailies could not.* Moreover even in the

---

* In 1970 the two widest read dailies, the *Mirror* and the *Express*, had nought and four constituency reports respectively. The *Telegraph*, *Guardian* and *Times* had 62 (72), 44 (87) and 40 (69) (1966 figures in brackets). *1970* p. 232.

heavy papers page traffic* would normally be concentrated on the news pages – and most obviously the lead story – which were likely to have a national focus. The regional daily press was already a pale shadow of its former self by the 1945 election. In the elections after the First World War the circulation of the regional dailies and evenings was about one-third greater than the national dailies. After the Second World War the nationals were 50 per cent larger than the others and by 1970 twice as big. The number of regional dailies had dropped too, and their character as foci of regional election coverage was lessened by a tendency to adopt a national approach to the main stories themselves. Another important determinant of papers' attitudes was their readership profiles. The heavy papers had mainly middle-class audiences with high terminal education ages: the tabloids had lower-middle and working-class audiences. These differences were critical to their news values and also, indirectly, to their space.

The first attitude to stress, whatever their audiences, is that in general *the media disliked 'quiet' elections*. Producers of *Campaign Report* wanted a certain pair of contributors in 1966 because, among other things, they might stage 'a bloody good row'.[44] 'Quietness' goes against every journalistic canon of good news: it implies familiarity, predictability, insignificance, absence of stress, conflict and excitement – a 'Small Earthquake in Chile – Not Many Hurt' situation. Media want the opposite. The typical images of 1945–70 were the obvious ones of clashes, struggles, fights, battles and races. This in itself, as the 1970 Nuffield study points out, could lead to a fundamental misunderstanding of the nature of elections: '. . . The two sides seldom encounter each other on the field, either in routine constituency electioneering, or in the arguments launched in Smith Square or on the air. Each party tends to campaign on its self-chosen battleground against straw men of its own devising. There is no obligation to answer the challenges of the other side; the general view is that it is a strategic mistake ever to do so . . . In fact, in describing an election the metaphors of fashion shows or beauty contests might be quite as appropriate as those of battle'.[45] In other words, the basic framework within which the media defined the nature of the campaign (including, of course, the use of the word campaign) imposed on the parties a false relationship.† Perhaps for that reason the media seem to have had a golden-age myth about

---

* 'Page traffic' denotes the proportion of respondents in readership surveys who read any given page of a paper.

† Not all elections fitted the Nuffield analysis equally well. In 1945 and 1950, for instance, the radio broadcasts assumed the form of a dialogue between succeeding party spokesmen.

general elections. In all eight of them from 1945 to 1970 there was more or less widespread discontent about the quality of the campaign. Even in 1945 – a ding-dong barney compared with most of the others – *The Times* was expressing its 'weary distaste' before the end.[46]*

It was this dislike of a 'quiet' election that enabled Labour to reap such swathes of publicity with the simple machinery of their daily press conference in 1959. The importance of the eagerness with which media pursued the 'unquiet' is that it presented a problem for a party whose strategy in fact required a quiet campaign. This was a much more common strategy than one might suppose. Indeed the party already in office pursued it more often than not. If the polls showed a healthy lead, it was the obvious course. Thus in 1955 and 1959 the Conservative planners sought to fight the election in a low key. The first time, the behaviour of the media helped them, and the Labour Party's own weaknesses no doubt made it easier. In 1959, however, Labour's aggressiveness – typified in its press conferences – galvanised the media, and the Conservatives found themselves having to step up their campaign in the last week. (They completely restyled their last two TV broadcasts, for instance.[47]†) In 1966 and 1970 it was the turn similarly of Labour to argue that making too much noise would be counter-productive. In 1966 Labour's 'relatively subdued campaign, giving no hostages to fortune, using few gimmicks', contrasted with 'the frenetic activity of 1964'.[48] The behaviour of the media coincided with these aims rather better in 1970 than 1966. By corollary, in 1970 it suited the Conservatives worse: party managers found a much more sluggish response than in 1966 to their daily initiatives in the press conferences and speeches.[49]

'Unquiet' campaigns held special importance for the Liberals. Butler and Stokes have shown that in 1964 and 1966 as many as 34 per cent of Liberal voters made up their minds how to vote after

---

* 1950, for journalists, 'was an election in which they had to go out and seek material rather than desperately endeavour to keep up with a fast moving campaign'. In 1951 there was much comment on 'the great seemliness' of the election. 1955, the press thought, was 'an essentially dull, demure, routine affair'. 1959 was brighter, though *The Times* again lamented the campaign's poor and cynical nature. In 1964 the *Express* grumbled that 'far too much time, far too many words, are being spent on trifling issues'. In 1966 'newspaper men found the election rather tiresome'. By the end of the first week in 1970 complaints of the election's depressing tone and triviality were widespread. *1950*, p. 164; *1951*, p. 97; *1955*, p. 96; *1959*, p. 111; *The Times*, 1 October 1964; *1966*, p. 149. *The Times* is not easily satisfied. 1970 was 'a tawdry business. It drags its slow length through a mass of mediocrity'.; *1970*, p. 231.

† The Conservative counter-attack in the last week 'was not so much a carefully prepared and timed assault as a militant response to a situation that threatened to get out of hand'. *1959*, pp. 68–9.

the campaign began, compared with 8–10 per cent for the other parties. Thus 'to a remarkable extent the Liberal vote is a "pick-up" vote, one that must be constantly renewed'.[50] We can reasonably infer, then, that the Liberals depended extremely heavily on their publicity: they had everything to gain from confrontations (even from talk about confrontations), from the perpetuation of the press conferences and the development of TV reporting.

Dislike of quiet elections is a general quality. It can be divided into two simple features which affected the nature of 'the national campaign' to some degree, whether quiet or not. The first was the familiar *attraction of media to personalities* – to men not measures. 'The vast majority of his audience can never have seen Mr Eden in the flesh', the 1951 Nuffield study remarked wide-eyed of the first-ever Conservative election TV broadcast, 'and this appearance of the Deputy-Leader of the Conservative Party speaking in a pleasant and statesmanlike way must be regarded as compelling electioneering'.[51] The reliance of TV upon pictures and movement obviously biases it towards personalities. In the press, specially the mass circulation papers, the same emphasis rests on deeply held assumptions about readers' interests.

Sometimes the attraction to personalities coincided with party strategy. The best example was probably the Conservatives' concentration on Winston Churchill in 1945. 'Help him finish the Job' was the slogan. His press coverage was overwhelming. In 1970 Labour planners seem to have accepted that Wilson was their strongest electoral asset and to have gone along with his predominance in media coverage (though at the press conference he always had colleagues with him).[52] At other times it might not actually conflict with party strategy, though it meant the people who caught the public eye were not necessarily those who carried most weight outside the campaign: people like Charles Hill in 1951, Morgan Phillips (a party official, almost totally unknown before his press conference triumphs for Labour in 1959), Quintin Hogg in the later 1950s and 1960s, and George Brown in 1970. Also, leaders who were believed to be weak media personalities – notably Home in 1964 and Heath in 1966 – had no alternative but to put on the best show they could.

Most often, however, the stress on personalities distorted party intentions: either the wrong personalities got the coverage, or parties wanted to stress policies and not personalities at all. The two big examples of the former were Aneurin Bevan and Enoch Powell. The Conservatives were bound to hammer away at the Bevanite split in the Labour party in 1951, specially as it appeared to be widening at the party conference held not long before the campaign.[53] Bevan was regarded as 'the most colourful personality in the Labour Party as well as a possible source of indiscreet indications of its disunity', and he was 'assiduously reported'.[54] Charles Hill, in the most famous radio election broadcast of all time, made much of him ('The end is Nye', etc.). Labour tried to damp the issue down by ignoring it, but the damage to the party's intentions is reflected in the fact that eventually Mr Attlee felt obliged to defend the leadership emphatically in his closing election broadcast.

The example of Enoch Powell is discussed at length in the last section of Chapter 4. Certainly his astonishing media coverage, particularly on TV during the four-day national newspaper strike about wages, threatened to blow the Conservative strategy far off course in the last week of the campaign. Other examples were more a matter of emphasis. In 1950 Churchill was again 'as news alone . . . the outstanding figure of the campaign'; yet with the trauma of 1945 behind them the Conservatives were trying hard this time to *avoid* a campaign built exclusively around him.[55]* In 1959 the Conservatives wanted to prevent Mr Macmillan getting disproportionate coverage, being sensitive to charges of their 'cult of personality' and the Supermac image; but they were not really successful.[56]

Media stress on personalities when the parties wanted to stress policies was a matter of modest emphasis as well as more substantial bias. In 1959 the Nuffield study noted that the press 'did not reflect the emphasis of the first Labour TV broadcast upon pensions; even the *Daily Herald* placed its stress on Mr Gaitskell's remarks on foreign policy because what the leader of the party said was automatically regarded as more important than the major point that the programme was designed to make'.[57] That sort of practice was habitual. Again, a programme like *Election Forum*, with the party leaders getting through questions at the rate of one a minute, inevitably 'conveyed more about personalities and political styles than it illuminated policies'.[58] But sometimes a party's *general* strategy was geared very strongly towards projecting a set of policies. As with the question of 'quiet elections', an opposition party more often than not had a strategy of that sort (though in the later years a wider acceptance of the complex nature of the party images in the voters' minds may have encouraged planners to blur the distinction between policies and personalities). Thus in 1959 Labour concentrated with much preparation and care on trying to put across its economic programme. In 1966 the Conservative party managers aimed to fight constructively on the radical ideas they had been formulating in opposition, rather than defend their 13 years of rule and hammer away at Labour. (The latter would have been tempting

---

* Churchill did 4 out of 10 election broadcasts in 1945 but only 1 out of 8 in 1950.

for its popularity among activists in the constituencies.) In 1970 the Conservatives again concentrated on policies, though this time they also had more to attack. In these situations the media's news values were a constant threat to the successful implementation of a party's strategy.

The second feature of mass media which can be linked to the dislike of quiet elections is *a liking for clear-cut issues*. Issues should not be confused with policies. The term was used very loosely by mass media. It amounted to a feeling that elections ought to be about some *thing* and not just about rival *persons*. The feeling was not inconsistent with liking personalities. Media liked both – lively, colourful people having lively, colourful arguments about some thing over which they disagreed and which mattered. It is not unfair to suggest that for the media the ideal election issue in 1945–70 was a subject which could easily reduce to simple terms; which involved principles more than complex facts and ends more than means; which was 'fresh' and not 'stale'; which differentiated the parties with tidy polarity; and which was 'real' (that is, consistent with the media's view of political priorities). The media themselves did not need to discuss them at any length: by their nature, issues could be distilled if necessary into a few drops of pungent prose, in a paper like the *Mirror*. On the evidence of Butler and Stokes, issues were conceived in much the same terms in the electorate at large.[59]

This view of and liking for issues clearly had a variety of effects upon the nature of national campaigns in 1945–70. It was shown, for instance, in the devout attention to the party manifestos. These never bore much relation to subsequent events. They were couched in anodyne prose; and they were sometimes prepared with a haste that may have reflected their true insignificance (specially for a party in power).* But for the press their great virtue was as single authoritative documents defining party policy. They were nearly always printed in full by the heavy papers and discussed prominently by the others. They were normally one of the main items of Liberal publicity.

The status accorded the manifestoes could not positively harm a party's election plans. Other aspects of the concern with issues could. It might contribute greatly to a party's difficulty in fighting a 'quiet' election, for instance, or a 'men not measures' one. Or suppose there were *no* issues plainly differentiating the parties. The 1945 Nuffield study reported that several papers remarked on the fact that people were interested in bread-and-butter issues which hampered heroic orations and old-style campaign thumping. Indeed with obvious exceptions like 'nationalisation', British politics between 1945 and

* The press conference to launch Labour's manifesto in 1970 had to be delayed for half an hour while the final version was rolled off. *1970*, p. 150.

1970 was not characterised by chasm issues; and some of those which did appear – unilateral nuclear disarmament, the EEC, immigration – never yawned before the voters in elections. As with their conception of elections as a battle, so the media generally sought to impose on campaigns their expectations of a dialogue about 'issues'. If there was none (in the sense here meant), they tended to declare the election boring in images of Tweedledum and Tweedledee and to blame the parties for ignoring the 'real' issues.

Allied to this were two other problems. First was the question whether issues can be discussed effectively on television at all – an element of the trivialisation charge. On balance, the 'bloody good row' syndrome attractive to *Campaign Report*'s producers tended to reinforce the media's view of an issue, rather than the approach favoured by, say, Labour in 1959 and Conservatives in 1966 and 1970. The latter, aiming to put across policy initiatives, required a more expository and less dialectic approach.* The second problem was the 'issue-a-day' approach to electioneering. This was characteristic of BBC's television coverage in 1966. It was a habit that obviously might suit parties variously. In 1966 Labour disliked its implied pressure, since they had a 'quiet' strategy. The same practice in 1964, on the other hand, would have suited the Conservatives well, since their own strategy tended towards an issue a day anyway. The other implication of the practice was its effect on attempts to sustain a single issue. The Nuffield study quotes a Conservative in 1966: 'In my view, the people who say that we made a mistake in not pushing Europe harder have got to show how it could have been kept in the headlines. I just don't think it was possible. The press was already getting bored.'[60]

The most extensive effect of the media's concern with issues, however, was probably not on how far an election was about issues of any kind but on the detailed question of *which* issues. Here there were two ways in which the development of a campaign was out of the hands of the party strategists and in those of the reporters from the start. There were the explicit choices of the media about the 'important issues' (often in practice the result of chance phrases like Churchill's 'Gestapo' smear and George Brown's '3 per cent mortgage' claim in 1964;† and there was the less predictable matter of

---

* The difficulty is that which defeated Harold Wilson's attempt to explain devaluation to the uninitiated in 1967, when he used the barnacle phrase about 'the pound in your pocket' being worth the same as before. For the full text and a gloss on the context, see *1970*, p. 5n.

† Brown's suggestion that interest on mortgages might be cut to 3 per cent was one of the big debating points of the campaign. It was originally made to an audience of 18 people. *1964*, pp. 113–14.

connections between the election and independent, spontaneous news stories (e.g. about strikes). The extent of this effect is such that to survey it fully would mean a detailed account of every campaign. Only a few illustrations can be given here: more can be seen in the next section, in the context of press partisanship.

One index of parties' preferred priorities is the content of their own broadcasts. In 1959 Trenaman and McQuail compared these with the contents of other broadcast programmes and the press. Two subjects – nationalisation and industrial relations – figured scarcely at all in the party broadcasts but quite significantly everywhere else; and the theme of 'prosperity' got twice as much attention elsewhere.[61] The Nuffield study did a similar exercise about radio and TV alone in 1966. The EEC received far 'too much' coverage and the social services too little. Neither party in 1966 wanted Europe to be an issue, not least because they were unsure if there were any votes in it. But the media were very keen, and their extensive coverage eventually helped force Wilson to speak out on the issue.[62]

Party leaders also found, in contrast, that speeches they did make attracted little attention. Wilson apparently excused his failure to make constructive policy speeches in 1966 partly because his detailed policy statements in 1964 had poor coverage.[63] In 1970 the Conservative stress on the economic theme was deliberate, but 'it was in part reinforced by the failure of other themes to evoke a response from the press, let alone the public'.[64]

Some news stories that suddenly became important political symbols during a campaign live on in their shorthand names, like the 'Jasper affair' of 1959 and the 'Noose trial' of 1966. The Jasper group of property companies became the subject of a major City scandal early in the 1959 campaign. A QC was appointed to investigate it. It never became a specific party issue, though Labour speakers made pointed remarks about the 'casino mentality of the City of London'. For the media, however, it was first-rate copy; 'the press was far more ready than the parties to point to its electoral implications, while at the same time neglecting the pensions issue, which by general agreement of those in the field, was at that stage in the campaign arousing much more interest among voters'.[65]* The 'Noose trial' in 1966 was the name given to an incident in which eight factory hands in the BMC works at Cowley were 'tried' before several hundred colleagues and fined £3 each for failing to join an unofficial strike. During the trial a noose was dangling in the background. The press seized on this as an excellent story, and it dominated the headlines in the first week of the campaign. Leaders in both parties commented at length on its implications, and some Conservative

* The *Daily Herald* at one point had a headline 'THE JASPER ELECTION'.

papers (chiefly the *Daily Telegraph*) squeezed the last ounce of advantage out of it.[66]

The last of the mass media attitudes to elections that needs attention here was their *obsession with forecasting results*. This used to be a matter of inspired guesswork. Lord Beaverbrook raised a *Daily Express* reporter's salary by £10 a week for predicting the result in 1935 to within 44.[67] *The Times* used to gather forecasts from each constituency and do a big eve-of-poll sum like the football pools. Charting the ebb and flow of a campaign and gauging its effects was a journalistic craft. The development of opinion polls threatened to make it obsolete. Perhaps for that reason the *Express* was reluctant to take its own poll more than semi-seriously until the election of 1970, when it sponsored one of the established organisations. Despite such mixed feeling, the spread of polls between 1945 and 1970 was, after broadcasting, the most noticeable innovation in media coverage. There were more of them, including in provincial papers; and succeeding Nuffield studies comment on the increasing attention they received. In 1945 the *News Chronicle* alone published polls (and not all of them were national forecasts). They proved reasonably accurate, and in 1950 the *Chronicle* featured them more prominently, making their neck-and-neck forecast the headline story on the eve-of-poll.

The big development did not come until 1959. Four of the nine national dailies then ran polls at least weekly, each on a different day. They were dignified by one of the new sponsors being a heavy newspaper, the *Daily Telegraph*. By 1966 *The Guardian, Financial Times, Sunday Times, Observer* and the *Economist* had also joined in. *The Guardian*'s experiment was not successful (they sponsored a firm using unsatisfactory techniques) but in 1970 *The Times* took their place. In that year there were five different national polls, two of which were producing two sets of national findings. Their impact was much more widespread than before, however, because all attempts at exclusive publication were dropped. They ranked fourth equal and sixth out of a list of eleven topics on ITN and BBC–1 news; and they were the main election story on seven and six evenings respectively in three weeks.[68] In the national press, one-third of the lead stories on the election were about polls. In 1966 the proportion had been one-tenth. Papers reported their competitors' polls as readily as their own.

Although parties had started commissioning private polls as early as 1950, 1951 seems to have been the first election in which they paid much attention to the public polls. Then and afterwards the polls more often than not (the exceptions being 1955 and 1964) showed a clear lead for one of the parties at the start of the campaign.

Whatever happened then, the parties were bound to react, in their morale if not their actions. The general pattern was this: if the lead stayed up or rose (1955, 1966, 1970), the trailing party became depressed and frustrated and the leading party worried about complacency. If the lead faltered (1951, 1959), tension mounted all round. The 1951 Nuffield study's analysis is typical: the polls initially showed a 10–13 per cent lead for the Conservatives. Naturally enough, then, they 'were a potent source of depression to the Labour Party at the outset, but later on the relatively sharp trend they showed did much to worry the Conservatives. However, they continued to show a Conservative lead adequate to ensure victory, and a number of speakers thought it necessary to give warnings against over-confidence inspired by the polls.'[69] A measure of Labour's depression is that the party's General Secretary was stung into describing the polls as 'a new technique of propaganda . . . calculated to sow the seeds of depression in the ranks of the Labour movement'.[70] In 1959 a Tory lead of 5–8 per cent diminished during the campaign, and the trend contributed to a resurgence of 'the spirit of 1945' detected in the Labour party. Equally, however, 'Conservative agents spoke of workers being spurred to action by the first adverse trends'.[71] Spokesmen commented on the polls at the party press conferences, and they reinforced the feeling at Conservative headquarters that Labour's early initiatives were bearing fruit and must be countered more strongly. This in turn led to a change in campaign tactics, with a modification of the 'quiet' approach, restyled party broadcasts and so on.

The most depressing polls of all, however, were in 1966 and 1970. The two main polls in 1966 put Labour 10 per cent or more ahead throughout the entire campaign. This took much of the steam out of the contest and created among Conservatives, as the *Telegraph* put it, 'a helpless sense of predestination'.[72] A similar situation existed in 1970, though the Labour lead was lower. Right at the end, one or two polls suggested an upturn in Conservative fortunes. Conservative strategy may not in fact have been much affected, since it was based primarily on their own private polls. Morale, on the other hand, was: 'it does seem probable that Mr Heath was almost the only leading Conservative, who in private as well as in public, behaved as though he was unfalteringly convinced that his party was going to win'.[73] In that situation the overwhelming tendency of the press was to anticipate the result as certain and even to begin shifting its interest to the next object of speculation – the future of the defeated leader.

(c) *A changing tradition of partisanship in the press*

The values and attitudes of the press permeate the most distinctive feature of its behaviour at elections – its long tradition of partisanship. In Chapter 6 this has been described as a parallelism between the press and the party system, with deep historical roots and a formerly strong organisational basis. By 1945 the tradition was already past its peak. Between then and 1970 it declined further. The aim of this section is to examine briefly the kind of modifications in the period and to consider their effects on the nature of the national campaign in elections.

Unlike the growth of broadcasting and opinion polls, the decline in partisanship was spasmodic and uneven. Some papers were already relatively non-partisan and remained so; others moderated their partisanship only little. The decline was therefore general and relative. Almost without exception every national daily paper and most Sunday papers came off the fence at every election (see Chapter 6, Table 6.1). By 1970, however, it was more a matter of tensing up and taking a leap than of easing smoothly on to trodden ground. In the 1960s a study of press partisanship *between* elections would show far more differences from behaviour *at* elections than in the late 1940s and early 1950s.

One important element was a decline in unquestioning or 'official' loyalty. The demise of the *Daily Herald* – which in this context is measured from its takeover by IPC in 1962 – was a landmark. In 1945 the *Herald*'s role was symbolised by the fact that it organised a great Labour rally at the Albert Hall. Its entire coverage – selection and presentation of news and features – was geared to securing a Labour victory, then and in later elections. Among Conservative papers the *Telegraph* came nearest to being the official voice of the party. Comparing it to the *Herald*, the 1950 Nuffield study suggested the hallmark of an official paper was that all its 'themes and leader subjects seemed to be raised first in speeches or party declarations'.[74] Such papers followed the leadership and preached orthodoxy, rather than finding initiatives of their own. In 1950 '. . . the *Herald* judged its news by the test of whether it would help the party'.[75] There was no Labour paper of which that could be said in 1970; nor a Conservative paper either, for by then the *Telegraph* seemed to show more independence in its approach – giving space for features by Labour leaders, for instance.

The balance of papers changed too. Once *The Guardian* gently abandoned the Liberals and the *News Chronicle* died there was no Liberal paper after the 1959 election; and although the number of voters reading Conservative and Labour papers was reasonably balanced, the number of Conservative papers was greater than of Labour – and their support tended to be given earlier and more forcefully in 1966 and 1970.

The familiar techniques of partisan bias could be found in any election – and are well documented in the Nuffield studies. But other, more impartial habits grew beside them, like the custom of inviting leaders of all parties to contribute feature articles. In 1945 the Nuffield study could find only one article actually by a Conservative leader (excluding Lord Beaverbrook) even in the Conservative press.[76]* In 1955 the *Mail, Mirror* and *News Chronicle* all found space for the opponents, and in the 1960s the practice spread wider still. The *Mirror* latterly developed the habit too of staging an elaborate performance of weighing pros and cons before deciding which way to vote: 'First the Inquest – Then the Verdict' was its theme in 1966, and it examined party policies and personalities before plumping for 'Wilson and his team'. The *Sun*, both before and after it became a tabloid under Rupert Murdoch's control, went through a similar exercise.

The significance of the *Mirror*'s performances in the 1960s – important to Labour because it was the only mass circulation daily supporting the party – is brought out by comparison with its earlier practices. In these it had extended its Labour propaganda even into its strip cartoons (until 1955) with a vigorous and singleminded commitment from the start of the campaign. 1945 was undoubtedly its triumph, though its slogan 'Vote for Him', evoking a variety of associations about men in the Forces, made only an implicit appeal. The only comparable performance was that of the *Express* in the same year. Lord Beaverbrook was still a very active associate of Churchill, and the paper was in a position unique in the period 1945–70 of being controlled by a direct participant in the party battle. The paper made what proved to be a disastrous miscalculation of the popular mood, interpreting the people as fretting to be set free from the necessary controls of wartime and filled with repressed vitality. It gave tremendous coverage to Churchill and to Beaverbrook's own speeches and pursued a most aggressive anti-Labour campaign.

The decline of full-blooded campaigns must also have been affected to some extent by changes in the party situation itself. 1955 and 1959 in particular were elections where partisanship could not express itself in conventional terms, inasmuch as differences were about ends more than means and sometimes fairly subtle. Perhaps consensus politics encouraged a trend in the press towards pro- or anti-government views more than pro or anti a party. In the 1960s the

---

* There were great restrictions on space, of course.

issue of entry into the Common Market fortuitously muted the partisanship of the *Express* and *Mirror* – the former because entry infringed a deep Beaverbrook tradition of loyalty to the Commonwealth, and the latter because its controllers' enthusiasm for Europe clashed with Labour's equivocation and caution.

Opinion polls may have made a difference as well. It was bad enough in 1959, when for a fortnight three Conservative papers had to highlight evidence of significant increases in Labour support. In subsequent elections it was much worse, specially in 1966, when the same papers and others too had to accept a massive Labour lead that showed no sign of diminishing. 'For all the good that it has done Mr Wilson's critics it seems that the General Election campaign need not have taken place', the *Telegraph* commented sourly. Obviously there was nothing the papers could do except put the boldest possible face on the situation but it was undoubtedly a constraint. The *Express*, for example, simply would not have been able to fight the sort of campaign it fought in 1945. Papers had to gear their approach to independent estimates of the electorate's mood, instead of to their own wishful thinking.

It can be argued, finally, that the growth of broadcasting moderated the techniques of partisanship too. Editors now knew that virtually everyone was exposed to direct political argument and would have some difficulty in avoiding all unsympathetic points of view. It is unlikely that Laski or Bevan could have been painted in the same lurid colours daubed by Conservative papers in the 1940s and 1950s if the public had been used to seeing them in person – not just at elections but in between times too – as they became familiar later with a potential bogeyman like Enoch Powell.

The great advantage of a partisan press – so long as its distribution retained a reasonable balance – was that it gave each party the confidence of knowing there were papers on its side. The 'official' paper, as defined above by the Nuffield study, was obviously a tremendous boon. The qualities which in 1955 made the *Herald* seem if anything 'a little duller and more orthodox' than ever to the Nuffield study[77] may well have seemed to the party leaders veritable virtues. Partisan papers did the parties' work with and for them – challenging and exposing the other side's arguments and expounding their own. Certainly it meant each leader faced prejudiced and hostile papers too, which would do their best to distort and destroy his strategy (or so it seemed). But the loyalty of a party's own papers provided a secure instrument for implementing its own campaign aims. On the face of it, therefore, the decline of partisanship reduced the parties' control over what constituted the national campaign.

In fact the consequences were rather more complicated. Firstly, some of the most popular papers in the period – notably the *Mirror* and *Express* – were very far from 'official'. As we have seen, they were apt to define the campaign in their own way, which might coincide with a party's goal of victory but deviated often from its preferred strategy. Secondly, the implications of papers' loyalties were complicated by the kind of factors discussed in previous sections – for example the emergence of issues linked to spontaneous stories like the 'Noose trial'. These should not need further detailed illustration. The important point is that their treatment by one party or paper often provoked a reaction from opponents, introducing a dialogue whose course could not be predicted. The warmonger issue in 1951 was a particularly good example. A few Labour speakers, without apparently intending any great stress on it, suggested a Conservative government might be likely to go to war with Russia. The Labour leaders in fact rejected specific allegations. But the *Daily Mirror* seized on the issue (see below) and the Conservatives themselves unwittingly spread it by the heat and frequency of their denials. Three out of their five broadcasts mentioned it, as well as a major speech by Churchill and speeches by less prominent candidates.[78]*

The existence of these factors within the framework of a partisan press reduced the consequences of growing non-partisanship. While the predictability of wholehearted support was a loss, the unpredictability of its forms made that support a sometimes disconcerting blessing: Churchill blamed Beaverbrook's performance in the *Express* for his defeat in 1945. What the election would be 'about' was now little more unpredictable than before.

The best example of all to illustrate the arguments in this section – the changing nature of partisanship and the unpredictability of its forms – is the decline of stunts and scares. The greatest stunt of the century was the Zinoviev letter in 1923 (see Chapter 1); but the Laski stunt in 1945 and 'Whose Finger on the Trigger?' in 1951 were in the same tradition. Massive, shrill newspaper coverage was designed to appeal sensationally to emotions of fear if not of panic, and to raise a particular issue above all others as the basis for electoral decision. These two were the last stunts of the period, however. 1955 saw a reaction almost to the extent of anti-stunt stunts. In the extreme case the *Mirror* charged that 'The Hydrogen Bomb should not become a scare issue of the general election' – no one had tried to make it one – and pledged that it would 'take no part in scare campaigns by one side or the other.' The only paper to

* Petrol rationing and 'atom talks' with the Russians were issues that developed strongly.

practise the technique thereafter was the tabloid *Sketch*, and it too had given up by 1970.

The nub of the Laski affair was the relationship between the Labour party's National Executive Committee and a future Labour government (or 'boss rule', as the Conservatives called it); and, latterly, a statement attributed to Laski that the party might have to use violence to achieve socialism. The first arose out of Laski's comments as chairman of the party on an exchange of letters between Churchill and Attlee, about Labour representation at forthcoming peace talks.[79] The second stemmed from a speech by Laski. The Conservatives took up Laski's first comments in their party broadcast the same evening. The question at issue was whether a Labour government would be able to decide its foreign policy independently (an aspect of a familiar Labour controversy about policymaking). Mr Attlee rebuked Laski, and the Conservative press jumped in. The *Express* gave nearly a quarter of its whole election coverage to the affair. It was featured every day from 16 June to polling day (5 July), more often than not on the front page and five times as the lead story. The paper harped on Laski as a sinister figure with dictatorial pretensions ('Gauleiter Laski') and showed the incident and its repercussions as evidence of a major split in the party.[80] Its report of Laski's speech ('Socialism Even if it means Violence') led Laski to issue writs for libel, though he eventually lost the case.[81] Arthur Christiansen, the paper's editor, admitted in his memoirs that he thought 'we had an election weapon as good as the Zinovieff letter . . . It was all-in wrestling, hand-to-hand fighting, commando stuff, and we were, we thought, very good at it.'[82]

'Whose Finger on the Trigger?' also led to writs – by Mr Churchill, who was paid damages by the *Daily Mirror* out of court after the election. Early in the 1951 campaign the *Mirror* asked 'Whose Finger do you want on the trigger?' This provoked Churchill into commenting that it would not be a British finger that would pull the trigger of a third world war; whereupon the *Mirror* cast doubt on Churchill's capacity to restrain American fingers. Continuously it handled the theme in different ways – embroidered reports of a rumour that Churchill would deliver a 'peace ultimatum' to Stalin, prominently displayed letters and so on. In the final days 'Whose Finger on the Trigger?' became a banner headline. On polling day it was featured above a large drawing of a pistol, photographs of Attlee and Churchill and the headline 'Today YOUR Finger is on the trigger'. The Nuffield study concluded that the paper showed 'more unequivocally than ever that its basic technique had more in common with the advertising than the editorial world'.

III. CONCLUSIONS: THE FUTURE PATTERN

What difference did mass media make in the general elections between 1945 and 1970? The focus of this essay has not been on direct differences in particular results nor on their effects upon the salience of elections: completely different data are needed for those questions. The analysis has concentrated on the interaction of media and politicians in the national campaign. We can now summarise the arguments and draw out some conclusions.

The chapter's main contention has been that the very existence of a national campaign was conditional upon the presence of the media: they were no mere eavesdroppers of an independent argument but participants – whether or not they were partisan. Their general effect was to help define an evolving campaign pattern, made up of all their coverage, especially including their reports of party leaders' activities and, in the case of broadcasting, the leaders' actual appearances.

The particular effects of the media included, first, integrating the campaign – giving it a spurious impression of order and logic and relating the parties to each other in a dialogue which otherwise would not exist. Detailed election round-ups in the papers each Sunday, for example, could be quite influential over politicians assessing the progress of the campaign and planning the next phase. The value to the Liberals of being brought into this dialogue was enormous. In a number of other ways too that party depended virtually for its very recognition as a national party on the behaviour of the media. Jo Grimond had every reason to say in 1964 that TV was 'the Liberals' greatest asset'.[83]

Another important element in the media's definition of the campaign was that, more than the parties themselves, they struck the balance between issues and personalities, seeking continually to impose a differentiation on the parties, in the interests, presumably, of clarifying the choices open to the electorate. They sought also, doubtless for the same reasons, to avoid a 'quiet' campaign. Within that balance they were equally important in ranking specific personalities and issues. Their choices, moreover, did not always correspond to party preferences. In addition they highlighted certain completely extraneous events like the Noose trial, to which the parties reacted, incorporating them into the campaign. All these effects operated within a framework of partisan press attitudes and broadcasting neutrality; and in general the effects were of the same kind in 1970 as in 1945.

There were, however, substantial differences in the direction of those effects – in the kind of pattern campaigns took. If any single election was a watershed it was 1959. That was critical in the development of the polls, of broadcasting, and of the parties' sophistication in managing the media. These were developments which contributed to the increasing *presidentialism* of British elections. That is a difficult characteristic to pin down, but there seems no doubt that it grew. The Conservative campaign in 1945 concentrated heavily on Winston Churchill. But imagine it in the context of 1970: Churchill continually on TV, in the news bulletins and election broadcasts; Churchill at the daily press conference; Churchill given space in the *Mirror*. Presidentialism is relative, in other words; and the behaviour of the media in 1945 shaped a campaign into a less presidential mould than in 1970.

Two possible implications of presidentialism are worth stressing. Firstly the concentration of attention on the party leader might have populist consequences. Performance on TV could become a factor in the initial choice of leader. Whether this would ever make much difference to the choice is arguable: it may be that the qualities making a good TV performer are very similar to those traditionally sought in a leader anyway. What is perhaps more serious is the possibility that frequent TV contact with the electorate and the ensuing tendency to reduce problems to simple terms might lead to unreasonably high expectations of results, culminating in disillusion and a collapse of the legitimacy of the political system. Secondly, the party leader's command of TV raises the possibility of him virtually taking over the complete national campaign. All kinds of persons and information might bear on his strategy, but its implementation would rest with him: indeed Labour's national campaign in 1970 already went some way in this direction.

1959 was also quite an important year in the changing partisanship of the media. In the press this consisted in a decline in papers' unwillingness to recognise merit in opponents and faults in their own party. In broadcasting it was a decline in the completeness of neutrality. The end of the parties' monopoly of election programmes introduced an element of 'random partisanship', in the sense that, as has been argued, the broadcasters' own programmes might now coincidentally favour the strategy of one party more than another.

The significance of this change is extremely important. By 1970 the media as a whole were detached as never before from the party system. In 1945 they stood towards one end of a spectrum: there were still a few 'official' party papers, and on the air the parties had absolute control over the very limited number of election programmes broadcast. By 1970 they had shifted far towards the other end. In an

era of universal suffrage the parties had paradoxically lost control
over the means of appealing to the electorate.

This decline appeared to have three consequences. First, the
parties had to work a bit harder to get attention. Second and more
important, they could not set the tone of their coverage so successfully. For example the media would not now accept so readily the
parties' own definition of the important issues. Harold Wilson had
to hope the *Mirror* would see things his way: Clement Attlee could
be certain the *Herald* would. There was a major shift in control over
the picture of the national campaign from the politicians to the
journalists and TV producers. The third consequence is less definite.
Studying the Nuffield accounts one is left with the impression that,
notwithstanding the media's role in creating party dialogues,
national campaigns were *less* of a dialogue in 1970 than in 1945.
In the early studies there is a strong sense of the parties talking to
and with each other, of a debate conducted on a national hustings
through the press and party broadcasts. Various media characteristics continued to promote this debate – their anxiety to find issues
to differentiate parties and to promote confrontations on TV, for
instance. But by 1970 the parties seemed to talk *to* and *about* one
another yet not so much *with* each other as formerly. Several
explanations could account for the change. It might be that elections
were becoming rituals – gradually divorced from the realities that
would souse an incoming administration and wash out many of its
aspirations. Perhaps the change was a reflection too of the obsession
with 'images' and the recognition that 'debate' in fact had no place
in the voters' make-up. Even if those suggestions are plausible,
however, the decline in dialogue seems also to have been a result of
the decline in media partisanship.

The change in partisanship was one of a number of ways in which
the press and TV became increasingly interconnected as elections
went by. One might almost say they converged. Television made
news in the papers: programmes were reported – and arguments
about programmes just as much. In return the press fed TV with
opinion polls and often made the running at the morning press
conferences. For broadcasters seeking criteria to guide their own
non-partisanship, the definitions and reports of newspapers must
have been the obvious source.

There were good reasons to suppose that this convergence would
continue, barring an upheaval in the party system. The number of
national daily papers might continue to fall, probably reducing the
likelihood that those remaining would see virtue in deep or lasting
loyalty to a party. Also the scale and complexity of modern government, plus its changing social context (less deference, better education,

etc.) would arguably confirm the tendency of the press to strike an anti-government stance regardless of party – a stance of 'positive criticism', suspicious of government and well equipped to expose it. These factors might in addition cause the press to redefine news values so that traditional short-run news took up proportionately less space and intensively researched features and specialist journalism, of a kind previously associated with magazines and Sunday papers, took up more. The remaining British dailies, that is to say, might become more like the *New York Times*. In the context of a general election, even if the leader columns still plumped for particular parties, the weight of the contents of the press would not be highly partisan.

If on the other hand press partisanship did not decline in that way, it remains possible that convergence would continue as a result of movement in broadcasting. By 1970 broadcasting may have reached a plateau in its capacity to cover elections, but it was certainly not in a position of equilibrium. For several reasons one could expect a further loosening of the constraints on the broadcasters' discretion. Firstly the constraints were to some extent self-maintained, if not actually self-imposed. (Cf. Chapter 5 which documents the self-imposition of the old Fourteen Day Rule.) Apart from Granada's innovations in the late 1950s the BBC took the main initiatives in pushing back the boundaries of coverage; but even the BBC was generally cautious. Consistent with the Reith tradition, many influential broadcasting executives no doubt shared the view of party leaders that the development of election programmes was fraught with dangers and must be carefully and responsibly controlled. There were, to be sure, severely practical justifications for caution too, ranging from brief gestures of disapproval like Wilson's refusal to grant the BBC a victory interview in 1966 to more rumbling threats about the level of the licence fee (which provides the BBC's revenue) or the advertising levy on ITV.

Self-restraint was likely to change (or be redefined) with the passing of the Reith tradition. More important, it can be argued that the broadcasters' discretion would inevitably widen because the original decision in 1959 to let them do their own programmes undermined most of the ground on which the practice of neutrality rested. With that decision the logical justification vanished not only for those practices which were straightway forsaken, like the omission of the election from news bulletins, but also for those which were *not* (apart from those required by the Representation of the People Act), like the cancellation of comedies and children's programmes that might be construed as having partisan implication. The *principles* of non-partisanship remained the same. What changed was the critical matter of who had the power to interpret them in practice. After 1959 this power shifted progressively to the broadcasters. The politicians could now hold the line only by sheer power politics, exercised as likely as not after the event – Wilson's snub being a small example. Blumler's 1966 study shows that certain broadcasters behaved in just the same way, testing the limits of their discretion by pushing hard up against them. Once the broadcasters were allowed to make their own election programmes, the power to define impartiality effectively passed to them (within broad limits). Before 1959 partisanship could be measured in quantitative terms ('how many minutes of party broadcasts each?'): after 1959 it needed a qualitative judgement, and the question 'Who is to judge?' could in the nature of things more often be answered by the people actually making programmes than by party leaders and managers. In the last resort, moreover, the politicians must know that it would be far more trouble than it was worth for them to force a reversal in the direction of election broadcast coverage. The broadcasters, always able to plead that they were in good faith trying to act according to reasonable standards of impartiality, could push after 1970 against an open door that still had some way to swing.

Further convergence of the press and TV would consist, then, in four tendencies: a continuing decline in traditional press partisanship (between, even more than at, elections); a more compact, 'magaziny' national press (with a gaggle of more or less ephemeral and underground journals scooting about in its shadow); broadcast programmes increasingly free of rules imposed from outside about party balance at election time; and an orientation in current affairs broadcasting, probably, that was similar to what has just been called 'positive criticism' in the press.

Such convergence, whether or not it continued in the way sketched out, could cause serious dislocation in the political system. It is debatable whether political parties can effectively sustain mass support without the opportunity for their leaders to project themselves and their policies as they themselves wish, and whether general elections can operate as an instrument of effective representation in the absence of well organised and coherent parties. On a less speculative plane, it is quite certain that no government would allow the broadcasting organisations to deviate from the political mainstreams for long without putting in chairmen of the BBC governors and the IBA whose task was to paddle them back on course. In an extreme case we might also find repressive legislation against the press, if governments felt their capacity to fulfil their legitimate functions was nullified by press activity.

On practical as well as theoretical grounds, therefore, we might expect that extreme detachment between the media and the parties would be a matter of concern both to the media and the parties – particularly in elections, when competition is at its height. How could the media and the parties be joined together again without returning to the old type of press industry and the days of Lord Reith?

One possibility is commercial advertising. If the parties have lost control of media organisations then it is reasonable to suggest they should be allowed to buy control of media contents. Party advertising in the press already has quite a long history, but it has not been allowed on TV.[84] On the other hand the party political broadcasts already amount to free advertising, so the main form expansion could take would be the short 'spot' commercials of a minute or so in length common in the United States. These might be attractive to viewers, but given their brevity they would be one step further away from the rational ideal of political argument. Less romantic is the objection to them on grounds of cost. It is most unlikely that the parties would want to become embroiled in the business of raising money simply to compete in advertising time, specially with the extreme example before them of the escalating fortunes spent on campaign advertising in the United States.

A second possibility is to extend the principle of 'free advertising'. This could solve problems both for the parties and the broadcasters. The logical conclusion of the freedom given to the broadcasters since 1959 is that they should be subject in elections to no rules and conventions imposed by the parties: all questions of how much attention to give the election, what issues to discuss and speeches to report, and whether to permit contributors to 'editorialise', would be entirely within their own discretion. The parties would have no right to impose their own standards of bias and triviality. In return the parties should be given the opportunity to sponsor parallel coverage of the election on their own terms. This might include an element of programmes like the existing party broadcasts; but it would go much further, to include their own commentaries, feature programmes and news reports, pitched at whatever level of partisanship they chose and done explicitly under their respective labels. With four channels available each party could have 30 or 45 minutes a night on one of them (not necessarily the same each night) without the air being saturated by politics, even granted the broadcasting organisations' own coverage. Assuming production facilities and personnel were made available, the task of putting together such a nightly programme need not be beyond the parties' resources. The same idea could easily be applied to the press. Each party could be allocated a number of pages of advertising in each national newspaper (by the same method that party broadcasts are fixed, perhaps). They would be paid for out of public funds. What the papers contained would be up to the parties.

Those ideas follow logically from the developing position of the media; and by giving back the parties direct control over a section of media content, they would free the media organisations (mainly the broadcasters) from external constraints over their own programme content. If such a proposal was too drastic, however, various minor changes might happen instead, some of which were prevented after 1959 by little more than the determination of the party leaders. The simultaneous transmission of party broadcasts might go. As Blumler and McQuail have pointed out, this would help to make space for smaller parties on the air.[85] The same authors found evidence in their survey of electors that more inter-party debates would be welcome,[86] and they discussed ways in which these might be organised, though whether the idea would ever be very popular with politicians is questionable.

A number of other developments would be consistent with trends in the media. Local radio should be able to make an original contribution to electioneering. BBC-TV and ITV between them surely ought to be able to find a way of getting any candidate who wanted it at least 10 minutes on TV in his region: *Election Marathon* cannot be the limit of their ingenuity. Whether the Liberals deserved the amount of attention they got on national TV in 1966 and 1970 is open to question. There is room for expansion of programmes spotlighting issues in depth. The mechanics or context of elections offer scope too for more investigation of subjects like party organisation, the formation of policy in opposition and the election's implications for senior civil servants. Non-party organisations with political views could be given the chance to discuss the campaign from their perspectives – Trade Unions, pressure groups, students, immigrants, etc. Particular newspapers – the weeklies would be obvious choices – could be given a programme to deal with the election however they liked.

Detailed speculation about the activity of media in future elections takes us beyond the scope of the survey. What is certain, however, is that the nature of the campaign and the behaviour of the media will continue to be closely interlinked. The effect of media, as this analysis of the 1945–1970 campaigns has sought to show, will continue to be much wider and more complex than election studies have commonly indicated.

9

Private Eye: the politics of the Fool

In the early 1960s Britain had a 'satire boom'. On the stage it was typified by a student revue, *Beyond the Fringe*, and the success of *The Establishment* nightclub. On television it was launched by *That Was The Week That Was* (which 'made' David Frost). In print it was led by *Private Eye*, described in the press as 'the satirical fortnightly' until familiarity made a label as unnecessary as for *Punch*.

The satirists' success came partly from their freshness of approach. *Beyond the Fringe* broke away from the frothy, inconsequential, often camp revues of the 1950s. *That Was The Week That Was* guyed politicians and public figures with a freedom that drenched the unsuspecting viewer, drowsy with the staidness of the BBC, like a cold shower. *Private Eye* exploited new techniques of ridicule like the 'bubble' caption superimposed upon a photograph.

Equally fresh were the satirists' subjects. The name of the night-club, *The Establishment*, indicated the range of their targets. Politicians in particular came under fire, with the mass media that linked them to the public. 'Fears in the medical profession that the mange which had attacked Mr Macmillan's moustache might have spread to his brain are now lessening', *Private Eye* remarked in typical mockery both of the Prime Minister and the oblique style of conventional political comment. Mr Macmillan could soon return to the House of Commons, 'Our Political Correspondent' explained; but his medical advisers 'state that he is in no condition to do anything but convalesce – which he will probably do, encased in plaster, propped up on the Front Bench alongside the stuffed effigies of Mr Selwyn Lloyd and Mr R. A. Butler which have, of course, been there for some time.'[1] In *Beyond the Fringe* Peter Cook, wearing a rubber mask of Macmillan, depicted a tired, fumbling figure, describing his meeting with the 'young, virile' President Kennedy.

This kind of writing and acting simply had not existed in Britain within living memory. Many people were in the mood for it. *TW3* had an audience of 12 million at its height. The mood changed and the boom subsided after about two years, roughly at the time of Mr Macmillan's retirement in October 1963. But *Private Eye*, unlike the satirical TV shows, managed to survive a drop in circulation – in a mere three months – from 90,000 to 25,000. It found new readers under the Labour government and was still established with a circulation of more than 70,000 ten years after its first appearance.

The boom was not just a social phenomenon. The satirists played – and *Private Eye* continued to play – a political role. Despite the destructive connotations of satire this role was well within the values of 'the system' itself. Even in its earliest days *Private Eye* never resembled the underground press of the late 1960s which, in contrast, tended to grope for the values of 'alternative societies'. *Private Eye* pilloried Westminster politicians but not the Westminster system of politics. Indeed it was very much a product of the Establishment itself. Its founders were public school graduates of Oxford and Cambridge. (One of them taught at Eton after leaving Oxford.) They did not need to tout dummies of the magazine around, seeking backers: one of the founders, Andrew Osmond, put up the capital himself. (Osmond later joined the Foreign Office; wrote some successful novels with a colleague; resigned, and by 1971 was back at *Private Eye* as Managing Director.) Their attitude was one of detachment more than alienation. In that sense it is significant that the first editor, Christopher Booker, was active in the Liberal party, which in the early 1960s might be seen as a home for those who could not identify with the two big parties but did identify with the system containing them. An alienated middle-class graduate in 1961 would more likely have sought expression through the Campaign for Nuclear Disarmament and the *New Left Review*.[2] In brief, *Private Eye* might be described as *rebellious*, not *revolutionary*.

Being a uniquely 'satirical' magazine *Private Eye* had a political role quite distinct from that of ordinary newspapers or magazines. It changed a little after the Macmillan era, becoming more concerned than before to retail information as well as comment. But its role in the 1960s generally can best be analysed by comparison with the subtle political role of the mediaeval court jester, or Fool.

The Fool may now be more familiar through literature than history: he is an important foil in some of Shakespeare's plays – for example *King Lear* and *A Midsummer Night's Dream* (Bottom the weaver is turned literally into an ass in the dream).[3] But in history the existence of the Fool seems as old and common as the idea of kingship itself. There was a Fool at the court of the Pharaohs. In Charlemagne's time the fame of Buhlul, Fool of Caliph Harun al-Rashid, was widespread. In England there were Fools at the court of Edmund Ironside before the Norman Conquest; and

Duke William brought Fools with him in 1066. The Fool with a significant but implicit political role developed in Europe in the Middle Ages and flourished under feudalism and absolute monarchy. In Czarist Russia, for example, his role became elaborate and well-entrenched.[4]

The essence of the Fool's position is his exemption from the normal rules of society. In his primary form he may be, literally, an idiot, 'who seems to have originated somewhere outside society and its normal laws and duties and to continue to belong to the "outside" from which he came',[5] or his deformity may be physical: the earliest known Fool was a negro dwarf at the court of Pharaoh Pepi I. The humour of clowns and circuses is still closely linked to deformity – dwarfs and fat or bearded ladies. In either form the idiot or grotesque Fool is funny because of his unavoidable incongruity with society: he is in it but not of it.

But the Fool may also be artificial: someone who is not really an idiot but who *plays* the Fool. He is licensed by the King to ignore and flout the rules of society, and this must include ignoring the rules about the sanctity of the King himself, whom he can use as a butt for jokes, insults and obscenities. The fact that he is not a real idiot gives him an important extra dimension. His political role becomes that of *ritualised rebellion*: that is, the King, by tolerating – indeed encouraging – his Fool to break the rules, shows his own strength and provides an outlet for the frustrations of his subjects. The Fool thus strengthens the system; although he may weaken the position of those who presently control it.

It is in those terms that the role of *Private Eye* is best analysed. In a complex, large-scale society there cannot be one King and one Fool: the roles have been institutionalised. In the private retinue surrounding public men – the Private Office of Ten Downing Street or the White House Office of the American President – there may indeed be men with an element of detachment from the political and administrative empires about them; who thereby possess rare, disinterested wisdom and frankness akin to the Fool's.* One cannot know if they are regarded in this way by those around them. But certainly they are not visible to the people, as was the historic Fool, who traditionally appeared with the King in public rituals. For a modern society as a whole the idea of kingship is institutionalised in some concept like 'the Establishment' – to use the phrase appro-

---

* John Wyndham, later Lord Egremont, private secretary to Mr Macmillan in Downing Street (whose complete detachment from the Westminster and Whitehall hierarchies is nicely symbolised by the fact that he was unpaid) seems to have occupied some such position. See his memoirs, *Wyndham and children first* (1968) and his obituary in *The Times* (7 June 1972).

priate to the origins of *Private Eye*; while the idea of the Fool is expressed inevitably through the institution of a mass medium. To each man his own conception of 'the Establishment'; and to each his choice of Fool. For some 90,000 in the Macmillan era, the choice was *Private Eye*. Many of them, no doubt, also laughed at Peter Cook's impersonations of Macmillan and the weekly songs and sketches on *TW3*.

Although the roles are not institutionalised, the relationship of King and Fool remains. In the top corner of the cover of each issue of *Private Eye* is a little cartoon of a helmeted crusader. He wears the lost, helpless look of a Fool. His sword is bent and useless, like the clown's rubber club or cardboard dagger that confounds our expectations of hard wood and steel. The rules of war and the might of its weapons for him are turned topsy-turvy; yet, while looking absurd himself, he mocks the little crusader who for years was pictured on the masthead of Lord Beaverbrook's *Daily Express*: Beaverbrook's earnest campaigns, by implication, were themselves just as foolish and ineffective, though backed by wealth and position.

I. ORIGINS AND AIMS OF PRIVATE EYE

Before examining further the nature and implications of *Private Eye*'s political folly we should see how far its origins and aims fit the analysis. The Fool, it has been noted, 'seems to have originated somewhere outside society . . .'[6] Looked at from the point of view of the established press – *Punch* as well as the political weeklies – this was certainly true of *Private Eye*. The path of most aspirant journalists with the background and education of *Private Eye*'s founders was a spell in the provinces or a fairly humble position on a national paper, leading to greater things. This was true not only of 'serious' journalists but of humourists too: Bernard Levin and Michael Frayn, both of a slightly earlier university generation but contributors to the satire boom, started respectively on *The Spectator* and *The Guardian*. But the founders of *Private Eye* struck out on their own: content, design, production and distribution were original, drawing not at all on the resources of the existing industry.[7]

In one sense *Private Eye* was a development from the magazine of Shrewsbury School. Christopher Booker, editor for the first two years, his successor Richard Ingrams, and the cartoonist William Rushton, who did most of the illustrations in the early days, were all at Shrewsbury together.* Booker went on to Cambridge, Ingrams

---

* Paul Foot, who added an element of exposure journalism to the magazine in the late 1960s, was also at Shrewsbury.

to Oxford and Rushton to London as a Solicitor's Clerk. Booker and Ingrams had intended 'one day' to start a magazine. But the person whose energy really got *Private Eye* started seems to have been Peter Usborne, another Public School boy who worked with Ingrams at Oxford on *Mesopotamia*, an undergraduate magazine whose style and content clearly anticipated the *Eye*. When he left Oxford in 1961 Usborne contacted Booker, who went down from Cambridge a year earlier and worked for the Liberal Party magazine *Liberal News* (for which Rushton did cartoons). Booker had recently left it and was thinking seriously about a humorous radical magazine. Usborne suggested he join up with the *Mesopotamia* people and sent a long memo about the idea during the summer of 1961 from the United States where he had a job with *Time* magazine. On his return there were meetings in pubs; plans were settled (the name took quite a time to decide) and the first issue appeared on 27 October 1961.

Usborne, Booker and Osmond were thus the active founders. Usborne provided the organising energy and production skills. Booker, because of his experience as a journalist, was made editor. Osmond put up the £300 capital.

The originality of content has already been indicated. The satirical element had been faintly foreshadowed (without the obscenity) by changes in *Punch* under the recent editorship of Malcolm Muggeridge and by the Westminster commentary of Taper (Bernard Levin) in *The Spectator* – both of whom Booker acknowledges as influences. Design and production undoubtedly could be said to 'originate somewhere outside society'. Usborne had discovered the cheapness of offset-lithography compared with normal printing; and 'letraset' – 'instant lettering' for headlines, etc. – had just come on the market. The result was a magazine of highly experimental design, produced by an unfamiliar process and looking as though it was typed instead of printed. The first few issues were on cheap yellow paper. The magazine was not distributed by the established companies either. Osmond drove round Chelsea and Kensington distributing it to the cafés and restaurants.

Five hundred copies of the first three issues were published. Others were sent free, in the hope of getting publicity, to prominent or influential people (some of whom the editors were acquainted with; Booker, of course, having worked for the Liberal Party, had good contacts there). Circulation soon started to rise by about a thousand copies an issue. (Osmond got his money back several times over within a few months: later, with fluctuations in its fortunes, the ownership changed and became more complex.) When the magazine did try to get distributed by a major firm, W. H. Smith, it was refused. Smiths maintained that their legal advisers warned them not to handle it. This extended even to the handling of a Penguin Books anthology from *Private Eye* in 1965. The result was a longstanding grudge. Smiths ('W. H. Smug') became a *Private Eye* butt. Eventually distribution was taken over by a newcomer to the field, Charles Harness, who was building up a distribution service for magazines. The first big publicity came in *Time and Tide* and *The Observer*. By July 1962 circulation was about 15,000. Then, with the first major cracks in the Conservative Government's self-confidence – it was in July that Macmillan sacked a third of his cabinet – the satire wagon began to roll and the magazine took off towards its peak of 90,000 a year later. Thereafter the paper got closer and closer to the centre of the system to which it was Fool.

Just as its origins fitted the idea of the Fool, so did *Private Eye*'s aims. Booker wanted a platform for his brand of angry Liberalism (the second issue contained a full-page article about the Liberal Leader Jo Grimond; impatient at his ineffectiveness, though admitting that at least he was concerned for the right issues). But he wanted social satire and humour too: for some time the magazine described itself on page 2 as a 'fortnightly lampoon'. Much of the humour, in his own words, was just 'cock-snooking, like little boys in class' – critical, detached, but secretly admiring or acknowledging the authority of the masters.* In the early issues there was a kind of randomness about the contents and the subjects pilloried which coincides with the disordered nature of the Fool and enables one easily to understand the query (raised by a critic at the time) 'When are you going to develop a point of view?' The novel, irregular layout confirmed this impression.

Where Booker looked to the *Punch* of Muggeridge and – more perhaps – of its republican days in the early 1840s, Ingrams, who joined the magazine properly soon after it started, looked to Claud Cockburn's news-sheet of the 1930s, *The Week*.[8] This had some of the qualities of the Fool, and to that extent many parallels can be found with *Private Eye*. It had similarly unconventional origins: financed on a shoestring, produced on a duplicating machine from a pokey attic room, and distributed through the mail. Unlike *Private Eye* it was orientated very largely towards facts and rumours; but Cockburn had a similar determination to keep it detached from the Establishment. As a journalist abroad he had increasingly felt that anyone frequenting 'any kind of club or other meeting-place

---

* Like little boys' jokes, too, the humour was often lavatorial. A typical Rushton cartoon headed 'Leonardo: The Final Heave' showed a man about to be sick into a lavatory. The reference is to an attempt by public subscription to buy 'for the nation' a Leonardo Da Vinci cartoon which would otherwise probably have been sold abroad.

where, say, diplomats, lawyers, bankers and newspapermen gathered together and talked, must have been deeply aware of the strange contrast between the colourful information and significant rumours – for rumours can often be as significant as facts – circulating in the clubs, and the awfully tight-lipped drabness of the newspapers being sold on the club doorstep . . . What informed people were really saying – and equally importantly, the tone of voice they were saying it in – were scarcely reflected at all in the newspapers.'[9] Returning to England, he started *The Week* to meet that need. As he remarks, he had frequently to fight off help that would have prevented him through sucking him into the system: 'I had to keep firmly in mind that what we were running was a pirate craft and we could not burden ourselves with conventional navigators and mates, however skilled and knowledgeable.'[10] His eccentric design and production methods were therefore, as for *Private Eye*, a positive help. By not fitting in to the system, like the Fool, he found he was freely able to publish information that found no outlet elsewhere: 'Sometimes it came from frustrated newspapermen who could not get what they considered vital news into their own papers.'[11] His point about rumours is significant too: to the uncomprehending Fool the distinction between facts and rumours is meaningless. Furthermore the reactions of the authorities were exactly what one expects of those inside a society trying to 'place' the inherently unplaceable Fool: 'obviously the authorities would much rather deal with people who are visibly members of some recognised political organisation, and I had a lot of evidence that they were considerably worried by not knowing what I was "as"'.[12]

Many of those comments could be made with little change about *Private Eye*. In view of Ingrams' interest in *The Week*, that is no coincidence. The connection was made explicit when Cockburn actually joined *Private Eye* in 1963 as guest editor and later as a regular columnist. His influence was partly responsible for the considerable increase in the magazine's factual content. Previously, though their roles were similar, a comparison of the magazines would show a substantial difference in substance. *The Week* was not illustrated and not satirical. It was essentially a *news* sheet, with a bias towards foreign affairs (and finance, to some extent). It was unquestionably more influential, in the sense of receiving close attention from political élites at home and abroad: it was informative, not just amusing.*

---

* *The Week* 'took off' when the Prime Minister, Ramsay MacDonald, criticised it at a press conference. In its heyday (it closed in 1941) it was essential reading for those who would be informed. Cockburn lists some of its subscribers (the Foreign Ministers of eleven nations, etc.) in Cockburn, *I Claud* (1967), pp. 139–40.

It would probably be a mistake to define the aims of *Private Eye*'s founders too sharply. According to Booker they had no clear expectations about what they hoped to achieve. This in itself, however, is consistent with the aimlessness of the Fool. To the extent that the aims were explicit, they fit well the character and role of the Fool. This character must now be further explored.

II. PRIVATE EYE: THE CHARACTER OF A FOOL

The basis of the Fool's position – his exemption from the normal rules and conventions of society – supports a range of characteristics, all of which are related to one another and observable in *Private Eye*.

(a) Odd appearance

The analogy here is with the Fool's dress. This 'characteristically contains chaotic and disproportionate elements',[13] a description that might not unreasonably have been applied to the layout and design of the early *Private Eye*. Even the publication of the magazine *fortnightly* was untypical: British magazines tended to come out weekly or monthly. *The Week* looked equally odd. Cockburn recalls his partner wanting it to look 'neat'. What Cockburn wanted was for it to be noticeable – hence the use of brown ink on buff-coloured paper: 'It was not merely noticeable, it was unquestionably the nastiest looking bit of work that ever dropped onto a breakfast table.'[14]

Willeford goes on to point out that the Fool's dress sometimes brings the chaotic elements together 'with a balanced and harmonious pattern', as in the diamond-patterned dress of a harlequin – originally just a jumble of patches.[15] So, as time went on, *Private Eye*'s design became familiar and predictable: a regular message from the remote and sinister proprietor Lord Gnome; the next instalment of familiar strip cartoons (such as the blundering sexual adventures of Barry Mackenzie) and of a series like Mrs Wilson's Diary – a sustained catalogue of trivialities and absurdities behind the doors of 10 Downing Street. In short, *Private Eye* developed a format. Its original eccentricity was superseded in the mid-sixties by the experimentation of underground papers like *IT, Oz, Gandalf's Garden* and many others. This change did not substantially affect its character as Fool, however: its design remained unorthodox by the standards of the established media.

(b) Unpredictable behaviour

The chaotic appearance of the Fool simply reflects his chaotic behaviour. Since he does not obey the rules of society his behaviour cannot be predicted by those who do. In the resulting incongruities and paradoxes lie much of the Fool's humour. Cockburn says people did not know how to place *The Week*: it was probably very much more difficult to place *Private Eye*. Take the matter of names, for example. In the list of those responsible for the magazine's administration real names appeared – Peter Usborne, Nicholas Luard. But what about Sir Charles Harness? In other weeks he appeared as Charles Q. Harness, or Charles Harness Esq. Did he exist at all? Might he be a knight (after all, they were a pretty upper-class lot)? Then Mrs O'Morgo-Ingrams: was she perhaps the same as Miss Mary O'Morgan? Had she married Ingrams since the last issue? Or did some of the others think she *wanted* to marry him (or had, secretly), or that he wanted to marry her? Or did he (or she) want to try to make the others think that she (or he) wanted to marry him (or her)? All the rational guidelines were lost.* The same was true of letters. Many of those published were jokes written by the editors; some with fictitious names (Sir Herbert Gussett was an early favourite), some with real names. Issue 19 included letters allegedly written by F. R. Leavis, Lord Beaverbrook and Lord Rothermere. More and more often as the years passed the letters were apparently genuine. Yet one could never be sure.

Private Eye carried its fun into the camps of other magazines too. Issue 18 announced a competition (First Prize £5: but did they mean that, or was it part of the spoof?) to see who could get the largest number of bogus letters published in *Time and Tide*, a right-wing weekly. Subsequent issues reprinted successful letters and gleefully reported the measures taken by *Time and Tide* to check the credentials of their correspondents.

Further illustrations of the unpredictable or 'illogical' nature of the magazine's content include the following:

the habit of breaking off a parody in mid-sentence with the note 'contd. on p. 94' (there never was a page 94, of course), instead of rounding it off in a conventional way;

the use of nicknames or misspellings: Sir Alec Douglas-Home was always called Baillie Vass, after a Scottish newspaper transposed photographs of him and a Local Government representative called Vass; Harold Wilson was always called Wislon;

---

* In fact she was Miss Mary Morgan, an Irish girl, who married Richard Ingrams.

the introduction of a 'colour section' in which there was never any colour;

the series of 'True Stories' contributed by Christopher Logue (issue 15 onwards), which re-told stories published in the newspapers that were almost beyond belief themselves. The second one was about a man fined in Edinburgh for unscrewing his wooden leg and throwing it at a passing car. (When the police warned him he shouted abuse at them and did it again.) Issue 26 reprinted the names of the fifty mourners at a Requiem Mass in a provincial Irish town for Mrs Mary Kate McDermott: all of them were priests.

The inclusion of newspaper items containing (sometimes obscene) *double entendres* or printing errors – e.g. 'Three Battered in Fish Shop: Man gaoled for Assault'.

(c) Fantasy and make-believe

The Fool has no means of distinguishing truth and falsehood, reality and fantasy. In *Private Eye*, as in *The Week*, the distinction between rumour and fact (especially in the first couple of years) was unimportant. The humour frequently derived from putting false words into the mouths of real people or sensible words into the mouths of fictional people. 'Someone once asked me why I married the Queen', Prince Philip is made to say: 'And I replied, "Because she was there"'. The playwright John Osborne, one of the original 'angry young men' of the 1950s, remarks: 'There *must* be something inherently wrong with a society that can produce me.' The photographs of prominent people with bubble captions superimposed on them typify this technique. 'Brothers, what are we worrying about?' asks the bubble coming from George Brown, Deputy Leader of the Labour Party, addressing a public meeting. 'You, Brother', says the woman beside him – caught by the camera in a glum moment.

The list of fictional characters in whose mouths pertinent social comment was put is a long one. Lunchtime O'Booze, a Fleet Street journalist, crops up everywhere, revealing journalistic qualities normally hidden from the public. ('Aah, 'tis a sad day for Mother Ireland', says an old man who has just provided him with some local colour. 'Now perhaps you'd buy me that whiskey.') The gimmicks of the pop scene were exposed through such groups as Spiggy Topes and the Turds, and Len Greeb and the Yobboes. Columnist Maureen Cleavage asks Spiggy about 'the controversial microphone stroking that is the high point of his act. "Is it in any way sexually orientated?" His reply was revealing: "Of course it is, you idiot dolly. Look, are you a virgin or something?"' Again, has success spoiled the 'Les

Swindle' girls (who sing in the nude)? 'Greeb was unequivocal in his reply. "Yes," he said. "I've never seen such a repulsive load of old slags in my life. And I've seen a few."' Eric Buttock, MP, provided for several years a vehicle for some fairly shrewd Westminster comment (written in misspelt schoolboy English, modelled on the Geoffrey Willans/Ronald Searle book, *Down with Skool*).

The humour contains other elements of fantasy conventional in satire. The world of Mrs Wilson's Diary was obviously a make-believe world. The fable form was adopted for a long series called 'Aesop Revisited' in 1961–2, which mocked the pretensions of politicians, critics, playwrights and even the racing-driver Stirling Moss. Many stories made their point by the extension of actual situations to absurd lengths. At a time of art thefts in 1962 the *Eye* reported 'National Gallery Stolen' under a photograph of Trafalgar Square with the gallery blotted out and a dotted line showing where it ought to be. The story said the absence of the Gallery, 'which was not officially noticed until Friday of this week, has caused something of an uproar in artistic circles'. All airports were being 'subjected to a rigorous scrutiny'. The police were 'baffled by the fact that the thieves totally ignored St-Martins-in-the-Fields'.

(d) Emphasis on personalities

The Fool is by nature bad at argument. If he does follow a logical process of thought, it may still be absurd because he misunderstands the context or has missed out some of the premisses. He is much better at reacting to personalities. In *Private Eye* the personal characteristics of politicians were continually aped. Here the effectiveness of caricature and cartoon forms goes without saying: *Private Eye* provided an early forum for the work of such gifted caricaturists as Gerald Scarfe and Barry Fantoni, besides William Rushton. In prose, the age and appearance of Mr Macmillan were a frequent butt. Sir Alec Douglas-Home was another favourite. After an interview in 1962 with Kenneth Harris in *The Observer*, when Home was still Foreign Secretary (and a Peer), *Private Eye* printed its own version. It ended typically: '*Harris*: Lord Home, in closing, you'll forgive me for saying so, but you've always struck me as a somewhat ludicrous figure. I should like to thank you for giving me a chance, in this interview, to prove that this is indeed entirely the case. *Home*: Quite, quite. Many people who don't know me, and think I *look* ridiculous, are often surprised to find, when they get to know me better, that despite the fact that I'm quite a nice old bird, I really *am*.' When Wilson became Prime Minister his professed liking for HP sauce led to a stream of homely habits being described in Mrs Wilson's Diary to illustrate his implied 'greyness': a fondness for Wincarnis table wine, etc. For Heath, the twisted vowel sounds of his accent – childhood Kentish with an Oxford veneer – were often stressed. So far from being an irrelevance, personal characteristics were always at the centre of *Private Eye*'s comment.

Where the *Eye* did use argument, it showed the Fool's improper grasp of logic, turning conventional rationalisations on their head by altering or ignoring their original bases.* When Lord Beeching announced his plan to modernise British Railways, the magazine published its plan for Beeching: 'Beeching appointed at £24,000 to run B.R. Cuts down railways. Job smaller. Beeching no longer economical at the price. Arms and legs declared redundant. Without arms and legs Beeching totally redundant. Sacked.' At about the same time, when Britain's independent deterrent was in question, *Private Eye* made its own suggestion: 'What you want,' it advised the Defence Minister, Peter Thorneycroft, 'is a British deterrent that is (a) cheap, (b) fools the Russians and (c) is not obsolete before manufacture. The answer is the Thorneycraft Mk. I., an entirely bogus missile, constructed of cardboard, pieces of string and old copies of the *Sunday Telegraph*. Provided that no one is ever actually allowed to *see* the missile, the Russians need never latch on . . .' Another perfect example of this inversion of argument followed the publication some years later of the Pope's encyclical condemning contraception. The *Eye* announced a further encyclical, *De Constipatione*, forbidding the use of laxatives. Constipation (like conception) was a natural God-given event, with which man had no right to interfere. The Pope's logic, by implication, was the silly rationalisation of a conservative old man.

(e) Lack of inhibitions

With no guidelines the Fool frequently disregards the niceties of normal behaviour. This has a reductive effect, sweeping away the conventions that differentiate men in society. His association with obscenity and sexuality is the clearest example. Stripped of social rank, all men are the same: only birth, reproduction and death are important. Hence satire, concerned to demolish its butts, has always contained a strong element of obscenity; and the Fool's attributes (notably his sceptre) often contained sexual symbolism. Other equally familiar instruments of ridicule were also used in *Private Eye*.

The distortions of caricature, misspelt names and warped logic

* Cf. 'The Fool effects an inversion of our assumed values and shows their arbitrariness. For him they are make-believe . . .' Willeford (1969), p. 136.

have already been mentioned. Another stock *Private Eye* technique was the continuous attribution of self-interested motives to its victims. Lord Gnome's messages were masterpieces of hypocrisy, typified by his ready threat of recourse against critics to his sinister solicitors, Messrs Sue, Grabbit and Runne. *Private Eye*'s cynical parody of the informal methods by which the Conservative Party used until 1965 to choose its Leader was another excellent example. When Mr Macmillan sacked a third of his Cabinet in July 1962, imitations of the conventional resignation letters were printed. 'Dear David,' the one to Sir David Eccles began, 'I know we have always regarded your position as Minister of Education as something of a private joke between us . . .' The letter to Selwyn Lloyd, Chancellor of the Exchequer, illustrates the structure of this form of ridicule neatly. Conventional, 'realistic' remarks begin the parody; to be followed by the self-revealing, hypocritical comment normally supplied by the reader but now expressed for him in the mouth of the victim. 'Dear Lloyd. We have worked closely together now on many problems for some years', the letter starts, in terms Macmillan might plausibly have used. Then comes the twist: 'and you know me well enough not to be surprised at my decision to stab you in the back.'*

To impute hypocrisy suggests politicians are not morally superior to ordinary people. To impute stupidity and incompetence suggests they are no cleverer; and this was also a common *Private Eye* technique. It was specially a weapon used against Sir Alec Douglas-Home. It is implied in the depiction of Parliament as a school in Eric Buttock's letters home; in the absurd age attributed to Mr Macmillan (often 104); and in the mediocrity of Harold Wilson's cultural and family life. In the arts *Private Eye* attacked both the hypocrisy and stupidity of the 'pseudo'. Clearly the *Eye*, as we have seen, thought the pop scene was a lot of humbug. Its attitude to fine arts was typified early on by a spoof competition to 'spot the art'. Underneath two drawings, identical but for a label in one of them with the name Duchamp on it, the text explained: 'One of the above exhibits is a hat-rack from the waiting room at Victoria Station. The other is "Hat-Rack 1962" by the French artist Marcel Duchamp. Which is which? Private Eye invites you to make your choice . . .' etc. In later years this attitude was formalised in a regular 'Pseud's Corner', to which readers were *genuinely* invited to contribute extracts from the press (for £1·00 prizes). In this specific area the magazine might see itself, compared with the established media, in the role of the little boy in the story of the Emperor's new clothes.

* This is the verbal form of the photograph 'bubble' joke. At *Private Eye* it was known as 'the Ingrams ending'.

Private Eye's obscenity was mild by the standards of the eighteenth century or the underground magazines of the late 1960s. But for 1961 it was quite outspoken – though that is the wrong word since it was visual more than verbal (apart from a few names like 'the Turds' pop group and press magnate Lord Gnome's ambiguous references to his 'organ'). Often it was merely cheeky and lavatorial. 'What's Macmillan like in Bed?' was the question on one front cover: 'See Page 14'. On page 14 there was just a cartoon of Mr Macmillan sitting up in bed reading a book, with a large caption saying: 'Much the same as everyone else, old cock!' The simple sexuality of the Fool was perhaps better seen in the early cartoons of 'Knifesmith'. These were drawn in crude, childlike outline, making a correspondingly simple point about the figure drawn. 'I have seven orifices', the caption below one of them went. 'I keep one clean with a brush, five clean with cotton products and one with paper. I have to keep on and on doing this.' Later the magazine's strip cartoons about Barry Mackenzie (the adventures of an Australian in London) and the Cloggies (a band of itinerant 'clog dancers') stressed sexual themes with a non-titillating directness completely in keeping with the unembarrassed reductive behaviour of the Fool.

(*f*) *Invincibility of the Fool*

Since he is beyond their reach, the Fool cannot be defeated under society's rules. To treat him as though he could is to make oneself ridiculous. He may be silenced: the game may be stopped. But that is not the same as winning it: indeed it may amount to the admission of defeat, if the reason for stopping it is frustration at the inability to win.

The obvious illustration of this characteristic in *Private Eye* was its ability freely to make uninhibited comment which in established media would have provoked libel actions and major damages. The same was true of *The Week*. Both magazines profited from being transparently incapable of paying large damages anyway (in itself a deterrent against actions) and from the probability that suing them would give the libel greater currency and make its victim look even more ludicrous. Cockburn has said, indeed, that this was the test he used in order to decide whether to print a libellous story: 'In case he brings an action, I asked myself, which of us in the end will look more ridiculous?'[16]

The Week was often threatened with libel but no action was ever brought or even settled out of court. *Private Eye* was less fortunate. The first action against it was brought in January 1963, some fifteen months after the magazine started, by a Rotherham alderman,

L. J. Tarbit, a former prospective Liberal parliamentary candidate.* This attracted little attention. But next month Randolph Churchill decided to sue. His larger-than-life personality and previous forays into the courts in libel actions ensured quite a lot of publicity which the magazine must have welcomed. Churchill had, perhaps, a few of the qualities of the jester himself: it is not in the least surprising that a man of his flamboyant personality was an early litigant. The same qualities made him content not to seek swingeing damages that might have closed the magazine down.[17] In the first ten years there were over a dozen actions reported in *The Times* – almost all by journalists, politicians or show business people: a typical reflection of the *Eye*'s range of subject matter.[18]

Only two put the magazine in real difficulty. In 1966 an award of £5,000 (plus about £3,000 costs) to Lord Russell of Liverpool, who was not in the least put off by the 'Fool' character of the *Eye*, led to a public appeal for funds, complete with a Charity Matinée at the Phoenix Theatre.[19] Awards of £500 each to two journalists on *The People* in 1969 – plus costs amounting to £9,000 (the case took seven days) – led similarly to the 'Gnomefam' appeal.[20] The Russell case was the most elaborate, with a string of well known witnesses for the defence. Normally the actions were settled out of court. There were others, moreover, that were not reported in the press,† and some complaints led to injunctions against the magazine mentioning the victim in the future. The first of these was taken out by C. P. Snow.

III. The political role of the Fool: the significance of Private Eye

It has already been suggested that the Fool is in society but not of it. He contributes positively to the functioning of the social system, though not always to the maintenance of a given individual's role. His situation gives him a love/hate relationship with the system.

These suggestions can now be examined in detail.

(a) The Fool sustains the necessary mythology of kingship

The idea of kingship supposes 'perfection': yet the King himself is inevitably possessed of human frailties. The Fool, because he is

---

* See *The Times*, 4 January 1963. Alderman Tarbit died two weeks afterwards; which the *Eye* regarded as highly significant.

† Ingrams says *Private Eye* was sued by about 50 individuals in its first ten years and paid out nearly £50,000. *Life and times of Private Eye*, p. 11.

the only person apart from the King not subject to the King's laws, 'reflects' the King; and by concentrating in his own person the King's inadequacies, he assists the illusion that the King himself is perfect.*

The institutions and principles of modern British government equally depend on a sustaining mythology. The very idea of constitutionalism contains the doubtful notion that it will always seem more important to politicians to do things according to certain procedures than to achieve ends that may be inconsistent with them. The principles of collective and individual ministerial responsibility are partly mythical. The ideas that Parliament makes laws, that civil servants are accountable to Parliament and that general elections change governments need to be hedged about closely with reservations and careful definitions if they are to pass for accurate descriptions of government. Principles are necessary to the logic and rationality of the system: but to some extent they can never exist except in theory. All constitutions are prescriptive. Practice may resemble theory quite closely (it is perhaps fairly easy in Britain, where the constitution is unwritten and vague); or the theory may, as in the 1936 Russian constitution, represent an ideal towards which the system aims to move. In any case there will be a gap between how things are supposed to be done and how they are actually done. The same judgement may probably be made about models of government that aim simply to *describe* processes. In principle a completely accurate model of the British system of government could be described. But its detail would be so voluminous that it would become inaccurate as soon as constructed; it would need simplification if it was to be widely accessible and understood; and in both these ways a gap between theory and practice would open up.

It is the first type of model, however – the set of institutions and principles believed by those operating them and by the people at large to be the appropriate (i.e. the legitimate) machinery of government – to whose operation the Fool is important. He reminds us of the difference between the ideals of the theory, with its ritual and symbols – the mace, the crown, the judge's wig (stressing the impersonality of justice) – and the human nature of the practitioners. For example, by his emphasis on personalities and his uninhibited comment he shows that the distinction between the public and private life of a politician is a sham – itself a product of the attempt to distinguish the perfect system from the persons who operate it. 'The private life of a politician is his own affair' is a principle that

---

* Cf. Willeford (1969), p. 156. 'When the King was a syphilitic semi-imbecile, a jester even more grotesque may have served as a useful stage prop, disarming criticism by making the King look more nearly normal by comparison and thus making the make-believe of Kingship possible.'

can be accepted only if we believe that a politician's private attitudes and values can have no conceivable bearing on his public actions – a belief that assumes an artificially sharp distinction between a pure 'impersonal' system, and a private life-style.

Cockburn has indicated how essential to the satirist the existence of this difference between the theory and practice of the system is: 'What arouses the indignation of the honest satirist is not, unless the man is a prig, the fact that people in positions of power or influence behave idiotically, or even that they behave wickedly. It is that they conspire successfully to impose upon the public a picture of themselves as so very, very deep-thinking, sagacious, honest and well-intentioned. You cannot satirise a man who says "I'm in it for the money and that's all about it". You even feel no inclination to do so.'[21]

In this sense, then, the role of *Private Eye* was, like the Fool, to apprise the public of the realities coexisting with the necessary myths of the governmental system. It did this in relation to the establishment media as well as to politicians. Just as *The Week* was started to report what people were 'really saying' so the demand for *Private Eye* was created, as Cockburn remarked after his stint with the magazine, not by any means simply by what *Private Eye* did, but by what the rest of the British Press either could not or would not do.'[22] The press 'played the game'. *Private Eye* must not. Hence Cockburn, as guest editor, flouted a D Notice and published the name and address of the head of M.I.5. This (he says) caused an uproar, not least because, if he were allowed to get away with it, *the rest of Fleet Street would think it unfair.*[23]

The Fool's failure to distinguish truth and falsehood is important here. Cockburn was a fact and rumour man. *Private Eye* in contrast was a 'fantasy' paper, until, partly under Cockburn's influence, it began to inject more facts. But the importance of its contents was independent of truth or falsehood. What mattered, in the present analysis, was that by mocking the frailties of the system with the techniques described in the previous section it fantasised them. With its taunts of incompetence, gerontocracy, hypocrisy and cardboard missiles, it enabled its readers to laugh at a *picture* of the system. By reading the trivialities of Mrs Wilson's Diary, we could reassure ourselves that actual life at Number Ten – and the *actual* system – conformed to the idealised view. By lampooning the system as the exact opposite of 'very, very deep-thinking, sagacious, honest and well-intentioned', the *Eye* may have encouraged the reader to feel it could not be as bad as all that. To talk of cardboard missiles was to *avoid* engaging in argument about defence and to leave the 'system's' ideas on defence intact.

Willeford discusses the Fool's reinforcement of the make-believe essential to kingship in terms of the failure of kingly power to control lands beyond the kingdom and potentially, therefore, to control even the kingdom itself. The Fool embodies 'the possibility that the kingly office and the institutions may lose their power and meaning and that the realm beyond the borders of the kingdom may again become threatening. The jester diminishes the threat playfully by holding the possibility of the threat up to the imagination.'[24] That could be a fair summary of *Private Eye*'s role in relation to make-believe. The 'threat' of chaotic government – particularly in the last two years of the Macmillan era – was diminished by the 'playful admission' of its possibility.

(b) By tolerating the Fool the King shows his own strength

That is, he shows that his authority is strong enough to ignore even open rebellion. In general terms, the acceptance of the dominant values in a society may be measured by the degree of its toleration of deviance from them. Here one may note that the TV satire shows, reaching audiences of many millions and put out on a publicly controlled, non-partisan broadcasting system, proved to have a much lower threshold of tolerance and were abandoned after a few years; while *Private Eye*, though on the whole more deviant, had no difficulty (except financial) in continuing. Some of the later underground magazines, on the other hand, ran foul of the law since they were perceived as a threat to established values, despite their small circulations. In other words they were propagandists for 'alternative societies', not Fools for the existing one.*

(c) The jokes and insults of the Fool against the King are cathartic for the people

This point is closely connected to the previous one. The frustrations of the individual in a large-scale, modern society with a bureaucratised system of government may be alleviated by the antics of such as *Private Eye*.† One would thus expect the magazine's readership to be predominantly among people who to some extent cared about public affairs and wanted, in a vague or specific way, to 'participate'. Cockburn has described the type of people who contributed to the

---

* The outstanding example was the trial of the editors of the underground magazine *Oz* in the summer of 1971, on obscenity charges. See Tony Palmer (1971).

† In France the bureaucratic régime of General de Gaulle, with power concentrated strongly on the person of the President, equally produced a great success for the comedian Henri Tissot, who specialised in impersonations of the General.

Private Eye financial appeals: teachers and schoolboys, dons, graduate students and research workers, Trade Union officials, MPs, peers, journalists, show business people, advertising and city people.[25] None of those seems surprising; least of all the peers, who, within the political system, have many of the characteristics of the Fool themselves. One may note here, too, the willingness with which journalists plied *Private Eye* with information their own papers would not publish. It had a kind of safety-valve function, making the limitations of working 'in the system' more tolerable.*

The parallel both of this point and the one under the previous heading with the role of ritualised rebellions is an obvious one. In his essay on *The licence in ritual*, Max Gluckman examines the work of anthropologists on the great military rituals of the Swazis, performed at sowing, first fruits, harvest and before war. Their essence was to enable the subjects more willingly to tolerate the King by expressing in a 'game' their real resentments and fears. The rites affirmed the unity of the nation round the idea of kingship but admitted the conflicts round the person of the incumbent King – 'the resentment of his subjects against authority, the jealousy of his brother-princes who covet the throne, and so forth. Indeed the ritual exaggerates the conflicts. Whether or not princes covet the throne they are made to act as if they do so covet it.'[26] In just the same way *Private Eye* pilloried not the Westminster system but the incumbent rulers – the Prime Ministers of the 1960s and their associates; even to the extent of attributing presumed motives of self-interest and so on, like the Swazis, where there may have been no evidence of any. Why does the 'rebellion' go on? Because 'the Kingship is sacred, and its sacred strength is necessary for the nation . . . The acceptance of the established order as right and good, and even sacred, seems to allow unbridled licence, very rituals of rebellion, for the order itself keeps this rebellion within bounds. Hence to act the conflicts . . . emphasises the social cohesion within which the conflicts exist'. The people support the King 'despite the conflicts between them. Or, at least, if they don't support the particular King, they support the Kingship . . . Swazis were rebels, never revolutionaries.'[27]

Clearly, the magazine's role as purveyor of catharsis was unintentional and should not be exaggerated. The important point is that it was a distinctive role not performed systematically by other media. It was neatly encapsulated in the magazine's attitude to pop stars. Its mockery may have helped people to accept the fact (which many no doubt resented) that pop stars became in the 1960s a group with financial power and considerable influence on life-styles.

* Many stories were 'Fleet Street "rejects"', passed on to us by their disgruntled authors'. *Life and times of Private Eye*, p. 21.

Ordinary papers and the broadcast media ignored them or regarded them with deference and envy. The underground press, typically, treated them with utter seriousness. Only *Private Eye* played the Fool with them.

(d) Under some conditions the Fool may pose a definite threat to the incumbent King

Again the sysem itself may not be threatened; rather, the position of powerful individuals within it. In one sense the Fool presents a permanent threat. He symbolises the power of emotions, the limitations of rational behaviour and thus the existence of forces outside the control of kingship. In Willeford's words, 'The Fool helps to maintain a relativity between the King and his office and between that office and the facts of life and death.'[28]

Willeford quotes a story that is relevant here about the Caliph Harun al-Rashid. 'He once gave his buffoon Buhlul a document by which Buhlul was made governor of all the bears, wolves, foxes, apes and asses in the caliphate. "It is too much for me," Buhlul answered, "I am not ambitious enough to desire to rule all your holiness's subjects." The Caliph had offered him a position that comically and on a ridiculously inferior level paralleled his own; at the same time, the subjects to be governed by the fool were representative of forces that could in any case not be fully brought under the control of the caliph. In his rebuttal the fool not only reduced the entire human population of the caliphate to the level of animals; he also implied that the caliphate consisted only of forces that the caliph could not really control. By playing upon the inadequacy of the king's power, the Fool made a mockery of the kingdom: a kingdom composed only of bears, wolves, foxes, apes, and asses would be like one in which all the fools wear crowns. It would be no kingdom.'[29]

Private Eye, one might say, helped people to keep a sense of proportion. How much did the government really matter in our everyday lives? Not a great deal, after all; and Mr Macmillan and his colleagues were ordinary people not omnicompetent moguls. To read the heavy papers one might think that politics was the most important thing in the world and that politicians did actually run things. The Fool destroys such illusions. In doing so, however, he poses paradoxically a threat, for he reduces the possibility that the King *will* be able to run things.

In another sense the extent to which the Fool threatens the King depends on the terms of the game. The assumption on which the taunts and jokes of the Fool are tolerated is that the King's authority is suspended *voluntarily* and could be enforced at a word. That assumption may be challenged. If the King's tolerance is involuntary the Fool may truly threaten his authority. The game may become a grim reality, a struggle for power.* Even when the King's authority is apparently absolute we can never be completely sure, so long as the rules are suspended, that he can invoke them again. The Fool may always be a potential rival, a catalyst for opposition. (He has obvious affinities here with the Hero, who may be the supporter of the King, yet become his rival and successor, like Mark Antony.)

Naturally one could not see the editors of *Private Eye* as potential leaders of a coup. The nature of any 'threats' the magazine posed, rather, lay in such differences as its distinctive character may have made to the course of political events. Its first successful 'threat', which drew its existence to the attention of both a wider and more élite audience than before, came during the Profumo Affair in the summer of 1963. Rumours that Mr Profumo, Secretary of State for War, had been having an affair with Christine Keeler, a 'model' who was also associated with Captain Ivanov, a military attaché at the Russian Embassy, circulated for some months and culminated in a personal statement by Profumo in Parliament in March, 1963. Profumo denied any impropriety in his relationship and any breach of security. The rumours continued to circulate; but although documentary evidence also began to accumulate, the press was completely silent. Even before the March statement it had done no more than hint at the rumours. On 4 June Profumo relented and resigned, admitting that his parliamentary statement was untrue (though not in respect of the denial of breach of security).[30]

Private Eye could claim to have published the fullest story to appear about the rumours before they were publicly denied by Profumo in Parliament; and it was able to take the lead, for which it is given generous credit by Wayland Young in his careful study, *The Profumo Affair: Aspects of Conservatism*, precisely because it was Fool to the system. Its story was in 'code' (written by Lunchtime O'Booze): the characters were named James Montesi, Vladimir Bolokhov and Gaye Funloving. The characteristic confusion of fact, fantasy and rumour meant that it could go further in what it said than conventional papers. For Profumo to have sued would have been counterproductive. The *Eye*'s relationship to the established media ('Fleet Street's conscience') meant also that Stephen Ward, a friend of Christine Keeler closely involved in the affair, approached

---

* See Willeford, p. 155, for a description of Michel de Ghelderode's play *Escurial*, written in 1927. 'A King and his jester exchange roles in a grim game in which their mutual hatred and rivalry are openly expressed. Finally, both shout, "My crown! I am the King!", and the king puts an end to the game by having the jester strangled.'

it spontaneously with information. It was a story in which the barrier erected in society between the public and private lives of a politician broke down, and in which human feelings and sexuality were crucial. The weakness of Profumo (as 'King') and his deviance from the make-believe ideal of kingship (it was 'a great tragedy for the probity of public life in Britain' wrote *The Times*) were exposed by the Fool, and Profumo's position was successfully challenged. The fact that the affair was treated as such a crisis for the government requires a complex explanation in which the role of the mass media might not be very important. But the media certainly played a part in precipitating it, and the particular qualities of *Private Eye* made it perfectly suited to take an early lead.

Another, much more limited, way in which *Private Eye* occasionally 'threatened' individuals, specially in its early years, was the forms it obliged its victims to use in counter-attack. We have seen the drawbacks of libel actions – they might give even greater currency to the libel, and the magazine was at that time incapable of paying heavy damages. A few people, perhaps litigious or indifferent to publicity, took action nonetheless. But on at least two of those occasions the type of redress itself broke the normal rules of legal remedy and involved an element of playing the Fool. *Private Eye* may have lost in one sense; but it won in the sense of forcing its victim to fight on its own ground. Randolph Churchill's action was the best example. 'I'm fed up with lawyers and as I didn't want any money myself I decided to cut them out of the case,' he told *The Times*. 'I was told I might get damages of £100,000, but I didn't want to close the magazine down. I think it's quite amusing as long as it leaves me alone.'[31] His remedy was to make *Private Eye* buy a full-page advertisement in the London *Evening Standard* (whose circulation was many times greater; the existence of the libel thus reached a much wider audience). It contained a statement by Churchill and a letter of retraction by the magazine's editors.[32]

On a more modest scale the TV producer and scriptwriter Elkan Allan exacted an apology in the form of an 18-line insertion in the personal column of *The Times*.[33]

The most effective way of silencing *Private Eye* without running risks or meeting the magazine on its own terms seems to have been by requiring an agreement that a victim would not be criticised in future. A sign of its effectiveness, perhaps, is that the editor complained about the practice in a letter to *The Times*.[34] In 1967 an undertaking was given to Derek Marks, editor of the *Daily Express*, that 'none of us will publish anything in future that is defamatory of you or the *Daily Express* or anything which reflects directly or indirectly on your editorial competence or integrity'. A similar undertaking was given to the *New Statesman*; while *The Spectator* extracted an agreement that nothing would be published about it without its editor's written approval. This was 'stopping the game' with a vengeance.

(e) The Fool is a disinterested adviser to the King

Because he has no status inside society the Fool alone among the King's subjects can confidently be expected by the King to give him disinterested advice (especially if he is an artificial Fool). Although he may be a threat in the sort of circumstances just discussed, at other times he may be of great assistance to the King himself, quite apart from buttressing the institution of kingship. In this sense the element of the later *Private Eye* devoted to traditional exposure journalism can be seen as a straightforward contribution to the reduction of corruption and incompetence in public life. As guest editor, Cockburn hammered away at the point that 'a satirical paper cannot justify its existence only by satirizing what is already known. It must disclose news too.'[35] After Paul Foot joined the magazine in 1967 it became firmly established in the tradition of exposure journalism, both at the level of titbits of political and financial gossip ('In the City – By Slicker') and of more sustained digging. For reasons already discussed its exposures could often be made earlier than in established media and tended to concern subjects they neglected. Sometimes this neglect followed from the fact that established media, for commercial, partisan or more vaguely political reasons, lacked precisely the element of disinterestedness present in the *Eye*. Soon the magazine could claim a long list of matters which it had been the first to expose, many of them in the the fields of city, police, local government and the nationalised industries.*

(f) The role of the Fool means he is kept close to the King

Because the Fool's role gives him a kind of political power it is important to the King that he should not be far out of sight. 'The Roman Emperors took great care that the great mimes should be close to the throne . . . They had the power to turn the people

---

* 'There was most notably the Heart Transplant saga, when Foot, alone among British journalists, bothered to find out what was going on at Groote Schuur. There was Ronan Point – another technological disaster – and the long saga of the Concorde aeroplane; Israel, Greece and Northern Ireland; the Biafran civil war; the drugs industry; police and local government corruption; Porton Down – all these are stories which for one reason or another the national press do not report as fully as they might.' Ingrams (1971), p. 21. He could later have added Poulson to the list.

against the Emperor, and they were known to be afraid of nothing . . . With one laugh pitched to the exact pitch, the clown could destroy the Kingdom, as a singer will destroy a wineglass.'[36]

As the 1960s progressed, *Private Eye* became closer to those who worked 'the system'. The process was greatly accelerated by its role in the Profumo Affair, and by the gradual increase in its *factual* content discussed in the previous section.

Endless illustrations could be given to show how the King's embrace gradually enfolded it. In 1969 Granada Television, a bulwark of the Establishment media, gave it a special award as 'irritant of the year . . . for its exclusive stories which often provided the basis for newspaper stories and which made it required reading in Fleet Street and Westminster.'[37] In 1972 *Punch* dignified it with an eight-page parody.[38] In 1961 the magazine simply would not have been interested in membership of the Lobby Correspondents Group – the traditional focus of Westminster news-gathering: by 1971 it was visibly irked by exclusion, though enjoying the opportunity of ridiculing the system. In 1971 the reader could be fairly confident that contributions by a prominent mainstream comedian, Spike Milligan, and by the poet John Betjeman (a series on new architectural monstrosities) *were* by those people: in 1961 he could have been equally confident that they were not. Competitions and prizes in 1961 were bogus: in 1971 they were genuine. The editors and contributors increasingly wore the label of *Private Eye* when appearing on television and radio programmes, even when interviewing the Prime Minister.* As with *The Week*, the number of sources snowballed as the paper's role became clearer. Its regular Wednesday lunch for contributors in a pub opposite the office became an institution.† Perhaps the best symbol of *Private Eye*'s relationship with the established media by 1971 was, to quote *The Times*, its 'healthy audited circulation which its editor frequently, publicly and gleefully compares to that of the *Spectator* (to the detriment of course, of the *Spectator*)'.[39] Of its political respectability what better symbol could there be than Mr Wilson's invitation to the editor – and its acceptance – to a Downing Street reception?

* '. . . Mr Wilson was also interviewed by Mr Charles Douglas-Home, Defence Correspondent of *The Times*, and Mr Paul Foot, deputy editor of *Private Eye*' – *The Times* 17 April 1970.

† 'There are, we discovered, people in every organisation with a strongly developed anarchic streak, mischief makers, mavericks, who like nothing better than to throw a few spanners in the works now and then. These people exist in Fleet Street, the BBC, the Civil Service and the City – even the Conservative party. They are people who are against the Establishment – whatever party it may subscribe to – and it is from their ranks that the *Eye* draws its informants and its readers.' Ingrams (1971), p. 21.

IV. THE FOOL'S LOVE/HATE RELATIONSHIP
WITH THE KING

The character and political role of *Private Eye* as Fool gave it a
love/hate relationship with the system. The Fool loves the King
because his security is linked to the King's security. Without the
King as a butt, he has no role. At the same time he hates the system
because he is excluded from its normal social values and relationships: he exists only on the King's sufferance. In the same way
Private Eye depended upon those in the Establishment for its
material (and some of its readership) while constantly insulting them.
It showed contempt for 'pseuds and bores', yet it never stopped
writing about them. It parodied the styles of Fleet Street, yet with a
skill often equal to the originals. The perfect indicator of this
relationship was the paper's situation in the Macmillan era. Macmillan
was an ideal butt: so were the extraordinary events of his last
year in office – disastrous by-elections, the Skybolt rocket crisis,
the collapse of negotiations for entry to EEC, the Vassall spy case,
the Profumo affair, etc. When Macmillan went, *Private Eye*'s
dependence upon him was dramatically revealed in the tumbling
circulation – reduced by nearly three-quarters in a few months to
25,000.[40] The paper probably then had three choices. It could quietly
die, just as the King's Fool might be removed when the King died.
It could conceivably have risked trying to turn itself into a more
underground magazine, detaching itself from the system. Or it
could yield gracefully to the system's patronage, becoming less a
natural Fool and more consciously a licensed one, performing a
particular, predictable role. The latter must have seemed the obvious
choice. The Fool managed to adapt successfully to the accession
of new Kings.

References

1. The nature and production of mass media effects

1. See P. Watzlawick et al., *Pragmatics of human communication* (1968), pp. 75–8.
2. Max Gluckman, *Custom and conflict in Africa* (1955), pp. 130–1.
3. The *Mirror*'s relationship with its readers has been the subject of a detailed study at the Centre for Contemporary Cultural Studies, University of Birmingham.
4. See e.g. Raymond Williams, *Communications* (1966); Denys Thompson (ed.), *Discrimination and popular culture* (1964). For the argument as applied to TV see Richard Crossman, *The politics of television*, Granada Guidhall Lecture (1969).
5. Jeremy Tunstall, *Journalists at work* (1971).
6. For a limited but systematic study of foreign news values, see J. Galtung and M. H. Ruge, 'The structure of foreign news' (1965) in Tunstall (ed.), *Media sociology* (1970). Cf. J. Halloran et al., *Demonstrations and communication* (1970).
7. A highly readable and well illustrated discussion comparing press and TV is John Whale, *The half-shut eye* (1969).
8. Whale's *The half-shut eye* provides a wealth of examples of this kind to illustrate the impact of the television medium on British and American politics.
9. See Ole R. Holsti, Robert C. North and Richard A. Brody, 'Perception and action in the 1914 crisis', in J. David Singer (ed.), *Quantitative international politics* (1966) and Robert C. North's article of the same name in John C. Farrell and Asa P. Smith (eds.), *Image and reality in world politics* (1967). For a general discussion of the significance of communication processes in international politics, see Robert Jervis, 'Hypotheses on misperception', *World Politics*, Vol. XX, 3, 1968.
10. Mendelsohn and Crespi, *Polls, television and the new politics* (1970) similarly distinguish between 'direct' and 'indirect' political communication effects and stress the importance of the latter as opposed to the former.
11. Jay Blumler, 'Producers' attitudes towards TV coverage of an election campaign: a case study' in Tunstall (ed.), *Media sociology* (1970).
12. Harold Wilson, *The Labour Government, 1964–70* (1971), p. 456. For an analysis of the decision, see Colin Seymour-Ure, 'The disintegration of the Cabinet', *Parliamentary Affairs* XXIV, 3 (1971), pp. 201–2, and Samuel Brittan, *Steering the economy* (1970).

13. John Whale, *Journalism and government* (1972), pp. 99–100.
14. *Lord Denning's Report* (1963), pp. 42–3.
15. Lewis Chester et al., *The Zinoviev Letter* (1967), p. 14.
16. Ibid., where the letter is quoted in full, pp. xi–xiii.
17. Ibid., p. 205.
18. Ibid., p. xiii.
19. Ibid., p. xvii.
20. H. G. Nicholas, *The British General Election of 1950* (1951), pp. 109–11 and 140.
21. Gay Talese, *The kingdom and the power* (1970), pp. 5–6.
22. *Sunday Times*, 22 July 1962.
23. The role of the press in this situation is analysed more fully in Colin Seymour-Ure, *The press, politics and the public* (1968), pp. 289–300. See also Tunstall, *The Westminster Lobby correspondents* (1970).
24. Harold Wilson (1971), pp. 455–6.
25. Ibid., p. 457. Cf. Samuel Brittan (1970), pp. 360–1.
26. The data in this section is drawn from *Svoboda: the press in Czechoslovakia 1968* (1969) and interviews. The quotations are from pp. 115, 48 and 107. See also Stuart Hood, *The mass media* (1972).
27. Lord Boyle and Anthony Crosland, *The politics of education* (Maurice Kegan (ed.)) (1971), p. 109.
28. The source for these paragraphs is David Butler and Michael Pinto-Duschinsky, *The British General Election of 1970* (1971).
29. Cf. Jeremy Tunstall (1970(2)), pp. 101–2.

2. The political context of mass media effects

1. 'The structure and function of communication in society', reprinted in B. Berelson and M. Janowitz, *Reader in public opinion and communication* (1966), pp. 178–9.
2. See J. T. Klapper, *The effects of mass communication* (1960) and James Halloran, op. cit. (1965, 1970).
3. Denis McQuail, *Towards a sociology of mass communications* (1969), p. 71 and D. Chaney, *Processes of mass communication* (1972) pay special attention to this approach.
4. See section I (*e*) below, and Sidney Kraus (ed.), *The great debates* (1968).
5. See the general discussion of this question in Halloran (1970), pp. 53–66.
6. Quoted in Harold Herd, *The march of journalism* (1952), p. 241.
7. Quoted in Tom Clarke, *Northcliffe in history* (n.d.), pp. 152–3.
8. These details, and data throughout this section, are drawn from J. G. Blumler et al., 'Attitudes to the monarchy', *Political Studies*, XIX, 2, 1971, pp. 149–71.
9. E.g. Harry Street, *Freedom, the individual and the law* (1963), pp. 154, 171.
10. Cf. the comments of the Royal Commission on the Police, *Report* (1962), pp. 117–21.

11. Cf. the findings of a survey by the Television Commission of the ACTT, one of the TV industry's unions, *One Week: a survey of television coverage of union and industrial affairs in the week January 8–14th 1971* (1971).
12. Radio 4, 23 April 1971.
13. For discussions of this argument, as seen by the student of mass media, see e.g. John Whale (1967), Robert MacNeil, *The people machine* (1970), and Bernard Rubin, *Political television* (1967).
14. MacNeil (1970), p. 253.
15. Ibid., p. 294.
16. James Reston, quoted in MacNeil (1970), p. 292.
17. A. Barker and M. Rush, *The member of parliament and his information* (1970), p. 170.
18. See e.g. George Brown, *In my way* (1971), p. 47.
19. For detailed analyses see Wayland Young, *The Profumo Affair* (1963); Seymour-Ure (1968), pp. 266–76 and 288–9.
20. K. and G. Lang, *Politics and television* (1970), pp. 30–1.
21. This account is drawn from Bernard Rubin (1967), pp. 34–6, and K. and G. Lang (1970), pp. 24–9.
22. Richard M. Nixon, *Six Crises* (1962), p. 100.
23. Lang (1970), p. 27.
24. George Brown (1972), pp. 161–7.
25. Quotations from ibid., p. 166.
26. George Brown (1972), p. 167.
27. Some of it is collected, and more is referred to, in Sidney Kraus (ed.) (1968).
28. Lang (1970), p. 213.
29. Pierre Salinger, *With Kennedy* (1967), p. 80.
30. *Boston Herald*, 10 November 1960. Quoted Rubin (1967), p. 18.
31. Nixon (1962), p. 357.
32. Kraus (1968), p. 258.
33. MacNeil (1970), p. 169; Theodore H. White, *The making of the president 1960* (1961), p. 291.
34. Ibid., pp. 290–1.

3. The Times *and the appeasement of Hitler*

1. *House of Commons Debates*, 14 Dec. 1950, Vol. 482, c.1367.
2. Martin Gilbert, *The roots of appeasement* (1966), p. 195.
3. The development of appeasement can be traced in many of the sources quoted in this chapter. For general reference one may single out: Margaret George, *The warped vision: British foreign policy 1933–39* (1965); Martin Gilbert (1966); Martin Gilbert and Richard Gott, *The appeasers* (1963); Keith Middlemas, *The diplomacy of illusion* (1972); Keith Robbins, *Munich 1938* (1969); A. J. P. Taylor, *The origins of the Second World War* (1961); Sir John Wheeler-Bennett, *Munich, prologue to tragedy* (1948 reprinted 1963).
4. Rt Hon. the Earl of Avon, *The reckoning* (1955), p. 21.

5. Lord Vansittart, *The mist procession* (1958), p. 364.
6. Francis Williams, *Dangerous estate* (1957), p. 271.
7. John Evelyn Wrench, *Geoffrey Dawson and our times* (1955), pp. 432–3.
8. Ibid., p. 361.
9. *The Times*, 23 September 1938. Quoted in *The history of The Times* Vol. IV (1952), p. 939.
10. Ibid., p. 962.
11. For details see C. L. Mowat, *Britain between the wars* (1959), p. 542.
12. Gilbert and Gott (1963), p. 26.
13. *History of the Times* (1952), p. 945.
14. *History of The Times* (1952), pp. 781–2.
15. Colin Coote, *Editorial* (1965(2)), p. 169.
16. *The Liddell Hart memoirs* (1965), Vol. II, p. 149.
17. Wrench (1955), p. 69.
18. Quoted anonymously, *History of The Times* (1952), p. 1067.
19. H. Nicolson, *Diaries and letters, 1930–39* (1966), p. 359.
20. Neville Thompson, *The Anti-Appeasers* (1971).
21. *History of The Times* (1952), p. 770.
22. Wrench (1955), p. 373.
23. See Chapter 6. Good examples are *Le Monde* (France), *Neue Zürcher Zeitung* (Switzerland) and *Christian Science Monitor* (USA). For their editorial policymaking procedures see C. Seymour-Ure 'Policy-making in the press', *Government and Opposition*, Vol. IV, no. 4, 1969, pp. 425–525.
24. Thomas Jones (1954), p. 161; cf. Liddell Hart (1965), Vol. 1, p. 289.
25. Harold Macmillan (1966), pp. 437, 444–5.
26. William Shirer, *Berlin Diary* (1941), p. 44.
27. N. H. Baynes, *The speeches of Adolf Hitler* (1942), pp. 1400–1. Cf. The Earl of Halifax, *Fulness of days* (1957), p. 186.
28. Sir Nevile Henderson was British Ambassador to Berlin, 1937–9.
29. Baynes (1942), pp. 1678–9.
30. *Documents on British foreign policy* (Third Series), Vol. II. Sept. 6, 1938, p. 257.
31. Ibid., Vol. I, pp. 369–70.
32. Sir Nevile Henderson, *Failure of a mission* (1940), p. 65.
33. Loc. cit.
34. *Documents* 3s. Vol. III, pp. 389; Vol. I, pp. 80–2.
35. *Documents* 3s. Vol. I., pp. 444, 472.
36. Ibid., Vol. V, p. 65.
37. Rt Hon. the Earl of Avon, *The Eden memoirs: Facing the dictators* (1962), p. 508.
38. Ibid., p. 177.
39. *The Spectator*, 7 April 1939.
40. Wheeler-Bennett (1963), pp. 96–7.
41. *History of The Times* (1952), p. 929. Wrench (1955), p. 371. See also McLachlan (1971), pp. 146–52; Gannon (1971), pp. 178–83.
42. *The Times*, 7 September 1938.
43. Wrench (1955), pp. 371–2.
44. *Documents* 3s. Vol. II, p. 271n.

45. *History of The Times* (1952), pp. 933–4.
46. Ibid., p. 934n.
47. Duff Cooper, *Old men forget* (1953), p. 226.
48. Thomas Jones, *A diary with letters* (1954), p. 407.
49. Colin Coote, *A companion of honour* (1965(1)), p. 162.
50. Rt Hon. the Earl of Avon (1965), p. 21. Letter to J. P. L. Thomas.
51. *Documents* 3s. Vol. II, p. 271n.
52. Ibid., p. 293. Cf. 'Chips' Channon, a British delegate: 'Everyone is indignant with "The Times" for its article last Tuesday, which they pretend has strengthened Hitler's hand . . .' Robert Rhodes James (ed.), *Chips. The diaries of Sir Henry Channon* (1967), p. 164.
53. Nicolson (1966), *Diary*, 9 Sept. 1938, p. 352.
54. See e.g. Thomas Jones (1954), p. 407; Rhodes James (1967), p. 164.
55. *History of The Times* (1952), Quoted p. 933.
56. I. Maisky, *Who helped Hitler?* (1964), p. 81.
57. Liddell Hart (1965), Vol. II, ch. 1ff.
58. *The Times*, 14 June 1938.
59. Wrench (1955), p. 83.
60. *Dictionary of National Biography 1941–50*, p. 205.
61. Vansittart (1958), p. 364.
62. Wrench (1955), Diary, 14 September, p. 376.
63. Diary, 24 Sept., Ibid., p. 377.
64. Quoted in F. Williams (1957), p. 273. Dawson's activity is nicely evoked there.
65. Wrench (1955), p. 377.
66. Claud Cockburn, *I Claud* (1967), p. 179.
67. Ibid., p. 179.
68. Michael Astor, *Tribal Feeling* (1963), p. 146. The house came into the public eye again in the early 1960s because of its part in the Stephen Ward and Profumo affairs.
69. Cockburn (1967), p. 180.
70. Gilbert and Gott (1963), pp. 55, 354.
71. 1 April 1938 (approximately). Wrench (1955), p. 366.
72. *History of The Times* (1952), p. 893.
73. Wrench (1955), p. 402.
74. A. J. P. Taylor (1965), p. 418.
75. F. Williams (1957), p. 273.
76. Liddell Hart (1965), Vol. II, p. 149.
77. *The Times*, 6 February 1852.
78. F. Williams (1957), p. 275.
79. Ibid., p. 274.
80. *History of The Times* (1952), p. 1008.
81. Loc. cit.
82. Loc. cit.
83. Report of the Merger of *The Times* and *The Sunday Times*, H.C. 273, 1966–7, pp. 39–40.
84. *History of The Times* (1952), p. 907.
85. Loc. cit.
86. Quoted by Martin Gilbert (1966), pp. 143–4.

87. Shirer (1941), p. 33.
88. Ibid., p. 68.
89. *Ambassador Dodd's diary 1933–38* (1941), p. 422, 17 June 1937.
90. Vansittart (1958), p. 507.
91. Martin Gilbert (1966), p. 165.
92. Sharf, *The British press and the Jews under Nazi rule* (1964).
93. *History of The Times* (1952), p. 908.
94. Ibid., p. 594. Author's italics.
95. McLachlan (1971), p. 129. The misleading crudity with which the charge has sometimes been made is discredited in Appendix III of McLachlan's book, pp. 282–3. Cf. Gannon, *The British press and Germany 1936–39* (1971), pp. 123–6.
96. See, e.g. McLachlan (1971), p. 136; Gannon (1971), pp. 124–5.
97. Liddell Hart (1965), Vol. II, p. 180.
98. Ibid., p. 197.
99. Ibid. p. 147.
100. Wrench (1955), p. 380.
101. F. Williams (1957), p. 275.
102. Ibid., p. 380.
103. *The Times*, 13 July 1939.
104. See *History of The Times* (1952), p. 971.
105. Coote (1965(2)), p. 185.
106. Cooper (1953), p. 227.
107. *History of The Times* (1952), p. 571.
108. Ibid., See Ch. XIII passim. Cf. Steed's role in the Chanak crisis, with a critically timed letter in *The Times* from Bonar Law, pp. 737–8.
109. *History of The Times* (1952), p. 756.

4. *Enoch Powell's 'earthquake'*

1. Quoted in David Butler and Michael Pinto-Duschinsky, *The British General Election of 1970* (1971), p. 76.
2. E. J. B. Rose et al., *Colour and citizenship: a report on British race relations* (1969), p. 606. For a full analysis of the development of British policy, see chs. 16, 26, 27, 29.
3. Ibid., Appendix III.4.
4. See Hugo Young's analysis in the Runnymede Trust's *Race and the press* (1971).
5. For a chronology and analysis of the period see *Colour and citizenship*, p. 699ff., and Paul Foot, *The rise of Enoch Powell* (1969), pp. 104–11.
6. Ibid., p. 614.
7. Foot (1969), p. 111.
8. See Foot (1969), p. 96. For some details of his disagreements with Conservative economic policy, see Butler and Pinto-Duschinsky (1971), pp. 69–70.
9. Foot (1969), pp. 58, 53.
10. Ibid., p. 39.

11. Interview with Paul Foot. Ibid., p. 35.
12. Foot (1969), p. 101.
13. The Birmingham speech was made at the Midland Hotel, to an audience of about 85 at the Annual General Meeting of the West Midland Area Conservative Political Centre. Both speeches were published in full, with a detailed commentary, in Bill Smithies and Peter Fiddick, *Enoch Powell on immigration* (1969); in Tom Stacey, *Immigration and Enoch Powell* (1970); and in Powell's own book, *Freedom and reality* (1968). The Birmingham speech is also reprinted in *Race*, Vol. X, No. 1, 1968, together with the text of the letters exchanged between Mr Heath and Mr Powell upon his dismissal from the shadow cabinet; part of a speech by Mr Hogg on the second Reading of the Race Relations Bill, 23 April 1968; and the full text of a speech on 4 May 1968 by Mr Roy Jenkins, Home Secretary until shortly before.
14. Gallup, May 1968.
15. This postbag was discussed in two articles by Diana Spearman in *New Society*, 9 May 1968 and 27 June 1968. My calculation of 180,000 possible signatories is based on the fact that her sample of 3,347 'pro' letters contained 5,570 signatures.
16. Ian Trethowan, *The Times*, 26 April 1968.
17. *Frost on Friday*, London Weekend Television, 3 January 1969. Printed in Smithies and Fiddick (1969), pp. 95–129.
18. E. J. B. Rose (1969), p. 740.
19. *New Statesman*, 26 April 1968.
20. Young (1971), pp. 29–30.
21. Smithies and Fiddick (1969), p. 14.
22. See Rose (1969), p. 10 and ch. 2 passim.
23. Paul Hartmann and Charles Husband, 'The mass media and racial conflict', *Race*, Vol. XII, 3, 1971. Cf. Rose, (1969), p. 591.
24. For a brief discussion, see Rose (1969), pp. 588–604.
25. Ibid., p. 590.
26. Ibid., p. 553.
27. Ibid., p. 567, p. 570. Cf. Gallup poll:
'Do you think that on the whole the country has benefited or been harmed through immigrants coming to settle here from the Commonwealth?'

	August 1965	October 1967	May 1968
Benefit	16	9	16
Harmed	52	60	61
No Difference	20	19	14
Don't Know	12	12	9

28. *Frost on Friday*, 3 January 1969; in Smithies and Fiddick (1969), p. 114.
29. *New Statesman*, 26 April 1968.
30. Smithies and Fiddick (1969), p. 15.
31. *The Guardian*, 20 May 1970.

32. *Crossbow*, April–June 1968, p. 26.
33. Quoted in the *Observer*, 28 April 1968.
34. *Guardian*, 20 May 1970.
35. Loc. cit.
36. Quoted, *The Times*, 26 April 1968.
37. Foot (1969), p. 65.
38. *Frost on Friday*, 3 January 1969, in Smithies and Fiddick (1969), p. 96.
39. Paul Foot gives a good impression of Powell's activity from 1966 onwards – and the extent of its deviations from Conservative orthodoxy. Foot (1969), pp. 96–101.
40. Ivan Yates, *The Observer*, 28 April 1968.
41. Butler and Pinto-Duschinsky (1971), p. 78.
42. Smithies and Fiddick (1969), p. 33.
43. For a short but useful discussion of Nietzschean themes in Mr Powell's thinking, see Robert Jackson's article, in form a book review, in *The Times*, 24 September 1970. See also the same author's earlier article about Mr Powell, *The Times*, 24 April 1969.
44. E. J. B. Rose (1969), p. 740.
45. Harold Evans, *The Listener*, 16 July 1970, p. 76. Cf. Nicholas Deakin, 'The Commonwealth Immigrants Bill', *Political Quarterly*, Vol. XXXIX, No. 1, 1968, p. 37; *The Listener*, 30 October 1969, p. 586.
46. Hugo Young (1971), p. 31.
47. E. J. B. Rose (1969), p. 741.
48. Hartmann and Husband (1971), p. 270.
49. *Daily Mail*, 2 July 1970; a story about illegal immigrants.
50. Hartmann and Husband (1971), p. 274. A serial investigation into immigrants in *The Times* in the early 1960s carried the general title 'The Dark Million'.
51. Ibid., p. 279.
52. *The Listener*, 16 July 1970, p. 77. Evans' paper is reprinted in an extended form in the booklet *Race and the press* (1971), pp. 42–53. Cf. Eric Butterworth's article about tendentious reporting of a Bradford smallpox outbreak in 1962 in the *Yorkshire Post*. *Race*, Vol. VII, 4, 1966, pp. 347–65.
53. Tunstall (1970(2)), p. 15.
54. *Frost on Friday*, 3 January 1969; Smithies and Fiddick (1969), p. 112.
55. For accounts of this period see E. J. B. Rose (1969), pp. 616–18, and Butler and Pinto-Duschinsky (1971), pp. 75–8.
56. Speech at Swansea, 4 May 1968; published in *Race*, Vol. X, No. 1, 1968, p. 101.
57. 23 April 1968. 763 *H.C. Debates*, c. 75.
58. Loc. cit.
59. See Smithies and Fiddick (1969), p. 81.
60. Smithies and Fiddick (1969), pp. 13–14.
61. *Frost on Friday*, in Smithies and Fiddick (1969), p. 97.
62. Dick Pixley, *The closed question* (1968), pp. 61–2.
63. Ivan Yates, *The Observer*, 28 April 1968.
64. 27 April 1968.
65. In Smithies and Fiddick (1969), p. 63.

66. Pixley (168), p. 62.
67. Gordon K. Lewis, 'Protest among the immigrants', *Political Quarterly*, Vol. XL, 4 (1969), p. 428.
68. E. J. B. Rose (1969), p. 607.
69. There is no scope for such a discussion here. A concise one, written fairly close to the events, is in E. J. B. Rose (1969), ch. 29, pp. 605–28. N.O.P. published the following poll, taken between 3–9 March 1970. Q.: '. . . And do you think that Mr Powell's speeches have improved or worsened relations between white and coloured people in Britain, or have they made no difference?'

Percentages	All	Con.	Lab.	Lib.
Improved	8	7	8	7
Worsened	44	41	44	52
No Difference	45	49	44	39
Don't Know/No Answer	3	3	4	2

70. Foot (1969), pp. 119–22.
71. In John Wood (ed.) (1970), p. 15. The context is 1970, but Mr Cowling's analysis appears to be applicable to the period since 1968.
72. Hartmann and Husband (1971), p. 270.
73. See Nicholas Deakin (1968), p. 44.
74. E. J. B. Rose (1969), p. 616.
75. Ibid., p. 617.
76. Harold Evans, *The Listener*, 16 July 1970, p. 78.
77. 21 April 1968. Cf. *Guardian*, 23 April; *Daily Mirror*, 25 April; *Daily Telegraph*, 26 April.
78. The full text is published in *Race*, Vol. X, 1, 1968, p. 99. The account of Heath's actions is taken from Alan Watkins, *New Statesman*, 26 April 1968.
79. Foot (1969), p. 116.
80. Hartmann and Husband substantiate this point with some interesting examples (1971), pp. 276–7.
81. N.O.P., May 1968.
82. N.O.P., October 1968.
83. Butler and Pinto-Duschinsky (1971), p. 79.
84. Wood (ed.) (1970), p. 56.
85. Foot (1969), p. 118.
86. George Gale in Wood (ed.) (1970), p. 56.
87. Quoted, ibid., pp. 112–13.
88. Butler and Pinto-Duschinsky (1971), p. 350.
89. See ibid., pp. 252–5.
90. Ibid., p. 160.
91. *The Times*, 15 April 1971.
92. Butler and Pinto-Duschinsky (1971), p. 163.
93. Ibid., p. 161.
94. Loc. cit.

95. Ibid., pp. 406–7.
96. Butler and Stokes (1971), p. 529.
97. Ibid., pp. 420ff.
98. Quoted, Wood (1970), p. 119.

5. Parliament and television

1. The data is reported in detail in Charles Wilson (ed.) *Parliaments, people and mass media* (1970), Appendix 1, pp. 109–22.
2. Ibid., p. 3.
3. Quoted in Robin Day, *The case for televising parliament* (1963), p. 16.
4. E.g. in the House of Commons, 15 March 1963, 673 *H.C. Deb.* c.1715–1820; 14 May 1963, 677 *H.C. Deb.* c.1131; 28 May 1965, 713 *H.C. Deb.* c.1033–1133; and see below in text. Robin Day's pamphlet (1963) was widely discussed. Cf. Granada TV, *Prelude to Westminster* (1963). Newspaper articles in the early 1960s included Howard Thomas, *Sunday Times*, 21 October 1962; Malcolm Muggeridge, *Daily Herald*, 19 March 1963; Jo Grimond, *Observer*, 21 February 1965; and various leader comments and reports of politicians' speeches. An early academic discussion was Allan Segal's in Bernard Crick, *Reform of Parliament* (1964).
5. 24 November 1966, 736 *H.C. Deb.* c.1730. 19 October 1972, 843 *H.C. Deb.* c. 583–4. There was a free vote on each occasion. Party managers had expected the proposal to be carried in 1972. Its failure was attributed to absenteeism.
6. Butler and Stokes (1971), p. 42.
7. Ibid., p. 271.
8. See Ch. 8 below. Cf. Trenaman and McQuail, *Television and the political image* (1961); Blumler and McQuail, *Television in politics* (1968); and the Nuffield College general election studies by David Butler and others, published by Macmillan in 1960, 1965, 1966, 1970.
9. Capt. I. Fraser, 25 March 1925, 182 *H.C. Deb.* c.428; Lt-Cmdr Kenworthy, 1 April 1925, Ibid., c.1339, 1814, 186 *H.C. Deb.* c.1978–9; Mr Smithers, 30 November 1925, 188 *H.C. Deb.* c.1804.
10. Mr Day, 29 October 1936, 316 *H.C. Deb.* c.25–6; Mr Day, 7 February 1938, 331 *H.C. Deb.* c.669–70; E. Smith, 20 April 1939, 346 *H.C. Deb.* c.496 and 19 September 1940, 365 *H.C. Deb.* c.192–3; Mr Bevan, 29 June 1944, 401 *H.C. Deb.* c.912; Cmdr. King-Hall, 30 June 1944, ibid., c.976.
11. 20–21 January 1942, 377 *H.C. Deb.* c.199–202, 382–3.
12. W/Cmdr Cooper, 21 August 1945, 413 *H.C. Deb.* c.444; Mr Gordon Walker, 11 December 1945, 417 *H.C. Deb.* c.213–14.
13. *Report of the Broadcasting Committee 1949*, Cmd. 8116 (1951), p. 68.
14. Butler and Stokes (1971), p. 269.
15. 3 November 1959, 612 *H.C. Deb.* c.865–7.
16. *Report from the Sel. Comm. on Broadcasting etc. of Proceedings in the House of Commons. H.C. 146, 1966–7. A concise discussion of it

and its aftermath is in D. W. Limon, *The Table*, Vol. XXXV (1966), pp. 69–73.

17. 736 *H.C. Deb.* c.1730.
18. 15 June 1966. The vote was 56 to 21. 275 *H.L. Deb.* c.136.
19. 14 February 1968.
20. 19 February 1968.
21. The resolution was passed on 11 December 1967; 756 *H.C. Deb.* c.94–137.
22. *The Times*, 30 April 1968.
23. Select Committee on House of Commons Services, 9th Report, H.C. 448 (1967–68); 1st Report, H.C. 48 (1968–9).
24. Robert Sheldon, 791 *H.C. Deb.* c.1617–1718.
25. Report from the Select Committee on Broadcasting (Anticipation of Debates), H.C. 288 (1955–6), memorandum from the BBC, pp. 30–1.
26. Ibid., pp. 23, 25.
27. Report of the Broadcasting Committee (1951), pp. 68, 197.
28. Select Committee on Broadcasting (1955–6), p. 26.
29. Ibid., p. 27. See also the comments of Mr Crookshank, leader of the Commons, on 30 November 1955, 546 *H.C. Deb.* c.2440. Cf. Burton Paulu, *British broadcasting in transition* (London, Macmillan, 1961), p. 96.
30. 30 November 1955, 546 *H.C. Deb.* c.2315–2446.
31. 562 *H.C. Deb.* c.1095–7; 25 July 1957, 574 *H.C. Deb.* c.91–2W.
32. 23 February 1955, 537 *H.C. Deb.* c.1277.
33. H.C. 288 (1955–56), p. iii.
34. *Yesterday in Parliament*. Licence, clause 13(2), *BBC Handbook*, 1970, p. 168, p. 284. The programme is only on sound.
35. Average estimated audiences for those programmes in 1955, the year the Fourteen Day Rule was abandoned, are as follows (1971 figures for comparison):

	1955 (UK pop. aged 16+)	1971 (UK pop. aged 5+)
Yesterday in Parliament		
Winter:	750,000	1,350,000
Summer:	350,000	1,100,000
The Week in Westminster		
Winter:	1,500,000	300,000
Summer:	750,000	150,000

Source: BBC Audience Research Department.

36. 102 *H.C. Deb.* 4s. c.784.
37. 102 *H.C. Deb.* 4s. c.688, 784. Chester and Bowring, *Questions in parliament* (1962), p. 84.
38. *Observer*, 20 June 1965.

39. 16 June 1965.

40. The other tribunal members were Lord Caradon (former Labour minister) and Sir John Foster, Q.C., M.P. The eight participants were: Rev. Ian Paisley, Democratic Unionist Party and M.P. for North Antrim; Gerard Fitt, Social Democratic and Labour Party M.P. for Belfast West; Robert Cooper, co-chairman, Alliance Party; Neil Blaney, former Minister of Agriculture, Republic of Ireland; David Bleakley, Northern Ireland Labour Party, former Minister of Community Relations; Bernadette Devlin, Independent M.P. for Mid-Ulster; Michael Kennedy, Fianna Fail, a junior minister in the Republic government; John Maginnis, Unionist M.P. for Armagh.

41. For details see *The Times*, 5–7 January 1972.

42. *The Times*, 19 February 1968.

43. See Norman Gash (1953), ch. 15. Cf. Butt (1969), pp. 77–8.

44. The sustained argument for the idea is the pamphlet by Robin Day (1963).

45. Dame Joan Vickers, 24 November 1966, 736 *H.C. Deb.* c.1650.

46. William Deedes, 28 May 1965, 713 *H.C. Deb.* c.1050.

47. *The Times*, 19 February 1968.

48. *Lewis Fry Memorial Lectures*, Univ. of Bristol (1948), p. 7.

49. Quoted in I. K. MacKay, *Broadcasting in Australia* (1957), p. 77.

50. Dr A. J. Forbes, 'The broadcasting of parliamentary debates in Australia', *Journal of the Parlts. of the C'wealth*, Vol. XLV, 2, April (1964), pp. 128–34; A. R. Browning 'Broadcasting of parliamentary proceedings in Australia', *The Table*, Vol. XXXV (1966), p. 81.

51. H. N. Dollimore, 'Parliamentary broadcasting in New Zealand', *The Table*, Vol. XXXV (1966), pp. 87–8.

52. John Mendelson, 28 May 1965, 713 *H.C. Deb.* c.1087–90.

53. Gerhard Loewenberg, *Parliament in the German political system* (1966), p. 425.

54. Maurice Edelman, 21 November 1969, 791 *H.C. Deb.* c.1684.

55. David Wood, *The Times*, 19 February 1968.

56. Fred Peart, speech to the Inter-parliamentary Union, quoted in Charles Wilson (1970), p. 40. Cf. Select Committee on Broadcasting etc. (1966–7), pp. xx–xxiv, where similar arguments are discussed in some detail.

57. Charles Wilson (1970), p. 39.

58. Select Committee on Broadcasting etc. (1966–7), pp. xx, xxiv. Cf. Iain Macleod, 15 March 1963, 673 *H.C. Deb.* c.1972.

59. Select Committee on Broadcasting etc. (1966–7), p. xxii.

60. 7 July 1967.

61. 28 May 1965, 713 *H.C. Deb.* c.1043.

62. Blumler and McQuail (1968), pp. 97–100. Their data was made available to the Select Committee on Broadcasting etc. (1966–7), Appendix 22, pp. 138–41.

63. Select Committee on Broadcasting etc. (1966–7), Appendix 30, pp. 152–4.

64. Ibid., p. xxviii, para 68.

6. *Newspapers and party systems: connections*

1. *Democracy and the organisation of political parties*, trans. Fredk. Clarke (1902), 2 vols., Vol. I., p. 409. Ostrogorski himself held impressively 'modern' and sceptical views about what people read and why, and what influence it had on their behaviour. The results of survey research 50 years later would have held few surprises for him. (The possibility remains, of course, that for his own time he may have been wrong.)

2. Robert Michels, *Political parties* (1959), p. 130.

3. Rather than reprint an entire bibliography of political parties and comparative politics, perhaps the author may refer readers to the bibliography of a book which provided a helpful frame of reference for the present study, Jean Blondel's *Introduction to comparative government* (1970). The judgement offered on this page is based on the use of that bibliography, supplemented by later publications.

4. Included in this category are books like those co-authored by Brzezinski: Brzezinski and Huntington, *Political power USA/USSR* (1963), and Friedrich and Brzezinski, *Totalitarian dictatorship and autocracy* (new ed., 1965). In the latter, monopoly party control of mass media is offered as one of six distinguishing characteristics of totalitarian dictatorship. An example of a text which is extremely disappointing about press/party relationships is R. T. McKenzie's *British political parties* (new ed., 1963).

5. *Public opinion and American democracy* (1964), p. 392.

6. Cambridge, Mass., M.I.T. Press, 1963.

7. See Leonard Shapiro, *The Communist Party of the Soviet Union* (1953), pp. 37–43; M. Duverger, *Political parties* (1954), p. 150.

8. Alan Bullock, *Hitler: a study in tyranny* (1961), pp. 113–18, 215.

9. Thomas L. Hodgkin, *African political parties* (1961), p. 32.

10. Cmd. 7700, pp. 101, 106.

11. Quoted in Mark W. Hopkins, *Mass media in the Soviet Union* (1970), p. 57.

12. *Mein Kampf* (1933), Vol. I, p. 264. Quoted, Hale (1964), p. 75.

13. Cf. Hodgkin (1961), p. 55.

14. An inventory of party functions is offered in chapter 7.

15. J. Blondel (1970), p. 102.

16. R. J. Minney, *Viscount Southwood* (1954), p. 233.

17. See G. D. H. Cole, *A history of the Labour Party from 1914* (1948), p. 127, pp. 151–2.

18. Maurice Edelman, *The Mirror* (1966), pp. 184–90.

19. William Rust, *The story of the Daily Worker* (1949), p. 10.

20. See Colin Seymour-Ure, 'Policy making in the press', *Government and Opposition*, IV, 4 (1969), pp. 481–4; and the official history by David Ayerst, *Guardian*, Collins, 1971.

21. Ibid., p. 451.

22. A variety of examples is quoted and discussed in Seymour-Ure, *The press politics and the public* (1968), Chapter 2, esp. pp. 70–94.

The Leeds studies on Television and elections (Trenaman and McQuail, *Television and political image* (1967); Blumler and McQuail, *Television in politics* (1968)), also contain supportive evidence.

23. Butler and Stokes (1971). Ch. 10. Examples quoted from pp. 284–5.
24. See Ch. 7.
25. The account here is drawn mainly from Hopkins (1970), pp. 139–47; and for another useful discussion see Ch. 5 of Frederick C. Barghoorn, *Politics in the U.S.S.R.* (1968).
26. For a description of *L'Humanité's* role in the P.C.F. before 1952, see Alain Brayance, *Anatomie du P.C.F.* (1952), pp. 173–90.
27. A. Y. Pers, *The Swedish press* (1966), p. 22.
28. Rosalynde Ainslie, *The press in Africa* (1966), p. 70.
29. E. Lloyd Sommerlad, *The press in developing countries* (1966), p. 47.
30. Roy Pryce, 'The Italian local elections, 1956', *St. Antony's Papers*, No. 3 (1957), p. 69.
31. Pers (1966), p. 14.
32. Hopkins (1970), p. 144–6.
33. Ibid., p. 142–3.
34. John C. Merrill, *The élite press* (1968), p. 192.
35. See the very thorough analyses by Svennik Hoyer, Nils Thomsen and others in *Scandinavian Political Studies*, Volume 3, 1968. Other data, both for Scandinavia and the Benelux countries, much of it rather dated, is in Icko Iben, *The Germanic press of Europe* (1965).
36. Iben (1965), p. 20, p. 44.
37. Hopkins (1970), pp. 316–17.

7. *Newspapers and party systems: contexts*

1. UNESCO's *Statistical Year Book* publishes lists of newspapers and circulations. This was the source for the figures in e.g. B. M. Russett and others, *World handbook of political and social indicators* (1964).
2. Cf. D. Cater, *The fourth branch of government* (1959), p. 154.
3. E.g. Eric Moonman (ed.), *The press: A case for commitment*, Fabian Tract 391 (1969).
4. A detailed description of the scheme is in Nils Andren (1968), pp. 221–9.
5. Sommerlad (1966), p. 43.
6. For a further account of this episode see Seymour-Ure (1969), pp. 473–5.
7. Weidenfeld and Nicolson (1970).
8. Ibid., p. 139.
9. Ibid., pp. 141–3.
10. Sommerlad (1966), p. 31.
11. *The Times*, 17 December 1970.
12. Blondel (1970), pp. 143–52.
13. Ibid., Appendix pp. 532ff.
14. Ibid., pp. 157–9.
15. Ibid., pp. 111–12.

16. See David Butler and Michael Pinto-Duschinsky, *The British General Election of 1970* (1971), pp. 241–2; and Chapter 8 below.
17. *Sochineniya*, 35 vols. (4th ed., 1941–52), Vol. 5, p. 9. Quoted, Hopkins (1970), p. 20.
18. See J. Lapalombara and M. Weiner, *Political parties and political development* (1966), p. 20.
19. Thomas Hodgkin, *African political parties* (1961), p. 32.
20. Ibid., p. 32.
21. Ibid., p. 32.
22. *The politics of modernisation* (1965), p. 183, cf. p. 383.
23. Quoted, Seymour-Ure (1969), pp. 495–6.
24. Epstein, *Political parties in western democracies* (1967), p. 258.
25. Blondel (1970), Ch. 7, pp. 99–111, 116–19.
26. (1965), pp. 295–300.
27. See Blondel (1970), pp. 174–5.
28. Ibid., Ch. 8 passim.
29. Ibid., p. 133.
30. James S. Coleman and Carl Rosberg, *Political parties and national integration in tropical Africa* (1966), pp. 299–300.

8. *Mass media and British general elections, 1945–70*

The Nuffield studies are referred to in these references simply by the date of each election: R. B. McCallum and A. Readman, *The British General Election of 1945* (1947); H. G. Nicholas, *The British General Election of 1950* (1951); D. E. Butler, *The British General Election of 1951* (1952); D. E. Butler, *The British General Election of 1955* (1955); D. E. Butler and R. Rose, *The British General Election of 1959* (1960); D. E. Butler and Anthony King, *The British General Election of 1964* (1965); D. E. Butler and Anthony King, *The British General Election of 1966* (1966); D. E. Butler and Michael Pinto-Duschinsky, *The British General Election of 1970* (1971).

1. *Political change in Britain* (1971), pp. 50, 52. The authors comment: 'The influence attributed to elections is the more impressive in view of the fact that these conversations were held outside the context of an election campaign.' pp. 50–1.
2. Ibid., pp. 516–21.
3. Ibid., pp. 509–10. The authors go on to show how this knowledge evaporates in a matter of weeks.
4. Ibid., pp. 41–2.
5. *1955*, p. 96.
6. Butler and Stokes (1971), p. 513.
7. Ibid., pp. 503–4.
8. *1959*, p. 110.
9. *1945*, pp. 142–3.
10. *1951*, p. 77.
11. *1959*, p. 76.
12. Trenaman and McQuail (1961), p. 71.

13. *1964*, p. 167.
14. Ibid., p. 162.
15. *1966*, p. 127.
16. *1970*, p. 204.
17. Whale (1967), p. 124.
18. 'Producers' attitudes towards television coverage of an election', *Sociological Review Monograph*, No. 13, 1969. Reprinted in Tunstall (ed.) *Media Sociology* (1970).
19. Ibid., p. 415.
20. *1959*, p. 78.
21. *1966*, p. 146.
22. Ibid., p. 147.
23. *1945*, p. 154.
24. *1970*, p. 207.
25. *1964*, p. 168.
26. *1966*, p. 130.
27. *1959*, pp. 52, 116.
28. Ibid., p. 53.
29. *1945*, p. 154.
30. *1966*, p. 130.
31. *1964*, p. 171.
32. *1966*, pp. 125–6.
33. *1950*, p. 145.
34. *1964*, pp. 157–8. *1966*, pp. 126–7. *1970*, p. 203.
35. *1966*, p. 151.
36. A number of references are quoted in *1970*, p. 200.
37. *1970*, p. 248. *1955*, p. 49.
38. *1966*, p. 131, p. 134.
39. *1966*, p. 134.
40. *1966*, p. 138.
41. *1966*, p. 130.
42. *1964*, p. 162. Opinion poll figures provided further evidence.
43. *1966*, p. 139.
44. Blumler, in Tunstall, *Media Sociology* (1970), p. 421.
45. *1970*, p. 137.
46. *1945*, p. 182.
47. *1955*, p. 94. *1959*, p. 68.
48. *1966*, p. 179.
49. *1970*, p. 144.
50. Butler and Stokes (1971), pp. 507, 513.
51. *1951*, p. 77.
52. *1970*, pp. 146–7.
53. *1951*, pp. 110–12.
54. *1951*, p. 99.
55. *1950*, pp. 91, 143.
56. *1959*, p. 73.
57. *1959*, p. 111.
58. *1964*, p. 161.
59. Butler and Stokes, pp. 218–20.

60. *1966*, p. 188.
61. Trenaman and McQuail, pp. 58–60.
62. *1966*, p. 188.
63. Loc. cit.
64. *1970*, p. 144.
65. *1959*, pp. 110–11, 51, 57–8.
66. *1966*, pp. 108–10, 150, 187–8.
67. William Barkley (1959), pp. 53–4.
68. *1970*, pp. 210–11.
69. *1951*, p. 240.
70. *1951*, p. 88.
71. *1959*, pp. 105–6.
72. *1966*, p. 160.
73. *1970*, pp. 165–6, 170.
74. *1950*, p. 175.
75. Ibid., p. 176.
76. *1945*, p. 203n.
77. *1955*, p. 103.
78. *1951*, pp. 118–28. Other good illustrations are in *1950*, ch. VII.
79. *1945*, pp. 144ff.
80. This data is drawn from a study by A. C. H. Smith, Elizabeth Immirzi and Trevor Blackwell at the Centre for Contemporary Cultural Studies, University of Birmingham. It is to be published by Chatto & Windus.
81. An account of the case is given in Joseph Dean, *Hatred, ridicule and contempt* (1964).
82. *Headlines all my life* (1961), p. 240.
83. *1964*, p. 170.
84. Party advertising in Britain is discussed fully, with comparative examples, in Richard Rose, *Influencing voters* (1967).
85. Blumler and McQuail (1967), p. 284.
86. Ibid., p. 286.

9. *Private Eye: the politics of the Fool*

1. *Private Eye*, 13 July 1962.
2. Cf. Frank Parkin's book on the CND – *Middle class radicalism* (1968).
3. On the Fool in literature the standard work remains Enid Welsford, *The Fool: His social and literary history* (1935, reprinted 1968); and there is quite a body of other work. For present purposes the author found most stimulating *The Fool and his sceptre* (1969), specially Chapter 9. Generally the Fool in politics has been neglected, although some political philosophers have found the Fool analogy useful: see e.g. Leszek Kolakowski, 'The Priest and the Jester', in *Marxism and beyond* (1971), pp. 31–58 (esp. pp. 55–8).
4. See W. Willeford, *The Fool and his sceptre* (1969), pp. 157–61. Even Rasputin, *éminence grise* of the last of the Czars, seems to have had

some of the qualities of a Fool. Tolstoy gives Count Rostov a household Fool in *War and peace*.

5. Willeford (1969), p. 13.
6. Ibid., p. 154.
7. Richard Ingrams has described the foundation of *Private Eye* in his introduction to *The Life and times of Private Eye* (1971).
8. *The Week* is also discussed in chapter 3.
9. Claud Cockburn, *I, Claud* (1967), pp. 131–2.
10. Ibid., p. 136.
11. Ibid., p. 149.
12. Ibid., p. 146.
13. Willeford (1969), pp. 15–16.
14. Cockburn (1967), p. 136.
15. Willeford (1969), p. 16.
16. Cockburn (1967), p. 145.
17. *The Times*, 13 March 1963.
18. The actions (references are to *The Times*) included: Ald. L. J. Tarbit (4.1.63); Randolph Churchill (21.2.63, 2.3.63, 13.3.63, 16.3.63); Wolf Mankowitz (20.12.62, 13.6.63); Spike Milligan (18.9.63); Edward Martell (3.12.63); Colin Watson (*The Guardian*) (20.12.63); M. P. Daubeny (15.5.64); Lord Russell of Liverpool (1–4.2.66); Quintin Hogg, M.P. (11.3.66); Elkan Allan (27.4.66); Sir Cyril Black, M.P. (13.6.67); Derek Marks (*Daily Express*) (17.11.67); Ian McColl and others (*Scottish Daily Express*) (14.3.68); Paul Johnson (*New Statesman*) (21.3.68); Hugh Farmer and Denis Cassidy (*The People*) (6.2.69); Nora Beloff (*The Observer*) (30.10.72).
19. *The Times*, 1, 2, 3, 4, 16 February 1966. The offensive article had appeared in 1962.
20. Ibid., 6 February 1969.
21. Cockburn (1967), p. 407.
22. Ibid., p. 433.
23. Ibid., p. 411.
24. Willeford (1969), pp. 157–8.
25. Cockburn (1967), pp. 431–2.
26. Max Gluckman, *Custom and conflict in Africa* (1955), p. 124.
27. Ibid., pp. 125–6.
28. Willeford (1969), p. 162.
29. Ibid., p. 161.
30. The official inquiry into the affair is *Lord Denning's Report*, Cmnd. 2152. See also Ron Hall and others, *Scandal '63* (1963), Wayland Young, *The Profumo Affair: Aspects of conservatism* (1963). For the role of the press, see Colin Seymour-Ure (1968), pp. 266–76.
31. *The Times*, 13 March 1963.
32. The page is reproduced in Ingrams (1971), p. 73.
33. *The Times*, 27 April 1966.
34. Ibid., 26 April 1969. See also Michael Foot's speech condemning the practice, *The Times* 24 April 1969; and correspondence on 10 and 13 May 1969.
35. Cockburn (1967), p. 409.

36. Robert Payne, *The Great God Pan: A biography of the tramp played by Charles Chaplin* (1952) quoted in Willeford (1969), p. 163.
37. *The Times*, 8 January 1969. The award was one of the annual Granada Awards for journalism, made by the TV programme, *The Papers*.
38. *Punch*, 26 April 1972.
39. *The Times*, 4 May 1971.
40. Cf. Christopher Booker, *The Neophiliacs* (1969), pp. 215–16, where the author describes Macmillan as 'the man who had been the *raison d'être* for Britain's "satire movement".'

Bibliography

Ainslie, Rosalynde, *The press in Africa* (London, Gollancz, 1966).

Almond, Gabriel, and Powell, G. B., *Comparative politics* (Boston, Little, Brown, 1966).

Amery, L. S., *My political life* (London, Hutchinson, 1953), 3 vols.

Andren, Nils, 'Sweden: State support for political parties', *Scandinavian Political Studies*, Vol. III, 1968.

Apter, David, *The politics of modernisation* (Univ. of Chicago Press, 1965).

Association of Cinematograph, Television and Allied Technicians, *One week: a survey of television coverage of Union and industrial affairs in the week January 8–14, 1971* (London, ACTT, 1971).

Astor, Michael, *Tribal feeling* (London, John Murray, 1963).

Avon, Rt. Hon. the Earl of, *The Eden memoirs: Facing the dictators* (London, Cassell, 1962).

Avon, Rt. Hon. the Earl of, *The Eden memoirs: The reckoning* (London, Cassell, 1965).

Ayerst, David, *Guardian* (London, Collins, 1971).

Banks, A. S., and Textor, R. B., *Cross-polity survey* (Cambridge, Mass., M.I.T. Press, 1963).

Barghoorn, Fredk. C., *Politics in the U.S.S.R.* (Boston, Little, Brown, 1966).

Barker, A., and Rush, M., *The member of parliament and his information* (London, Allen & Unwin for P.E.P. and Study of Parl. Gp., 1970).

Barkley, William, *A reporter's notebook* (London, Oldbourne Press, 1959).

Baynes, N. H., *The speeches of Adolf Hitler* (London, O.U.P., 1942) 2 vols.

BBC handbook (London, BBC, annual).

Berelson, B., and Janowitz, M., *Reader in public opinion and communication* (Glencoe, Free Press, 1966).

Birch, A. H., Campbell, Peter, and Lucas, P. G., 'The popular press in the British general election of 1955', *Political Studies*, Vol. IV, 3, 1956.

Birkenhead, the Earl of, *Halifax* (London, Hamish Hamilton, 1965).

Blondel, Jean, *Introduction to comparative government* (London, Weidenfeld & Nicolson, 1970).

Blumler, Jay, and McQuail, D., *Television in politics* (London, Faber & Faber, 1968).

Blumler, Jay, 'Producers' attitudes towards television coverage of an election campaign: a case study', *Sociological Review Monograph* No. 13, 1969. Reprinted in Tunstall (ed.) (1970(1)).

Blumler, Jay, et al. 'Attitudes to the monarchy', *Political Studies*, Vol. XIX, 2, 1971.

Booker, Christopher, *The neophiliacs* (London, Fontana Collins, 1969).

Boyle, Lord, and Crosland, Anthony, *The politics of education* (ed. M. Kogan) (Harmondsworth, Penguin, 1971).

Brayance, Alain, *Anatomie du P.C.F.* (Paris, Denöel, 1952).

Brittan, Samuel, *Steering the economy* (Harmondsworth, Penguin, 1970).

Brown, George, *In my way* (Harmondsworth, Penguin, 1971).

Browning, A. R., 'Broadcasting of parliamentary debates in Australia', *The Table*, Vol. XXXV, 1966.

Brzezinski, Z., and Huntington, S., *Political power USA/USSR* (London, Chatto & Windus, 1963).

Bullock, Alan, *Hitler: a study in tyranny* (N.Y., Bantam, 1961).

Butler, D. E., *The British General Election of 1951* (London, Macmillan, 1952).

Butler, D. E., *The British General Election of 1955* (London, Macmillan, 1955).

Butler, D. E., and King, Anthony, *The British General Election of 1964* (London, Macmillan, 1965).

Butler, D. E. and King, Anthony, *The British General Election of 1966* (London, Macmillan, 1966).

Butler, D. E., and Pinto-Duschinsky, Michael, *The British General Election of 1970* (London, Macmillan, 1971).

Butler, D. E., and Rose, R., *The British General Election of 1959* (London, Macmillan, 1960).

Butler, D. E., and Stokes, Donald, *Political change in Britain* (Harmondsworth, Penguin, 1971).

Butler, Lord, *The art of the possible* (London, Hamish Hamilton, 1971).

Butt, Ronald, *The power of parliament* (London, Constable, 2nd ed. 1969).

Butterworth, Eric, 'The 1962 smallpox outbreak and the British press', *Race*, Vol. VII, 4, 1966, pp. 347–65.

Cater, D., *The fourth branch of government* (N.Y., Vintage, 1959).

Chaney, D., *Processes of mass communication* (London, Macmillan, 1972).

Chester, D. N., and Bowring, N., *Questions in parliament* (Oxford, Clarendon Press, 1962).

Chester, Lewis, et al., *The Zinoviev Letter* (London, Heinemann, 1967).

Christiansen, Arthur, *Headlines all my life* (London, Heinemann, 1961).

Ciano, *Ciano's diary* (London, Heinemann, 1947).

Clarke, Tom, *Northcliffe in history* (London, Hutchinson, n.d.).

Cockburn, Claud, *I, Claud* (Harmondsworth, Penguin, 1967).

Cole, G. D. H., *A history of the Labour Party from 1914* (London, Routledge, 1948).

Coleman, James S., and Rosberg, Carl, *Political parties and national integration in tropical Africa* (Univ. of California Press, 1966).

Cooper, Duff, *Old men forget* (London, Hart-Davis, 1953).

Coote, C., *A companion of honour* (London, Collins, 1965(1)).

Coote, C., *Editorial* (London, Eyre & Spottiswoode, 1965(2)).

Crick, Bernard, *Reform of parliament* (London, Weidenfeld & Nicolson, 1964).

Dalton, Hugh, *High tide and after* (London, Muller, 1962).

Day, Robin, *The case for televising parliament* (London, Hansard Society, 1963).

Deakin, Nicholas, 'The Commonwealth Immigrants Bill', *Political Quarterly*, Vol. XXXIX, 1, 1968.

Dean, Joseph, *Hatred, ridicule and contempt* (Harmondsworth, Penguin, 1964).

DeFleur, M. L., *Theories of mass communication* (N.Y., David McKay, 1966).

Deutsch, Karl, *The nerves of government* (N.Y., Free Press, 2nd ed. 1966).

Dodd, W. E., *Ambassador Dodd's diary, 1933–38* (London, Gollancz, 1941).

Dollimore, H. N., 'Parliamentary broadcasting in New Zealand', *The Table*, Vol. XXXV, 1966.

Duverger, M., *Political parties* (London, Methuen, 1954).

Edelman, Maurice, *The Mirror: a political history* (London, Hamish Hamilton, 1966).

Egremont, Lord (John Wyndham), *Wyndham and children first* (London, Macmillan, 1968).

Epstein, L. D., *Political parties in western democracies* (London, Pall Mall, 1967).

Foot, Paul, *The rise of Enoch Powell* (Harmondsworth, Penguin, 1969).

Forbes, A. J., 'The broadcasting of parliamentary debates in Australia', *Journal of the Parliaments of the Commonwealth*, Vol. XLV, 2, 1964.

Friedrich, C., and Brzezinski, Z., *Totalitarian dictatorship and democracy* (Harvard, new ed. 1965).

Galtung, Johan, and Ruge, Mari Holmboe, 'The structure of foreign news', *Journal of International Peace Research*, Vol. I, 1965; reprinted in Tunstall (1970(1)).

Gannon, F. R., *The British press and Germany, 1936–39* (London, O.U.P., 1971).

Gash, Norman, *Politics in the age of Peel* (London, Longmans, 1953).

George, Margaret, *The warped vision* (Pittsburgh U.P., 1965).

Gilbert, Martin, *The roots of Appeasement* (London, Weidenfeld & Nicolson, 1966).

Gilbert, Martin, and Gott, R., *The appeasers* (London, Weidenfeld & Nicolson, 1963).

Gluckman, Max, *Custom and conflict in Africa* (Oxford, Blackwell, 1955).

Granada TV, *Prelude to Westminster* (London, Granada, 1963).

Hale, Oron J., *The captive press in the Third Reich* (Princeton U.P., 1964).

Haley, Sir William, *Lewis Fry memorial lectures* (London, BBC, 1948).

Halifax, the Earl of, *Fulness of days* (London, Collins, 1957).

Hall, Ron, et al., *Scandal '63* (London, Heinemann, 1963).

Halloran, J. D., *The effects of mass communication* (Leicester U.P., 1965).

Halloran, J. D., (ed.), *The Effects of TV* (London, Panther, 1970).

Halloran, J. D., et al., *Demonstrations and communication* (Harmondsworth, Penguin, 1970).

Hartmann, Paul and Husband, Charles, 'The mass media and racial conflict', *Race*, Vol. XII, 3, 1971.

Henderson, Sir Nevile, *Failure of a mission* (London, Hodder & Stoughton, 1940).

Herd, Harold, *The march of journalism* (London, Allen & Unwin, 1952).

Hitler, A., *Mein Kampf* (Volksausgabe, 1933) 2 vols.

Hodgkin, Thomas L., *African political parties* (Harmondsworth, Penguin, 1961).

Hood, Stuart, *The mass media* (London, Macmillan, 1972).

Hopkins, Mark W., *Mass media in the Soviet Union* (N.Y., Pegasus, 1970).

Iben, Icko, *The Germanic press of Europe* (Munster, Verlag, C.J. Fahle, 1965).

Ingrams, Richard, *The life and times of Private Eye* (Harmondsworth, Penguin, 1971).

International Press Institute, *Svoboda: the press in Czechoslovakia, 1968* (Zürich, I.P.I., 1969).

Ismay, Lord, *Memoirs* (London, Heinemann, 1960).

James, Robert Rhodes (ed.), *Chips, the diaries of Sir Henry Channon* (London, Weidenfeld & Nicolson, 1967).

Jones, Thomas, *A diary with letters* (London, O.U.P., 1954).

Key, V. O., *Public opinion and American democracy* (N.Y., Knopf, 1964).

King, Anthony, 'Political parties in western democracies', *Polity*, Vol. II, 2, 1969.

Klapper, J. T., *The effects of mass communication* (N.Y., Free Press, 1960).

Kolakowski, Leszek, 'The priest and the jester', in *Marxism and beyond* (London, Paladin, 1971).

Kraus, Sidney (ed.), *The great debates* (Glos. Mass., Peter Smith, 1968).

Lang, K. and G., *Politics and television* (Chicago, Quadrangle, 1970).

Lapalombara, J., and Weiner, M., *Political parties and political development* (Princeton U.P., 1966).

Lasswell, H., 'The structure and function of communication in society', in Berelson and Janowitz (1966).

Lewis, Gordon K., 'Protest among the immigrants', *Political Quarterly*, Vol. XL, 4, 1969.

Liddell Hart, B. H., *The Liddell Hart memoirs* (London, Cassell, 1965) 2 vols.

Limon, D. W., 'Broadcasting the proceedings of the House of Commons', *The Table*, Vol. XXXV, 1966.

Loewenberg, G., *Parliament in the German political system* (Ithaca, N.Y.; Cornell U.P., 1966).

Lord Denning's Report, Cmnd 2152 (London, HMSO, 1963).

McCallum, R. B., and Readman, A., *The British General Election of 1945* (London, O.U.P., 1947).

MacKay, I. K., *Broadcasting in Australia* (Melbourne U.P., 1957).

McKenzie, R. T., *British political parties* (London, Heinemann, new ed. 1963).

Mackintosh, John, *The government and politics of Britain* (London, Hutchinson, 1970).

McLachlan, Donald, *In the chair: Barrington-Ward of The Times* (London, Weidenfeld & Nicolson, 1971).

Macleod, Iain, *Neville Chamberlain* (London, Muller, 1961).

Macmillan, Harold, *Winds of change* (London, Macmillan, 1966).

MacNeil, Robert, *The people machine* (London, Eyre & Spottiswoode, 1970).

McQuail, Denis, *Towards a sociology of mass communications* (London, Collier-Macmillan, 1969).

Maisky, I., *Who helped Hitler?* (London, Hutchinson, 1964).

Mendelsohn, H., and Crespi, I., *Polls, television and the new politics* (Scranton, Pa.; Chandler Pub. Co., 1970).

Merrill, John C., *The élite press* (N.Y., Pitman, 1968).

Michels, Robert, *Political parties* (N.Y., Dover, 1959).

Minney, R. J., *Viscount Southwood* (London, Odhams, 1954).

Monopolies Commission, *Report on The Times Newspaper and the Sunday Times Newspaper*. H.C. 273 1966–7 (London, HMSO, 1966).

Moonman, Eric (ed.), *The press: a case for commitment*, Fabian Tract 391 (London, Fabian Society, 1969).

Mowat, C. L., *Britain between the wars* (London, Methuen, 1959).

Nicholas, H. G., *The British General Election of 1950* (London, Macmillan, 1951).

Nicolson, H., *Diaries and Letters 1930–39* (London, Collins, 1966).

Nihon Shinbun Kyokai, *The Japanese press* (Tokyo, Nihon Shinbun Kyokai, annual).

Nixon, Richard M., *Six crises* (London, W. H. Allen, 1962).

Ostrogorski, M., *Democracy and the organisation of political parties*, trans. Fredk Clarke (London, Macmillan, 1902) 2 vols.

Palmer, Tony, *The trials of Oz* (London, Blond & Briggs, 1971).

Parkin, Frank, *Middle-class radicalism* (Manchester U.P., 1968).

Paulu, Burton, *British broadcasting in transition* (London, Macmillan, 1968).

Payne, Robert, *The great god Pan: a biography of the tramp played by Charles Chaplin* (N.Y., Hermitage House, 1952).

P.E.P., *Report on the British press* (London, P.E.P., 1938).

Pers, A. Y., *The Swedish press* (Stockholm, 1966).

Pickersgill, J. W., *The Mackenzie King record* (Toronto, Univ. of Toronto Press, 1960).

Pixley, Dick, *The closed question* (London, Geoffrey Chapman, 1968).

Powell, Enoch, *Freedom and reality* (Kingswood, Surrey, Elliot Right Way Books, 1968).

Pryce, Roy, 'The Italian local elections, 1956', *St Antony's Papers*, No. 3 (London Chatto & Windus, 1957).

Report of the Broadcasting Committee 1949, Cmd 8116 (London, HMSO, 1951).

Report of the National Advisory Commission on Civil Disorders, Kerner Commission (Washington, D.C., Government Printer, 1968).

Reston, James, *The artillery of the press* (N.Y., Harper, 1966).

Robbins, Keith, *Munich 1938* (London, Cassell, 1968).

Rose, E. J. B., et al., *Colour and citizenship: a report on British race relations* (London, O.U.P. for Inst. of Race Relations, 1969).

Rose, R., *Influencing voters* (London, Faber, 1967).

Royal Commission on the Police, 1962. *Report*, Cmnd 1728 (London, HMSO, 1962).

Royal Commission on the Press. *Report*, Cmd 7700 (London, HMSO, 1949).

Rubin, Bernard, *Political television* (Belmont, Calif.; Wadsworth Publ. Co., 1967).

Runnymede Trust, *Race and the press* (London, Runnymede Trust, 1971).

Russett, B. M., et al., *World handbook of political and social indicators* (New Haven, Yale U.P., 1964).

Rust, William, *The story of the Daily Worker* (London, People's Press Printing Society, 1949).

Salinger, Pierre, *With Kennedy* (N.Y., Avon Books, 1967).

Scandinavian Political Studies, Vol. III (Oslo, Universitetsvorlaget, 1968).

Schapiro, Leonard, *The Communist Party of the Soviet Union* (London, Methuen, 1953).

Select Committee on Broadcasting (Anticipation of Debates), *Report*, H.C. 288 (1955–6), (London, HMSO, 1956).

Select Committee on Broadcasting etc. of Proceedings in the House of Commons, *Report*, H.C. 146 (1966–7) (London, HMSO, 1967).

Select Committee on House of Commons Services, *Ninth Report*, H.C. 448 (1967–8) (London, HMSO, 1968).

Select Committee on House of Commons Services, *First Report*, H.C. 48 (1968–9) (London, HMSO, 1969).

Seymour-Ure, Colin, *The press, politics and the public* (London, Methuen, 1968).

Seymour-Ure, Colin, 'Policy-making in the press', *Government and Opposition*, Vol. IV, 4, 1969, pp. 425–525.

Seymour-Ure, Colin, 'The 'disintegration' of the Cabinet', *Parliamentary Affairs*, Vol. XXIV, 3, 1971.

Sharf, William, *The British press and Jews under Nazi rule* (London, O.U.P., 1954).

Shirer, William, *Berlin diary* (London, Hamish Hamilton, 1941).

Smithies, Bill, and Fiddick, Peter, *Enoch Powell on immigration* (London, Sphere Books, 1969).

Sommerlad, E. Lloyd, *The press in developing countries* (Sydney U.P., 1966).

Spearman, Diana, 'Enoch Powell's postbag', *New Society*, 9 May and 27 June 1968.

Spender, J. A., *The public life* (London, Cassell, 1925) 2 vols.

Stacey, Frank, *The British Ombudsman* (Oxford, Clarendon Press, 1971).

Stacey, Tom, *Immigration and Enoch Powell* (London, Tom Stacey, 1970).

Street, Harry, *Freedom, the individual and the law* (Harmondsworth, Penguin, 1963).

Sykes, Christopher, *Nancy: the life of Lady Astor* (London, Collins, 1972).

Talese, Gay, *The kingdom and the power* (N.Y., Bantam, 1970).

Taylor, A. J. P., *Beaverbrook* (London, Hamish Hamilton, 1972).

Taylor, A. J. P., *English History 1914–45* (London, O.U.P., 1965).

Taylor, A. J. P., *Origins of the Second World War* (London, Hamish Hamilton, 1961).

Templewood, Viscount, *Nine troubled years* (London, Collins, 1954).

Thompson, Denys, *Discrimination and popular culture* (Harmondsworth, Penguin, 1964).

Thompson, Neville, *The Anti-Appeasers* (London, O.U.P., 1971).

The Times. History of The Times (London, The Times Publ. Co., 1952) Vol. IV.

Trenaman, J., and McQuail, D., *Television and the political image* (London, Methuen, 1961).

Tunstall, Jeremy, *Journalists at work* (London, Constable, 1971).

Tunstall, Jeremy (ed.) *Media Sociology* (London, Constable, 1970(1)).

Tunstall, Jeremy, *The Westminster Lobby correspondents* (London, Routledge, 1970(2)).

UNESCO. *Statistical Yearbook* (Paris, UNESCO, annual).

Vansittart, Lord, *The mist procession* (London, Hutchinson, 1958).

Watzlawick, P., et al., *Pragmatics of human communication* (London, Faber & Faber, 1968).

Weiss, Walter, 'The effects of the mass media of communication', in G. Lindzey and E. Aronson, *Handbook of Social Psychology* (Reading, Mass.: Addison-Wesley, 1969) 5 vols.

Welsford, Enid, *The Fool: his social and literary history* (London, Faber & Faber, 1935, reprinted 1968).

Whale, John, *The half-shut eye* (London, Macmillan, 1967).

Whale, John, *Journalism and government* (London, Macmillan, 1972).

Wheeler-Bennett, Sir John, *Munich: prologue to tragedy* (London, Macmillan, 1948, reprinted 1963).

White, Theodore H., *The making of the President 1960* (N.Y., Atheneum, 1961).

Willeford, William, *The Fool and his sceptre* (London, Edward Arnold, 1969).

Williams, Francis, *Dangerous estate* (London, Longmans, 1957).

Williams, Francis, *Press, parliament and people* (London, Heinemann, 1946).

Williams, Raymond, *Communications* (London, Chatto & Windus, 1966).

Wilson, Charles (ed.), *Parliaments, people and mass media* (London, Cassell for the Inter-Parliamentary Union, 1970).

Wilson, Harold, *The Labour Government 1964–70* (London, Weidenfeld & Nicolson and Michael Joseph, 1971).

Wood, John (ed.), *Powell and the 1970 Election* (Kingswood, Surrey, Elliot Right Way Books, 1970).

Woodward, E. L., Butler R., et al., *Documents on British foreign policy*, Third series (London, HMSO, 1947), Vol. II.

Wrench, John Evelyn, *Geoffrey Dawson and our times* (London, Hutchinson, 1955).

Young, Hugo, 'The treatment of race in the British press', in *Race and the press* (London, Runnymede Trust, 1971).

Young, Wayland, *The Profumo Affair: aspects of conservatism* (Harmondsworth, Penguin, 1963).

Index

L'Action Tunisienne, 194
Age, 180
Al Ahram, 181, 197
Aitken, Sir Max, 163
Almond, Gabriel, 44, 157
Appeasement, and *The Times*, ch. 3
    passim; justifications of, 69–70; *see
    also The Times*
Apter, David, 194
Arbeiter-Zeitung, 170
Asahi, 171
Ashanti Pioneer, 186
Astor, Col. J. J., 71, 162
Astor, Lord, 84
Astor, Michael, 86n.
Attlee, C. R., 139, 142, 145n., 235;
    and 1945 election, 206, 232; and 1951
    election, 222
Australia, parliamentary broadcasting
    in, 137, 149, 151
The Australian, 171, 180
Avanti, 157
Azikiwe, Dr, 157, 194

Baldwin, Stanley, and Zinoviev letter,
    30–1; and Geoffrey Dawson, 83, 85;
    and press barons, 156–7
Balfour, A. J., 144
Barrington-Ward, Robin, 89n., 91; on
    Munich, 68; in First World War, 69;
    and Sudetenland, 82; access to
    politicians, 82–5; and Liddell Hart,
    93–4
Bay of Pigs, and *New York Times*, 32
B.B.C., and devaluation of 1967, 33–4;
    and election broadcasting, 138; and
    Fourteen Day Rule, 140–3
Beaverbrook, Lord, 27, 156, 162, 226,
    229, 230, 231, 243
Beneš, E., 78, 80
Benn, A. Wedgwood, and Enoch
    Powell, 132, 133
Betjeman, John, 263
Beuve-Méry, H., 172
Bevan, Aneurin, 111, 114, 139, 221–2,
    230
Bevin, Ernest, 161, 164
Beyond the Fringe, 240
Bild-Zeitung, 171
Birch, Nigel, 101
Blondel, Jean, 184ff.
Blumler, Jay, 23, 43, 213, 237, 239
Booker, Christopher, 241, 243, 244, 245,
    247
Boothby, Lord, 84
Bowden, Herbert, 150n.

Boyle, Lord, and cabinet agenda, 36
Bracken, Brendan, 162
Brand, Lord, 88
British monarchy, entrenchment of, 51;
    TV and, 148n.
Broadcasting, effects of on Parliament,
    144–9; effects on of Parliament,
    138–43; and Representation of the
    People Act, 138–9; Fourteen Day
    Rule, 140–3; in general elections,
    206–18; *see also* B.B.C.
Brown, George, 24n.; resignation as
    Foreign Secretary, 59–60; and 1970
    election, 215, 221; and '3%
    mortgages', 224; and *Private Eye*, 249
Buckle, G. E., 70n., 83, 93
Buhlul, 241
Die Burger, 170
Burnham, Lord, 162
Butler, David, 114, 115, 130, 132, 133n.,
    135–6, 165n., 203, 220, 223
Butler, R. A., 82n., 240
Butt, Ronald, 144n.

Cadbury family, 162
Callaghan, James, and devaluation of
    1967, 34
Campaign Report, 213–14, 219, 224;
    and Enoch Powell, 132
Cape Times, 180
Carr, E. H., and *The Times*, 70
Chamberlain, Austen, 97
Chamberlain, Neville, 67; values
    Dawson's opinion on Germany, 74;
    and Sudetenland crisis, 79; relation-
    ship with Dawson, 83, 86
Christian Science Monitor, 171, 181
Christiansen, Arthur, 232
Churchill, Randolph, 254, 261
Churchill, Winston, 50n., 85, 95; on
    appeasement, 67; and Colin Coote,
    70; and Vansittart, 83; wartime
    speeches not recorded, 139, 150;
    against broadcasting Parliament,
    142–3; and *Daily Herald*, 164;
    'Gestapo' speech, 206, 217, 224; and
    1945 Conservative campaign, 218,
    221, 229, 231, 232, 234
'Cliveden set', 74, 84–5
Cockburn, Claud, 84–5, 245–6, 247,
    248, 250, 256, 257
Coleman, Terry, 114
Commonwealth Immigrants Act 1962,
    99
Communication, medium of defined,
    16; inevitable, 15

Congress, United States, and TV, 26; and Presidency, 55; broadcasting of Senate committees, 137, 146
Cooper, Duff, 81, 94–5
Coote, Colin, 96; and *Times* atmosphere, 70; and *Times* Sudetenland leader, 81
Corriere della Sera, 198
Cowling, Maurice, and Enoch Powell, 125
Crisis definition, role of media in, 39–40, 54; and Enoch Powell, 127
Crosland, Anthony, 56n.
Crossman, Richard, and devaluation of 1967, 33–4; and broadcasting Parliament, 139
Czechoslovakia, in 1938, 24–5; and Hitler, 31; and *The Times*, 31, 78–82; and Warsaw Pact forces, 1968, 34–5

D Notice system, 179, 256
Dagens Nyheter, 171
Daily Chronicle, 162
Daily Express, and Abyssinian crisis, 76; and Kenya Asians, 101, 118; and Enoch Powell, 102; political attitudes of, 162, 168, 171; and general elections, 226, 229, 230, 231, 232; and *Private Eye*, 243, 261
Daily Express (Nigeria), 187
Daily Herald, and Cecil King, 27; and Zinoviev letter, 30; in 1930s, 49; and G. K. Chesterton, 161n.; as party paper, 161–2, 164, 168, 196; and general elections, 222, 230, 235; demise, 228
Daily Mail, and Zinoviev letter, 29–30; and Macmillan cabinet changes, 32–3; and Northcliffe, 48–9, 156; and Abyssinian crisis, 76; and Enoch Powell, 102; political attitudes, 162, 168, 171; and general elections, 229
Daily Mirror, and Second World War, 17; and Cecil King, 27; and Enoch Powell, 102, 110; and *Daily Herald*, 161–2; political attitudes, 168; and general elections, 203, 223, 229, 230, 231, 232, 234, 235
Daily News, 162
Daily News (New York), 180
Daily Sketch, 162, 168, 232; and Enoch Powell, 110, 132
Daily Telegraph, and Kenya Asians, 101, 118; and Enoch Powell, 102; and Conservative party, 160, 162, 168; and general elections, 226, 227, 228, 230
Daily Worker, 162
Dalton, Hugh, 57
Daniels, G. E., 92
Dawson, Geoffrey, 17–18, 24, 31, 67–8; on Munich settlement, 68; 'free hand' as editor of *The Times*, 71; character and career, 71–3; Sudetenland leader, 80–2; access to politicians, 82–7; and Abdication Crisis, 85n.; criticisms of, 87–98
Deedes, William, 149n.
Denmark, parliamentary broadcasting in, 137

Deutsch, Karl, 16
Devlin, Lord, 146
Le Devoir, 180
Donnelly, Desmond, contrasted with Enoch Powell, 135–6
Douglas-Home, Sir Alec, 101; on TV, 151; and 1964 election, 211, 214, 218, 221; and *Private Eye*, 248, 250
Dubcek, Alexander, 34–5
Dugdale, Baffy, 76n.

Ebbutt, Norman, 92
Eccles, Sir David, 252
The Economist, and Enoch Powell, 125; and general elections, 226
Edelman, Maurice, 152
Eden, Anthony, 32; on *The Times* in 1930s, 67, 78–9, 81; relationship with Dawson, 83; and 1951 election, 221
Effects of mass media, defined, 21–2; primary and secondary, 22, 41–2; production of, 23ff.; importance of timing in, 28–9; importance of frequency in, 35–7; importance of intensity, 37–40; on cabinet agenda, 36; study of unduly narrow, 41–3; on audiences, 43; levels of, 44–6; on U.S. Congress and Presidency, 55–6; on Enoch Powell, 128–9, 134; on general elections, 53, 202–5, ch. 8 passim
Eisenhower, Dwight, 58
Election Forum, 211, 218, 222, 239
Election Marathon, 210, 216
Electioneering, TV and style of, 214–15; 'presidential' character of, 219
Elliot, Walter, 81
Elliott, Philip, 43
Epstein, L. D., 195
The Establishment, 240
European Economic Community, B.B.C. debate on, 146; and 1966 election, 225, 230
Evans, Harold, 117
Evening Standard, 85, 261
Exposure journalism, 27–8

Fantoni, Barry, 250
Fiddick, Peter, 112, 114, 120
Le Figaro, 180
Financial Times, 162, 164, 169; and general elections, 226
First World War, outbreak of and communications systems, 21
Fool, *Private Eye* as, ch. 9 passim; characterised, 241–3
Foot, Paul, 101, 115, 125, 128; and *Private Eye*, 243, 262, 263
Fourteen Day Rule, 140–3
France-Soir, 180
Frost, David, and Enoch Powell, 113, 115, 121

Gaitskell, Hugh, 222
Gale, George, and Enoch Powell, 130
Gandalf's Garden, 247

Gannon, F. R., 87, 94
Garvin, J. L., 84
General election, *of 1924*, 29–30; *of 1945*, 206, 214, 218, 219, 220, 221, 222, 223, 226, 227, 228, 229, 230, 231, 234, 235; *of 1950*, 207, 220n., 222, 226, 228; *of 1951*, 207, 220n., 221, 227, 231, 232; *of 1955*, 207, 209, 220, 227, 229, 230, 231; *of 1959*, 209, 210, 211, 213, 214, 215, 216, 220, 222, 224, 225, 226, 227, 228, 230, 234, 236, 237; *of 1964*, 211, 214, 216, 218, 224, 225, 233; *of 1966*, 207, 211, 213, 216, 218, 219, 220, 222, 224, 225, 226, 227, 229, 230; *of 1970*, 207, 211, 212, 214, 215, 216, 219, 220, 221, 224, 225, 226, 227, 228, 229, 232, 234–5, 236
General elections, and intensity of media coverage, 38; party strategies and media strategy, 38–9; and mass media, ch. 8 passim; media dislike of 'quiet', 219–21
Gilbert, Martin, 69, 93
Globe and Mail, 171, 172, 180
Gluckman, Max, 15, 258
Gnome, Lord, 247, 252, 253
Gott, Richard, 69
Granada TV, Rochdale by-election 1958, 210; *Election Marathon*, 210
Grimond, Jo, and broadcasting of Parliament, 139, 153n.; and *Guardian*, 163; and general elections, 217, 233; and *Private Eye*, 245
The Guardian, and Enoch Powell, 110, 114, 133; political attitudes, 165, 168–9; and general elections, 226, 228; *see also Manchester Guardian*

Ha'aretz, 171
Hale, Oron J., 158n.
Haley, Sir William, 150
Halifax, Lord, on influence of *The Times*, 77; on Sudetenland leader, 78, 81; relationship with Dawson, 83, 86, 96; and Cliveden set, 84
Halloran, James, 43
Harness, Charles, 245
Hartmann, Paul, 116
Heath, Edward, 27; and Powell immigration speech, 101, 105, 118, 119, 120, 125, 129, 130, 131, 134; sacks Powell, 61, 126–7; and general elections, 214, 217, 218, 221, 227; and *Private Eye*, 251
Helsingin Sanomat, 171, 172, 180
Henderson, Nevile, 77
Hill, Charles, 221–2
Hitler, Adolf, foreign policy, 67; complaints about British press, 77–8; and Sudetenland leader, 79–82; and German press, 157–8, 159
Hoare, Sir Samuel, 75, 86
Hogg, Quintin, and Enoch Powell, 119, 126, 131; and 1964 election, 212, 221
Hore-Belisha, L., 82
House of Commons, question of televising, 26, ch. 5 passim; *see also* Parliament

Hoy (Cuba), 187
L'Humanité, 170, 197
Husband, Charles, 116
Hustings, 210, 216

Ideology, and newspapers, 192–5
Ingrams, Richard, 243–4, 246
Inskip, Tom, 81
Iremonger, Tom, 149n.
Iskra, 157
IT, 247
I.T.N., and general elections, 226
Izvestia, readers' interests, 19, 173; as government paper, 170, 172

'Jasper affair', 225
Jenkins, Roy, and Enoch Powell, 118, 126
Johnson, Lyndon, 22, 55, 117n.
Jones, Thomas, 69n., 76, 81; and Cliveden set, 84; and Geoffrey Dawson, 85
Jordan, Colin, 110, 112
Judicial system, entrenchment of, 51–2

Kennedy, Joe, 84
Kennedy, John F., 240; debates with Nixon, 61–2
Kennedy, Robert, 55, 61
Kenya Asians, citizenship issue, 100–1; and Enoch Powell, 116, 118, 130–1
Kerner Commission, 117n.
Key, V. O., 157
Kilmuir, Lord, 33
King, Anthony, 199, 202n.
King, Cecil, 27, 162
King, W. L. Mackenzie, 73n.
Komsomolskaya Pravda, 170
Korean War, TV and, 27
Krasnaya Zvezda, 170

Lansbury, George, and *Daily Herald*, 161
Laski, Harold, 230, 231, 232
Lasswell, Harold, and study of mass media, 41–2
Law, A. Bonar, 97
Lenin, V. I., and *Iskra*, 157; and role of the press, 158–9
Levin, Bernard, 243, 244
Liberal News, 244
Liddell Hart, B., on Munich, 71, 81, 82; criticism of Dawson, 87–8, 90; 'repeatedly gagged', 93–4
Lloyd, Selwyn, 25, 33, 240, 252
Lloyd George, David, 86; distrust of Northcliffe, 49–50; and *Daily Chronicle*, 162
Lloyds Weekly News, 48
Lobby correspondents, status of, 36; and *Private Eye*, 263
Lothian, Lord, 84–5, 86, 92
Low, David, 85

Ma'ariv, 171
McCarthy, Joe, 58
MacDonald, J. Ramsay, 85, 161; and
  Zinoviev letter, 29–30; and *The Week*,
  246
McLachlan, D., 87, 93
Macleod, Iain, 101; and broadcasting
  Parliament, 139
Macmillan, Harold, and cabinet
  changes of 1962, 25, 28, 32, 59; on
  The Times and the Abyssinian crisis,
  76; on *The Times* Sudetenland leader,
  81; and 1959 election, 222; and
  Private Eye, 240–1, 245, 252, 253,
  259, 264
McQuail, Denis, 43, 225, 239
Mainichi, 171
Maisky, L., 81
Manchester Guardian, 162, 163; *see also
  Guardian*
Manchester Union Leader, 59
Marks, Derek, 261
Mass media, distinctive features, 16ff.;
  effects of, defined, 21–2; functions of
  in general elections, 204
Massey, Vincent, 73n.
Matthews, George, 162
Maudling, Reginald, 101, 146–7
Mayhew, Christopher, 207
Mbadiwe, Dr, 171
El Mercurio, 171
Mesopotamia, 244
Michels, R., 156
Milligan, Spike, 263
Milner, Lord, 'Kindergarten', 72
Milwaukee Journal, 180
Le Monde, 172, 180; ownership, 171
Morning Advertiser, 164
Morning Star, 162; *see also Daily
  Worker*
Mosley, Sir Oswald, 112, 125n.
Muggeridge, Malcolm, 244, 245
Murdoch, Rupert, 162, 183
Murdock, Graham, 43
Muskie, Edmund, 59
Mussolini, B., 75, 77; and *Popolo
  d'Italia*, 157

The Nationalist, 193
Nea, 187
Neue Zürcher Zeitung, 171, 172, 181, 183
New Left Review, 241
New Statesman, and Enoch Powell, 112,
  114, 118n.; and *Private Eye*, 262
New York Post, 58
New York Times, 236; and Vietnam,
  40; political attitude, 171; west coast
  edition, 180
New Zealand, parliamentary broad-
  casting in, 137, 149, 151
News At Ten, and Enoch Powell, 132
News Chronicle, 181, 228, 229
News of the World, and Enoch Powell,
  110, 119
News values, 18, 96; and Enoch Powell,
  116–17, 120–2; and general elections,
  218–27; and press partisanship,
  228–32

Nicolson, Harold, 74, 75, 76n., 81
Nigerian civil war, and *Sunday
  Telegraph*, 54–5
Nixon, Richard, 1972 election
  campaign, 26; televised veto, 55;
  'Checkers' speech, 58; debates with
  Kennedy, 61–2
Nkrumah, K., and press, 186, 193, 194,
  199
'Noose trial', 225, 231, 233
Northcliffe, Lord, 17, 27, 90, 196;
  effect on political system, 48–50;
  and *Daily Mail*, 48–9; and Baldwin,
  156
Northern Ireland, media coverage of,
  46; B.B.C. debate on, 146

O'Booze, Lunchtime, 249
Observer, and Enoch Powell, 123; and
  general elections, 226; and *Private Eye*,
  245
Odhams Press, 161
Opinion polls, 226–7, 230, 235
Osborne, John, 249
Osborne, Sir Cyril, and Kenya Asians,
  101, 102
Osmond, Andrew, 241, 244
Osservatore Romano, 198
Ostrogorski M., 156
Oz, 247, 257n.

Panorama, and Enoch Powell, 110–11;
  and general elections, 210, 211,
  218
Parliament, and televising of debates,
  ch. 5 passim; effects of on broadcasting, 138–43; effects of broadcasting on, 53, 144–9; proposal to
  televise, 1966, 139–40; 'bypassing' of
  by TV, 145–50; *see also* House of
  Commons
Parliamentary Commissioner for
  Administration, and publicity, 56
Parties, affinities with newspapers, 52–3,
  158–9, ch. 6 passim, ch. 7 passim;
  and the British press, 160–9; and
  press abroad, 169–76; left wing
  'underrepresented', 173; 'paralleling'
  press systems, 173–6; types of and
  types of press, 185–200; ideologies
  and newspapers, 192–5
Party manifestos, press attitudes to,
  223–4
'Peace Ballot', 69
Peart, Fred, 150, 152
The People, and Enoch Powell, 121, 162
Philippines, parliamentary broadcasting
  in, 137
Phillips, Morgan, 215, 221
Pinto-Duschinsky, Michael, 114, 115,
  130, 132, 133n.
Pixley, Dick, and Enoch Powell, 123,
  125
Popolo d'Italia, 157
Powell, G. B., 44, 157
Powell, Enoch, 21, 27, ch. 4 passim;
  role in the political system, 50;

Birmingham speech on immigration, 20 April 1968, 103–5; media coverage, 39, 57, 105–11; position in Conservative party pre-1968, 101–3; 'Tiber foaming with much blood', 105, 121; aims and techniques, 113–16, 118–20; 'shaking inevitabilities', 115; effects of Birmingham speech, 122–36; fired from shadow cabinet, 126–7, 129–30; and 1970 general election, 131–6, 212, 214, 221–2, 230

Pravda, 169–70, 172

President, United States, and TV, 26, 55–6; and press, 178, 196

Private Eye, ch. 9 passim; problems of sueing, 25, 28; and judicial system, 52; circulation, 241; founded, 243–7; and *The Week*, 245–6; and libel actions, 253–4

Profumo, John, 28, 57, 260, 261, 264

Punch, 243, 245, 263

Race Relations, public attitudes to, 111–13, 117–18; effect of Enoch Powell on, 122–6

Race Relations Act 1965, 100

Race Relations Act 1968, 100

Radio, decline of in elections, 206–9

Rand Daily Mail, 180

Rees-Mogg, William, 164, 165n.

Representation of the People Act 1949, 209, 211, 236

Representation of the People Act 1969, 211

Reston, James, 32n.

Ribbentrop, J. von, 78

Roosevelt, F. D., 'Fireside chats', 55

Rose, E. G. B., 125

Rothermere, Lord, 27, 156, 162, 196

Runciman, Lord, 80, 81

Rushton, William, 243–4, 245

Rusk, Dean, and Vietnam, 55

Russell, Lord, of Liverpool, 254

Russell, William Howard, 21

Saint Louis Post-Dispatch, 180

Salinger, Pierre, 61

Sandys, Duncan, and Kenya Asians, 100–1, 102

Scarfe, Gerald, 250

Scott, C. P., 162, 163

Shackleton, Lord, 140

Sharf, William, 93

Shawcross, Hartley, 207

Shirer, William, 77, 92

El Siglo, 171

Smithies, Bill, 112, 114, 120

Spectator, and Sudetenland, 79; and *Private Eye*, 262, 263

Spender, J. A., 95, 144n.

Springer, Axel, 171, 183

Stacey, Frank, 56n.

Steed, Wickham, 74, 89n., 93, 97

Stewart, Michael, and Nigerian civil war, 54; and televised teach-in, 146

Stokes, Donald, 135–6, 165n., 203, 220, 223

Süddeutsche Zeitung, 178

Sudentenland, *The Times* leader on, 79–82

Sun, and Enoch Powell, 102, 133; launched, 162; political attitude, 168; and general elections, 229

Sunday Citizen, 162

Sunday Express, and Enoch Powell, 102, 115, 127

Sunday Mirror, and Enoch Powell, 105, 121, 162

Sunday Telegraph, and Nigerian civil war, 54–5; and *Private Eye*, 251

Sunday Times, and Macmillan cabinet changes, 33; and Enoch Powell, 128, 134; and general elections, 226

Sunday Times (Johannesburg), 181, 194

Svenska Dagbladet, 171

Sweden, parliamentary broadcasting in, 154

Sydney Morning Herald, 180

Tarbit, L. J., 254

Taylor, A. J. P., 87–8, 91ff.

Television, effect of on Parliament, 53 and ch. 5 passim; and general elections, 206–18; displaces 'real' election campaign, 212–13; and party election press conferences, 215; election 'confrontations', 216–17; 'trivialises politics', 217–18; interaction with press in elections, 235, 237

Television Act 1954, 209

That Was The Week That Was, 240, 243

The Question of Ulster, 146

The Week in Westminster, 143

The World This Weekend, and Enoch Powell, 110

This Week, 211

Thompson, Neville, 74

Thomson, Lord, 18, 91, 161, 163

Thorneycroft, Peter, 101, 251

Thorpe, Jeremy, and Enoch Powell, 131–2

El Tiempo, 171

Time and Tide, 245, 248

The Times, and appeasement of Hitler 17–18, 24–5, ch. 3 passim; leader on Sudetenland, 31, 79–82; and devaluation of 1967, 34; and Abyssinian crisis, 75–6; readership in 1938, 75; and opinion abroad, 76–82; influence as a pressure group 85–7; criticisms of its appeasement policy, 87–98; and Enoch Powell, 111, 134; and proposal to televise Parliament, 140, 147, 150, 152, 153; ownership of, 162, 163; political outlook, 164–5, 168–9; price, 182; costs of production, 183; and elections, 217, 220, 226, 261

Timing of communications, importance of, 28–9

Tonight, 210

Trenaman, J., 225

Trethowan, Ian, 118n.

Tunstall, Jeremy, 18, 117

24 Hours, and 1966 election, 23; and Enoch Powell, 111

Uhuru, 193
United States of America, election TV, 26; *see also* Congress, President
Usborne, Peter, 244

Vansittart, Lord, 67, 89, 93
Vima, 187
Violence, mass media and, 45
Völkischer Beobachter, 158

Wall Street Journal, 180
Walter, John, IV, 71, 73
Washington Post, 180
Watergate, Senate hearings, 55
Watkins, Alan, 112, 114, 118n.
The Week, 81; and Cliveden set, 84; and *Private Eye*, 245–6, 247, 248, 249, 253, 256, 263
Die Welt, 171
Werth, Alexander, 92
West African Pilot, 157, 194
West Germany, broadcasting of Bundestag, 151

Westminster Confidential, 28
White, Theodore H., 62
Whitelaw, William, and Enoch Powell, 133
Willeford, W., 247, 255n., 259, 260
Williams, Francis, 87–90; on Geoffrey Dawson, 67–8
Williams, Harold, 89
Wilson, Harold, and devaluation of £, 24, 33–4, 145, 147; and Enoch Powell, 131, 134; on broadcasting technique, 209n.; snubs B.B.C. in 1966, 214, 236; and general elections, 214, 217, 224, 225, 235; and '£ in your pocket', 224n.; and *Private Eye*, 248, 250, 252, 263n.
Winn, Anthony, 95
Wood, David, and broadcasting of Parliament, 147
Wyndham, John, 242n.

Yesterday in Parliament, 35, 143
Yomiuri, 171
Young, Hugo, 112, 118
Young, Wayland, 260

Zinoviev letter, 29–31, 231, 232